G000271286

Spreading the Risks

Spreading the Risks

Insuring the American Experience

By JOHN A. BOGARDUS JR.

With ROBERT H. MOORE

POSTERITY PRESS

© 2003 John A. Bogardus Jr.
All Rights Reserved

Bogardus, John A.
  Spreading the risks: insuring the American experience / by John
  A. Bogardus Jr. with Robert H. Moore.
     p. cm.
  Includes bibliographic references and index.
  ISBN 1-889274-16-X
  1. Insurance—United States. 2. Alexander & Alexander—History.
  3. Insurance companies—United States. I Moore, Robert H.
  (Robert Henry), 1940-II. Title.

  HG8531.B64 2003
  368.006573—dc21   2002069385

First Edition

Posterity Press, Inc.
P.O. Box 71081
Chevy Chase,
Maryland 20813

www.PosterityPress.com

Printed in the United States of America

Designer: Susan Lehmann
Picture Editor: Carol Haythorne

Cover: *A personification of insurance graces a policy certificate issued
by Manufacturers' Accident Indemnity Company of Geneva, New York.
It insures against injury and death from causes including such illustrated risks as train derailment, shipwreck, or industrial accident in 1889.*

For Lela Bogardus

and

In memory of the employees

of Aon, Marsh & McLennan

and the other insurance organizations who were lost

in the September 11, 2001 terrorist attacks.

Contents

Illustrations

Foreword

As a former chairman and CEO of a global insurance brokerage, Jack Bogardus was in an excellent position to appreciate the linkage between his industry and America's social and economic growth. *Spreading the Risks* is a testimony to his determination to record the life and times of his industry. After years of research, and in concert with Robert Moore, Bogardus has given us an unsurpassed overview of America's commercial insurance development from the colonial period to the present.

The book shows how the insurance industry evolved as a counterpoint to major American social and economic events. It effectively uses personal histories to illustrate the industry's expansion. These are memorable stories about individuals and organizations from various regions of our nation whose triumphs and failures reflect an ever-changing business.

The saga of American insurance touches our lives in surprising ways. In my case, the narrative reminded me of my grandfather who ran the Hartford Insurance Agency in Vicksburg, Mississippi, and of two uncles who were general agents for Penn Mutual in Boston and for Massachusetts Mutual in Jackson. I still treasure their letters written to me as a child on stationery with impressive company letterheads.

I also remember stories from my home state about one

of America's great literary figures, Eudora Welty. Her father, Christian Welty, was President of Lamar Life Insurance Company whose new headquarters in Jackson, Mississippi, became the city's first skyscraper. It was a thirteen-story white gothic building with gargoyles carved in the shape of alligators and a tower with a Seth Thomas–designed clock looking down on the governor's mansion. The building symbolized the New South's arrival in Jackson, and when it opened on January 17, 1925, Lamar agents presented Christian Welty with insurance applications totaling a million dollars.

Eudora Welty began her writing career preparing copy for Lamar's radio station, WLDX, which was housed in the building's clock tower. In her first paying job, Welty wrote mule feed commercials, life insurance playlets, and feature articles on local talent such as the Leake County Revelers. Thus, one of our nation's greatest writers began her career nestled within her father's insurance world.

During my tenure as chairman of the National Endowment for the Humanities, I frequently stressed that rediscovering America's past could help us better understand what it means to be a citizen of the twenty-first century. In like spirit, *Spreading the Risks* offers poignant stories from across several centuries of our country's experience that demonstrate the intimate ties between insurance and American history. Just as we endured decades of upheaval after separating from the British Empire, our insurers fended for themselves in difficult decades of trial and error.

Disastrous fires in the eighteenth and nineteenth centuries dramatized America's risk management needs. In 1835, a three-day conflagration destroyed New York City's business district, wiping out 700 commercial and private buildings. A similar fire in 1845 destroyed fifty-six acres of homes, offices, and warehouses in Pittsburgh. In 1849, St. Louis lost half its business district and twenty-seven steamboats in a three-square-mile fire. Poorly capitalized insurers could cover only a small part of such losses. On October 8, 1871, the most famous nineteenth century conflagration began. In Chicago, more than 2,000 acres burned, leaving 250 dead and 98,500 homeless, and destroying 18,000 to 20,000 buildings worth $150 million to $300 million. Although Aetna Insurance Company paid Chicago clients about $3.5 million in losses, seventy other companies were forced out of business.

While insurance companies struggled with these tragic losses, the industry also responded to the nation's remarkable industrial development. As Thomas Edison invented the light bulb, George Eastman discovered the Kodak box camera, and William Le Barron Jenny erected the first iron and steel skyscraper, insurers adapted to new technology and were an indispensable part of America's growth. In 1903, the Wright brothers flew the first airplane, and in 1904, the first trans-Pacific cable was laid. Throughout the country, bold new inventions appeared and cities were born; new technology, communication, and modes of transportation evolved—all were secured by insurance.

As the twentieth century begins, Jack Bogardus focuses on C. B. and W. F. Alexander, two West Virginia brothers who founded Alexander & Alexander. He traces the extraordinary growth of the small family-owned business, which would become a publicly owned corporation and the world's second largest insurance broker. The Alexander brothers responded to the country's expansion by successfully placing coverage for the oil, automobile, airline, and film industries. When an A&A acquisition placed insurance for the first metal-clad dirigible, losses from "upside-down flying, looping-the-loop, spinning, rolling, hedge hopping, or other aerial acrobatics" were wisely excluded.

Bogardus uses Alexander & Alexander as a lens through which we explore the role of major twentieth-century American brokers. Like its counterparts, A&A became a global presence through aggressive mergers. In the 1970s, the company negotiated $35 billion of construction coverage in Saudi Arabia. Rapid expansion led to revolutionary changes in corporate culture and leadership as A&A and others moved from closely held businesses to publicly traded companies.

Jack Bogardus rose through corporate ranks to become CEO of A&A in 1978. Under his leadership, company revenue topped a billion dollars in 1986. He also oversaw acquisition of Alexander Howden, a British company whose financial problems haunted A&A for years. The level of intrigue at both Howden and Lloyd's during this period reads like a John Grisham novel.

From British coffeehouses to fires in colonial American cities, from the 1906 San Francisco earthquake to the September 11, 2001, World Trade Center loss, Bogardus documents the insurance industry's pivotal role in American history. By spreading risks, insurers and brokers have helped shield each generation of individuals and corporations from financial ruin, and they have contributed immeasurably to our nation's extraordinary growth. This powerful story will help both business professionals and the general reader better appreciate the challenges the American insurance industry has faced and how it continues to secure our future.

William R. Ferris
Professor of History
University of North Carolina at Chapel Hill
Chairman, National Endowment for the Humanities
(1997–2001)

Preface

On July 1, 1950, I reported for work at Alexander & Alexander, Inc. as a trainee and had the misfortune to ride up in the elevator with A&A's chairman. He took one look at me and asked: "Why aren't you wearing a hat?" Thirty-eight years later, I retired as chairman of the company. Hats were no longer required.

This minor modification offers a hint about changes in property/casualty insurance over the last fifty years. In fact, industry alterations have been revolutionary and profound. As the twentieth century progressed, they occurred at an ever-accelerating pace. And then, the twenty-first century barely had begun when the greatest cataclysm ever to rock the industry occurred. The terrorists' destruction of the World Trade Center, and the related tragedies in Washington, D.C., and Pennsylvania, will reverberate around the world for years to come.

Having spent my entire career in insurance, as my father did, I have witnessed many global disasters and triumphs. I believe an examination of our industry's incredible changes can be instructive to those who work in insurance today, as well as to business executives, government officials, and the general reader.

My research for this project began thirteen years ago. This combined with career experience led me to several conclusions. First, the task of examining evolving eighteenth and nineteenth century public and private risks offers insights into the origins of American insurance, its almost 300-year development, and its uncertain future. Second, much has been written on specific types of insurance companies, but little broad-based material has been published on the industry's progression since 1720. Third, although insurance company histories are common (and often available through corporate publications), the distribution system, especially the role of brokers, is largely ignored. Therefore, I am offering an overview of the industry's response to American property/casualty risks from the 1700s to 2002.

In much of the narrative, I will be using A&A's development to tell the story. While brokers' strategies and solutions to challenges vary, all have organized themselves around responding to clients' changing needs. The A&A employees cited here have counterparts in other brokerages. Further, our heavy reliance on acquisitions for growth in recent decades mirrored the expansion strategies of major competitors. We became the world's second largest broker before we, in turn, were acquired by Aon in 1997.

I also have devoted substantial attention to Lloyd's; this acknowledges its long-standing importance as the world's most famous and glamorous insurance market. Lloyd's has responded to the risks of many large multinational companies, and United States brokers routinely rely on it for complex placements. However, Lloyd's periodic problems poignantly epitomize lessons to be learned from the vulnerability of large institutions—old and new.

Lloyd's weaknesses grew out of several conditions. These included the extraordinary excesses of certain high-profile underwriters and several insurance brokers, as well as some disastrous underwriting. In the end, many individuals suffered financial ruin, and Lloyd's existence was seriously threatened. This threat was rekindled by the tragic events of September 11, 2001.

Since the industrial revolution, insurance has constantly

evolved to help underwrite America's unique economic expansion. Few other industries reflect our free enterprise system so well. Despite its invaluable contributions to national and global economic growth, however, the industry has a somewhat checkered image, which is reflected in comments like those in this note received by a Baltimore-based A&A salesman in the 1930s: "Dear Ed, Sorry I won't be able to renew my insurance with you, but my brother was injured in an accident and has a hole in his head, and since he can no longer work, he has gotten an insurance agent's license and is going to handle my insurance policies."

Although dated, this ingenuous and comic exchange echoes a serious image problem persisting into the twenty-first century. For millions of people, insurance represents a necessary evil. It costs money, sometimes a lot, and too many Americans can recount an unpleasant insurance-related incident. Additionally, the insurance policy often is replete with fine print and forbidding language with which even industry professionals sometimes struggle. With this in mind, I have tried to portray our business objectively, reporting on both its strengths and weaknesses.

Our industry will continue to change, with its most daunting challenges yet to come. These include complex risks generated by national and global transformations, the impact of international terrorist networks, and unforeseen catastrophic liabilities. Having risen to meet the challenges of centuries, it is likely the industry will meet future needs as well; but none should take this for granted. Our industry is an interdependent global system. Virtually every major social, political, and economic upheaval triggers vibrations that impact the entire system. Insuring tomorrow's risks will require concentrated energy, creativity, cooperation, and wisdom from old and new industry thinkers, their clients, and their governments.

Greenwich, Connecticut
June 2002

Acknowledgments

Spreading the Risks, which began as a history of Alexander & Alexander, evolved into an overview of how the American insurance industry developed. This project extended over many years and required the help and support of a diverse group of people.

I worked very closely with my friend and colleague, Robert Moore. He is a talented writer with extensive insurance experience, and I could not have written this book without his collaboration. Although his involvement and advice since 1998 have been invaluable in every facet of the project, the responsibility for the final text is mine alone.

Robert's wife, Patricia, with her considerable professional editorial experience, also took an active interest in the book. Her thoughtful and meticulous contributions were indispensable.

The years of research and periodic frustration were made bearable by the encouragement and counsel of my wife, Lela. Her unswerving support has always been there for me throughout our fifty-two-year marriage.

Warren Hope, an author and student of the insurance business, helped launch the project. I am especially indebted to Ronald W. Vinson, who provided sections from his and John Cosgrove's unpublished manuscript, "Challenging Risks: The Saga of American Insurance." This was particularly pertinent for the period from 1794 to 1820.

Former colleagues Horace Holcomb and Gary Sullivan followed the book's progress and supplied constructive suggestions. Past Alexander & Alexander directors Richard Alexander, Joseph Barr, Roswell Dunn, and Philip Ness also furnished useful background information. Historical Alexander & Alexander data collected by a previous A&A corporate secretary, Jack Pritchard, were essential. Also, my former colleague Dewitt Waltmon gave me Herbert Alexander's unpublished transcript, which discussed the founding of Alexander & Alexander. This unique document was most informative.

Principals of major insurance brokerages offered historical material about their companies. They included Hawley T. Chester Jr. (Johnson & Higgins), Melvin Holmes (Frank B. Hall), Richard Page (Fred. S. James), Alan Parry and John Swinglehurst (Sedgwick Group), Frank Tasco (Marsh & McLennan), John Tucker (R. B. Jones), and William Wilson (Reed Stenhouse). Their goodwill and cooperation were especially encouraging, and they provided much instructive information.

The historian and biographer Joseph J. Ellis helped me focus on the big picture in the early chapters when I was bogged down with detail. Coletta Kemper of The Council of Insurance Agents & Brokers and William Steinberg of The Hartford commented constructively on portions of the manuscript at various stages. Victoria Larson of TEXERE publishers also made useful suggestions.

In writing about the dynamics of the Lloyd's market, I am indebted to Murray Lawrence, a friend and a former Lloyd's chairman, whose introductions to various senior underwriters made my task much easier. London-based Peter Tritton was also helpful in developing Lloyd's materials.

Jean Lucy, librarian at the Insurance Library Association of Boston, located rare and fragile books covering essential aspects of early American insurance. My every request was tended to promptly, with courtesy and efficiency. Additionally, Hal Keiner, former Cigna archivist, generously made his facilities available.

Mariam Touba, reference librarian at the New-York Historical Society, tracked down an important but obscure mid-eighteenth-century newspaper ad. My thanks to William A. Bridge, who permitted use of pictures he took as the World Trade Center collapsed.

Philip Kopper of Posterity Press and his able associate, Carol Haythorne, were supportive in guiding the manuscript through the publication process and helpful in choosing illustrations and developing captions.

I also thank my faithful typist, Marilyn Codd, who must have been exasperated with me at times but never showed it.

PART I

DEVELOPMENT AND EXPANSION OF INSURANCE:
Antiquity to the Modern Era

CHAPTER 1

Origins: From the Code of Hammurabi to Lloyd's of London

Risk—the possibility of loss—is as certain as life and inevitable as taxes. Accidents occur, fires ignite, rains fall, catastrophes happen. "Acts of God" interrupt our lives daily. While we cannot prevent these, we can compensate or be compensated for them. Managing risk—improving one's position in the likelihood of risks—is as old as biological evolution. Minnows swim in schools to improve the odds some will survive the predations of bigger fish. Wolves hunt in packs to reduce each hunter's peril when bringing to bay quarry as large as moose. Risk protection has been a primary goal of humans and institutions throughout history. *Intelligently protecting against risk is the essence of insurance.*

For millennia, various groups, including benevolent nobles and nervous merchants, have attempted to protect against fortuitous loss. The precursor of insurance—as a separate, specific, and definable way of treating risk—dates back at least 5,000 years to interest rates in Mesopotamia. By 3000 B.C., interest rates were evident in Babylon, the nexus of well-traveled trade routes, which linked population and cultural centers throughout the Middle East and beyond. Caravan operators and traders were at the mercy of acts by God or man, by enemy or friend. They needed loans to purchase goods and finance cargo shipments. In addition to interest on the capital, the merchants also charged a "risk premium" reflecting a venture's riskiness.[1]

[1] The risk premium could amount to double the interest charge, or more. Borrowers often posted all their property, and sometimes family members, as collateral; if cargo was lost, they and their families might be sold into slavery.

Thirteen centuries later, insurance emerged in a form similar to what we know today. The Code of Hammurabi, circa 1755 B.C., offered a basis for institutionalizing insurance. It formalized concepts of "bottomry" referring to vessel bottoms and "respondentia" referring to cargo. These provided the underpinning for marine insurance contracts. Such contracts contained three elements: a loan on the vessel, cargo, or freight; an interest rate; and a surcharge to cover the possibility of loss. In effect, shipowners were the insured and lenders were the underwriters.

By 750 B.C., this practice was common, and risk sharing was refined into a concept known as "general average," which became a fundamental doctrine of maritime insurance. General average is a partial loss falling on all interests in a maritime venture; all parties share, on a pro rata basis, a partial loss that affects them all (e.g., jettisoning of cargo to save the vessel). In Athens, this risk-sharing principle led to the birth and growth of the first insurance exchange.

After Greece declined, Rome continued such practices and also advanced early forms of life insurance.[2] Rome's fall, circa 450 A.D., nearly took the precursors of insurance with it, but vestiges continued throughout the Middle Ages in merchant and artisan guilds. These provided forms of member insurance covering risks like fire, flood, theft, disability, death, and even imprisonment. During the feudal period, early forms of insurance waned as travel and long-distance trade declined; but transportation, commerce, and insurance would reemerge in the fourteenth through sixteenth centuries.

In fact, marine insurance appeared in Italian port cities as early as the twelfth century. And, the Hanseatic League actually produced detailed regulations for marine policies used in Lombardy by 1300. Venice became an insurance center. Policies (derived from the Italian word *polizza*, meaning a promise or undertaking) were given to those insuring marine risks. Shipowners and merchants offered policies to individuals who signed their names and recorded risk percentages at the bottom of the contract, hence becoming known as "underwriters."

[2] Members of *collegia* regularly contributed to a fund, out of which their own burial expenses eventually were paid.

Other early European underwriting examples abound. Evidence suggests that a bank in Bruges, Belgium, also offered insurance in the twelfth century, but the first organization formed specifically to write commercial insurance there dates from 1310. After merchants paid a percentage of the risk, the Bruges Chamber of Assurance covered their goods.

Marine insurance developed haphazardly in Britain. Italian merchants insured fourteenth- and fifteenth-century London exports, which suggests they were the ones who brought marine insurance to Britain. In the next century, policies providing the basis for the British Admiralty Court's first civil actions were written in Italian and adapted from the 1523 Ordinance of Florence. In 1574, Queen Elizabeth I granted Richard Candler the right to establish an insurance office in the Royal Exchange Building; the office could prepare policies and register them for a fee. Also, English law began dealing with insurance in the 1601 Francis Bacon Bill.[3] Throughout the seventeenth century, marine insurance was written primarily by shippers and traders as a sideline.

Fire insurance probably originated as a commercial product in Hamburg and other German cities during the thirteenth century. When London's Great Fire took place in 1666, however, there was no fire insurance in Britain. Shortly thereafter, Nicholas Barbon, a former doctor, opened an office to underwrite such protection. Others joined him in 1680 to start The Fire Office, the first joint-stock company for fire insurance in London and perhaps the world. Renamed The Phoenix Office in 1705, initially it insured buildings but not furniture, fittings, or goods.

Although Spain had life insurance by 1100, this type of policy evolved slowly and was introduced elsewhere in Europe during the 1700s and 1800s. England's first recorded life policy dates from 1583. Under the sponsorship of "friendly societies" (similar to fraternal orders in the United States), such insurance grew quickly. However, sparse vital statistics and lack of actuarial science caused many early life insurers to fail. The present form of life policies

[3] The bill's preamble read in part "by means of which policie of assurance it comethe to passe upon the losse or perishinge of any shippe there followeth not the undoinge of any man but the losse lighteth rather easilie upon many, than heavilie upon few." Again, sharing risk is at the heart of the idea.

Venice, a thriving port since Medieval times, became one of Europe's first insurance centers due to its stature as a capital of Renaissance commerce. The first forms of insurance were placed on goods in commerce—spices and fabrics traveling the Silk Road; furs, grain, and precious metals carried in ships. One legacy of the innovative Italians, our word "policy" derives from polizza, a promise or undertaking. When such a promise was reduced to writing and a person agreed to its terms, he wrote his name under the text to become the policy's "underwriter."

originated with England's Society for Equitable Insurance on Lives and Survivorship founded in 1762.

English insurance "brokers" appeared in the seventeenth century. Shipowners sent clerks to solicit signatures for risk participation; the clerks performed a "broking" function (i.e., they placed risks with underwriters). Becoming skilled in analyzing risks and locating insurers, some branched out and independently provided insurance advice.

As capitalism developed, English institutions changed fundamentally. The middle class gained power through its mobile cash and credit resources and challenged the nobility whose wealth was rooted in land. In this context, coffeehouses became popular; London's first opened in 1652. In less than fifty years, the city had 3,000 coffeehouses that had become hubs of social, intellectual, and business life.

By 1688, merchants and others who wrote insurance as a sideline gathered at Edward Lloyd's Coffee House. Actively trying to attract seafarers, it soon became a commercial center. Lloyd's auctioned various items and was particularly hospitable to shipping interests. When Edward Lloyd died in 1713, his son-in-law, William Newton, succeeded him; the Coffee House subsequently passed through many hands. Although marine underwriters gathered at Lloyd's in the early 1700s, it is impossible to pinpoint when it became a true insurance marketplace. Most likely, Lloyd's developed gradually as it offered more comprehensive news of world shipping.

British maritime trade grew significantly from 1690 to 1720 and expanded the need for insurance. In 1717, promoters sought government charters for two marine insurance companies—the Royal Exchange Assurance Corporation and the London Assurance. They wanted to eliminate competing corporations, groups, or partnerships from marine insurance. Their chances were bleak until, in time-honored fashion, they offered King George I a bribe. His influence prevailed, and the charters were granted under the 1720 Bubble Act.[4]

The two new companies also hoped to take over most marine insurance handled by individual underwriters. Ironically, under the act, individuals actually received competitive protection from other insurance organizations, which were now outlawed. In fact, the chartered companies wrote mostly fire insurance and for years left the marine insurance market to individuals.

Lloyd's gained considerable prominence by midcentury. Unfortunately, it gradually became infiltrated by persons of dubious character. Gambling was so rampant that when newspapers published names of prominent people who were seriously ill, bets were placed at Lloyd's on their anticipated dates of death. Reacting against such practices, seventy-nine merchant underwriters broke away in 1769 and two years later formed a "New Lloyd's Coffee House" that became known as the "real Lloyd's."

The first Lloyd's Committee was established in 1771 to create and monitor a self-regulating code of behavior. Now a society, Lloyd's was made up of a group of independent men allied by mutual interests. It relocated to the Royal

[4] This broader legislation responded to the "South Sea Bubble," a notorious failure of a stock company organized to monopolize Britain's South Sea trade. When its shares became disastrously overinflated, the company's collapse caused financial panic throughout the country.

Exchange Building in 1774, where it provided Lloyd's first true underwriting room and where it remained for fifty years. John Julius Augerstein, later called "the Father of Lloyd's," became chairman in 1795 and initiated many organizational changes and efficiencies.

London's fledgling insurance business faced catastrophic losses like those of today's insurers—but with a crucial difference. There was no "reinsurance" to spread risks among insurers. (Reinsurance is the spreading of one insurer's risk by selling a portion of it to other insurers.)[5] Reinsurance was illegal in Britain between 1745 and 1864, because it was believed to facilitate gambling by enticing those inclined to wager. The fallacy of this ban became obvious in 1780. French and Spanish fleets captured fifty-five of sixty-three vessels in a consolidated convoy of troopships and merchant vessels of the East India and West India Companies. When this generated an unprecedented loss of £1.5 million, many Lloyd's underwriters defaulted on their obligations.

[5] Although different reinsurance methods have appeared over the centuries, the principle remains the same: to spread the risk among insurers.

Fire insurance underwriters also faced challenges. A 1782 act imposed heavy premium taxes that insurers were responsible for collecting. Although Lloyd's underwriters were not subject to the taxes, they subsequently were penalized and not allowed to write fire insurance from 1790 to 1810. After this restriction was removed, a stamp duty was imposed. Such measures dictated that, for many years, Lloyd's wrote little if any fire insurance.

Gradually, Lloyd's became more cohesive and professional. In 1800, its underwriting room was restricted to merchants, underwriters, insurance brokers, and bankers—any of whom needed to be recommended by two or more members. A subscription fee of £15 helped control chaotic overcrowding and eliminate undesirables. Those paying this fee were called "subscribers." After a Trust Deed took effect in 1811, they agreed to abide by a code of rules and become subject to a central disciplinary committee. After 1843, the term "subscribers" applied principally to brokers.

Lloyd's prospered with the British economy. During the

Sir Brook Watson, a godfather of insurance, understood risk better than most. As a boy he went to sea where at 17 he lost his leg to a shark attack immortalized in a painting by John Singleton Copley. Watson became a military emissary, merchant, government official, Lord Mayor of London, and chairman of Lloyd's in 1797. Founded a century earlier by shipowners who joined forces to share the costs of losses at sea, Lloyd's became the world's most famous insurance market. Watson helped found Lloyd's Patriotic Fund in 1803 to aid war veterans and dependents—one of the first charitable trusts to help individuals in need.

Napoleonic Wars, insurance rates generated large profits. Prices of goods moved upwards, benefiting underwriters. In 1811, Lloyd's was London's only marine insurance market. However, with the 1812 Battle of Waterloo, Lloyd's first golden age ended. By 1818, commodity prices and wartime premiums fell as competition heated up from new, powerful insurers. Further, Lloyd's ostensible monopoly on marine insurance was eliminated by decree in 1824, opening up such underwriting to others. Interestingly, nearly all newly formed insurers wrote fire and life insurance, not marine.[6]

Lloyd's suffered a thirty-year period of difficulty. It had 2,150 subscribers in 1814, but membership dropped to fewer than 1,000 by 1843; only 190 of these were professional underwriters. As the 1850s approached, things improved, and the last vestiges of the Coffee House also disappeared. Lloyd's then established four subscriber cate-

[6] Although a few strong companies wrote marine insurance and were competitive with Lloyd's, there were not enough to constitute a serious threat.

[7] Only underwriting members could sign Lloyd's policies. Nonunderwriting brokers were annual subscribers. Merchants' Room subscribers included merchants, bankers, and traders who were encouraged to make market investments. Captains' Room subscribers were seafaring men who sometimes sold ships and goods at auction.

gories: underwriting members, nonunderwriting brokers, Merchants' Room subscribers, and Captains' Room subscribers.[7]

The Captains' Room subsequently became a separate club opened to others for an annual fee, but it was not successful. Likewise, the Merchants' Room lasted only ten years due to the pressure for space. And in 1846, just two member categories remained—underwriters and nonunderwriters; the latter group subsequently would decline to only a few. At midcentury, Lloyd's remained a small institution that provided facilities for marine insurance transactions. Finally, two decades later, the foundation was laid for building a renowned organization.

The Lloyd's Act of 1871 created its first detailed constitution sanctioned by Parliament and established the Lloyd's Society as a legal entity. In essence, this certified the economic importance of insurance. The act defined the Committee of Lloyd's authority and duties, delineated rules for underwriting and nonunderwriting members, addres-sed punishment of members, and gave the Committee the right to grant admission to the Underwriting Rooms to persons—called "associates"—not engaged in the insurance business.

In the 1880s, men of exceptional vision and perseverance laid the groundwork for Lloyd's emergence as a creative force in almost every line of insurance. Three men stood out: Henry Hozier, Frederick William Marten, and Cuthbert Heath.

Henry Hozier, an extraordinary innovator, was Lloyd's secretary from 1874 to 1906. After the telegraph was invented, he developed a code signal system for collecting and distributing intelligence worldwide; this permitted the posting of vessel locations at sea.

Frederick William Marten, an underwriter, sought to increase his business in the 1880s by promoting the concept of a large Lloyd's syndicate. Until then, syndicates usually consisted of one or as many as six members (later called

"Names") for whom an underwriter wrote business. Marten shocked the Lloyd's community by forming a twelve-member syndicate. Large syndicates ultimately helped Lloyd's regain business lost to insurance company competitors.

Cuthbert Heath joined Lloyd's as a clerk at eighteen. Well educated but hard of hearing, he was encouraged by his influential family to pursue an insurance career, believing it would not entail undue pressure. Undeterred by his disability, he became a marine underwriter at twenty-two and immediately made his mark by underwriting nonmarine insurance. In time, Heath would become known as the "Founder of Modern Lloyd's."

In 1885, Heath wrote Lloyd's first reinsurance contract for a fire insurance company. He then provided coverage for profit losses caused by fire. Although this prompted vigorous protests from those fearing fraudulent claims, Heath persisted, and other underwriters soon followed his lead.

During an epidemic of burglaries in 1889, he began underwriting burglary insurance. This led to broadened protection under an "all-risk jewelers policy" on personal jewelry, and to the commercially important "jewelers block policy."[8] After the Employer's Liability Act of 1880 and Workmen's Compensation Act of 1897 prescribed employer liability for work-related injuries, the Heath syndicate was the first to offer relevant coverage.

[8] Such policies provided protection inside and outside a jeweler's premises on an "all-risk basis" (i.e., they insured property against loss or damage from every cause except war, which was and is generally excluded).

As the twentieth century began, Heath was the first underwriter to significantly develop retail insurance. When a smallpox epidemic struck Britain, he offered individuals insurance provided they were vaccinated, thus inducing many to become vaccinated. Heath also played a key role in opening up the American insurance market for Lloyd's. He developed "excess-of-loss" coverage (now a standard form of reinsurance) in response to Hartford Fire Insurance Company's inquiry about catastrophic insurance. Sensing the potential for U.S. business, he established a brokerage for that purpose in 1902.

Heath became legendary in American insurance circles after San Francisco's 1906 earthquake. While many insurers delayed paying claims until they could determine whether policies provided coverage, Heath cabled his claims representatives: "Pay all your policyholders in full irrespective of the terms of their policies." Additionally, Heath wrote Lloyd's first American automobile insurance policy in 1907 and a year later began a close business relationship with Chicago broker Rollins Burdick Hunter.

It is difficult to imagine a U.S. insurance industry without the British experience as a model. Despite Heath's influence and those preceding him, American insurance would develop somewhat differently from that in the United Kingdom, as we shall explore. Many factors contributed to this, among them America's size, geographic diversity, and fierce independent spirit.

CHAPTER 2

Insurance in America: The Beginnings

William Penn founded Pennsylvania in 1681, and within twenty years its capital surpassed Boston as the most important colonial town. From its beginning, Philadelphia attracted immigrants. With a favorable location, an appealing layout, and benevolent Quaker governance, the city boasted of 5,000 residents by 1700. As population grew, so did various industries such as shipbuilding, shipping, and transatlantic trade. These activities helped Philadelphia become the insurance capital of British North America, a position it held for more than a century.

Penn cited insurance several times in his writings. For example, in 1705 he noted that "J. Askew ensured [for] £100, upon thy letter, but the ensurer [went] broke, and the 20 guineas [premium] lost. . . . Ensurers fail much." This reflects a commonly held and well-founded eighteenth-century view.

There appears to be no reference to indigenous American underwriting before 1721. Insurance, limited to marine risks, was modest and awkward. It was underwritten an ocean away by British insurers—they controlled policy terms and prices. Claims took months to be settled. When King George granted charters to two English companies in 1720, it seemed they acquired monopolistic control over marine underwriting, even in the colonies where royal charters applied, of course. However, in 1721, John Copson demonstrated that such controls did not extend to individuals when he announced he would open an insurance office in Philadelphia:

Assurances from Losses happening at Sea, are being found to be very much for the Ease and Benefit of the Merchants and Traders in general; and whereas the Merchants of this City of Philadelphia and other Parts, have been obliged to send to London for such Assurance, which has not only been tedious and troublesome, but even very precarious. For remedying of which, An Office of Publick Insurance on Vessels, Goods and Merchandizes, will, on Monday next, be Opened, and Books kept by John Copson of this City, at his House in the High Street, where all Persons willing to be Insured may apply: And Care shall be taken by the said J. Copson That the Assurors or Under Writers be Persons of undoubted Worth and Reputation, and of considerable Interest in this City and Province.[1]

[1] Advertisement in the *American Weekly Mercury*, May 25, 1721.

The advertisement implied a new office like others established later that century. Those with such offices performed brokering duties by finding individuals to underwrite specific risks. Often, they were underwriters themselves. Copson's venture probably was short-lived, and little is known about it. In *Ways and Means for the Inhabitants of Delaware to become Rich* (1725), Francis Rawle, a prominent Philadelphian, reported there were no insurance offices in that city then but said, "Now whereas there has [sic] been some Attempts made at Philadelphia [at establishing insurance offices] ... which dropt and prov'd abortive, (for what Reasons we never could learn). . . ."

Except for the ads, there appear to be no other records confirming the presence of an authentic American insurance office in Philadelphia before 1746. Moreover, earlier Philadephia references relate to English underwriters. However, there were ample opportunities for enterprising persons to experiment with marine underwriting. Rawle's book devotes a paragraph to advantages of marine insurance for "the industrious Adventurer."

Joseph Marion probably opened the first true American insurance office in Boston in 1724.[2] Four years later, he advertised the availability of fire insurance on household goods in the *Boston Newsletter*—a futile effort because the

[2] Notice of that office's opening was not found in surviving issues of three 1724 Boston newspapers, but subsequent references confirm this date.

public didn't appreciate its importance until much later. Marion's *Boston Evening Post* ads appearing late in 1745 read:

The Publick is hereby advertised that the Insurance Office first opened in Boston, Anno Dom. 1724 by Joseph Marion, Notary Publick is still held and kept by him on the North side of the Court house, near the head of King Street, where Money upon the bottom of ships and vessels may also be obtained for a reasonable premium. . . .[3]

Between 1720 and 1740, Europe's demand for wheat and flour increased; Philadelphia's port was busy. By 1740, more than 200 vessels called annually, and marine insurance was pivotal to foreign trade. Like the British, most early colonial underwriters were in shipping, and insurance became an important sideline.

Following the London pattern, coffeehouses emerged as practical and popular places for insurance negotiations and for receiving timely shipping news. In 1754, William Bradford established Philadelphia's London Coffee House (larger than an earlier version)—the center of insurance activity until the City Tavern superceded it about twenty years later. At the tavern, two insurance clerks were on duty from noon until one and from six until eight o'clock each evening. Although spirits were sold, establishments like City Tavern were business centers, similar to coffeehouses. Several catered to insurance interests by making space available for their transactions.

When six underwriters became partners in Philadelphia's Thomas Willing and Company in 1757, America's first group underwriting office opened. A merchant and shipowner, Willing was the cashier; his colleague John Kidd probably had initiated the partnership. Each equal partner could underwrite from £50 to £600 per risk. Apparently, the British permitted this office to operate because it conducted individual underwriting.

The earliest documented underwriting agreement was issued in 1762 in Philadelphia. Seventeen underwriters fixed a 1.25 percent commission rate for brokers, whose duty it was to collect and remit premiums. Claims assis-

[3] Another *Post* notice in March 1748 referred to "the first insurance office established in America and opened in Boston Anno Dom. 1724 by Joseph Marion. . . ." Marion's contemporaries apparently never challenged his assertion about establishing an office in 1724.

tance merited an additional 0.5 percent. Because of competitive pressures, most underwriters abandoned an attempt to standardize premiums four years later. In 1766, nineteen underwriters signed "Articles of Standards" for general business conduct, but they proved unworkable and were discontinued.[4]

Although many names of local insurance brokers and agents have survived in Philadelphia, relatively little is known about New York's early de facto brokers, but we do know where they conducted business. The first venue, Merchants' Coffee House, opened at the corner of Wall and Water Streets in 1744. The Tontine Coffee House, named for a kind of insurance lottery, was established across the street in 1791. Marine coverage was the focus; fire and health insurance were not yet significant factors, and the advent of casualty insurance was a century away.

New York's earliest known insurance broker, undoubtedly also an underwriter, was Anthony Van Dam, who placed similar ads in the *New-York Gazette* on August 27, 1759, and the *Philadelphia Gazette* on September 13, 1759:

> . . . the New York Insurance Office is opened at the House of the Widow Smith, adjoining the Merchants' Coffee House; where all Risks are underwrote at moderate Premiums. Constant attendance will be given from the Hours of Eleven to One in the Forenoon, and from Six to Eight in the Evening by Anthony Van Dam, Clerk of the Office, New York, August 21, 1759.

Van Dam was subsequently a warden of the Port of New York.

Fire insurance in the colonies did not develop until the eighteenth century. Widely scattered and mostly agrarian, the colonists assisted each other in repairing fire damages and replacing losses. In Boston, New York, Philadelphia, and other enterprising cities, authorities mandated elementary safety measures. As early as 1632, Boston prohibited thatched and wooden roofs. Then, after a devastating fire in 1653, the town fathers ordered:

[4] Although rate wars had developed in the 1760s, they quickly subsided. Bernard Webb has reported elsewhere, "In 1761, two competing brokers, Ezekiel Price and Samuel Phillips Savage, agreed to fix insurance conditions and rates; that agreement also did not last long."

That thear be a ladder or ladders to every house within this town, that shall rech to the ridg of the house, which every houshowlder shall provide for his house. . . . That every houshowlder shall provide a pole of about 12 feet long, with a good large swab at the end of it, to rech the rufe of his house to quench fire; that the seleckt men shall provide six good and large ladders for the towns use, which shall hang at the outside of the meeting house. . . .

In the area that became New York City, Dutch governor Peter Stuyvesant required regular chimney cleaning and inspection by the mid-1600s. And, by 1696, Philadelphia authorities did not permit smoking in the streets; further, households had to have a twelve- to-fourteen-foot swab

After marine risks, the hazard to be widely insured against was fire. In December 1835, a fire in a New York City warehouse spread because water to fight it froze in fire hoses and wells. Seen as far as Philadelphia, the fire razed 674 buildings in Manhattan's business district including its pride, the grand Merchants' Exchange (center). The disaster bankrupted 23 of 26 New York fire insurers and prompted reforms in building codes, fire resistant construction, and development of a piped-in water supply.

and a bucket. Early versions of fire engines also were acquired; Boston had one in 1653. Philadelphia purchased one in 1718; but thirteen years later when it dealt inadequately with a blaze, the city purchased two new English pumpers. New York also received a hand-pumped English model in 1731.

The next year, in Charleston, South Carolina, an effort to organize a local fire insurer failed; but in 1736 the Friendly Society was established to insure houses and tenements from fire. It was a "mutual society" (i.e., it was owned by its policyholders).[5] After a 1740 Charleston conflagration destroyed more than 300 houses, as well as stables and wharves, the Friendly Society dissolved and an ordinance took effect restricting houses to brick and stone construction.

Beginning in 1729, Benjamin Franklin's *Philadelphia Gazette* often focused on fire protection. Franklin subsequently organized the Union Fire Company, the first of several volunteer organizations. Such companies resembled clubs, mixing social functions with firefighting and striving to achieve civic status. Each owned a fire engine that was hand-filled, pumped, and drawn. Company identity was enhanced by distinctive uniforms, insignias, and unique painting of their engines.

By the mid-1700s, there were more than 2,000 houses in and around Philadelphia—none insured for fire—probably reflecting the difficulty of arranging London-based coverage. The challenge of long-distance communications made it inevitable that local competition would be preferable.

American initiatives often were based on British formats. For example, in 1752, Ben Franklin and others founded the Philadelphia Contributionship for the Insurance of Houses from Loss by Fire. It came to be known as Hand-in-Hand and issued policies for seven-year terms. Hand-in-Hand adopted the rules and practices of England's Amicable Contributionship, one of that country's oldest fire insurance companies. The company became America's first successful fire insurance firm and continued as the only one for thirty-two years.[6]

[5] The Society's Articles of Agreement read in part: "Whereas the Insurance of Houses against Fire hath by experience been found to be of very great service, to many Persons, who would otherwise have been reduced to Poverty and Want. And whereas, by reason of our Distance from Great-Britain, no Insurance Office there, will upon any Terms or Conditions, Insure any House in this Town from Loss by Fire; and it being natural for Men to form themselves into Companies and Societies, in order to guard against those Evils and Mischiefs, which separately and in their distinct capacities they would not be able to avoid. . . ."

[6] Incorporated in 1768, the Hand-in-Hand is still going strong and offers perpetual insurance for brick and stone buildings in Philadelphia and its surrounding area.

Not surprisingly, the American Revolution (1775–1783) stymied colonial insurance growth. Marine insurance continued as the most commonly held local coverage, and the greatest insurance challenge during the war years was hostile action because Britain controlled the seas.

Philadelphia's population increased during the hostilities and was 42,000 by 1781. The city nurtured the founding of new banks, which was an important trend for insurance companies. Banks frequently provided start-up capital, but they could also cause financial panics contributing to insurers' demise. The Pennsylvania Bank was established in 1780 to purchase provisions for the Continental army. The next year, the Bank of North America opened—the first conventional bank. A decade later, it bolstered the new currency by keeping records in dollars and cents instead of pounds, shillings, and pence.

In 1781, the colonies had fewer than ten manufacturing plants and a small merchant marine; seven of eight vessels arriving in American ports did so under foreign flags. Even after independence, America was economically dependent on England.

Britain's insurance industry continued dominating the market.[7] Lack of capital was the greatest obstacle to a competitive local underwriting presence. Some American insurers arranged a syndicate but could provide only a maximum of $25,000 coverage on a single risk. Conversely, British underwriters offered virtually any coverage amount, on any terms.[8]

Only one insurance company was domiciled in North America in 1782; but there were several insurance offices and about a dozen individual marine underwriters concentrated in Boston and Philadelphia.[9] Three years later, the Phoenix Assurance Company of London (Phoenix Assurance) became the first to accept American fire risks. Phoenix Assurance later pioneered the U.S. insurance agency system.

From the mid-1780s to the early 1790s, a number of

[7] Though two South Carolina insurers were established in 1776—the South Carolina Insurance Company and the Charlestown Insurance Company—apparently, neither survived Britain's occupation of Charleston.

[8] Curiously, English firms did not establish local claims facilities until the early 1800s. Perhaps there was not enough business to warrant this, or they preferred to keep business at home.

[9] Ezekiel Price, for instance, had operated a Boston marine office since 1759.

marine offices were launched, primarily in Philadelphia. Some who operated the offices were insurers before the war—prominent among them Issac Wharton, Samuel Lewis Wharton, and John Donnaldson—all of whom formed various partnerships while serving as both broker and underwriter.

Just a handful of fire companies emerged before 1794. One developed because the Philadelphia Contributionship stopped insuring houses fronted by trees. Fires spread from house to house via trees, and the trees hampered firefighting, thus increasing claims. A group who resented the tree restriction formed the Mutual Assurance Company for the Insuring of Houses from Loss by Fire.[10]

The Baltimore Insurance Fire Company, organized in 1787, was the nation's third stock insurer and the first to be incorporated. Because the value of American currency was unstable, the company was capitalized in pounds rather than in dollars. That same year, New York's first fire insurance company opened.[11]

America's technical advances helped drive the successes of financial institutions in Philadelphia and other cities. In 1787 for example, John Fitch, a Connecticut mechanic, operated a skiff on the Delaware River; the skiff was powered by a three-inch steam cylinder that moved six horizontal paddles on each side. This was the earliest recorded use of a steam-powered boat; but the next year, Fitch launched a primitive sixty-foot steamboat, which briefly carried passengers and goods between Philadelphia and Burlington, New Jersey. Unfortunately, the bright new technology also had a dark side. Increasingly common use of steam-powered transportation posed deadly risks for passengers and insurers alike.

When the Insurance Company of North America (INA) opened in 1792, the age of American insurance began in earnest. Originally, INA was conceived as a "tontine." Tontines dated to the seventeenth century and were a European form of life insurance lottery. Tontine subscribers con-

[10] This insurer was formed in 1784 and incorporated in 1786. It became known as "Green Trees" and provided keen competition for the Contributionship.

[11] The company, the Insurance Fire Office, was almost immediately renamed the Mutual Assurance Company for Insuring Houses from Loss by Fire in New York. Subsequently, it converted to stock form and in 1846 became the Knickerbocker Fire Insurance Company until it was liquidated in 1890.

tributed money to a pool that was invested and earned annuities for each member. As subscribers died, their balances were shared among the survivors. Each member's death increased survivor shares. When just one subscriber remained, he received the fund's balance.

INA's plan did not anticipate a last survivor. Instead, it had a predetermined termination date. After twenty-one years, assets would be divided among surviving shareholders. INA soon realized it could not raise adequate funding because tontines had lost popularity. Therefore, it adopted a resolution stating, "The Universal Tontine Association be and is hereby changed from its original objectives and converted into a Society to be called The Insurance Company of North America."

Headquartered in Philadelphia, INA began insuring vessels in 1793.[12] The company was incorporated a year later and its charter was amended to include fire insurance. Within a few days, the Insurance Company of the State of Pennsylvania also was incorporated. This company would become part of the American International Group Inc. (AIG).

[12] INA was the country's oldest surviving "independent" stock insurance company until 1999 when it was absorbed by ACE Ltd.

Conditions for marine and fire insurance underwriting looked promising. World events soon intervened, however. The next two decades brought war and challenges to freedom of the seas. English, French, and Spanish navies targeted American merchant ships. The nation's young shipbuilding industry was in turmoil; marine underwriters faced great uncertainty and hardship.

During the industry's formative years in the nineteenth century, banking, insurance, and occasionally other services were sometimes offered by the same company, particularly in New York State. In 1799, The Manhattan Company began with the purpose of providing a city water system. However, it was chartered with a proviso prepared by Aaron Burr, a member of the New York State legislature and subsequently a vice president of the United States. Burr's goal was to form a bank led by men connected to the Democratic Party that would rival the city's two Federalist-controlled banks. The Manhattan Company was allowed to use surplus funds for any lawful purpose connected with finance or operations. A bank was immediately formed, and for a time it also offered life insurance. Today, this institution is J. P. Morgan Chase & Co., the nation's largest bank.

Several marine insurers opened offices in New York City from 1797 to 1804. Unfortunately, the debilitating effects of European wars on shipping altered this pattern. Another development occurred in the city during the early 1800s. "Out-of-door underwriters" (brokers) set up street-corner offices; shaving insurance rates, they placed business with insurers who were willing to accept their lower prices. Their remuneration came through commissions, similar to what insurance agents received. New York's earliest stock fire insurance firm, The Eagle Fire Insurance Company, was established in 1804 and incorporated two years later with $500,000 in capital stock.[13]

[13] The Eagle Fire Insurance Company retained its name for 159 years until 1963, when it was purchased by the Continental Insurance Company of New York. The company was renamed The National Reinsurance Corporation. Subsequently, it was sold to the Lincoln National Corporation and finally to the General Reinsurance Corporation.

New insurance entities also opened in Massachusetts, Rhode Island, and Connecticut. With ocean access, these states were particularly desirable locations.

In 1795, the Massachusetts Fire Insurance Company was the first U.S. insurer to advertise for out-of-state clients. The company accepted insurance proposals from any U.S. citizen, a practice adopted by INA a year later. A rival to this company, Massachusetts Mutual Fire Insurance Company, was formed in 1798 by Paul Revere and others.

Towns like Salem, Massachusetts, also attracted insurers. Salem was an active privateering port during the Revolution and War of 1812. Ships departing from there sailed all over the world. Understandably, Great Britain forbad its West Indian possessions from trading with Americans. In response, vessels from Salem traveled around the Cape of Good Hope. A very profitable China trade resulted, and new insurers reaped significant benefits.

Newport, Rhode Island, enjoyed extensive West Indies trade. Vast quantities of sugar were imported and used primarily to manufacture rum. By 1765, Newport claimed twenty-two distilleries and Providence had a large number by 1800.

Thanks chiefly to the efforts of John Brown, president of the Providence Bank, the Providence Insurance Company opened in 1799. Brown was rather parsimonious about other senior officers' remuneration. He observed that "if the Salleries [were] fixed too high it [would] have a bad effect—in Respect [to] our other Institutions all-ready Astablished." He suggested not more than $1,000 per year be split—70 percent for the president and 30 percent for the secretary. The president's salary was subsequently capped at $800 annually and the secretary's at $200.[14]

Connecticut's prominence as an insurance center dates from the late eighteenth century. After the Revolutionary War, it (like most of America) was largely agrarian with no manufacturing facilities. Because Connecticut's deep rivers offered access to the Atlantic Ocean, it was a distribution center. Since vessels and their cargoes required protection, a vigorous insurance market developed.

Connecticut's underwriting business began with individuals and then expanded to partnerships and companies.[15] The Mutual Insurance Company of the City of Norwich was its first insurance company.[16] Originally a marine insurer, by 1818 it offered only fire insurance on buildings, with a $1,000-per-risk limit. In addition, The Hartford Insurance Company, formed in 1796 and incorporated in 1803, operated until 1825 when it was reconstituted as the Protection Insurance Company.

The industry also developed outside the Northeast in states like Maryland and Virginia. Baltimore, Maryland, strategically located between Philadelphia and Washington, D.C., gained visibility. In 1794, the Baltimore Equitable Society for Insuring Houses from Loss by Fire was formed to insure property in that city and within a five-mile radius. The company was created to address the many brush and wood fires that swept the region and terrified its population.

[14] Another Rhode Island firm, The Washington Insurance Company, began in 1800. In 1820, it joined with the Providence to form the Providence Washington Insurance Company. A few decades later, the company offered both fire and marine insurance. It remained independent until it was acquired by PW Investors, Inc. (a New York-based investment company). In 1989, it was purchased by yet another entity controlled by Baloise Holding Company of Basel, Switzerland.

[15] Similar to other cities, Connecticut's coffeehouses were popular for conducting insurance transactions. In Hartford, Morgan's Exchange Coffee House, opened by J. P. Morgan's grandfather, was a favorite.

[16] Chartered in 1795, this company operated well into the twentieth century.

The original and only successful
STEAM FIRE ENGINE BUILDERS.
BUCKEYE WORKS, CINCINNATI, O.

In 1852, A. B. & E. Latta, of Cincinnati, Ohio, developed an engine to replace the devices that were pumped by teams of men (see lower left in image on page 17). Latta's machine used a coal-fired steam engine to power the pump; teams of horses hauled it through the streets. It went into service in 1853 when the Cincinnati Fire Department became the first full-time paid department in the nation.

Also in 1794, the Virginia legislature granted a corporate charter to the Mutual Assurance Society on Buildings Against Fire of the State of Virginia. John Marshall, later the chief justice of the United States, helped organize this company. It became the first American company to offer "perpetual insurance," a type of policy that required a premium deposit and remained in effect until there was a total loss or the deposit was withdrawn.

By the mid-1790s, underwriting concentrated in Pennsylvania, New York, Massachusetts, Connecticut, and Maryland. Fifteen insurance companies (incorporated and unincorporated) wrote marine, fire, and/or life insurance in these states. When the nineteenth century began, total fire insurance premiums exceeded marine premiums. As many as thirty-five insurers were underwriting fire and marine risks, and they represented some 10 percent of the authorized corporations.[17]

Between 1800 and 1810, more than fifty charters for American insurers were issued; and in the nineteenth century's first decades, hundreds of other insurers formed. Most failed, leaving policyholders and investors high and dry. Although causes of failure varied, the new companies shared underlying weaknesses. Often, they were undercapitalized, and individual investors defaulted on their posted collateral notes. Many companies did not establish sufficient reserves for paying claims. Most insurers focused on limited geographic areas and, consequently, were especially vulnerable to local fires, storms, and other catastrophes. Further, it would be years before logical rating systems developed to assist in establishing adequate prices.

Until about 1815, Philadelphia remained the young country's most important city; its community leaders were in manufacturing, banking, and insurance. Technological inventions and improvements became commonplace. In 1808, Philadelphia's firefighting equipment was greatly improved after a riveted hose was invented. The hose was made of folded rawhide or leather and enabled engines to fight fires from greater distances. By 1810, Philadelphia had thirty-five fire companies with side-braked engines; nine hose companies used hoses of $2\,{}^1/_8$ to $2\,{}^1/_2$ inches in diameter, significantly improving water flow.[18]

The nineteenth-century historian J. A. Fowler reported that Philadelphia and environs had nearly 100,000 people by 1808, about 16,000 dwellings, and numerous other buildings. Approximately 60 percent were brick; the others were wood. A breakdown of manufacturing plants suggests the kinds of risks being covered: twenty-seven tobacco and snuff factories; fifteen cotton, woolen, and other textile factories; eighteen distilleries; seventeen carriage makers; eleven breweries; ten sugar refineries; seven paper mills; three iron foundries; and two glassworks.

Many significant insurance companies were headquar-

[17] Fire policies usually required annual premiums and, like Hand-in-Hand's, were written for seven years; this type of policy was common for many years.

[18] Brakes were the handles or levers used to pump early hand fire engines.

tered in Philadelphia. These included the Union and the Phoenix Insurance Companies; both started in 1803 and were chartered a year later. Isaac Wharton, the prominent broker and individual insurer, became the Phoenix's first president.

The respected veteran Israel Whelen died in 1806 and was succeeded by his son, Israel Whelen II, who was an organizer of the American Fire Insurance Company of Philadelphia in 1810.[19] The following year, eleven insurance companies were issuing policies from their Philadelphia headquarters, but only INA had fully paid-up capital.

Although British insurers were often used, the fledgling U.S. insurance market now provided virtually any coverage required for marine and fire risks. Nonetheless, many other perils, including earthquake, remained uninsurable.

On December 16, 1811, a massive quake was felt along the nation's midsection, from Canada to New Orleans and as far east as Boston. The initial quake and two enormous aftershocks on January 23, and February 7, 1812, were the strongest ever chronicled in the contiguous United States. It is estimated they ranged between 8.4 and 8.7 on the Richter scale.[20]

The quake's epicenter was near the town of New Madrid in the Missouri Territory where it created utter turmoil. All of New Madrid's houses collapsed, the Mississippi River changed its course, flooding was rampant, whole islands disappeared, and many vessels were lost on the river. Outside the epicenter, most log cabins withstood the shock, but their stone chimneys caved in. Bricks fell as far away as Georgia and South Carolina.

Despite the quake's devastation and the War of 1812, the second decade of the nineteenth century should have been prosperous for marine underwriters. Shipbuilding continued and included the 1818 launching of the world's first steam warship, the *First Fulton*, shortly after the death of its designer, Robert Fulton.[21] American ships were busy in foreign trade as well as on coastal and inland waters. Whaling and fishing were major businesses. Even with such positive trends, the next few decades would be difficult for stock companies writing marine coverage.

Fierce rate wars raged constantly. Competition came from new insurance companies that sprang up along the eastern seaboard. They sought to capitalize on shipping activity, with particular emphasis on Boston and New York, where business was brisk. The emerging industrial revolution also had an unsettling impact on an agrarian society. Artificially high land values contributed to bank failures and massive unemployment. Financial panic was rife during 1818 and 1819, ushering in a four-year depression. Another huge foreign trade decrease and a significant drop in merchant marine tonnage hampered marine insurance. Most insurers initially survived this crisis, but many failed later due to their impaired financial conditions.

Paradoxically, this uninviting climate did not deter new insurer formation. Some established headquarters farther west as canal and road building coincided with increased westward migration. The new insurers discovered that safety was an increasingly serious public issue. Frequent steam explosions and fire risks were constant threats.[22]

In the early 1820s, Massachusetts and New York were leaders in establishing new insurers. Although weak financial structures resulted in many short-lived firms, there were notable exceptions. New York City's North River Insurance Company was one. Capitalized at $350,000 in 1822, it later became part of the Crum & Forster Group of insurance companies, as did the United States Fire Insurance Company, founded in 1824.

Another firm, the Atlantic Insurance Company, opened in 1824; after two reorganizations as a stock company, it was mutualized in 1842.[23] Additionally, Philadelphia's Franklin Fire Insurance Company was organized in 1829 with many of the city's business leaders subscribing to the paid-in capital of $400,000.[24]

With insurance companies proliferating, it was natural they would have listings on the fledgling stock exchanges. In their unpublished manuscript, "Challenging Risks: The

[22] Philadelphia led the nation with advanced firefighting brigades. The Fire Association of Philadelphia, founded in 1817 by volunteer firemen, consisted of companies that also insured property. When it reincorporated in 1881, the Fire Association became exclusively an insurer. Its name changed to the Reliance Insurance Company in 1958, and the company was active until filing for bankruptcy in 2001.

[23] Atlantic Mutual still earns high respect today.

[24] Charles J. Martin was the company's first New York City agent. He later became the second president of the Home Insurance Company of New York (the Home). In a quirk of fate, the Home acquired the Franklin in 1948.

Saga of American Insurance," Ronald Vinson and John Cosgrove reported that in 1792, more than twenty stockbrokers gathered at a Wall Street location to formalize a working arrangement, which was the forerunner of the New York Stock Exchange. They noted, "The brokers traded government and corporate securities from the Tontine Coffee House, alongside individual insurance underwriters."

In 1817, the New York Stock & Exchange Board came into existence with twenty-four stockbrokers. Within ten years, it listed more than one hundred different securities, including twelve banks and nineteen insurance companies. Twelve years later in Philadelphia, there were fifteen banks and twelve insurers listed on the city's stock exchange.

As America moved from colonial status to thriving independence, and from an agrarian to a preindustrial economy, the insurance business developed from a handful of men into a significant industry. As the U.S. economy expanded, the industry grew in counterpoint. Insurance became more sophisticated, offering new types of coverage and diversified services for an increasingly complex country.

CHAPTER 3

Raising the Ante: The American Insurance Industry Comes of Age

The maturation of American insurance involved a distinct change, a metamorphosis, as the individual underwriter gave way to the insurance company and an evolving system that would require individual agents and brokers. Generally speaking, both agents and brokers acted (and act) as middlemen between insurance buyers and insurers. They differ in that an agent conducts business on behalf of one or more insurance companies. A broker, on the other hand, provides access to a multitude of insurance companies or markets; brokers are also licensed agents in some states.

The first American insurance agency opened in Charleston, South Carolina, in 1795. Originally called Davis & Reid and later renamed the Vigilant Insurance Office, it advertised "a choice of underwriters, as well as all possible indulgence in the payment of premiums." This office soon represented the new South Carolina Insurance Company[1] and the Charleston Insurance Company, which were formed in 1796 to offer marine coverage. Initially, insurers required brokers to process applications for which the South Carolina paid brokers 2.5 percent of the premium. That requirement was shortly rescinded in favor of a 2.5 percent discount to any purchasers submitting their own applications.

In 1797, Davis & Reid accepted a novel invitation from

[1] An earlier company with the same name did not survive the American Revolution.

the Insurance Company of America (INA) to process applications for fire insurance. It was a test, an experiment. Its
trial period lasted about a year before INA's directors decided it was "not expedient to have an agent in Charleston
authorized to take risques against fire." Apparently, they
feared agents might favor clients at the company's expense.

The launching of America's agency system reflected
leadership of the Mutual Assurance Society on Buildings
Against Fire of the State of Virginia, the Phoenix Assurance
Company (London), and INA. When the Mutual Assurance
Society won a 1794 charter, it was developed as a statewide
insurance company. Its charter identified agents by name in
twenty-three Virginia towns. In 1800, the appointment of
an agent in each county was authorized. Although restricted to that single state (which then included what became
West Virginia), it functioned as an agency system.

Other insurers sought agents to build their fire insurance
portfolios as the most cost-effective method of geographic
expansion. INA was also a leader in creating agencies. On
October 6, 1807, Alexander Henry made an impassioned
plea to his fellow INA board members to establish agencies
beyond the Allegheny Mountains. He was appointed to
chair a committee to explore expansion, and the committee's favorable recommendation was implemented in the
following January.

One INA historian says the company's first agents were
appointed on January 26, 1807, while Vinson and Cosgrove
indicate in their unpublished manuscript that Charles Ellis
of Burlington, Vermont, and James Ewing of Trenton, New
Jersey, were appointed four days earlier. These agents were
granted modest responsibility. INA's board carefully
instructed the executive charged with agent appointments
to "appoint trusty persons . . . at such places as he shall
think advisable to act as Surveyors and Agents . . . whose
duty it shall be to Survey and Certify the situation of all
Buildings and property on which insurance is required, at
the expense of the persons applying therefore." The home
office accepted business and set rates, but coverage on a risk
could not exceed $10,000. Unlike some of its competitors,

INA gave little authority to its agents before the Civil War.

At least two INA historians cite 1807 or 1808 as the starting date of the American agency system. In any case, this distinction belongs to the Phoenix Assurance. Thomas H. Montgomery, in his nineteenth-century INA history reports, "This extension of the company's business found a motive in the establishment of the Phoenix Insurance [sic] Company of London of agencies in this country; and as their experiment had been successful, the time had arrived for the North America to secure the like footing at distant places."

The Phoenix was considering U.S. operations as early as 1789, when it presented a fire engine to Charleston, South Carolina, as a marketing ploy. By 1798, it was receiving insurance offerings from Meins & Mackey, a Savannah, Georgia, broker. Clive Trebilcock has noted that, in 1804, the Phoenix appointed its first U.S. agency, Theophylact and Andrew Bache of New York City.[2] In their first month, the Baches sold eighteen policies for total premiums of $1,128.25. By the year's end, they had developed premiums of $25,000 and received commissions of 7.5 percent. Since communications between London and New York were very slow, Phoenix's New York agency could provide insurance of up to $40,000 on fireproof stores and their contents; American underwriters could not offer such high coverage limits. The agency could also settle claims and immediately draw bills on London for full settlements.

[2] This office was subsequently inherited by Thomas Satterthwaite in 1814.

The Phoenix built its agency force in response to an increasing number of insurance applications. They appointed Israel Whelen of Philadelphia and Maynard Davis of Charleston as agents in 1805, and by the end of 1806 additional agents were appointed in New Orleans, Baltimore, Boston, Norfolk (Virginia), Middletown (Connecticut), and Savannah (Georgia). From 1806 to 1815, New York State was the company's second most profitable foreign agency site. During this period, the Phoenix sold itself based on its financial strength, rather than on price.

Trebilcock also notes that Jenkins Jones, Phoenix's London home secretary from 1805 to 1833, traveled to

America and achieved some success in establishing fire insurance rates at profitable levels. However, he acknowledged the tough competition from American insurers. Jones reported, "Baltimore had a particularly aggressive concern [firm] which grasped at all risks, and to any amount, at the most trivial premiums." He also cited a Boston insurer and several mutual insurers as being very competitive. By 1810, some states, including Pennsylvania, had banned foreign insurers; New York followed suit in 1814.

The Hartford Fire Insurance Company (Hartford Fire), formed in 1810, was another insurer that appointed agents. Although one of today's foremost companies, its early years were precarious—as is typical for new insurers. Fortunately, its losses were modest even though its two employees—the president, Nathaniel Terry, and secretary, Walter Mitchell— had no prior insurance background and were frequently absent from the office. In today's parlance, it was dumb luck.

Some sources suggest that the company was founded for altruistic reasons because Terry received no salary during the first thirteen years. Most likely, his lack of compensation reflected the concurrent jobs he held as president of the Hartford Bank and as mayor of Hartford. In any event, he devoted limited time to insurance.

During the period from 1829 to 1835, the Hartford Fire was basically bankrupt and stayed in business by obtaining loans through Terry's influence. Richard M. Bissell reports that "as collateral for outstanding indebtedness, ready assets and even premiums were pledged. Any nonpledged funds were routinely paid as dividends." By 1835, the company was in such desperate condition that Terry and Mitchell were terminated by the shareholders. Thereafter it moved rapidly ahead.

John Trumbull of Norwich, Connecticut, grandson of the state's Revolutionary War governor, became the Hartford Fire's first agent. Signing on in 1810 as a surveying agent, he was limited to surveying properties to be insured and then forwarding his reports to the company for underwriting decisions.

A year later, the Hartford Fire appointed its first out-of-state agent in Conandiague, New York. By 1819, only sixteen Hartford Fire agents had been appointed. Initially, they were paid fifty cents for each policy processed; after 1819, a 5 percent commission replaced the flat fee.

Contemporary records suggest that in about 1819 there were fewer than 100 agents in the United States. But because of the paucity of accurate records, this figure probably understates the facts. An accurate count is further complicated because most were only part-time agents. As the century progressed and the nation developed, agent training increased significantly, as did the authority given them.

During 1819, eighteen insurance companies were established in various states. By far the most significant was the Aetna Insurance Company (Aetna), or "Little Aetna" as it came to be known.[3] One of its first priorities was to treat agents well. It chose agents with great care, treated them as professionals, and became extremely influential in developing the American agency system. Many early agents were current or former residents of Hartford known by one or more of Aetna's directors.

[3] Aetna was absorbed by the Connecticut General Corporation in 1962.

A letter from Aetna in 1820 to Stephen Tillinghast, its first agent in Providence, noted:

Agents of insurance companies have generally no other power and direction than simply to deliver instruments as drawn by the officers of the company. The Aetna agents are quite differently intrusted [sic] and empowered, and the highest confidence is reposed in their integrity and intelligence. In most cases they determine the rate of premiums and fill up and countersign blank policies with which they are previously furnished, without reference to the office.

Aetna produced a *Book of Instructions* for its agents in 1819, which was revised over the years. Considerable thought went into defining a successful agent. While these traits are not unique, those cited in the *Book of Instructions* have stood the test of time. For example, Aetna advised:

There is probably no occupation in life where it is so necessary to combine the caprices of mankind, and to deal with humanity

in such various phases, as the solicitation of insurance; and no class of men, consequently require in such degree, that peculiar tact which a close knowledge of human nature gives its possessor than insurance agents.

An agent who talks to all men in the same strain, using the same arguments in every case, will hardly reach the maximum of success. The successful agent has to study his subject as a physician does a patient—they do not all require the same treatment. Most men have some keynote—some chord—by touching which you lay bare the soul. It may vibrate ever so slightly, but vibrate it will, according to the nature which animates it; and this is all that is necessary. Many men, keen judges of humanity, understand this principle thoroughly, and can touch these keys with a delicacy of finesse indicating genius, if not positive intuition.

This judgment can be a science in which all, by study, practice and observation, can become more or less proficient.

In 1821, the country's population reached 9.6 million, more than a 30 percent increase in one decade. That same year, Aetna became the first U.S. insurer to appoint Canadian agents and write Canadian business. At the time, only the Phoenix Assurance (from 1804) and the Quebec Fire Assurance Company (from 1818) offered coverage in Canada. Also in 1821, the Hartford Fire enacted one of the earliest American reinsurance contracts when it reinsured the New Haven Fire Insurance Company. Four years later, both Aetna and Hartford Fire issued the earliest insurance poli-

America's insurance industry grew more complex as the nation's economy evolved— a process of starts, stops, and overlapping stages. Witness the clipper Flying Cloud *(far left) which still sailed to San Francisco Bay after steam-powered* John L. Stephens *began carrying passengers who came from New York via Panama. For safety's sake and doubtless to satisfy insurers, both would use the services of the pilot schooner in this 1855 lithograph.*

cies to an American university, Yale. Also in 1825, Aetna
probably became the first insurer to designate a "Special
Agent" to appoint and supervise new agents.

The American agency system matured slowly. Spotty
records preclude a definitive picture, but most agents initially represented only one insurance company—except in
the South. With few insurers headquartered there, agents
often dealt with many insurers. In 1821, the agency of
Robertson & Barnewell of Mobile, Alabama, acted as agent
for fourteen insurers, seven located in New York City.

Fire insurance was difficult for agents to sell unless there
had been recent fires. Agents rarely marketed it aggressively before 1820—perhaps because of their limited duties and
authority. A Philadelphia agency, Ralston & Lyman, did
seek clients by citing the low cost of fire insurance. Other
agents advertised their ability to place risks located any-
where in the United States or Canada.

In the 1820s, the number of agencies mushroomed. The
opening of the Erie Canal in 1825 provided access to the
Midwest and beyond. Now New York City goods could be
moved to Buffalo in ten days instead of thirty, and cheaply
at that, while midwestern farm products could be shipped
east. As people moved westward, insurers quickly learned
that agents were their principal source of new business.

Simultaneously, railroads began carrying passengers.
The first locomotive to run on American rails was built by
John Stevens of Hoboken, New Jersey, in 1825. The Baltimore and Ohio Railway (B&O) was chartered two years
later, and in 1830 became the first common carrier, operating a horse-drawn carriage over a thirteen-mile track. In
1831, the B&O ran a coal-burning locomotive from Baltimore to Frederick, Maryland, a distance of sixty-one miles.
The first U.S. locomotive built for sale, *The Best Friend of
Charleston*, was constructed in New York City in 1830 for
$4,000. On Christmas, it pulled a "passenger train" over six
miles to become the first scheduled American steam train.
In 1833, the 136-mile track from Charleston to Hamburg,

South Carolina, became the longest continuous railroad in the world. Railroads would play an indispensable role in the early growth of major insurance brokers.

Hartford Insurance Company enjoyed an exemplary record for deploying an agency system. Reorganized during 1825 and renamed the Protection Insurance Company, it was licensed to underwrite fire and certain "inland marine" coverages.[4] The Protection was particularly aggressive in the early appointment of agents. Appointees included Ephraim Robins of Cincinnati, who in 1826 was probably the country's first "General Agent." In this role, his responsibility was broader than a special agent's, usually covering a branch or larger territory. While he appointed (and presumably trained) many agents, Robins also managed the company's agency and brokerage business in his territory.[5]

Agency development was constrained between 1827 and 1835, as a series of states imposed taxes on nonresident insurers to raise general revenue. Begun in Massachusetts, taxes ranged from 4 to 20 percent of premiums, and even leading companies lacked the capital to meet new state requirements. Aetna, for instance, could not write insurance in Massachusetts and Pennsylvania because it lacked the minimum capital of $200,000. Because of such restrictions, many agents were forced to switch insurance company representation or drop agency activities completely. It took a major conflagration to demonstrate the folly of state restrictions.

The New York City fire of 1835 began an era of crippling catastrophes. On a cold December night, with the temperature falling to seventeen degrees below zero and winds rising to gale force, a fire started in a warehouse, according to Edwin Burrows and Mike Wallace. Stove coals apparently ignited gas escaping from a broken main, and the city burst into flames, radiating a glow visible from New Haven to Philadelphia. Firefighters' hoses froze, and nearly 700 commercial and private buildings, including most of New York's business section, were destroyed in three days. The estimat-

[4] Inland marine insurance encompasses a variety of disparate assets. Coverages deal mostly with moving or movable property, such as anything in transit—jewelry, fine arts, musical instruments, and scores of other articles.

[5] The Protection appointed some 250 agents before failing financially in 1854.

ed loss was $20 million, an extraordinary figure for the time. Out-of-state fire insurers contributed $2 million. The Hartford Fire's payment of $65,000 was one of the few losses that an insurer was able to pay in full. With collective assets of less than $10 million, all but four fire insurers based in New York defaulted and went bankrupt.

This disaster highlighted the vulnerability of concentrated underwriting in a single area of high risk. The need for underwriters from out-of-state insurance companies to spread the risk was clearly demonstrated, and state taxes were subsequently reduced or eliminated.

During the 1830s, the insurance community faced a serious dichotomy. On the one hand, signs of the Industrial Revolution were appearing, and underwriters were encountering an array of new insurable risks.[6] On the other hand, many of the same obstacles remained that had impeded progress before, such as undercapitalization and rate wars. After a string of promising underwriting years, sudden catastrophic events imperiled many companies. These roller-coaster conditions would continue throughout the nineteenth century.

Still, the early 1830s were years of hope and progress. The physicist Joseph Henry had constructed a primitive electromagnetic motor in 1829. Cyrus Eaton demonstrated a mechanical reaper in 1831 and three years later patented an improved model—a machine that would eventually increase the farm worker's productivity exponentially. This coincidentally fueled the movement of rural laborers to urban manufacturing centers. Later in the decade, John Deere invented the steel plow, which replaced the fragile wood and iron tool, further bolstering farm productivity. In 1839, Charles Goodyear developed "vulcanization," a process making the use of rubber possible. Elias Howe's sewing machine, introduced in 1845, sewed 250 stitches a minute, seven times faster than by hand.

Newspapers developed during this same period. The first successful penny daily, the *New York Sun*, appeared in 1833,

[6] Until about 1856, when it was phased out, some underwriters wrote slave insurance, as slaves were considered property.

followed two years later by the *New York Herald*, a four-page penny daily. During the next decade, the rotary press enabled rapid and efficient newspaper printing, leading to the founding of the *New York Times* in 1851.

By fostering the Industrial Revolution, these and other innovations accelerated insurance growth. Insurance facilitated manufacturing expansion by limiting the exposure to risk, thus encouraging new industrial opportunities, which enlarged markets for insurance. As the surge of new insurers continued between 1832 and 1837, twenty-six companies were formed, nineteen confining underwriting to fire insurance.

The advent of the true American clipper ship, which succeeded the Baltimore clipper, created optimism among marine underwriters. The era began in 1832 when the *Ann McKim* was launched in Baltimore. American clippers would rule the seas until just before the Civil War. Faster and cheaper to sail than the British broad-beamed ships, they were also safer in poor weather. While the old sailing vessels took 150 to 200 days to go from New York to San Francisco, *Flying Cloud* set a record in 1851 by covering the distance in eighty-nine days. The clippers briefly bolstered the fortunes of American marine underwriters, but the frequency and size of claims soon changed the underwriting mood from enthusiasm to despair.

The steamship also made steady headway. The *Savannah* crossed the Atlantic by sail and steam in 1819. The *Great Western*, in 1838, became the first to make the passage under steam power alone; scheduled oceanic steamboat service began a year later. Additionally, by 1834, steamboats were commonplace on America's rivers, with almost 500 in service during 1835. While these vessels were initially more appealing to underwriters than the sailing craft, flatboats, and rafts they replaced, the risk of explosion was considerable. Accidents were frequent, and safety measures became an urgent need.

A depression that began in 1837 extended well into the

1840s, creating such havoc that many insurers folded. In Philadelphia and Hartford, even some of the better-managed companies failed. Hoping to survive, several failed Philadelphia stock insurers reappeared briefly as mutuals.

Signs of economic recovery began in the mid-1840s. Philadelphia's reign as financial capital ended, and New York City assumed this mantle. New York's population and its port activity moved rapidly ahead of its rival. While Philadelphia remained an important insurance center, it had to share that distinction with other northeastern cities. Fortunately, it would be spared the worst of the crippling fires that plagued other urban centers.

By 1845, industrialization was in full swing, bringing prosperity and optimism. Not even a short war with Mexico (1846–47) impeded momentum. Upcoming decades would usher in changes that few had envisioned. Between 1842 and 1870, the country's population doubled to 39 million people, a figure that eclipsed the individual populations of Italy, France, Japan, and the United Kingdom. American innovation flourished. In 1837, Samuel Morse exhibited the electric telegraph. Tapping out his first telegraphic message, from Washington, D.C., to Baltimore in 1844, he asked, "What hath God wrought?" By 1861, use of the telegraph was common, greatly expediting business transactions and revolutionizing military communications—just in time for the Civil War.

As remarkable as these developments were, railroad expansion contributed most to America's unprecedented prosperity. Among the chief beneficiaries were the railroads themselves. The Pennsylvania Railroad, formed in 1846, became America's most powerful corporation, growing larger through acquisition. By 1852, its track extended to Pittsburgh. A $600,000 investment in three small intermediary lines permitted track to reach from Pittsburgh to Chicago in 1858.[7] The Rock Island Railroad spanned the Mississippi River in April 1856 with a wooden bridge, making it much easier for freight and passengers to travel west.

[7] Railroad travel remained difficult. While one could travel from New York to Chicago by 1854, the journey required changing trains and crossing the Hudson River at Albany by ferry in summer and by sleigh in winter.

Although much of the country enjoyed vigorous economic activity as industrialization progressed, the insurance industry was not prospering. By 1845, only half of the original 150 marine insurers remained. A century later, just 20 survived.

Mutual marine insurers in particular experienced multiple catastrophes. Of the fifty or so companies formed between 1820 and 1850, most had disappeared by the late nineteenth century. The Atlantic Mutual Insurance Company, an exception, survived a series of catastrophic marine disasters that plagued the industry during the 1850s.

Property and marine insurers faced innumerable obstacles in the 1840s and 1850s. Fire was the greatest threat. In 1845, New York City was enveloped by a second huge fire, which destroyed 450 buildings and many ships. To survive and preserve its financial integrity, Aetna assessed its directors for funds. A third conflagration struck in 1853, and

The success of the world's first oil well, drilled in 1859, quickly spawned a forest of derricks in Titusville, Pennsylvania. Drilling, transporting, refining, and retailing oil products came to be dominated by John D. Rockefeller's empire. Starting as Standard Oil of Ohio in 1870, it revolutionized America's corporate model, while oil itself revolutionized manufacturing and transportation. These industries offered as many new opportunities as risks, which insurers learned to cover through experience, savvy, even trial and error.

many vessels were lost, including the clipper *Great Republic*, then the largest U.S.-built merchant ship.

Other cities were similarly affected. In Pittsburgh, some 1,000 buildings, including homes, offices, and warehouses covering fifty-six acres, were consumed in an 1845 inferno. The fire began in a crowded group of wooden structures near a river, and many vessels were destroyed. Only about 25 percent of the buildings and boats were insured. During the late 1840s, St. John's, Newfoundland; Nantucket Island, Massachusetts; Albany, New York; and St. Louis, Missouri, suffered crippling fires. On May 19, 1849, St. Louis lost half its business district and twenty-seven steamboats in a three-square-mile area after the steamer *White Cloud* caught fire. In these instances, the Hartford Fire paid between $54,000 to $84,000 in losses.

Marine underwriting continued to be treacherous. Following horrendous payouts in 1853, the next year proved even worse. Unusually powerful winds destroyed a number of New York's fleet of prime steamships, packets, and clippers, along with many ordinary freighters. Clipper ships in particular seemed to face one weather- or fire-related calamity after another. Frequent fraudulent claims arose as vessels were scuttled by crews to collect insurance. Claims on nonexistent cargoes were often filed after ships were lost, and marine underwriters were inevitably victimized. Atlantic Mutual paid $4.5 million in claims for 1854 alone. This far exceeded annual premiums, forcing the company to forgo a policyholder dividend for the only time in its history.

An Atlantic Mutual historical review recalls an incident from the 1870 "disaster book" that reflects the ingenuity of fraudsters:

Early in the year, the steamship George Washington left New York for New Orleans. Atlantic had $83,400 at risk on the hull and cargo. Fire broke out below decks a few days after she left port. The captain traced the source of the smoke to a lower hold where he found a smoldering 4-foot-square box marked "Handle With Care—Keep Dry." Its owners had claimed that the box contained valuable machinery.

The captain soon found that the contents could loosely have been labeled machinery, but it was of the type to be made famous many years later by Rube Goldberg. It consisted of a one-gallon can of spirits of turpentine, a soda-water bottle filled with gasoline, two cigar boxes in which nestled several families of white mice, a highly explosive compound of potassium chloride, and packing of straw and sawdust.

The bizarre contents were arranged in such a way that the mice would nibble at one of the containers and set off the explosive. This in turn would ignite the turpentine, gasoline, straw and sawdust. The fire would then gain headway in the lower hold and would wipe out ship, cargo and crew, destroying all evidence in the process. Thus the incendiary box—worth about $10—would return many times its value to the shippers, including $83,400 from the Atlantic. Thanks to a vigilant captain and crew, the diabolical plan failed.

Problems with fraud paled in comparison with the constant threat of steamship explosions, which produced thousands of injuries and fatalities. Paddle boats were common on navigable rivers by the 1840s, but they were poor insurance risks. Cargo was often the only risk underwriters would cover, presumably because frequently it could be salvaged. The seriousness of steam boiler explosions led Congress in 1838 to enact the first legislation dealing with this type of risk, as the law established standards for boiler testing, inspections, and liability. This legislation, relatively toothless at first, was considerably strengthened in 1858.

After 1840, various states began to regulate insurers. Some efforts were meritorious, others self-defeating, while in general state rules kept the business fragmented. Pennsylvania began scrutinizing insurers' annual reports in 1842; this positive action contrasts with New York legislation that opened a Pandora's box in 1849. Entitled "An Act to Provide for the Incorporation of Insurance Companies," the law permitted creation of mutual fire insurance companies capitalized by notes. It also allowed immediate acceptance of risks, even if the companies had no cash on hand. Sixty mutual fire companies were formed during the next several years, and predictably more than 80 percent failed by 1860, with losses exceeding $2 million.

New York passed another questionable bill in 1849 and

strengthened it in 1853. The measure precluded a company from providing both fire and life coverage. Because of the importance of selling both forms of insurance in New York State, Aetna was forced to divest itself of its subsidiary, Aetna Life Insurance Company, which it had formed in 1850.[8] On a progressive note, in 1853, New York required its insurers to establish an unearned premium reserve reflecting that portion of premiums not yet earned during the policy period.[9]

Various states instituted more formal approaches to insurance supervision. New Hampshire and Vermont, for example, established insurance departments in 1852, and Massachusetts followed three years later. The nation's first insurance commissioner was appointed by Massachusetts in 1858.

Western expansion created opportunities and pitfalls. The 1849 California gold rush contributed to a shipbuilding boom and sparked rapid formation of insurers. As with New York State's fire mutuals, few were adequately capitalized or properly staffed. Most that survived the country's financial crash of 1854 fell during the 1857 and 1858 business collapses.

Failure of the New York City branch of the Ohio Life Insurance & Trust Company actually triggered the panic of 1857. Although Ohio Life & Trust wrote a small number of life insurance policies, it was primarily a bank, and its failure came from the watering and inflating of stock values. Unscrupulous promoters drained the underlying companies of assets, so their securities had no backing to support the prevailing prices. As a national consequence, U.S. silver coins became worth more than their face value. Subsequent events caused approximately 13,000 businesses, including sixteen of Philadelphia's twenty-six insurers, to collapse.

Remarkably, notable successes occurred in the midst of chaos. Several companies with impressive financial strength and excellent management were chartered. For example, the Dividend Mutual Insurance Company, formed in 1849, was renamed the Glens Falls Insurance Company in 1864.[10] The Springfield Fire & Marine Insurance Company began in

[8] The Aetna Life Insurance Company became Aetna Casualty and Surety Company in 1917 and Aetna Life and Casualty Company in 1967. It was renamed Aetna Inc. in 1996. (Referred to hereafter as Aetna L&C.)

[9] Massachusetts had adopted similar legislation in 1837.

[10] Both the Glens Falls and the Niagara Fire Insurance companies, which opened in 1850, were eventually purchased by the Continental Insurance Company.

1849 and the Hanover Fire Insurance Company in 1850.[11] Three other major twentieth-century insurers, Home Insurance Company, Continental Insurance Company, and Saint Paul Fire and Marine Insurance Company, were established in 1853.[12]

The Home and Continental companies eventually operated nationally and survived well into the twentieth century, when they were acquired by other insurers. The Home's sponsorship was especially noteworthy. Its board of forty-five directors drew from New York City's mercantile business leaders. Within a few decades, the company became the country's largest fire insurance underwriter.

Not surprisingly, New York City became headquarters for significant insurers because its prominence as a financial center was developing dramatically. Wall Street was well on its way to becoming America's financial capital, and eight rail lines served the city, which by then boasted twenty daily newspapers.

Hartford's visibility as an insurance center also grew. Although one of its most significant insurers, The Travelers, was not yet formed, the Phoenix Insurance Company (Hartford) opened for business in 1854, capitalized at $200,000, and drew many of its first employees from the defunct Protection.

Marine insurers' business deteriorated precipitously during the Civil War. In the twenty years before the war, American foreign trade increased from 763,000 to 2,500,000 tons. Aggressive activities of the British and Confederate navies abruptly reversed this.

The British, in particular, played a decisive role in restricting ocean shipping. Their reliance on southern cotton was a major incentive for aiding the Confederacy, and the Royal Navy inflicted enormous losses on Union ships. They also provided the South with two powerful warships, *Alabama*, built in Birkenhead, England, in 1862, and *Shenandoah*, built in Glasgow, Scotland, and commissioned in late 1864.

[11] The Hanover removed "Fire" from its title in 1958 and was absorbed by the Allmerica Property & Casualty Companies Inc. in 1992.

[12] The Saint Paul had to sell its office furniture to survive an 1857 financial crisis, yet remains an important insurer today.

The *Shenandoah* targeted Union whalers and ranged as far as the Bering Sea. Its goal was to disrupt the supply of whale oil, which was used as a lubricant and lamp fuel. *Shenandoah* seized or destroyed forty Union ships. The *Alabama* was even more effective, destroying or capturing during a twenty-one-month stint sixty-five Union vessels worth more than $6.5 million.

Concerned about tremendous losses, Atlantic Mutual's president, John Devine Jones, met with President Lincoln and agreed to provide war risk insurance for federal shipping. In return, he asked the government to file claims against the British crown at the war's end. He sought reimbursement of all losses paid by insurers that had been caused by British action. The final figure was $12 million in gold plus $3.5 million of interest, a sum decreed by a tribunal and specifically designated as reimbursement for insurers.

Based on some 10,000 claims, Atlantic Mutual's portion was more than $1.6 million. Unfortunately for Atlantic Mutual and other American insurer claimants, Congress reneged on reimbursement after Lincoln's assassination. Instead, the earmarked money was eventually dispersed among other claimants, including uninsured shipowners, merchants, and those Congress felt "deserved payment."

The war created problems for many southerners insured by northern companies. A few months after the presidential election in 1860, southern agents received instructions from northern insurers to decline all applications and not renew policies. However, the integrity of many insurers survived the war. Vinson and Cosgrove reported that clients of a Charleston, South Carolina, agent lost three buildings to fire when they were still insured under a prewar Hartford Fire policy. The agent told the policyholders to fill out proofs of loss. He wrapped these documents and applicable policies in watertight material and buried them in a field. After the war, and four long years after the loss, all articles were retrieved, and the Hartford paid the claim.

Although the Civil War's end brought renewed prosperity to much of the country outside of the South, America's merchant marine and marine underwriters did not share the good fortune. Rebuilding the U.S. Navy took precedence over augmenting the merchant fleet, and the situation was complicated by a mounting preference for new British ships over American clippers. Even before the war, Great Britain was building iron ships propelled by steam.[13] Although iron was replacing wood for ship construction, the United States was slow to develop its abundant resources of coal and iron. As a result, between 1865 and 1872, foreign ships, most of them British, handled 70 percent of international transport. This in contrast to the 1850s clipper era, when U.S. ships carried 70 percent of combined imports and exports. After the war, reflecting their diminished use, a third of the ships of U.S. registry were sold to foreigners at bargain prices.

British underwriters also undercut American insurers by offering lower rates for British than for U.S. ships. There was even a disparity on the rating of sailing vessels. According to Lloyd's, research indicated that the white oak used in constructing American ships afforded two-thirds the useful years of British oak.

[13] In 1855, the first iron Cunard steamer crossed the Atlantic Ocean in nine and a half days.

Most other U.S. economic sectors thrived as industrialization continued gaining momentum. In 1861, the first transcontinental telegraph provided a communications underpinning for progress in almost every industrial area, and in 1866 Cyrus Field laid the first Atlantic cable. In 1859, Edwin L. Drake drilled the world's first oil well in Titusville, Pennsylvania, and in 1865 the first oil pipeline was laid, also in Pennsylvania, covering a distance of six miles. Five years later, John D. Rockefeller founded Standard Oil Company of Ohio. The petroleum industry opened a significant new class of business for insurers and brokerages. The risks involved were extremely complex and challenging, and agents usually were not equipped to handle them.

Between 1865 and 1875, two other significant developments aided insurers. U.S. manufacturing plants grew from 123,000 to 252,000, offering the insurance industry further

[14] In 1868, Westinghouse developed the air brake, greatly increasing railroad safety.

[15] Two railroad insurance syndicates, Eastern Railroad Syndicate and Railway Underwriters, underwrote most railroad risks. In 1919, Eastern was renamed the Railroad Insurance Association. Other insurer associations underwrote petroleum and, eventually, aviation risks, because of the huge values involved.

growth opportunities. The railroads' rapid progress produced a national railway system. The Central Pacific and Union Pacific Railroads joined at Promontory Point, Utah, in 1869, linking the continent by rail.[14] The 1853 founding of Cornelius Vanderbilt's New York Central Railroad also stirred up competition. This amalgamation of ten small independent northeastern roads immediately rivaled the B&O, the Erie, the Pennsylvania, and other eastern railroads.[15]

As with steamboats, increased railroad activity resulted in a proliferation of serious accidents. Between 1853 and 1863, some 1,356 railroad and steamship accidents cost 4,691 lives and injured another 6,614 victims. The *New York Times* reported in the five months after the Civil War that at least 3,181 individuals had died in railroad mishaps, steamship accidents, explosions of powder magazines, and the collapse of buildings. One of the most tragic accidents occurred with the sinking of the Mississippi River steamboat *Sultana*, which was carrying about 2,100 passengers, including some 1,500 Union soldiers who had just been repatriated from Confederate prisons. Seven miles from Memphis, a series of boiler explosions destroyed the boat, killing almost 1,600 people.

The double spiral continued: As old industries broke fresh ground and modern industries developed, insurers found new customers and covered emerging forms of risk. New coverages encouraged further innovation in commerce and industry. The road was not even, and rates of invention far from swift. Yet, on balance, the nineteenth century was a time of mechanical and economic progress, which meant considerable growth and diversity of coverages for insurers.

CHAPTER 4

Phoenix (and Others) Rising: Foundings, Fires, and Finances

Necessity is the mother of invention, and the compelling need for accident insurance sired one of the industry's giants. The Travelers Insurance Company, soon to be known as "The Travelers" (Travelers), was organized in Hartford, Connecticut, on April 1, 1864, by James Batterson. Its purpose was to serve modern and forward-looking people who were using the latest travel methods by "insuring travelers against the loss of life or personal injury while journeying by railroad or steamboat."[1]

The first printed policy was issued to Batterson himself. It agreed to pay him or his beneficiaries for personal injury or death from any accident caused by "outward and visible" means. Inevitably, there were numerous and interesting policy exclusions, such as death or injury caused by dueling or fighting, suicide, war, riots or invasion, intoxication of the insured, riding races, or willful exposure to unnecessary danger or peril.

A West Coast Travelers contract from this period declared that, "No insurance is granted against any fatal or non-fatal injuries caused by Indians . . . or while the insured is taking part in gymnastic sports." In a symbolic gesture (perhaps foreshadowing corporate public relations), the Travelers insured a Hartford banker against the risk of walking from the post office to his home. The banker paid a two-cent premium.

[1] While there are references to U.S. accident insurance from the early 1850s, the Travelers is usually credited with developing this coverage and giving birth to casualty insurance.

On December 6, 1864, five months after accident insurance was introduced, the first accidental death claim was paid to the widow of a conductor who fell between train cars. Other early claims included an engraver from Lynn, Massachusetts, who was in a covered wagon when a gust of wind ripped off its top. He was deposited among some rubbish and severely bruised. A commercial traveler from York, Pennsylvania, sprained his back pulling on a boot, and a carpenter from Pittsburgh broke a collarbone when he became entangled in his partner's hoopskirt while dancing.

In his Travelers' history, George Malcolm Smith recounts a bizarre incident involving a Reverend Mr. Petrey of Stamford, Kentucky. During a visit to one of his brethren, the Reverend had "scarcely seated himself in the parlor before a hen flew into the house and attempted to alight on a rifle hanging on the wall. The weapon fell and was discharged, the ball striking the preacher . . . lockjaw ensued, and he died two days later."

By the end of 1864, after only eight months in business, the Travelers had appointed 247 agents and written 2,880 accident policies with premiums of almost $50,000. The Travelers agents also found that they could easily add life insurance and began to offer life policies.

Although it was no simple matter to introduce new and unfamiliar products to a skeptical public, 40,000 accident policies were sold during the first two years. A Civil War major who became a Travelers agent reported, "I first besieged my friends and acquaintances for the favor. I recited accidents I gathered from the street and from the few newspapers published in 1865. Every morning and every evening I loaded up with items. No merchant, banker, traveler or stay-at-home could escape my ammunition. . . ."

Within months of the Travelers' opening, some seventy accident insurance companies had been formed, but rate cutting was rampant, and most companies soon folded. Of the early Travelers agents, at least one office remained an independent agency as late as 2002—Wilcox-Lumpkin Company of Columbus, Georgia, which had been originally appointed in 1866.

As in many professions, insurance agents were not without personal risk. A Travelers insurance company internal publication from the 1870s describes the tragic plight of one of its agents:

Mr. Fred W. Rice, but lately appointed agent of the Travelers at Scranton, Pennsylvania, came to his death in a shocking manner. . . . He was engaged in canvassing Delaware & Hudson Canal Company employees for accident insurance. He had just been talking with one of the men of the necessity for being insured in his perilous occupation when he made a misstep and fell down a shaft, a perpendicular fall of 350 feet. He was, of course, crushed into a shapeless mass, with nearly every bone broken. He was young, full of energy and promise, a good worker and a valuable man. A host of friends mourn his sad fate.

Safety concerns were responsible for other new coverages. The Hartford Steam Boiler Company evolved during 1866 from the Polytechnic Club, whose purpose was boiler safety.

Frequent reports of calamities involving both people and property encouraged the public to purchase more accident and fire insurance. Increased demand fueled further expansion of agencies as well as brokerages. As the business of agents and brokers matured, their differences became more distinctive. Agents benefited from the country's westward expansion, and their numbers increased greatly. San Francisco emerged as the West Coast insurance center where underwriting decisions were made and where agents congregated. But the Phoenix Insurance Company forced a change in San Francisco. Shortly after opening in 1854, it deployed agents up and down the West Coast with underwriting authority and advertised in local papers. These were shrewd strategic moves.

The insurance broker emerged gradually. In the United States, "broker" seldom evoked the negative connotation it did in the early days in England. There, brokers preferred to be known as "office-keepers," since the word broker connoted disreputable traders involved in shady practices. Until recent times (when some real scoundrels occasionally appeared on the scene), U.S. brokers were usually individuals of integrity who ran professional offices and managed money conservatively. Unlike many early agents for whom insurance was a part-time activity, most brokers worked full-time in the business.

Business complexity created the need for new insurance approaches. This benefited brokers who gained in visibility and prestige. Brokers' access to multiple insurers enabled them to place risks that agents, who usually worked with only a few insurers, could not accommodate. Even so, brokers struggled for years to be fully accepted by insurers and insurance buyers.

With the exception of Corroon & Black, the principal twentieth-century U.S. brokerages were formed between 1845 and 1900. Johnson & Higgins, or "J&H," was the first.[2] J&H was established at 90 Wall Street in New York City in 1845 as a partnership under the name of Jones and Johnson.

[2] Several major brokers were referred to by their initials and came to be known as "alphabet houses."

Jones and Johnson had been employees of the Atlantic Insurance Company, precursor of Atlantic Mutual Insurance Company. Originally they were marine average adjusters, or claim handlers, a business that led naturally to marine insurance brokerage. In 1847, A. Foster Higgins, age sixteen and a native of Macon, Georgia, joined the firm. Higgins left a year later for Atlantic Mutual but rejoined in 1851. When he became Johnson's partner in 1854, the partnership changed to Johnson & Higgins, the name it retained for the next 143 years.[3]

[3] Johnson died in 1881, while Higgins retired in 1887 and died in 1916 at the age of 85.

Between April 1855 and 1856, J&H adjusted sixty-six cases on which Atlantic Mutual was the insurer. The vessels included eighteen ships, fifteen barks, six brigs, and twenty-four schooners. J&H's nearest competitor adjusted forty Atlantic Mutual cases in the same period. (During the Civil War, J&H owned a wrecking schooner, and the federal government asked the company to help raise a sunken Union ship.) Although other brokers were active in marine insurance, significant competitors did not appear until years later.

Fred. S. James & Co., Inc.[4] (James & Co.), began in 1858

[4] The firm's first name, unusually, carried a period, because Mr. James preferred to be known as Fred rather than his given name, Frederick.

when Alfred James opened an agency on Old Courthouse Square in Chicago.[5] In 1864, his brother Fred, fourteen years his senior, joined the firm. The two gained invaluable experience adjusting client losses caused by the spectacular 1871 Chicago fire. When Alfred left a year later to join Northwestern National Insurance Company, Fred continued as Fred. S. James & Co., Inc. By 1879, the company represented seven insurance carriers and operated as a brokerage.[6]

Frank B. Hall & Co. grew from a brokerage that was founded in 1863, when Horace Moody and Charles Mann formed Moody and Mann in New York City. (Frank Hall, whose name the firm eventually adopted, did not enter the insurance business until 1893.) The two partners, Moody and Mann, complemented each other. Moody was young, scholarly, and well spoken, while Mann was older, more introspective, and more experienced. Moody led the early operation, but Mann steered it through the turbulent Civil War years. A third man, Henry Stewart, was crucial to its future success. In 1862, at age thirteen, Stewart emigrated from Newfoundland to America and, by his late teens, was employed by the firm. Shortly thereafter, its name was changed to Moody, Mann & Stewart.

The business was roughly divided into three parts: average adjusting, insurance brokerage, and overdue insurance. The third component addressed a serious need for shipowners. In the days before radio, ships requiring repairs during a voyage often landed at remote locations. Since it was difficult to report their plight, it was not uncommon for sailing ships to be overdue for three or four months, sometimes a year. After a delay of two or three months, the original marine insurers would often reinsure the vessel and its cargo—thus "overdue insurance."

The same process occurred at the end of six months, and again in the ninth month if the ship was not sighted. After nine to twelve months, reinsurance premiums might be 90 percent of the ship's worth. In a daring but successful bit of underwriting, Mann, Moody & Stewart often acted as the last group of reinsurers. With the advent of Marconi's radio

[5] Earlier, Alfred had served two years as an employee of the Home Insurance Company.

[6] James & Co. was acquired by Transamerica in 1983 and sold to The Sedgwick Group in 1985.

signaling system in the late 1890s, the need for overdue insurance vanished.

Charles Mann retired before 1870, leaving the business in the capable hands of Moody and Stewart. In 1883, Horace Moody died, and Henry's son, Cecil P. Stewart, was taken into the partnership. The firm became Henry Stewart & Son, with the two men specializing as average adjusters.

Marsh & McLennan Companies, Inc. (M&M), another historically important company, traces its origin to 1871, when brothers named Bomar from Kentucky formed a Chicago insurance agency. When R. A. Waller, also from Kentucky, joined in 1874, the firm became Bomar & Waller. Upon the Bomars' 1877 retirement, the agency became R. A. Waller. Henry Marsh and Donald McLennan did not join as partners until 1904, and the Marsh & McLennan name was adopted in 1906.

Among several signs that agents and brokers were coming of age was the formation of the National Association of Local Fire Agents in 1869. The association helped agents communicate on industry issues. In 1896, it became the National Association of Insurance Agents and developed a huge membership. It was the precursor to the largest agent group, the Independent Insurance Agents Association (IIAA).[7]

[7] The New York Board of Insurance Brokers, formed in 1862, was probably the earliest brokers association.

Underwriting fire insurance remained most insurers' preference. In the mid–nineteenth century, new fire insurance companies appeared in droves as others foundered. In 1866, the National Board of Fire Underwriters was organized. Its objectives were "to establish and maintain, as far as practical, a system of uniform premium rates, to establish and maintain a uniform rate of compensation to agents and brokers, and to repress incendiarism and arson. . . ."[8]

The objectives of the National Board of Fire Underwriters were difficult to enforce, and two years later thirty-seven fire insurers drew up a document titled the "Chicago Compact." It stipulated that no company would continue to do business through any agent who wrote a fire policy at a rate

[8] Widespread arson prompted a controversial policy, the "Hamburg Form." It provided that, in case of fire, the insuring company should pay no more than three-fourths of the actual loss, since a large percentage of fire losses were believed to be the work of arsonists.

lower than the National Board's promulgated rates. New insurers, seeking market share, often ignored this edict, staking survival on the law of averages. If enough companies were formed, a small percentage would be successful, and survivors would gradually expand.

The importance of rating discipline is reflected by insurers' horrendous post–Civil War experience. For example, American-insured fire losses accelerated from $29 million in 1864 to $43 million in 1865. The *Insurance Chronicle* noted that, "Competition had become unscrupulous and reckless; premiums were computed with the view of obtaining, rather than compensation for, the risks; underrating was substituted for underwriting. . . ."

Massive fires between 1865 and 1872 led to the demise of many insurers. Some of these catastrophes wiped out entire towns or cities. Two fires in Maine, one at Augusta and the other in Portland, destroyed most of each city. Vicksburg, Mississippi, was likewise decimated. In 1871, the town of

Despite new firefighting tools and regulations, fires remained cataclysmic. The Chicago fire in 1871 spread over five square miles of the city and burned into the psyche of America, fueled in part by this Currier & Ives lithograph, which heralded losses "to the amount of 200,000,000 dollars." The fire tested the resources of 200 property insurance companies and bankrupted scores of them. Boston burned a year later, reinforcing the tragedy of catastrophic losses in urban disasters, losses that stimulated new approaches to underwriting.

[9] Every wooden structure in town was destroyed, except a small shack and a crude cemetery cross. In just four hours, the wind-driven blaze ravaged an area at least ten miles east to west and forty miles north to south, wiping out every town and hamlet in its path. More than 1,200 people perished, including 600 in Peshtigo who died within minutes of the fire's start.

Peshtigo, Wisconsin, situated amid lush pine forests and the site of a large sawmill and woodenware factory, burned.[9]

Even Philadelphia was not spared, suffering record fire losses in 1866 and 1869, while calamities in Chicago and Boston broke the underwriters' backs. Chicago had experienced a population explosion with little if any organized planning. Of the city's 60,000 buildings, 40,000 were of frame construction. The *Chicago Tribune* observed that many facades shielded wooden barns. There were "miles of fire-traps, pleasing to the eye, looking substantial, but all sham and shingles." Disaster struck on October 8, 1871, the same day as the Peshtigo inferno.

Tradition accuses a certain Mrs. O'Leary's cow of kicking over a lantern in her barn, but that may be apocryphal, and the real cause remains unknown. The Chicago conflagration razed more than 2,000 acres during the two days it burned, causing 250 deaths and leaving some 100,000 people homeless. Between 17,000 and 20,000 buildings were destroyed or damaged, fewer than half of them insured. Property damage estimates varied, ranging from $150 million to $300 million.

Accounts differ as to the number of insurance companies involved, but there were more than 200. Approximately 70 were immediately forced out of business. No more than 55 could pay their claims in full. Panic by claimants initially was averted when Aetna and the Phoenix of Hartford promptly presented claim checks of $7,500 and $10,000, respectively, to their first two claimants. Aetna also pledged full payment of its $3.75 million loss. This was the greatest aggregate claim that a U.S. insurer had ever paid.

Other companies also suffered enormous losses but met their claims. The small Springfield Fire & Marine paid $450,000 with a capital of only $500,000 and had to assess stockholders $325,000. London underwriters paid out approximately $6 million, 90 percent of their losses.

The Fireman's Fund Insurance Company (formed in 1863) had losses that wiped out its assets. A stockholder's assessment of $250,000 was necessary for survival. Typical of those insurance companies that failed was the Merchants' Insurance Company of Hartford. Chartered in 1857, its loss of over $1 million represented more than five times its capital.

The Chicago fire commanded the attention of fire underwriters. A London underwriter correctly identified Boston, with its crowded quarters in the wholesale district and highly combustible mansard roofing, as especially vulnerable. In November 1872, Boston burned.

While less devastating than the Chicago fire, the Boston blaze spread chaos. Sixty-six acres were engulfed, destroying some 750 buildings. Incredibly, all but sixty-seven were constructed of granite or brick and considered mainly fireproof. The total loss was $75 million, of which about $56 million was insured. Thirty-three Massachusetts-based underwriters paid out some $36 million, and more than twenty soon failed, including seventeen of Boston's nineteen stock insurers.

The high ratio of failures dramatized the inadequate spread of risk. The causes for insurer failures were not new. Requirements for forming underwriting companies were too lenient, and reinsurance was not a widespread or sophisticated practice.

Fire rates jumped considerably after the Chicago and Boston catastrophes. In spite of the National Board's efforts, however, the new rates were generally inadequate. Newly formed insurers, desperate for business, offered insupportable rates to attract clients. By 1876, the National Board permanently abandoned any effort to control fire rates.

Fortunately, many cities began taking corrective actions, and fire prevention ordinances were tightened. Cincinnati's move to create a professional fire department was followed by New York City in 1865 and Philadelphia in 1871, then other cities fell in line. Various states also enacted legislation requiring insurers to adopt more stringent reserve levels and to procure reinsurance above defined levels. The strongest insurance companies were able to augment their assets. For example, during 1874, INA increased its capitalization from $500,000 to $1 million. In 1875, the Aetna

To span the Mississippi on piers 500 feet apart, pioneering engineer James Eads used the "canted lever" or cantilever. To build piers in 1869, he sank a "pneumatic caisson," a big bottomless box, to the riverbed. Workmen climbed down a shaft into the box and—breathing compressed air—dug it deeper by shoveling up the mud, which was pumped to the surface. Reaching bedrock, the caisson was left as the pier's base and filled with concrete. After men began to die mysteriously, doctors identified "caisson disease" i.e., the bends. Thus the St. Louis Bridge expanded medical knowledge as it aided travel and stimulated movement of people and goods, all of which engaged the growing insurance industry.

L&C followed suit, bumping its capital from $150,000 to $750,000.

Though America was increasingly prosperous, excessive speculation led to economic turmoil. A financial panic in 1873 produced more than 10,000 business failures, including many insurance companies. Speculative borrowing from 1868 to 1873 had been uncontrolled. While deposits were rising by only $43 million, bank loans nationally had increased by $283 million. Although the country was temporarily spared an economic disaster in 1873, another recession hit between 1877 and 1879. The low point was reached during 1878 as business failures mounted, and fierce labor strife broke out at the B&O Railroad. A yellow fever epidemic compounded the chaos when it erupted in the south, killing tens of thousands. Conditions became so severe that life insurance companies suspended writing new business in the affected areas.

Despite financial crises in 1884 and 1893, the U.S. economy grew dramatically in the last two decades of the nineteenth century. Fueled by a steady infusion of immigrants, America's population expanded to 76 million by 1900. John Cosgrove reported that, "By the 1880s, the value of manufactured goods surpassed that of farm products for the first time . . . in 1894, the country became the leading manufacturing nation in the world."

Inventions cut across all lines. Thomas Edison epitomized the entrepreneur on the cutting edge of new technology, inventing the phonograph in 1877 and three years later developing the first practical light bulb. George Eastman perfected the Kodak box camera in 1888. Steel came of age during the 1880s, and in 1884, William LeBaron Jenney designed and built the nation's first skyscraper, a ten-story iron- and steel-framed building in Chicago, for the Home Insurance Company of New York. The production of Bessemer steel I-beams in Pittsburgh in 1889 made possible the era of steel-skeleton skyscrapers. In 1890, Chicago erected the first entirely steel-framed building.

Other innovations would be of even greater importance for the insurance business, particularly the development of new modes of public transportation. In 1885, two Germans, Carl Benz and Gottlieb Daimler, developed products of lasting significance. Using a single-cylinder engine, Benz built the first successful gasoline-driven motor car, while Daimler, at the same time, was turning out the first motorcycle.

The first viable American electric trolley line was introduced in Richmond, Virginia, in 1887. This marked the advent of modern urban transportation and created new markets for accident and liability insurance.

A. A. Pope manufactured the first American bicycles in 1877, and twelve years later, the first safety bicycles were built on a large scale. The design was labeled "safe" because it featured two wheels of equal size, as opposed to the earlier design of one large and one small wheel.[10] Safety was a concern from the start, especially since more than a million bicycles were in service by 1893. Not only were riders vic-

[10] This was the "penny-farthing" vehicle, named for the English coins of dissimilar sizes.

timized by their own carelessness, they also became targets of horse-drawn carriages, which ran them down for amusement. By 1894, the Travelers averaged a bicycle accident claim a day during the spring and summer. Whether caused by irate drivers or cyclists' carelessness, knee injuries were particularly serious.

By the end of the 1880s, the question of liability for injury was being addressed more frequently. In 1889, the Travelers became the first American public liability insurer. Coverage was normally an adjunct to employers' liability coverage and written as a single policy. As the Industrial Revolution evolved, the requirement that the plaintiff prove negligence or other fault supplanted the ancient legal principle of strict liability. Vincent Covello and Jeryl Mumpower noted that, by 1850, the law stated that "the plaintiff must come prepared with evidence to show that the intention was unlawful, or that the defendant was at fault; for if the injury was unavoidable, and the conduct of the defendant was free from blame he will not be liable."

Moreover, they wrote, "an injured party could seek redress only if there was proof of negligence and, according to the principle of privity, only from the party contracted to supply a product." This narrow concept of liability remained in force until after World War I. When the Travelers commenced writing public liability insurance, the unfortunate practice of "ambulance chasing" began to spread. Lawyers, operating on a contingent fee basis, frequently urged clients to press claims for injuries.

Technology and invention created new opportunities for insurance. In turn, insurance affected the behavior of people and the practice of law. New statutes and case law eventually affected technology—especially with changes in product liability. At the dawn of the twentieth century, insurance was becoming an indispensable part of the fabric of our economy and our culture.

CHAPTER 5

Your Car Has Arrived: Agents and Brokers Speed Ahead

U ntil astronaut Neil Armstrong set foot on the moon and took his "giant leap for mankind," the greatest milestone in travel of the last century was arguably the progression from horse and buggy to automobile. While the airplane would affect how many people travel, and eventually how *most* people travel distances in industrialized countries, automobiles have become part of everyday life. The profound effect of the auto's emergence on life in the United States was mirrored by its impact on the insurance industry.

By 1887, American inventors were experimenting with a variety of vehicles powered variously by steam, electricity, and gasoline. Ransom E. Olds, a machinist in Lansing, Michigan, completed building a buggy driven by a gasoline-fueled steam engine. Also in 1887 an electric car, powered by storage batteries, was driven on New York streets. Five years later, William Morrison of Des Moines, Iowa, drove his first electric car in Chicago, then built a dozen by the end of 1895. But it was the onset of gasoline-powered automobiles that truly fueled the revolution.

Initial credit goes to a pair of bicycle designers from Springfield, Massachusetts, the Duryea brothers. In 1892, they constructed their first gasoline auto. Assembled in a loft, the vehicle suddenly moved forward and plunged through a door to the street below. Four years later, the brothers produced thirteen two-passenger, two-cylinder runabouts in Springfield, marking the first time an automobile company produced more than one car from a single design. The American automobile industry was launched.

The cutting edge of automobile production was represented by the Olds Motor Vehicle Company. Formed in 1897, ten years after Mr. Olds assembled his gas-powered "buggy," it was the first true auto company. Although it produced only four vehicles, in 1901 its successor, the Olds Motor Works, introduced the concept of mass production by building 425 curved-dash Oldsmobiles. By 1903, the company was producing 4,000 cars annually. Entrepreneur Henry Ford made his Model T affordable to most Americans, thereby providing a seminal boost for the insurance industry. He had built his first horseless carriage, the Quadricycle, a strange contraption, in 1896.[1] Seven years later, he incorporated the Ford Motor Company and soon sold its first Model A car to a dentist.[2]

As portentous as these events may have been, automobiles were not readily accepted by many Americans—including insurers. INA president, Charles Platt, insisted, "I'll never insure a gasoline can on wheels, the noisy stinking things!" The insurance trade journal *Spectator* reinforced this position by suggesting:

> The motormen—chauffeurs is the general term—driving automobiles are usually reckless, rushing madly past frightened teams [of horses] without attempting to slow down . . . nervous horses are sure to be alarmed at such apparitions . . . [underwriters] might serve the cause of public safety by refusing to insure anyone who has acquired the automobile habit.

At the turn of the century there were 8,000 automobiles on American roads, a figure that would jump to 78,000 by 1905, or nearly tenfold in five years.

More cars powered by steam and electricity than gasoline were built during the centennial year. Shortly thereafter, steam-powered vehicles became less prevalent, and by 1920 they were rare. Electric automobiles experienced the same decline, as gasoline became the fuel of choice—and of the future.

[1] With a body resembling a small crude wooden box, this vehicle had a single seat, a steering tiller, bicycle wheels, an engine cylinder fashioned from a steam engine's exhaust pipe with a wooden flywheel, and an electric bell on the front.

[2] A new Model A was introduced in 1928.

As popular as automobiles were in certain quarters, insurers responded cautiously. The Travelers recognized a need for liability protection and issued the first third-party automobile insurance policy in 1897. Placed by an independent agent, it was written for Gilbert J. Loomis of Westfield, Massachusetts, a mechanic who had built his own one-cylinder car. Mr. Loomis drove automobiles until 1956, and his only claim over that fifty-nine-year period was for a minor dent caused when he hit a stalled car. It wasn't until 1902, when the Boston Insurance Company pioneered automobile fire, theft, and then collision coverage, that auto insurance was listed in insurers' rating manuals.

Shortly after writing the Loomis policy, the Travelers sold another liability policy, this one to the owner of an electric vehicle. The $11.25 annual premium for liability provided $5,000 coverage for any one person's claim and $10,000 for any one accident, however many people were involved. The earliest automobile liability policies were written on "team forms," designed for horse-drawn conveyances, to cover damages frequently caused by runaways and kicking or biting horses.

There was no mad rush to offer auto liability coverage. The vast majority of fire and marine underwriters resisted writing liability insurance until the uncertainties could be better evaluated. Many agents and brokers benefiting from automobile insurance soon took advantage of a need for coverage generated by new equipment that revolutionized communications and improved office efficiency.

Other insurance forms came to the fore, including burglary coverage, fidelity bonds, and more. By 1885, the need for burglary insurance was addressed through a policy offered by the American Protective Mutual of Reading, Pennsylvania.[3]

The fidelity bond, which guarantees an individual's honesty, was first underwritten by a U.S. insurer through the Fidelity & Casualty Company in 1880. The bond reimbursed employers for pecuniary loss occurring through

[3] This coverage, introduced in England as early as 1865, was popularized by Lloyd's underwriter Cuthbert Heath starting in 1887.

employee dishonesty. The Fidelity & Casualty was an important insurer. Founded in 1876 as the Knickerbocker Plate Glass and Accident Insurance Company, it was almost immediately renamed Knickerbocker Casualty Company of New York, and again renamed as Fidelity & Casualty Company in 1880.[4]

Other new coverages offered during the last two decades of the nineteenth century included a smorgasbord of protection. Tornado insurance was first written by the Springfield Fire & Marine on an Iowa risk in 1882.[5] Elevator, mortgage, credit, and title insurance all appeared. The surety bond, which guaranteed the performance of an undertaking, such as the construction of a building, was also offered. The Fidelity & Guaranty Insurance Company commenced business in 1896, and by 1910 was America's largest surety bond writing company.[6]

Not all insurers were eager to embrace new coverages. Vinson and Cosgrove report that, during the 1880s, a rare woman insurance agent, a Mrs. Dodds, asked her company's general agent in Cincinnati whether she could offer windstorm protection, only to be admonished:

Wind Storm being entirely foreign to the business of fire insurance in which we are engaged, we have nothing to do therewith. Neither do we suppose that any other reputable fire insurance co. does, but only such companies as must resort to some ludicrous method or worse in order to get any business. . . . If against Wind, why not also against Rain, Hail, Crushing by snow, accidents caused by faulty construction of buildings, etc. etc. etc.? The proposition, Mrs. Dodds, is too absurd for any strictly legitimate fire insurance company to consider for a moment.

Various business innovations paved the way for insurance office efficiencies. Shortly after inventing the telephone in 1876, Alexander Graham Bell called a Travelers insurance agent to purchase an accident policy. This was the first known business transaction conducted by telephone. The first U.S. public telephone appeared in 1877, and by 1895, 300,000 had been installed and rapidly became essential to insurance agents and brokers.

[4] In 1929, stock control of the Fidelity & Casualty Company was gained by the Continental Insurance Company and the Fidelity-Phenix Fire Insurance Company, which the Continental absorbed in 1958. The Fidelity and Deposit Company, formed during 1890 as the Fidelity Loan and Trust Company of Baltimore City, became one of the country's foremost fidelity bond underwriters. The Fidelity and Deposit Company was subsequently acquired by the Maryland Casualty Company, and in turn by the Zurich Insurance Group.

[5] In 1884, the Phoenix Insurance Company wrote individual policies for risks of cyclone, tornado, and hurricane.

[6] Fidelity & Guaranty became the United States Fidelity & Guaranty Company (USF&G) and was bought by the St. Paul Companies, Inc., in 1998.

The typewriter was also indispensable. While the first typewriter patent was granted to William Burt of Detroit in 1829, it wasn't until 1874 that a practical unit appeared, the original Remington Rand. The Metropolitan Life Insurance Company purchased a Locke & Bates typewriter in 1877 for $125. However, business was slow to embrace the typewriter, and only 5,000 were sold before 1880. By the late 1890s, the equipment was in general use and instrumental in integrating many women into the workforce. The typewriter was a bonanza for the labor-intensive insurance industry. Similarly, the wireless telegraph, available from the late 1890s, became invaluable.

With innovations contributing to more efficient work, attention also focused on employee welfare. Benefit plans began to be offered. The American Express Company introduced the first employer-sponsored pension plan in 1875. Benefits equaled 50 percent of average pay earned in the final ten employment years, but were capped at $500 annually. In 1883, the Denver and Rio Grande Western Railway's Hospital Association adopted the country's first dental insurance plan.

The integration of leisure time with business development also took a noteworthy turn in the 1880s. John M. Fox of Philadelphia encountered golf on a trip to Scotland in 1885, and subsequently introduced the game to Americans. The nation's first true golf club opened in 1887 in Foxburg, Pennsylvania, and the first eighteen-hole course was completed in 1893 in Wheaton, Illinois.

Although the amount of time agents and brokers devote to golf may be exaggerated, many billions of insurance dollars have been negotiated, directly or indirectly, on courses all over the world. A tongue-in-cheek observation in an Aetna L&C internal publication cited golf courses for "making it possible for insurance agents and doctors to lead fulfilled and happy lives."

By the turn of the century, huge monopolies were being created. This pattern developed even though Congress had

passed the Sherman Antitrust Act in 1890 to inhibit formation of monopolies. John D. Rockefeller's Standard Oil
Company of New Jersey, formed in 1899, at one point controlled some 85 percent of the nation's oil refining capacity.[7] In 1901, the J. P. Morgan banking group started the
United States Steel Corporation, which ultimately controlled almost half of America's steel-making capacity.

[7] In 1911, the U.S. Supreme Court ordered Standard Oil broken up into thirty-four separate companies.

Despite many acquisitions and failures, nothing resembling a monopoly developed within the insurance industry,
and it remained extremely fragmented. Far fewer new
insurers were launched, but those that came on the scene
tended to be conservatively capitalized. Chubb & Son
(Chubb), always a highly reputable firm, was formed in
1882 to manage insurance companies. It focused on marine
risks and specialty areas, such as personal insurance for
wealthy individuals.

Insurers had considerable flexibility in controlling policy conditions as the nineteenth century ended. After the
discovery of gold in Canada's Yukon Territory led to the
Klondike stampede, many life and accident companies said
they would invalidate coverage for policyholders participating in the rush. Conversely, during the Spanish-American
War of 1898, some insurers suspended—for patriotic reasons—policy clauses that precluded military service.

Alternatively, increased state regulation sometimes
resulted in conditions that insurers found restrictive and
unfair; this was illustrated by the "valued policy" that
applied to fire insurance. In the standard fire insurance policy, loss was based on the property's cash value when the
fire occurred, i.e., an "indemnity policy." However, starting
with Wisconsin in 1874, several states legislated valued
policies, in which coverage value was determined in
advance, i.e., a "guaranty policy." Insurers argued that the
standard fire policy should be one of indemnity, not guaranty. They also argued that valued policies increased moral
hazard, since the property's insurance value might be more
than the property was worth—making arson a temptation.
Despite such arguments, the insurers did not prevail. By
1915, valued policy laws were in force in twenty-two states.

In that year, the pioneer, Wisconsin, repealed its law because of large numbers of fraudulent claims.

During the final two decades of the nineteenth century, brokerages multiplied and became more easily distinguishable from agencies. At the end of 1882, America had 218 licensed insurance brokers. Although this number grew rapidly in just a few years, it was dwarfed by the number of insurance agents; INA alone boasted 2,200 in 1884.

While most insurers preferred to deal only with their own agents, they ultimately conceded that brokers were inevitable and a growing force. This was not always the case. As David Schiff has recently pointed out, in the mid-nineteenth century, and even later, many large companies despised brokers, considering them unnecessary and greedy. This feeling was passionately articulated in an 1868 circular signed by twenty-six insurance companies. It charged: "The insurance brokerage system is, in the judgment of the undersigned, an evil to both Insurance Companies and their customers, with little compensating good. . . . Customers can place their own insurance better than brokers can." Interestingly, most who signed the circular were out of business by 1908, while brokers generally prospered.

The most balanced attitude was summed up by Charles Platt, president of INA from 1879 to 1908. Addressing the issue of brokers' and agents' commissions, Platt defended the 15 percent commissions paid to INA agents, even though many other insurers paid less. He observed:

In the large cities of New York, Philadelphia, Boston, New Orleans, Pittsburgh and some others there is a class of men known as Brokers or Middlemen, through whose hands a very large proportion of the business of Fire Insurance passes. These men by active personal solicitation secure the control of the business of most of the large Manufacturing Concerns and Mercantile businesses and it is now the exception to a rule when such risks are placed directly by the assured with the Companies. The reason is a plain one. When large amounts of insurance are required and any one Company will not assume more than a limited line it becomes a very troublesome business and requires constant attention. Brokers are now the recognized medium and must obtain licenses from the State Authorities. Why not do away with this system? The reply is that no one Company can safely move in this direction for the result would be the alienation of the large portion of its business derived from Brokers.

The brokerage commission rate, 15 percent in Philadelphia, ran as high as 25 percent in New York City. Rates were volatile, however, and by 1886 the average New York rate had receded to 10 percent.

While the larger brokerages were advertising themselves as brokers, the line between agent and broker remained blurred. Where vital industry matters were involved, there was no distinction. Leading executives from various brokers and agencies collaborated to promote industry safety issues. When the World's Columbian Exposition of 1893 (i.e., the World's Fair) was being launched in Chicago, an auxiliary committee was formed that included such names as W. A. Alexander, R. S. Critchell, Fred. S. James, and R. A. Waller, all of whose firms became major Chicago agents or brokers.[8]

Since the early 1880s, insurers had developed a keen interest in inspections relating to electricity. On behalf of the Columbian Exposition, in 1893 the committee hired an industrial engineer, W. H. Merrill. He established a Chicago testing facility to evaluate the use of Edison's illumination.[9] The Underwriters Laboratories organization was subsequently launched with manufacturers paying to have their products tested. If the products passed the test, they received a seal of approval.[10]

[8] The committee's mission was to minimize the fire risk of inflammable structures.

[9] The Mutual Life Insurance Company of New York excluded death by electricity from a policy written for Thomas A. Edison.

[10] The Underwriters Laboratories became part of the National Board of Fire Underwriters.

The two dominant insurance brokers of the day, Johnson & Higgins and R. A. Waller (Marsh & McLennan), expanded rapidly through acquisitions. Henry Marsh and Don McLennan were responsible for their company's rapid growth. The Boston-born Marsh attended Harvard but left for Chicago before graduation. He joined R. A. Waller in 1885 (after a stint with the Fireman's Fund Insurance Com-

Bicycles brought a great leap forward after advances in metallurgy enabled the use of lightweight chain drives. The bicycle gave a man transportation for work and leisure. The biking craze made the 1890s "gay," killed the bustle and corset, and helped emancipate women, said the early feminist Susan B. Anthony. Thousands of firms made bikes and engaged in cut-throat competition to survive. One bicycle maker gave buyers theft and accident insurance with a purchase—though health policies might have been better as horsemen and carriage drivers made a sport of forcing bicyclists off the road in the early years of cycling.

pany) when the Waller agency's annual premium volume was $190,000. A natural salesman, Marsh mixed socially with business executives in Chicago and gained many useful contacts.

In 1894, the firm acquired the O. W. Barrett & Company agency, owned by H. J. Ullmann, who was adept in organizational and administrative matters. Two years later, it numbered some twenty employees. There was one woman employee and one typewriter, both unusual at the time. In 1899, after Waller's death, the agency was renamed Marsh, Ullmann & Co.[11] An attractive opportunity arose in 1901 when the United States Steel Corporation was formed. Marsh was invited to relocate to New York City and serve as insurance manager of the new enterprise, and the agency opened its New York office in January 1901.

[11] That same year, the company acquired the Hammond Fry & Sheldon Agency.

Meanwhile, Donald McLennan, fatherless at age fourteen, sought employment to help support his mother and siblings. He joined Stryker, Manley & Buck in Duluth, Minnesota, in 1891, which merged with the agency of Colonel C. H. Graves to become the Graves-Manley Agency four years later. Duluth, Minnesota, and Superior, Wisconsin, were sites of huge warehousing facilities for grain storage in winter, when the Great Lakes were unnavigable, and this created opportunities for railroads to transport grain. McLennan subsequently became acquainted with many senior railroad officials.

Graves-Manley was renamed Manley-McLennan in 1900. Owing to relationships with railroads, a second office opened in Chicago in 1904. Here, the company handled insurance for the Northern Pacific, Santa Fe, and most of the Great Northern railroad companies. The competitive Chicago environment became fierce, with Messrs. Burrows, Marsh, and McLennan each enjoying personal contact with top railroad executives.[12]

Both Marsh and McLennan had been promised the Chicago, Burlington & Quincy Railroad account by different directors. Burrow's close friend headed the Chicago, Rock Island & Pacific Railroad. Rather than "savage" one another, D. W. Burrows & Company, Manley-McLennan, and Marsh, Ullmann & Company agreed to merge, and did so in January 1905, forming Burrows, Marsh & McLennan. With combined annual premiums of $3 million, it became the world's largest nonmarine insurance brokerage.

Despite its railroad success, the firm had almost no marine insurance. If a London placement was needed, it was directed to E. Uzielli & Company. When the first marine risks of note emerged during 1905, both Marsh and McLennan journeyed to London and arranged for C. T. Bowring & Company to place the insurance. Bowring subsequently became Marsh & McLennan's principal London correspondent.[13]

Johnson & Higgins, by contrast, was devoted almost exclusively to marine insurance and average adjusting. Its first nonmarine director, W. E. Lowe, became a partner in

[12] Daniel Burrows headed another Chicago agency, D. W. Burrows & Company.

[13] During World War I, at Marsh & McLennan's instigation, Bowring acquired Uzielli.

1896 to focus on fire insurance development. J&H was the first major brokerage to start numerous branch offices. By 1901, seven new locations were open, beginning with San Francisco in 1883 and followed by Philadelphia, Boston, Baltimore, New Orleans, Buffalo, Chicago, and Seattle. The latter opened in 1901 in response to the shipping activity generated by the Klondike gold rush.

J&H was also the first major U.S. brokerage firm to work with a foreign associate and enter the realm of international business. In 1892, it started doing business with the London broker Henry Willis and Company, which merged with Faber Brothers in 1893 to form Willis Faber & Company, Limited (Willis Faber). It became London's foremost insurance brokerage. In 1899, J&H entered into an exclusive working arrangement with Willis Faber, which lasted nearly ninety-one years.[14]

J&H agreed to place with Willis Faber all its marine business underwritten in London. Willis Faber, in turn, refused to accept marine placements from any other American brokerage. The result was that most of the large U.S. fleets were handled through Willis Faber. Both firms were recognized for broking the hull insurance on the *Titanic*, which sank in 1912. Its hull was insured for £1 million, while Marquis James reports the total insurance on the ship was over $5.5 million.

In 1899, J&H changed from a partnership to a unique corporate setup, although the term "partner" continued to be used. Its directors owned the firm. Approximately 70,000 shares of stock were divided, with larger portions belonging to directors having the greatest responsibilities. When invited to join the board, a J&H staff member was required to purchase 500 shares. As his years on the board increased, he accumulated additional shares, possibly increasing to 2,500 or as many as 3,500 shares, depending on his value to the firm. Upon retirement, these shares were returned to the company in exchange for a certificate entitling the retiree to ten years of dividends. Eventually, the shares were redistributed to active members, who collected no dividends until the expiration of the retiree's ten-year contract. (Until the

[14] The relationship lasted until 1990, when Willis Faber merged with a U.S. brokerage firm, Corroon & Black.

late 1960s, the retirement payments were treated as capital gains.)

At the turn of the century, J&H had seventy-five employees and was the oldest and probably largest American broker. Most of the company's early acquisitions occurred before 1930. The purchase of Lethbridge & Davidge in 1900 strengthened its fire insurance operation. In 1902, the firm seized an opportunity to gain an important foothold in San Francisco, where it already had a small office. The city had much closer relations with London than with New York or other East Coast cities. Except for the Fireman's Fund Insurance Company's marine account, the local San Francisco insurance market was British-oriented.

However, an American company, W. C. Gibbs, controlled most of the West Coast average adjusting business. J&H purchased Gibbs in 1902, thereby gaining immediate access to potential clients with diverse insurance needs. After these acquisitions, J&H probably was comparable in size to Burrows, Marsh & McLennan.

Another important brokerage, Rollins Burdick Hunter, was founded in Chicago in 1897. Its founder, Charles Rollins, became principal broker for the Chicago stockyards. In 1907, Rollins helped the large meatpacker Swift & Co. form one of the earliest captive insurance companies, which he reinsured in London through C. E. Heath.[15] By 1908, Rollins was traveling back and forth to London, where he teamed up with Heath to place high-risk insurance coverages for the Chicago stockyards.[16]

Meanwhile, Fred. S. James & Co. and Henry Stewart & Son (later Frank B. Hall & Co.) continued to expand. James & Co. concentrated on fire risks. In 1887, the firm took in as a partner George W. Blossom, who was known as a dynamic fire insurance executive. His son later joined the company and rose to become its president.

James & Co. was an innovative brokerage firm. In 1900, it pioneered a broker's first formal loss control service by hiring a team of engineers. A year later, it became one of the

[15] See Chapter 21.

[16] Partly through acquisitions, Rollins Burdick Hunter remained among the ten largest U.S. insurance brokers until absorbed by its fellow brokerage, Aon, in 1982.

earliest firms to be granted a Lloyd's binding contract. By 1902, the firm expanded its specialty, fire insurance, adding suretyship to its services followed by liability coverages. Its first branch office was opened in New York City during 1904 and offered marine insurance in 1908. A San Francisco office was launched in 1918, followed by other branches during the 1920s.

Frank B. Hall established his insurance brokerage business in 1893. Although the firm grew slowly, its founder was imaginative and farsighted. Early in the 1900s, he traveled to London seeking a local correspondent and met with H. B. Sedgwick, one of the founders of Sedgwick, Collins & Co. Ltd. (Sedgwick). They launched an association that lasted more than seventy years.

Frank Hall also did outside work for James & Co. There, he first met Cecil Stewart, who had left his father and

Although trains were vehicles of manifest progress, they could shock America with their lethal power. In 1887 Harper's Weekly reported "one of the most terrible railroad accidents ever recorded." An excursion train derailed in Illinois, killing 16 and injuring 279. Still, railroads shrunk the nation and expanded its economy as they shortened travel times, brought distant markets to new farm regions, and relocated settlers who then patronized freight and passenger trains. And if these contraptions had accidents, insurance could partly compensate victims and families.

joined James & Co. as an average adjuster. The two men began a friendship that continued after Cecil moved on to a better position at The Texas Company. Frank Hall finally persuaded Cecil to join him, and they jointly arranged a merger with Henry Stewart.

Although an agreement was signed in 1912, Henry Stewart suffered a fatal heart attack before the two brokerage firms were physically combined. Frank Hall and Cecil Stewart then each took 50 percent ownership, under the name of Frank B. Hall & Co., Inc. At the start of World War I, marine insurance represented 90 percent of F. B. Hall's revenue. When Cecil Stewart bought out Frank Hall's interest in the brokerage in 1916, Hall retired, but the company continued to operate under the Hall name.

The turn of the century was a propitious time to enter the insurance business. With the growth of the American economy, ambitious agents interested in commercial business had excellent prospects. They were positioned to benefit from their clients' successes and a thriving economy as well as from their own skills in managing a business, attracting customers, and generating sales. From a twenty-first century perspective, it is startling how only a handful of the hundreds of insurers formed in the late eighteenth and the nineteenth centuries survived. The reasons for failure seem obvious in retrospect. One might have expected, though, that the trail of failure left by hundreds of bankrupt insurance companies would have highlighted pitfalls for others to avoid.[17]

While the introduction of the automobile overshadowed other industrial developments early in the twentieth century, many other breakthroughs affected business. In 1903, the arrival of a gasoline-powered tractor signaled the mechanization of farming. That same year, two Ohio bicycle mechanics visited the dunes of North Carolina's Outer Banks, where they cranked up a contraption with a gasoline engine and flew it—under its own power—for about 100 feet. In 1904, the first trans-Pacific cable was laid.[18]

[17] Fortunately, insurance companies had entered a relatively stable period by 1900. Most were adequately capitalized and could base their rates on more credible statistical data. Many of today's widely used forms of insurance coverage were available, although workers compensation and others had yet to be introduced.

[18] President Theodore Roosevelt used it to send a message around the world; the message returned to him in twelve minutes.

Extended life expectancy would have considerable impact on insurance. Men born in 1900 could expect to live only forty-eight years, and women, fifty-one. Leading causes of death were infectious diseases such as pneumonia, flu, and tuberculosis.[19]

The decades surrounding the turn of the century were dynamic. Changes were underway, new firms were being founded, new technologies were entering the American mainstream. These set off economic torrents that would revolutionize the world and lead to "the American Century." Among the future insurance industry giants, barely noticed in the early years of the twentieth century, was one then employing just four people, an obscure West Virginia agency, Alexander & Alexander (A&A).[20]

[19] By 1940, life expectancy would increase rapidly and the leading causes of death became the chronic degenerative diseases—heart disease and cancer.

[20] Some of the most prominent nineteenth century U.S. agencies would become part of A&A after it became public in 1969. These included Moore, Case, Lyman & Hubbard, Inc. (founded in Chicago in 1859); Field & Cowles (Boston 1867); OBrion, Russell & Co. (Boston 1876); Charles W. Sexton Company (Minneapolis 1884); R. B. Jones Corp. (Kansas City 1889); McKee, Geny & Thornton, Inc. (Nashville 1892); Detroit Insurance Agency (Detroit 1894); Hutchinson, Rivinus & Co., Inc. (Philadelphia 1897); and The Neale-Phypers Company (Cleveland 1890s).

PART II

THE PARADIGM
AMERICAN BROKERAGE:
1899 to 1968

CHAPTER 6

Alexander & Alexander: West Virginia Origins

The Alexander & Alexander story is the saga of a tiny rural insurance agency launched by two relatively unsophisticated brothers who eventually would compete as equals with big city brokers. And how they did it is equally remarkable. While many men and women made it possible, the accomplishment is primarily a testament to the herculean efforts of one man, W. F. Alexander. Nevertheless, the larger A&A story, extending over the course of the twentieth century, serves as an example—perhaps the paradigm—of the growth and change experienced by major U.S. brokerages. Like many others that remain unsung, the agency had a start that merits recalling, as it appears to have been typical in many ways.

The paterfamilias of Alexander & Alexander was Richard A. Alexander.[1] His paternal ancestry could be traced to sixteenth-century Scotland through John Alexander, the first of the family in America, who settled in Virginia between 1627 and 1644.[2] For six hogsheads of tobacco, John purchased 6,000 acres of land on the west bank of the Potomac River, across from the future capital city of Washington, D.C. His property (located in what is now Arlington) continued south, where he built a grand house, Abingdon, and surrounded himself with several families he

[1] Five of his progeny and two of his nephews would attain some degree of prominence in the insurance industry.

[2] The Alexanders of Scotland included among their number John Alexander, Lord of the Isles, who married Margaret, daughter of Robert Bruce II, King of Scotland. Lord William Alexander, born in 1582, was the progenitor of the Virginia Alexanders. His son, John, emigrated to America.

[3] The house survived until the 1940s, when it was destroyed by fire.

brought from Scotland.[3] All were related by marriage, and within three generations the area called Bellehaven belonged almost exclusively to his descendants. They were so many that, with the blessing of the General Assembly of Virginia, the place was renamed Alexandria.

Richard's maternal great-great-grandfather was John Augustine Washington, youngest brother of George Washington. Over several generations, close ties linked various members of the Alexander and Washington families—so close that three of Richard's children had the middle name of Washington. The ties were especially strong among those in the vicinity of Charles Town, part of the Old Dominion that became a new state, West Virginia, during the Civil War.

Richard A. Alexander was born in 1849. Though he possessed what was called a weak constitution, he prospered in Charles Town, a rural center in the northern panhandle of western Virginia some sixty miles from Abingdon and the nation's capital. He married Julia Lane, who bore him seven sons and a daughter there.

They lived in a spartan manner in a modest frame house that was heated only on Sundays. Four boys occupied a single bedroom furnished with two double beds, an arrangement that led to frequent squabbles. Religion played a major role in family life, with morning and evening prayers, in addition to an hour of Sunday school—mandatory for the children—followed by nearly two hours of church service.

Since the quality of public education was considered a disgrace, the children were initially tutored at home in small groups. Subsequently, the boys attended Charles Town Male Academy, which was staffed by former Confederate soldiers and attended by boys coming by horseback or buggy from farms as far as twelve miles away. When Richard's second son, Charles, graduated in 1895, he felt his education was the equivalent of two years of high school.

As was then common in rural West Virginia, Richard plied more than one trade. He sold fertilizer, a fact his sons went out of their way to downplay in later years. He was the

Jefferson County assessor for sixteen years, and also served as deputy sheriff. But as a man of principle, he refused to run for sheriff because in those days before surety bonds the job required posting a large personal bond; and he would not ask friends to take such a risk. Richard possessed noble qualities, several of which were essential gifts for a successful insurance agent: sound business judgment, compassion for others, good humor, and persistence.

In 1870, Richard Alexander opened an insurance agency in Duffields, a village nearby, and then moved the office to Charles Town. The Peabody Insurance Company of West Virginia was the first to be represented by his agency, and the Aetna Insurance Company the second. A surviving policy from 1875 shows Richard writing on behalf of the Home Insurance Company of Columbus, Ohio. Another surviving policy, issued by the Peabody, covers a wooden dwelling against fire for an annual premium of $2.40.

About 1878, local businessmen and farmers organized the Jefferson County Mutual Fire Insurance Company and

The new century, like Alexander & Alexander, is just a decade old when a Great Northern express presses its luck in a no-contest race with daredevil pilot Cromwell Dixon's biplane. Dixon will then win a $10,000 prize for a round-trip flight from Montana across the continental divide, but less than a month later die in a crash at nineteen. The railroads will continue to be one mainstay for A&A and the insurance industry, while aviation soon becomes another.

named Richard its secretary. As his interests diversified and the insurance agency business grew, he invited John A. Washington, an older cousin, to become a partner in 1883. Washington and Alexander became the agency's new name, with Washington's name first in deference to his age.

In 1885, Richard's nephew, fifteen-year-old Herbert Alexander, was hired as a clerk. Herbert would recall years later, "There were no typewriters then, and I had to write all letters, policies, daily reports et cetera with pen and ink. . . . We used renewal receipts for one-year policies and that saved some writing." Around 1890, Richard's eldest son, Richard Washington Alexander, was hired to assist Herbert. Herbert resigned on January 1, 1894, and bought a small agency in Martinsburg, fifteen miles away.[4]

Later in 1894, the elder Richard, never in robust health, died of pneumonia. After his death, another relative was brought into the agency, and it was renamed Alexander & Cooke. Richard W. Alexander then sold his interest to a cousin, and the agency thrived under the same name well into the twentieth century.[5]

During this period, two of the elder Richard's other sons entered the insurance field. Charles B. Alexander ("C. B."), the elder by three years, and William Fontaine Alexander ("W. F."). After graduating from the Charles Town Male Academy, his father having died a year earlier, C. B. sought career advice from a family friend. The friend, William L. Wilson, an older man and a member of President Grover Cleveland's cabinet, advised him to join the merchant marine.

Mindful that he might have inherited his father's constitution, C. B. signed up to go to sea. In 1895, he was assigned as a cadet on a new government-subsidized vessel, *St. Paul*, at $15 a month. The *St. Paul*'s maiden voyage included a visit to England, a fascinating experience for a young man who had never been more than about twenty miles from home. Although he was homesick and harassed as a raw recruit, C. B. stuck with the ship for a year and returned home in robust health.

W. F., meanwhile, had taken a position with a local

[4] Shortly thereafter, Herbert purchased two more agencies and enjoyed a monopoly in Martinsburg for several years. When he took in a partner in 1899, the agency was renamed Alexander & Trammel.

[5] In 1907, young Richard W. organized the Citizens Fire Insurance Company of Charles Town, West Virginia, with the help of his youngest brother, Walter, who was made secretary. Seven years later, Richard left to become a vice president of the Equitable Trust Company in Baltimore.

lawyer. Both boys, recognizing the need for some form of career training, enrolled in an evening course in stenography, which was becoming widely used. Another well-placed family friend, former state Senator Johnson N. Camden, then arranged for C. B. to work on the Monongahela Railroad, where he toiled eleven hours a day. This was followed by a three-year stint as the senator's private secretary, a position that involved extensive travel.

In 1897, W. F. joined the Washington and Alexander agency in Charles Town. One day, in a moment of boyish abandon, he rode his bicycle around the office. Failing to negotiate a turn in the cramped quarters, he smashed into a glass-fronted bookcase and seriously gashed his arm. The local doctor recommended amputation, but W. F.'s mother refused. The doctor then drove W. F. sixty-five miles in his carriage to Johns Hopkins Hospital in Baltimore, where the arm was saved.

W. F. was a dashing young man, full of confidence in his own abilities and very outgoing. At nineteen, determined to buy his own insurance agency, W. F. set his sights on the J. Carl Vance agency, the largest and most respected in Clarksburg, some 135 miles from Charles Town. This proved to be a bold and insightful selection.

Since the early 1800s, the Vance name was prominent in Clarksburg. J. Carl's father, John C. Vance, was born there and became an outstanding lawyer while building an enviable reputation as a political speaker. John Vance had organized the county's first company of volunteer Union soldiers, although he later became disenchanted with the war's direction. In April 1862, the Union confined him in Fort McHenry in Baltimore as a political prisoner of war.[6]

To buy the Vance agency, W. F. borrowed $5,000 from his mother. Mrs. Alexander loaned it with the proviso that W. F. include as co-owner his cousin Herbert, who was twenty-nine and had insurance experience from his years in Martinsburg. She was concerned about how well W. F., at age nineteen, would handle the investment. The agency was purchased on July 1, 1899, and Alexander & Alexander was born.

[6] After the Civil War, John Vance did as much as anyone to establish the Democratic Party throughout West Virginia, leaving a legacy that extended well into the twentieth century. His grandson— J. Carl's son, Cyrus Vance— had a distinguished career in government, including service as secretary of the army from 1962 to 1964 and secretary of state from 1977 to 1980.

At nineteen, W. F. may have been young and somewhat inexperienced, but his considerable talent was soon recognized. On July 28, 1899, the *Clarksburg News* cited an article in the "Spirit of Jefferson," a Charles Town publication, entitled "Well Recommended." It read:

It is with more than ordinary regret that we announce the departure of our popular young townsman, Mr. William F. Alexander, who leaves us today for Clarksburg, this state. Mr. Alexander will locate permanently at that point, entering into partnership with Mr. Herbert L. Alexander of Martinsburg, W. Va., under the firm name Alexander & Alexander, and will engage in the insurance business succeeding to the most prominent insurance agency in that city. Mr. Alexander comes of an insurance family, and the several years experience that he has had in the general insurance business with the firm of Washington & Alexander, which is one of the largest agencies in the state, has qualified him well in this line. We are sorry to lose such an enterprising young businessman from our community, and commend him to the good people of Clarksburg as being most reliable and capable. Mr. Alexander, of Martinsburg, is also an old insurance man, having fifteen years experience in the insurance business, and we bespeak for the new firm of Alexander & Alexander which succeeds to the J. Carl Vance insurance agency much success in this line, in which they are eminently qualified.

Presumably, W. F. had observed the ongoing transformation of Clarksburg from an agricultural backwater to an emerging industrial center. It benefited from the aggressive development of its natural resources—coal, oil, and gas—that was greatly aided by railroad expansions. Located in north-central West Virginia, Clarksburg is 270 miles east of Cincinnati, Ohio, and 275 miles west of Washington, D.C. The town of Philippi, where the first land battle of the Civil War was fought on June 3, 1861, lies just twenty miles away. Nestled between hills in a lovely but relatively unknown part of the country, the area was once called "the Switzerland of America." C. B. Alexander, in a letter, recalled of Clarksburg:

This town was the center of agricultural pursuits solely. The two streets, Main and Pike, ran through this interesting village between many hills which make the whole of the north central part of West Virginia picturesque. In these hills and the valley which ran between them covered with blue grass, some of the prize beef cattle of this country was raised, and this was the chief source of the agricultural countryside upon which this little town developed.

Settlers came to the area in 1770. Three years later, the town was founded and named in honor of General George Rogers Clark, the renowned trader, explorer, and Indian fighter. It was officially chartered by the Commonwealth of Virginia in 1785. In 1842, Clarksburg considered itself the nation's population center, with equal numbers of Americans residing to the east and west of its borders. The B&O Railroad's main line reached the area in 1856, paving the way for Clarksburg's rapid expansion thirty years later. The mining of nearby coal deposits brought waves of Irish, Italian, and Greek workers, which triggered dynamic growth.

Model of Yankee prosperity, Clarksburg, West Virginia, lies midway between Cincinnati and Washington (about 270 miles from each). When Alexander & Alexander settles on Main Street in 1899, Clarksburg is the hub of a region thriving with farming, manufacturing, and oil and gas wells, a boomtown that gives A&A a firm business base. Its population and economy will continue to grow through World War II, long after the firm moved headquarters to Baltimore and then New York.

The city's population stood at 3,000 in 1876 and was growing nicely when the Alexanders started their agency. Indeed, the population subsequently exploded, reaching 28,000 by 1920, the year Clarksburg became the center for manufacturing window glass in the United States.[7]

In the early decades of the twentieth century, Clarksburg was the center of oil and gas discovery. A local newspaper headline from February 1900 read, "More Oil Wells—Big Ones Coming in Almost Daily These Days." Accounts of coal discoveries and railroad activity were featured daily, livery stables were generally filled to capacity, and all the characteristics of a booming frontier town were in place. One front-page story noted the number of big factories in Clarksburg and reported that "New York capitalists want all our coal."

In addition to reporting boosterish good news, the *Clarksburg Daily Telegram* was filled with lurid accounts of rape, robbery, and other crimes. Deaths of local residents were recorded in minute and often gruesome detail, and local scandals, which were numerous, got prominent play. Front page headlines from the boom times included:

DIED WITH HIS FACE IN THE MUD
ED SOUTHWORTH HORRIBLY KILLED
FELL BETWEEN THE CARS OF MOVING FREIGHT TRAIN AND
THE ENTIRE TRAIN AND ANOTHER PASSED OVER THE BODY
REMAINS SCATTERED ALONG THE TRACK
BODY WAS DRAGGED SOME 20 YARDS WITH BOTH FEET
AND ONE LEG SEVERED

MRS. LONG GONE!
ALSO FRANK WATSON
BOTH SUDDENLY DISAPPEAR AT THE SAME TIME
AND THE TONGUES OF THE GOSSIPS ARE BUSILY WAGGING

Clarksburg's explosive growth quickly outstripped its infrastructure, and the town could not provide many basic services. An editorial in 1900 lamented, "Clarksburg needs a good sewer system, well paved streets, first class businessmen to manage her affairs, a board of public works, good order, street corners free from obstruction and profanity, a police service of highest efficiency, a street railway system

[7] Clarksburg's prosperity lasted only through World War II. As coal, oil, and gas resources diminished, the city's prominence gradually subsided. Its population had reached an estimated 35,000 in 1946, but by 1970 had declined to 25,000. The census figure for 1980 was 22,000; for 1990, merely 18,000; and under 17,000 in 2000.

and a new natural gas supply." Most of these requirements came, but slowly. The town acquired its first streetcar in April 1902; it ran on five miles of track, and the fare was five cents.

The little city's dynamic atmosphere was ideal for W. F. Alexander in the last summer of the nineteenth century. Young and energetic, with the pleasing outgoing personality of a successful salesman, he saw nothing but opportunity. Before the end of the year, W. F. and his cousin moved to new quarters in the Horner Building on Main Street, one of many fine new buildings raised in the opulent, late- Victorian style with Italianate and Renaissance Revival adornments.[8] Alexander & Alexander occupied Rooms 2 and 3 on the second floor of the building, which still stands today.[9]

When the Alexander cousins bought the older agency, the Vances were running a weekly ad in a local paper:

INSURANCE!

J. CARL VANCE

(SUCCESSOR TO JONES & REED)

GENERAL AGT

GOFF BLOCK CLARKSBURG W. VA.

The Alexanders followed suit:

ALEXANDER & ALEXANDER

(SUCCESSOR TO J. CARL VANCE)

GENERAL

INSURANCE AGENTS

HORNER BUILDING, MAIN ST.

CLARKSBURG W. VA.

THE LARGEST AND OLDEST AGENCY

IN THIS PART OF THE STATE.

During the partnership's first two years, Herbert Alexander spent two weeks in Clarksburg and two at his Martinsburg agency, 150 miles to the east. He reported that "Willie [W. F.] was a good solicitor, and we increased the business 50 percent the first year. We also increased it 50 percent the second year."

By the end of 1898, C. B. Alexander had left his position with Senator Camden and had clerked at Cousin Herbert's Martinsburg agency for six months. C. B. subsequently

[8] The building was owned by the Horner family, an old Clarksburg clan with interests in real estate and oil.

[9] Occupied for many years by G. C. Murphy Company, the building is partly vacant, but its facade remains impressive.

bought a half interest in an insurance agency in Bluefield, West Virginia, 200 miles south of Clarksburg on the Virginia border, although this proved an ill-advised venture.

The Bluefield business was controlled by a family who owned a competing agency. To compound C. B.'s problem, his partner turned out to be a Bible-toting Baptist with a tarnished reputation. Yet another of the agency's evangelical salesmen obtained insurance applications on nonexistent properties, discounted notes, and pocketed the commissions. The notes were never paid, and the agency faced financial ruin. Herbert and Richard came to the rescue and bought out C. B.'s partner, each assuming a quarter interest. They remained silent partners, but C. B. was not a salesman and the agency stagnated. When it was sold late in 1901, C. B. moved to Clarksburg to join Herbert and W. F. at Alexander & Alexander.

Despite their immediate success, Herbert and W. F. were completely dissimilar in style. Herbert was slow and methodical, while W. F. exuded energy and drive. Expanding the business was his top priority, but Herbert, with two widely separated agencies, couldn't give Clarksburg the attention it required. As a result, in early 1902, Herbert sold his interest in the Clarksburg agency to C. B. Thus began an exclusive partnership between C. B. and W. F., which would remain intact until W. F.'s death forty-five years later.

CHAPTER 7

Alexander & Alexander Comes of Age: Growing Up and Out

C.B. Alexander's brief and painful experience with his Bluefield agency affected him profoundly. It reinforced a deep conservatism, which once led him to remark that he was against "everything new that had ever been proposed." C. B. was unashamedly preoccupied with the financial and administrative side of the business. He developed a meticulous knowledge of insurance, a keen appreciation for client service, and a knack for hiring high-quality personnel.

In 1902, almost all of A&A's business was fire insurance, which was a challenging sale. Many locals harbored an innate aversion to any type of insurance; others thought it too expensive. Many West Virginia property owners had no protection against fire loss, and properties that were covered usually had inadequate valuations. Fire insurance required aggressive selling; its purchase was almost never initiated by the buyer.

W. F. Alexander, a master salesman with an absolute belief in his product, was greatly aided by a new advertisement he created in 1903. Below a realistic drawing of a fireman carrying a woman down a ladder amidst a raging fire, the bold copy suggested that the benefits of fire insurance could not be measured in dollars and cents. Another A&A ad offered accident, steam boiler, and employers' liability insurance, as well as fire insurance. Another highlighted large insurance lines; and W. F. clearly had his sights on commercial clients.

Like their competitors, the Alexanders were not immune to stretching facts to strengthen a message. For example, one early ad declared that the agency was established in 1870, as Richard A. Alexander's agency had been. A 1905 letterhead also listed Alexander & Trammell in Martinsburg and Washington & Alexander in Charles Town as affiliated A&A offices. While controlled by members of the extended family, these agencies had no financial connection with A&A.[1]

Involvement in industry affairs began in 1904, when the agency joined the National Association of Local Fire Insurance Agents (NALFIA) and C. B. attended its convention in St. Louis. Early the following year, A&A joined three other local agents in a hostile reaction to the venerable New York broker Johnson & Higgins. They believed J&H was using an insurer that was not licensed in West Virginia in order to illegally sell below tariff-controlled rates.[2]

C. B., assuming the protagonist role in petitioning the Association's Boston headquarters, asserted that the Globe & Rutgers and Springfield Garden Insurance Companies underwrote 40 percent of the J&H line; Lloyd's syndicates, 50 percent; and the Royal Exchange (London), 10 percent. "This looks like a bad bunch of insurance companies," C. B. reported to the NALFIA. He added, "The companies are ones that we are very surprised that this assured would be willing to take. However, that is his own look-out." It turned out that C. B. and his associates had received inaccurate information. In fact, J&H had quoted proper rates. Nonetheless, the West Virginians' action demonstrated local agents' determination to fight out-of-state competition.

By 1905, insurance flourished in Clarksburg, with thirteen agents, forty-two fire insurance company offices, and several others listed under the categories of casualty, liability, or disability providers. W. F. Alexander's activity targeted the rapidly expanding energy-related companies. During the next decade, his efforts would propel the agency into a

[1] Blood was thicker than water. In 1902, the agency hired a fourth employee, C. B. and W. F.'s younger brother, Harry, apparently at the insistence of their mother. Harry came on as a bookkeeper and stayed only a few years.

[2] The "tariff" applied to fire insurance rates involving whole classes without differentiation of individual risks (except penalties for unusually hazardous conditions).

regional force and provide the underpinnings for a national firm.

W. F. attracted his first major corporate account in 1905. Although surviving documentation is fragmentary, Sun Oil Company was probably the client, and its pumping stations the insured assets. Evidently W. F. called on Joseph Newton Pew Sr., who cofounded Sun in 1886. Pew was not as concerned about Sun's fire exposure as he was about natural gas explosions. W. F. assured him that explosions were covered by fire insurance. Returning to the office, he discovered that this was inaccurate, as the furthest extension of the fire policy was for lightning.

W. F. and C. B. immediately set out to secure explosion protection. They collaborated with a Colonel Leighton to write the "inherent explosion clause," which covered explosions in and natural to the insured's premises.[3] It was the first underwriting of the inherent explosion clause and was later incorporated into standard fire insurance policies.

Identifying conditions where no coverage existed and working with insurers to offer new forms of protection were important factors contributing to A&A's early success. Such industriousness led to more business, and that, in turn, required additional staff. In January, 1906, the agency hired Lena Rottencutter, its sixth employee (and first female worker). This remarkable woman accompanied C. B. Alexander when he moved to the Baltimore office in 1916 and became the chief file clerk.

Unofficially, "Miss Lena" was A&A's "housemother." She became the chaperone and code enforcer for female employees and a stalwart member of the Women's Christian Temperance Union.[4] Until sometime in the 1930's, women in A&A's Baltimore office were not allowed to wear dresses with short sleeves. If Miss Lena considered their dresses too short, she sent them home for appropriate attire. Married or engaged women were never hired lest they become pregnant and leave for "family reasons."[5] Respected throughout the organization, Miss Lena officially retired with a large party in 1955, only to return to work the next day as if nothing happened. No one had the heart

[3] Leighton's first name is unknown, though records show that he was later a president of the National Fire Insurance Company of Hartford.

[4] Miss Lena also belonged to the popular Storytellers Organization, an association of people who traveled throughout the area entertaining audiences of all ages.

[5] A firm as distinguished as Marsh & McLennan had a similarly draconian policy: If a single woman married, she was required to resign.

The San Francisco earth-quake of 1906 wrecked destruction for 400 miles. It destroyed thousands of build-ings, while its carnage and astronomical dollar damage were caused by gas mains that exploded and stoves that collapsed to spark fires that

to challenge her, and she worked two more years before leaving in 1957 at age seventy-seven.

Between 1906 and 1914, Alexander & Alexander experi-enced steady if unspectacular growth. Fire insurance con-tinued to account for almost all revenues. Huge conflagra-

tions, occurring ever more frequently, were widely reported and boosted interest in coverage. Individuals and commercial enterprises were increasingly receptive to fire insurance.

The early 1900s saw a series of extraordinary catastrophes: Chicago's 1903 Iroquois Theater fire claimed some 600 lives and led to new theater safety codes. The steamship *General Slocum* was lost to fire in New York's East River

roared through the city for four days, burning almost unchecked because water mains broke too. Still, insurance covered about half the estimated losses and provided some $200 million to start rebuilding the magnificent city on California's great bay.

killing 1,021 people in 1904. The great Baltimore fire the same year burned 150 acres. Even though most buildings were stone or brick and considered fireproof, the city's business center was destroyed with losses of $70 million to $90 million (of which some $50 million was insured). Firefighting assistance was sought from as far away as New York City, but to little practical purpose because the outsiders' hose couplings did not fit Baltimore's hydrants and hoses. Hydrant and hose couplings were subsequently standardized as a result.

The 1906 San Francisco earthquake, which commanded worldwide press coverage, devastated five square miles and measured 8.3 on the Richter scale. More than 28,000 San Francisco buildings were destroyed, half of them residential. Approximately 5,000 were steel, stone, or brick; most others were made of redwood. Nearly 700 people were dead or missing, and another 300,000 were left homeless. Estimates of losses ranged between $350 million and $400 million; only an estimated $180 millionto $235 million was insured, with U.K. underwriters responsible for $40 million.

There was much haggling over coverage terms. Some policies covered fire only, but others included seismic shock. Thirty-seven insurers assessed stockholders $32 million to meet liabilities. The INA and its recently established Alliance Insurance Company paid over $4 million in claims. Fireman's Fund Insurance Company stated it was the first major insurer to survive such massive destruction in its home city. It paid half its claims of $11.2 million in company stock and assessed shareholders $300 per share.

The San Francisco earthquake and other significant catastrophes had little or no direct impact on A&A. The firm did not handle marine insurance until the late 1920s. For example, A&A was not affected by the hurricane and tidal wave that demolished Galveston, Texas, in 1900 and claimed some 5,000 lives, or by the loss of the *Titanic* in 1912 with more than 1,500 lives.

A&A's absence from the marine business was only one sign of its parochialism. The company was also slow to sell auto insurance. Clarksburg was booming and cars were everywhere, yet A&A wrote almost no automobile coverage.[6] By the end of 1912, when more than 500,000 people were driving cars, Charles Kettering's electric starter was being introduced to replace the hand crank, and a new process was invented to improve refining oil into gasoline. That same year, the Aetna L&C pioneered an auto policy that combined liability, property, and fire coverages, a forerunner of multiline policies.

Employee benefit programs also received national attention. Montgomery Ward adopted the first group accident and sickness policy in 1910. A year later, the Equitable Life Assurance Society issued the first group life policy to the Pantasote Leather Company of Passaic, New Jersey. It would be years, however, before A&A either sold group insurance or adopted a group medical plan for its employees.

Other new forms of coverage met specific needs of the day. Many applied to only a single peril. Wind and tornado insurance, while available much earlier, became popular among farmers by about 1910. Hail insurance was widely marketed by 1914, and crop protection became available by 1919. Rain insurance was first written in 1920.[7] Since Clarksburg was still an active agricultural area, such new products would have interested local farmers, but there is no indication that A&A pursued the business.

W. F. remained focused on the larger commercial accounts and energy-related business, which were invariably produced through his efforts. These fueled the agency's growth. New clients were either companies headquartered in the Clarksburg area or were organizations with major local facilities. By 1907, A&A required additional office space; the agency moved into the new Empire Bank Building, a handsome seven-story steel structure. The first- floor portal was flanked by Corinthian columns, and the embellished, bracketed cornice above the top floor conveyed a Renaissance Revival theme. The Alexanders selected an office suite on the fourth floor—because it contained a toilet.[8]

An A&A ad in 1909 referred to real estate, although this

[6] Similarly, it offered no workers compensation insurance, which became available in 1910.

[7] The first rain policy insured a rodeo in Dewey, Oklahoma. The event was rained out, and the Hartford Fire Insurance Company paid the $2,000 claim.

[8] Like the Horner building, the Empire Bank Building is still in service today.

Every step of progress is fraught with peril. In 1904, a German-American church group in New York chartered the paddlewheel steamboat General Slocum *for its annual picnic on Long Island. When fire broke out in a forward cabin, years-old life jackets crumbled and lifeboats wouldn't budge from their cradles. As fire spread aft, the ship ran aground, its bow aflame and its stern in deep water of the notoriously swift-moving East River. Frantic passengers crowded the decks; faced with death by fire or water, many jumped with their clothes aflame and drowned, to be washed ashore (opposite). The death count reached 1,021; the captain was jailed for safety violations.*

apparently was a short-lived sideline. To this day, many smaller insurance agencies combine the selling of insurance and real estate.

In April 1910, Roy N. Jenkins was hired to assist in placing insurance. A recent graduate of Clarksburg High, he had worked at the local Empire Bank and planned to attend the University of Pennsylvania for three years and then go to Jefferson Medical College. The Jenkins family knew the Alexanders, and W. F. saw great potential in the young man. Using his persuasive powers, W. F. painted a picture of large earnings and unlimited opportunity. Jenkins succumbed and was probably the agency's ninth employee. He became a widely respected force in the industry for many years and served until 1962, when he retired as chairman of the board.

Liability insurance was not in demand until after World War I. Before that, there was relatively little specialization within insurance agencies and brokerages. Although most employees at Johnson & Higgins were dedicated to marine insurance and average adjusting, workers in a more typical agency handled all types of insurance and were technically proficient in each.

At A&A, the Alexander brothers and Roy Jenkins routinely made detailed inspections of client properties. Company files include C. B.'s 1912 report for the People's Natural Gas Company. Another inspection was written up by W. F. for the Philadelphia Gas Company in 1913. Roy Jenkins drew up a 1915 property analysis for Quemahoning Coal Company. Inspection trips were frequently necessary if neither speedy nor comfortable, as A&A personnel traveled by horse-and-buggy or horseback. On one occasion, Roy Jenkins stayed in a Bluefield, West Virginia, hotel room and left his slippers under the bed. He returned weeks later, took the same room, and found the slippers where he had left them—perhaps a reflection of contemporary mores and housekeeping standards.

The year 1914 was auspicious for Alexander & Alexander. W. F.'s securing of the Baltimore & Ohio railroad account represented the first truly national account and led to geo-

graphic expansion. The B&O was concerned that appointing A&A would cause Baltimore brokers and agents to object to an "outsider" servicing its account. W. F. removed these concerns by opening an A&A office in the Abell Building across the street from B&O headquarters and moving his family to Baltimore.

Although the B&O has always been considered the firm's first railroad account, some sources have claimed that the Missouri Pacific Railroad (MOPAC) preceded it. No conclusive evidence supports this, and the weight of evidence favors the Baltimore & Ohio. W. F. acquired the MOPAC account through a referral from one of its directors, Robert Lancaster Williams, a prominent Baltimore banker and financier. W. F.'s older brother, Richard, introduced the two men, and since Williams was a director of the Great Northern Railway, it is likely that he introduced W. F. to that railroad. In any event, W. F. had acquired at least part of the Great Northern Railway account by 1927. The MOPAC account was almost certainly produced during World War I, and was placed by W. F. in London through Lloyd's underwriter Cuthbert Heath.

In all likelihood, the MOPAC account was taken from Marsh & McLennan. Don McLennan had close ties to the Eastern Railroad Syndicate, which became the Railroad Insurance Association in 1919. It had underwritten the account and refused to accept A&A as the new broker. Although C. B. Alexander was concerned about U-boat activity in the Atlantic, W. F. insisted on traveling to London to find underwriting. Fortunately, MOPAC became the first major American railroad to be insured in London. Heath designated A&A to adjust losses up to $250,000. After three years, this arrangement was assumed by Lloyd's U.S. legal representative, Mendes & Mount.

In addition to opposing his brother's London trips during the war, C. B. also disapproved of Roy Jenkins's move to Baltimore in 1915. He felt the uncertainties of the move were too great for a man with a young family. As a practical matter, Jenkins was now W. F.'s principal placer of insurance and needed to be near him. In 1916, C. B. realized that if

A&A wanted to concentrate on large commercial accounts, its growth depended on Baltimore and areas far removed from Clarksburg. Reluctantly, he too moved his family to Baltimore where he established headquarters. By 1915 at the latest, A&A was identifying itself as an insurance broker rather than an agent.

With its growth and a new office, the company needed additional employees, and Citizens Fire Insurance Company of Charles Town became a valuable source of recruits. Citizens had moved its executive offices to Baltimore at the end of 1911 and shortly thereafter was acquired by the Fidelity and Deposit Company (F&D) of Baltimore. After Citizens was adversely affected by large fire losses in 1913 and 1914, F&D reinsured the Citizens' entire book of business and dissolved the company, making many employees suddenly available for hire.[9]

By 1918, A&A's railroad accounts required a full-time professional specialist, and Martin Root was employed in that capacity. There were now sixteen employees in A&A's Baltimore office and five in Clarksburg. Baltimore's total monthly payroll was $1,920. Women, invariably in clerical positions, earned as little as $11 a week, while men's salaries were $100 to $300 a month.

The company's annual premium volume slightly exceeded $2 million, with net income of about $200,000. There were not many larger American insurance brokers, yet A&A was tiny compared with what would become its future competitors. For example, in 1916, Marsh & McLennan's New York office had thirty-two employees, with a monthly payroll of $3,885. A&A was poised to leap to a higher plateau, however, and the war provided opportunities for innovation.

The United States entered World War I in April 1917, and the armistice ending hostilities was signed on November 11, 1918. No A&A employee served in the armed services, and the conflict had little effect on company business. The war's end coincided with the 1918 worldwide influenza epidemic, which claimed at least 20 million lives, an estimated 500,000 in the United States. Countless people were

[9] Several of these individuals later became senior A&A executives. A. D. Legg was employed in 1915 as Baltimore office manager. Arthur Wooddy, hired in 1918, became a senior vice president, a director, and C. B.'s right-hand man. Ralph Henderson, who had left Citizens and served two other agencies, joined A&A as a fire inspector in 1918. He became the firm's fifth president in 1955. Hutson Lee Sr. moved to Baltimore when the Georgia Home Insurance Company was acquired by Citizens, then worked briefly with the Maryland Casualty Company before switching to A&A in 1916 and becoming its first secretary and treasurer after incorporation in 1922. Scott Wysong, from Charles Town as were many of the others, was hired in Baltimore in 1915. Transferred to Clarksburg two years later, he managed that office until 1961. Some time during 1916, Sue Roseman was hired as a temporary employee in Baltimore; when she retired in 1964 after forty-eight years, she wryly noted that she was never informed of a change in her status.

left with permanent health problems, and the pandemic focused attention on an urgent need for health and disability insurance.

In another venue, late in 1917, President Wilson had ordered the nation's railroads to operate under government control. They were not returned to private control until several years later. A&A's client, the Chicago, Rock Island & Pacific Railroad, which had a poor roadbed, wanted passenger legal liability insurance. No U.S. insurance market was receptive, but Roy Jenkins was able to place coverage at Lloyd's. This represented one of the first third-party legal liability insurances placed on an American railroad.

The end of World War I ushered in an era of geographic expansion that helped to establish A&A as a national brokerage. Simultaneously, in China, a series of events began which led to the creation of a major force in international insurance. In 1919, American International Group, Inc., was founded in Shanghai by Cornelius Vander Starr. Its original mission was to service insurance needs of local U.S. companies' Shanghai operations. As American International Underwriters (AIU), it would become a formidable underwriter of U.S. international risks. When Maurice R. (Hank) Greenberg became CEO in 1968, the company undertook a variety of imaginative initiatives under his brilliant leadership and would be widely viewed as the world's foremost insurer.

In November 1919, W. F. Alexander opened an office at 45 John Street in New York, an increasingly important underwriting center for large accounts and a center of headquarters for many industrial companies.[10] Ralph Henderson left Baltimore in 1920 to run the Manhattan office, which included W. F. when he wasn't away selling insurance.

The Tulsa, Oklahoma, office also opened in 1919 to accommodate a large account, Cosden Petroleum. In producing this business, W. F. leveraged his contacts rather than relying on "cold canvassing," his usual approach. Josh Cosden, once a Baltimore streetcar motorman with ambition, had obtained a loan from a local lawyer and subse-

[10] In 1919, the agency also hired a female employee at $35 a week, namely Miss Helen Thompson, who was engaged as a secretary in the New York City office.

quently made major oil discoveries in Oklahoma. W. F. met him through the lawyer and won Cosden Petroleum's business in 1912 or 1913.[11] Cosden became a colorful oil baron, known around Oklahoma as the "Prince of Petroleum." The Tudor-Gothic Cosden Building, begun in 1918, was at sixteen stories Tulsa's first skyscraper, later renamed the Mid-Continent Tower.[12]

From a small hometown agency, A&A was growing into a firm eager to compete with established players regardless of location. C. B. Alexander's fiscal conservatism, combined with W. F.'s extraordinary salesmanship, gave the balanced leadership that provided the foundation for A&A to become a leading national brokerage.

[11] In 1986, Occidental Petroleum Corporation became the owner of Cosden and its successor, Mid-Continent Petroleum Company. In 1968, Occidental had acquired another long-time A&A client, Island Creek Coal Company.

[12] It survived in part because of its listing on the historic registry, although in 1980 a twenty-story tower was cantilevered over it.

CHAPTER 8

Emerging Personalities: Four Founders

In the early 1920s, though they operated on vastly different scales, Alexander & Alexander and Marsh & McLennan shared many similarities. This was particularly true of their leaders.

Henry Marsh and Don McLennan were primarily responsible for winning M&M's significant accounts in the early decades of the twentieth century. While their personalities and lifestyles contrasted sharply, both had the advantage of important social contacts, but Marsh sold more on the strength of personality and McLennan on his contacts and intimate business knowledge.

Marsh was a natural producer—suave, flamboyant, and confident in his ability to influence people and events. He was fearless and took risks to produce accounts. For example, early in 1910, he noticed in a newspaper item that Theodore N. Vail, president of the American Telephone & Telegraph Company (AT&T), was sailing at noon for London. Without baggage, Marsh boarded the ship and secured a deck chair next to Vail's, then booked passage on the same return trip as his quarry. He developed a relationship with Vail, and M&M was appointed AT&T's broker in September 1910.

Marsh and Burrows had also been friendly with the utilities tycoon Samuel Insull. When Insull enlarged his empire, M&M was installed to operate as the insurance department and handle insurance requirements for all of Insull's companies.

More conservative, McLennan built his reputation through friendship and insurance know-how. McLennan built special relationships with senior executives within the railroad industry; his expertise evolved, in part, through participating in personal inspections.

Little rapport existed between Henry Marsh and Don McLennan. Their personal habits and lifestyles were completely different. They only met when pressing business matters required. Personal antipathy ran so deep that Marsh considered giving his M&M stock to Harvard University so that McLennan could never fully control the company.[1]

Don McLennan managed the company by establishing policy but avoiding details. From the mid-1920s, he spent considerable time working on the affairs of companies in which he was a director. His board position with Continental Illinois National Bank and Trust Company gave him contacts that produced new business opportunities. By the early 1930s, his focus returned to insurance. In a 1933 *Colliers* article, Hugh S. Johnson listed his "Industry's All-American Team" and reported that "the Ulysses of business outside of banking in Chicago is Don McLennan—an insurance man who dreads publicity but is, in my judgment, the most respected businessman in the Midwest."

In the smaller partnership of Alexander & Alexander, W. F. Alexander more closely resembled Henry Marsh. A tall, spare man with large ears, he was attractive rather than handsome. Impeccably dressed, W. F. was a great charmer and popular with ladies, which got him in hot water periodically. He could be quite profane, yet he was considerate and compassionate to employees. Although lacking social contacts, he proved to be a dynamic and ingenious leader with a strong, aggressive personality. There can be little doubt that, in similar circumstances, W. F. would have jumped aboard a prospect's outward-bound liner, too. He had an insurance brokerage mentality and little interest in small accounts. He spent much of his time seeking business

[1] Instead, he ultimately sold it to the firm over a period of several years. He resigned as chairman at the beginning of 1935.

W.F. Alexander (left)
A founder and tireless
salesman.

C. B. Alexander (right)
The older brother and
sterner partner.

around the United States, traveling widely by every available means.

W. F.'s magnetic presence and attentiveness to people was irresistible. He understood intuitively when to press for a sale and when to back off. His son Richard recalled that his father had taken him as a boy on a trip to visit a prospective client in Philadelphia. The extended small talk seemed pointless to young Dick, but as his father told him later, W. F. had sensed that the prospect lacked the authority to name A&A the broker. W. F. took pains not to embarrass the man by pressing for a commitment. Dick also recalled his father saying, "When you put your client first, your reward follows!" A competitor's chief executive once called W. F. the greatest insurance salesman of his time and the "Tiffany" of the insurance business. His success confirmed this.

Paradoxically, C. B. was unlike his brother in almost every respect. Fairly tall and of medium build, he was not particularly attractive. He complicated his undistinguished looks by dressing sloppily. C. B. wore patched trousers and stained hats, occasionally putting the hats on backwards. Ironically, he was fastidious about his butler's appearance and dressed him to the hilt in plum and silver livery.

At times, C. B. was demanding and difficult, but he was

adept at hiring talent and selecting the best individual for a designated task. Although he required results, he was fair and gave employees free rein to accomplish their jobs. Like W. F., C. B. showed compassion for employees with problems and often personally paid their medical bills before the firm offered group health care insurance. He was a smart and very conservative financial manager—tightfisted, some would say. He only bought secondhand cars for himself and once, upon learning that A&A's treasurer purchased a new Cadillac, he called in auditors to check the books. Unlike W. F., C. B. preferred small accounts, believing that they minimized the impact of lost business.

At home, he was a good family man, and he enjoyed his evening libation. After moving away, he longed for Clarksburg. On one occasion, he got off the train there looking disheveled, with his collar in his hand, to the shock of those meeting him. Seeing the concerned looks on their faces, he said to one, "Nonsense, son, this is the way I left West Virginia." Another time, he was visited in Baltimore by Martin Root Jr. of the Clarksburg office. C. B. suddenly sent his chauffeur out to get some pebbles and told Root to put them in his shoes so he would feel at home.

In different ways, each brother possessed a commanding presence, and others often deferred to them. Yet both were convinced—falsely, as it turned out—that they would not live beyond forty-five, the age at which their father died. This led to W. F.'s urgency and drive to accomplish goals early in life and may have contributed to C. B.'s yearning for Clarksburg's rural life.

Unfortunately, conflicts between the brothers brought long periods when they avoided one another. One cause of friction was said to be C. B.'s wife, who felt that W. F. had not experienced the life tragedies she and C. B. had suffered. These included the loss of a daughter, killed in a car given as a graduation present, and a son's death in World War II. Mrs. Alexander exercised great influence over C. B. and stirred up differences between the brothers. This seemed to have affected C. B. more than his brother, but it certainly caused anxiety among others in the firm.

Despite differences, or perhaps because of contrasts in personality and style, their partnership thrived. It was a situation where complementary talents totaled more than the sum of their parts. Things that C. B. could not achieve while hunkering over his books in Clarksburg, W. F. could accomplish with a grand gesture.

For example, A&A picked up momentum in 1925 after W. F. secured the General Chemical account; developing this account came by a circuitous route. W. F. had obtained a noncancelable insurance contract for a prospective railroad account, but the railroad's CEO wanted to give the business to another broker and instructed the insurance manager to terminate A&A if he wanted to keep his job. W. F. then prevailed on the Hartford Fire Insurance Company to cancel the policy, and the grateful insurance manager told the story to a friend. The friend's counterpart at Gen-eral Chemical was so impressed that he called W. F. and subsequently awarded him General Chemical's account.

General Chemical, which manufactured industrial acids, was part of Allied Chemical & Dye, a five-company conglomerate formed in 1920 in response to the shortages of dyes, chemicals, and pharmaceuticals that had plagued American industries during World War I.[2] Within a few years, A&A got the insurance business for all five companies, and Allied became its largest account for several decades.

In 1925, A&A received national attention for the first time because of another sale by W. F., a transaction increasing the firm's premium volume to $6 million, a 43 percent increase over the prior year. However, it also demonstrated the uproar that could be raised by wronged or jealous competitors.

W. F. had made friends with an executive vice president of the Chrysler Corporation and proposed that, as a sales incentive, the automaker provide fire and theft insurance on new cars. The Palmetto Insurance Company of South Carolina, a subsidiary of Auto Insurance Company of Hart-

[2] The four other original components of the company were the Barrett Company, supplier of coal tar chemicals and roofing; National Aniline & Chemical Company, a dye concern; Semet-Solvay Corpo-ration, a coke manufacturer; and Solvay Process Company, a producer of alkalis and nitrogen materials.

ford, agreed to provide the coverage. Policies were issued as cars were sold and financed by Commercial Credit Corporation. Chrysler's distributors and dealers submitted daily delivery records to a newly formed A&A office in Detroit. Chrysler advertised this nationally by declaring that effective July 1, 1925, all cars sold would "include fire and theft insurance for 100 percent of the F.O.B. factory list price, prepaid for one year. . . ." A&A's competitors were furious at losing in a single stroke the insurance contracts that might have come to them from new Chrysler owners. An August 25, 1925, *Eastern Underwriter* editorial argued:

About the only change that the Chrysler plan effects is that throughout the country there were heretofore ten to fifteen finance companies participating in financing time-payment sales of Chrysler cars, between them controlling insurance business which passed through ten or fifteen agents or brokers. The number of brokers is reduced from ten or fifteen to one. . . . we find the editor of one important insurance publication complaining that admittedly there is nothing in it for any one but the broker.

Predictably, local agents and state insurance commissioners bitterly objected. New York State threatened to revoke A&A's license, and the plan was terminated abruptly in the summer of 1926. Cliff C. Jones, chairman of R. B. Jones, speaking as president of the National Association of Insurance Agents, hailed A&A's defeat as proof of the association's strength.[3] Addressing a convention, Jones fumed:

A year ago there were dark clouds on the horizon that looked ominous. We were indeed facing as defiant and as determined a challenge as was ever flung at the foundation of the American Agency System: the Chrysler scheme of wholesale insurance! . . . The justice and unselfishness of our position triumphed over the influences which Cossack-like would have ridden us into the dust with as little concern as the cruel soldiers of the Czars showed the Russian peasantry, and with the same results in insurance as were brought about in that unfortunate country.

The plan earned A&A premiums of $1,182,000 in 1925 and $1,414,000 in 1926. A&A's Detroit office needed twelve clerks (all women) to issue policies. Generally speaking, in the 1920s, there still were few women in the industry's pro-

[3] A&A would acquire R. B. Jones in 1978.

fessional ranks. In 1926, for example, the Aetna L&C appointed its first female officer—as personnel director. A&A's New York City office, a warren of three rooms with a staff of five, hired Cora Seiler that May. She became an indispensable secretary and administrative assistant to three A&A CEOs. Similar to Miss Lena, Cora became the unofficial "office mother" who knew everything about the company.[4]

In terms of personnel, a breakthrough came in 1927, when the firm began hiring a number of young men who would rise to eventually hold senior technical, sales, and management positions. The new hirings were also an acknowledgment that W. F. could not sustain A&A's growth single-handedly. Many of those new hires had never been to college, but this did not affect their success. Rodney Piersol joined Baltimore's accounting department in 1923. He transferred to New York in 1925, where he became a fixture until his retirement in 1966 as a director and senior vice president.[5] Among other important additions to the staff were Fred Schmidt, the first manager of the aviation department and later a manager of the Chicago office, and Roswell Dunn, W. F.'s son-in-law.[6]

Effective managers produced positive results through quite dissimilar methods. For example, the two most important New York departments were the casualty and property departments, eventually managed by George Falvey and Stanley Bolden, who were hired in 1928 and 1929, respectively. The fact that the personalities of these two men were radically different again demonstrates the value of diverse talents and suggests the futility of stereotyping successful managers. Falvey was small in stature—with a loud voice and a bit of a Napoleon complex. Managing by intimidation, he ran a tight shop, with employees who either feared him or were wary of him. Nevertheless, his results were excellent, and his authoritarian style was replicated by other A&A senior executives. Stanley Bolden, on the other hand, had a very quiet demeanor and ran a somewhat loose

[4] One of Cora Seiler's duties was to maintain an inventory of neckties especially for Roy Jenkins, who was color blind. On days when he arrived at the office with an ill-matched tie–suit combination, she corrected the matter from her stash of haberdashery.

[5] Over the years Rodney Piersol had various responsibilities. These included serving as A&A's senior contact with many insurance companies and with London correspondent brokers, principally Sedgwick, Collins & Company Ltd.; initiating the firm's first reinsurance broking contracts; establishing an aviation insurance department; and running the New York office. Although he often displayed a cold and brisk facade, Piersol was a sound insurance broker who helped many junior employees adjust to the business. As a major shareholder, he was elected a corporate director in 1947 and a senior vice president in 1962.

[6] Roswell Dunn, a Princeton University graduate, was perhaps A&A's first college man. He understood the importance of business production and recruited two future A&A CEOs. His various roles with the firm included managing the St. Louis and Atlanta offices as well as the Southeast Region.

Prosperity and the coming of age of automobile design combined as Americans took to the roads in increasing numbers, using such conveyances as this sporty 1924 Chrysler roadster and its trailer, a Chenango, designed to carry camping gear. About this time W. F. Alexander persuaded Chrysler Corporation to offer a year's free fire and theft insurance to every new car buyer, a dividend that competing insurance agents called unfair.

department. He delegated responsibility and expected it to be carried out effectively. Bolden was extremely knowledgeable about fire insurance and loss control services, and was highly respected by members of his department and A&A's top officers.

During 1927, the Baltimore office established a local agency department under C. B. Alexander's direction, and this department operated as a separate company, with its own accounting system, as it sought smaller commercial accounts. The business was generated by nonemployee "solicitors." This department was notoriously unprofitable because small commercial and personal accounts require extensive and costly services. If A&A had used this as an object lesson, it might have saved tens of millions of dollars over the years. Nevertheless, the department was a valuable training center for many who would later advance to senior positions, particularly because it handled the personal insurance needs of corporate client executives.

Between 1929 and 1934, the Baltimore office appointed

or hired a number of solicitors. As nonemployees, their compensation was based on a percentage of commissions on the business they sold. At the time, this was a frequent practice in the insurance agency/brokerage industry. Excepting life insurance, it was a flawed practice—in part because the profitability of an account was rarely considered when negotiating the commission percentage. Some Baltimore solicitors became regular employees and distinguished themselves in various ways, both inside and outside A&A. Latimer Stewart and Samuel Shriver illustrate this pattern.

Lat Stewart became A&A's first formal solicitor in 1929, and a very successful one. In the course of the next forty years—he became a salaried employee in 1950 and did not retire until 1970—he produced more large accounts than anyone except W. F. Alexander. With his engaging personality and open manner, he became the confidant of many employees.[7] Sam Shriver, a solicitor hired in 1933, became a regular employee in 1950 and a director in 1951.[8]

It bears mention, sadly, that C. B.'s son, C. B. Jr., joined the Baltimore office as a solicitor in 1930 and remained in this capacity. He joined the American Field Service during World War II and was killed in Germany on April 9, 1945, shortly before the war's end, the only fatality among A&A servicemen during the war.[9]

On balance, the solicitors made important contributions. Nonetheless, company morale suffered from having solicitors while promoting team effort. Fortunately, for A&A, solicitors were few.

Another key figure dating from this period was Frederick T. Drake, who joined A&A in Baltimore in 1918, learned the ropes for a decade, and then earned the chance to run his own show when A&A required another venue in addition to its offices in New York, Baltimore, Clarksburg, and Tulsa. Texas had become an important state for A&A by 1928, but because of rigid insurance laws protecting local agents, it presented the company with a challenge. Except for loss adjusting, local licenses were needed to conduct insurance business in the state, and to obtain a license, one had to be a resident.

[7] Latimer Stewart was elected a director in 1951 and offered the presidency of A&A after Ralph Henderson's retirement in January 1961. He declined the position, however, because it required moving to New York City. This was a prudent decision on his part as he would have been unhappy handling the necessary administrative responsibilities.

[8] Samuel Shriver became chief financial officer and eventually president on January 1, 1961. He was elected CEO in 1963 and chairman of the board later in the year. He took early retirement in 1966.

[9] General Charles de Gaulle awarded him the Croix de Guerre with Palm posthumously.

While establishing residency to become a Texan, Fred Drake was traveling by train from St. Louis to Dallas and fell into conversation with a stranger over breakfast in the dining car. The stranger said he was on an unpleasant mission—to arrest a fellow who was breaking Texas insurance laws. Drake said he knew many Dallas insurance people who might be of help. The stranger confided that the culprit was one Fred Drake! Fred excused himself and got off at the next station. He always felt it was the most providential breakfast that he had ever eaten, and he remained outside Texas until the new operation qualified as a legal entity.

In due course, Drake became a Texan—or a resident of Texas at any rate—in 1929. He opened F. T. Drake Insurance, a sole proprietorship, while continuing as an A&A vice president. Among his first accounts, the office handled the Humble and Magnolia Petroleum Companies, Lone Star Gas, and the Texas and Pacific Railroad Com-pany. W. F. Alexander Jr. (Fontaine), one of W. F.'s sons, who joined the firm in 1929, was placed with the Texas affiliate and eventually became its leader.

CHAPTER 9

The Roaring Twenties: New Venues

The Roaring Twenties, a vibrant decade in America's history, was for Alexander & Alexander as frenetic as the new rage in music—jazz. Opportunities arose in new forms of coverage, in new venues, and in new client companies for a firm whose partners had energy, skill, and daring.

Labor strife and strikes in 1919 generated riot and civil commotion coverage. The invention of the airplane in 1903 had spawned the aviation industry, whose growth multiplied the forms of transportation insurance. Group life, health, and disability insurance became new coverages.[1] After World War I, the need for accident and liability insurance developed rapidly.

Liability coverage arose partly as an outcome of a New York State appeals court decision in *MacPherson* v. *Buick Motor Company*. This case placed greater onus on manufacturers to produce quality products. The 1916 precedent established two areas of responsibility. Manufacturers became responsible for product defects causing personal injury. Also, the lack of "privity," i.e., private knowledge or inside information, did not limit plaintiff rights to receive compensation or recover damages for injuries. The ruling stopped short of establishing strict liability, but it began a movement that created massive liabilities by the century's end.

A&A's first casualty department was set up in the Balti-

[1] A&A purchased a group disability policy for its employees in 1921. The Alexander brothers took out life insurance policies with a combined face value of $90,000 for the company's benefit. "Key Person" life insurance has continued to be popular with corporations.

[2] In contrast, Marsh & McLennan was involved with both casualty and marine insurance from 1905.

[3] These included $45,000 to a boy partly paralyzed after being hit by a truck, $40,000 to a man hit by a truck, $45,000 to a man knocked from a motorcycle by a car, $40,000 for a broken leg in an auto accident, and $35,000 for a permanent ankle injury caused by a truck.

[4] Such reports and recommendations involved considerable costs, but price reductions were primarily achieved through fireproofing processes and wider use of sprinkler systems. Yet one effect was to squeeze profit margins for brokers and agents. A vice president of a respected New York brokerage lamented, "No broker can run his business on an average commission of 10 percent."

[5] Johnson & Higgins also handled some railroad business.

more office in 1919.[2] A liability insurance specialist was hired as department manager, and for several years he received a small percentage of all revenues his department generated. By 1920, the country took notice of the rewards for pursuing liability claims. In 1923, the *Eastern Underwriter* reported that in jury awards involving a variety of accidents, persons injured by motor vehicles might collect damages in the $40,000 range (the equivalent of a seven-digit sum today).[3]

Although A&A's future appeared promising in 1920, the insurance business was no gold mine for some. Published reports chronicled the demise of many small brokers, often because they failed to specialize and remain competitive with larger firms. Marsh & McLennan was formidable in this respect. For example, as early as 1910, the firm had offered loss control services, routinely inspecting clients' facilities and presenting comprehensive reports with detailed recommendations. Shortly thereafter, A&A was providing similar services.[4]

In 1920, the *National Underwriter* reported that Marsh & McLennan was the absolute leader in insuring railroads. Its engineering department spent $50,000 to $70,000 annually servicing railroad accounts. A&A's Baltimore office was also cited as having some good railroad business. This was probably the first mention of A&A in a national insurance publication, a bellwether of its growing size and importance. M&M dominated the Midwest's railroads and thus the national rail scene, yet A&A arguably held a solid second position nationally.[5]

With the coming of the new decade, W. F. Alexander's success in securing new business led to nine additional employees in one year. Virtually all of W. F.'s new accounts were railroad, coal, oil, or chemical companies. These were growth industries of the early twentieth century, and they became A&A's strength.

By 1922, A&A handled part or all of the insurance for these railroads: Baltimore & Ohio; Chesapeake & Ohio; Chicago & Alton; Chicago, Rock Island & Pacific; Denver & Rio Grande; Denver & Salt Lake; International & Great

Northern; Missouri, Kansas & Texas; Missouri Pacific; and Texas & Pacific.[6] W. F. Alexander was responsible for securing these as well as A&A's natural resource accounts.

By 1922, he had produced contracts with American Zinc, Consolidated Coal, Cosden Petroleum, Empire Refining, Hope Natural Gas, Humble Oil,[7] Island Creek Coal, Magnolia,[8] and Sun Oil. He secured a major portion of the Sun Oil account in 1915, although some business was already on the books. Two of A&A's earliest commercial clients, Hope Natural Gas and People's Natural Gas, were owned by Standard Oil Company of New Jersey.[9]

A&A's total premiums jumped to almost $5 million in 1920,[10] and new office space was required for both the Baltimore and the New York offices. In 1921, the Baltimore office moved into the Standard Oil Building at 503 St. Paul Place, and the New York office moved to 80 Maiden Lane, where it operated for thirty years. A small office opened in St. Louis, taking space in a Missouri Pacific building to service that railroad.

Owing to New York City's growing importance, in 1921 W. F. and Roy Jenkins started working in the city full time. They moved their families to New Jersey, and Ralph Henderson returned to Baltimore. New Baltimore hires included H. C. Gaston, who retired as corporate treasurer in 1958.

On March 24, 1922, Alexander & Alexander Inc. of Maryland was formed. All partnership assets were purchased except those of Alexander & Alexander of Clarksburg. C. B. and W. F. owned all but 180 of A&A's 2,000 common shares and all its 3,000 preferred shares. Preferred shares were retired occasionally, and then retired completely by April 30, 1934. At the end of August 1922, A&A's earned surplus was $126,000.

The principal reason for incorporation was to perpetuate the firm.[11] Clarksburg, at C. B. Alexander's insistence, remained a separate partnership until mid-1923. The Alexander brothers held all but a few shares. C. B. retained a special fondness for Clarksburg even after it was obvious that the office would never generate significant profits.

[6] The Southern Pacific Rail Corp. was added in 1925.

[7] Humble was later acquired by what is now Exxon Mobil.

[8] Later acquired by Mobil Oil Company, now Exxon Mobil.

[9] In 1943, they, along with two other companies, were spun off as a stock dividend to form Consolidated Natural Gas. Standard Oil was required to divest its natural gas utilities in order not to be considered a holding company.

[10] This excludes the Clarksburg office.

[11] A similar step was taken by Marsh & McLennan in 1923, when Don McLennan became president and for all practical purposes the CEO. Henry Marsh was chairman of the board.

The period 1921 through 1925 was one of consolidation. The staff only grew from thirty-six to forty-three; twenty-four were in the Baltimore office. Except in 1926, when the special program was offered to Chrysler, the annual premium volume from 1922 through 1927 was between $4 million and $4.5 million.[12] New business rolled in, but insurance prices were depressed.

[12] This figure probably excludes the Clarksburg and Tulsa offices, which were separate corporations and kept their own books.

While A&A's client list became ever more impressive, the firm remained small compared with Marsh & McLennan and Johnson & Higgins. These brokers possessed financial strength and invested in growth strategies, an option not open to A&A. J&H's marine dominance was reinforced by acquiring the marine and average adjusting agency of Wilcox, Peck & Hughes in 1924, which made J&H the world's largest insurance broker, according to *National Underwriter.*

It is debatable whether J&H or M&M was larger, but both were expanding rapidly. By opening additional offices and purchasing the marine insurance of San Francisco's Balfour, Guthrie & Co. in 1928, J&H strengthened its national representation. Knowing that ocean marine insurance is global, J&H's executives understood the potential benefits of operating internationally. The firm was working jointly in Canada with Willis Faber by 1906 and opened an office in Havana, Cuba, in 1921. Over the years, J&H's international connections provided successful entrée to numerous American companies.

M&M listed fourteen domestic offices in 1925 and a Canadian office. Its correspondent relationship with C. T. Bowring in Britain was the competitive equivalent of J&H's link with Willis Faber. M&M moved ahead aggressively and, in 1929, purchased J. B. F. Davies, one of the largest insurance agencies in the West, with offices in Los Angeles, Phoenix, Portland, and Seattle.

M&M was always progressive. It initiated a formal strategic planning process in 1919. By 1923, it had established a life insurance department. While such insurance would not

Tired Out!

IT sometimes happens that a woman, on the death of her husband, is left without any means of support. Her duties have not fitted her to meet the problems of making a living for herself and her children, and she has to fall back upon her skill with a needle. Such skill is so poorly paid that poverty and privation stare her in the face.

No man has any excuse for subjecting his wife to such a future. Whatever he earns, a part of it should be used to guarantee her against it.

The Travelers Insurance Company in its Guaranteed Low Cost Monthly Income Policy has the best safeguard ever devised for just this emergency.

The Travelers Insurance Company
HARTFORD, CONN.

Please send me particulars regarding Guaranteed Low Cost Monthly Income Policy.

Name _____ Business Address _____

Date of Birth _____ City _____ State _____

The Saturday Evening Post

Advertising, another flowering industry, would not be left behind in the first quarter of the 20th century, nor would insurers fail to pluck the heartstrings in their ads. Thus Travelers warned husbands, "It sometimes happens that a woman, on the death of her husband, is left without any means of support. . . . [or] of making a living for herself and her children, and she has to fall back upon her skill with a needle. . . . No man has any excuse for subjecting his wife to such a future" when life insurance offers "the best safeguard ever devised for just this emergency."

become an important product to most brokers until after World War II, it was a forward-looking step. M&M was ready when group life insurance became significant during the 1930s.

Reinsurance broking was where Marsh & McLennan made perhaps its most brilliant strategic move. In 1918, the company was appointed U.S. managers of the Union Insurance Society of Canton, an important Far East organization. This introduced M&M to reinsurance, and it began producing for the Canton group "facultative reinsurance"—i.e., the reinsuring of a particular risk or part of a risk.

Substantial protection was also needed for M&M's railroad accounts to cover the shipment of cotton. This necessitated a special form of insurance written through the Cotton Insurance Association, a group of American and British insurers. The Association's manager was Guy Carpenter, and M&M placed a special excess-of-loss reinsurance policy for his group. Carpenter then established a New York reinsurance office, Guy Carpenter & Company, in 1923. He mandated that M&M, which provided new business for his office, would take over the company after his death. When he died in 1935, M&M was suddenly launched as the country's foremost reinsurance brokerage and was positioned to become the world's foremost as well. Remarkably, no other U.S. brokerage concentrated on reinsurance until long after Guy Carpenter's dominance was apparent.

The Frank B. Hall brokerage was also on the move. In 1920, the firm opened a Los Angeles office to handle movie-related business produced by its new president, Arthur Hoyt. A year later, Hoyt resigned as president, preferring to concentrate on other company duties. Cecil Stewart took on a dual role as president and chairman and was determined to accelerate growth. To beef up the nonmarine business, he purchased a New York City brokerage—Monks, Goodwin and Shaw, Inc.—which also had a Boston office. At the same time, several top solicitors were hired. In 1922, a new office opened in Philadelphia and geographic expansion was under way.

Fred. S. James & Co. also opened more U.S. offices. Additionally, James & Co. advertised in a 1923 issue of *Insurance Index* that it was serving as U.S. managers for the General Fire Insurance and Urbaine Fire Insurance Companies in Paris, as well as the Eagle Star & Dominion Insurance Co. Ltd. of London.

R. A. Corroon Company, founded in 1905 and renamed Corroon & Reynolds in 1928, also was becoming a major player. For the next four decades, its primary focus would be the management and control of small insurance companies, while also building a brokerage operation. The company sold its insurers in 1964. In 1966, it acquired a large brokerage, C. R. Black Corporation; in 1968, it became Corroon & Black Corporation.

Despite expansion of their major competitors, the Alexander brothers engaged in no formal planning or sales strategy. The firm's progressive initiatives were mainly by-products of W. F.'s ongoing successes, which were quite remarkable given the advantages that Marsh & McLennan enjoyed. In addition to their supersalesmen Henry Marsh and Don McLennan, M&M launched a program as early as 1906 to hire well-connected college graduates, paying them a percentage of commissions the firm received on new business they initiated.

Although the acquisition of insurance agencies did not play a major role in A&A's growth until after World War II, some were acquired before then. The earliest was Clarksburg's Thorn Agency in 1923. A year later, the Franz Insurance Agency of Clarksburg was acquired for $4,196.24 plus a 5 percent commission on the first renewal of its policies. The Tulsa office purchased the local Hoffman, O'Connell and Dobron agency in 1925, and in 1930 the West Virginia corporation acquired the H. D. Talbott Agency.[13]

By the 1920s, A&A still did not have close connections with any London brokerages that served as conduits for placing Lloyd's business.[14] Possibilities improved in 1926, when Harvey Bowing, of Sedgwick, called on C. B. Alexander to persuade him of Sedgwick's expertise in placing fire risks in London. Gwillym Lewis, who headed Sedgwick's nonmarine department, also began cultivating C. B.

Contact between Sedgwick and A&A continued. In 1928, Sedgwick recommended to its U.K. client, Royal Dutch Petroleum, that A&A be selected to handle the eastern United States insurance requirements of its subsidiary, Shell Petroleum Corporation. W. F. already was calling on Fred Godber, Shell's president, and Sedgwick's suggestion facilitated the decision to hire A&A.[15] At this point, Sedgwick became A&A's principal London correspondent and remained so for more than fifty years.

[13] The Talbott office was purchased from trustees who included Louis A. Johnson, later President Truman's secretary of defense.

[14] A&A's modest marine insurance requirements were being handled through Frank B. Hall, and an occasional fire risk was placed in London through an excess lines broker, Hall & Henshaw.

[15] The account was split among three U.S. brokers—A&A, M&M, and F. B. Hall.

New forms of coverage proliferated in the 1920s as people encountered novel forms of risks. New York City had its first midtown air crash in 1929 when a chartered plane lost power at 3,000 feet, in sight of Central Park. In a "dead-stick" glide, the dashing pilot, Charles Reid (inset), grazed the roof of the 12-story YMCA building before crashing on a fourth-story ledge. He died, although his passenger, Robert Bailie, a lion tamer, jumped with a parachute and survived. This brush with fate came just three weeks after another crash, that of the stock market.

After World War I, the insurance industry had difficulty keeping pace with technological advances and with American industry's geographic expansion. This was particularly apparent in the petroleum industry. As oil production in Texas and Oklahoma mushroomed, vast amounts of high-priced crude oil were stored in large, wooden-roofed tanks, which were particularly vulnerable to lightning strikes. Additionally, refineries were often built without sophisticated engineering input. One unfortunate result was the use of "batch stills," in which the distillation of crude oil took place. These stills released large quantities of flammable liquid when a break or explosion occurred.

Insurers' field representatives often were not technically qualified to assess refinery risks or proficient in recommending improvements. Consequently, underwriters were cautious and accepted only very small lines on a risk. Several hundred policies were frequently needed to complete coverage on a large plant. This was a nightmare for brokers, who visited many insurers to secure the coverage, and it increased the potential for nonconcurrent policy conditions. The situation also frustrated insurance companies.

In a 1918 attempt to remedy these problems, several insurers joined to form the Oil Insurance Association (OIA). It provided training for inspectors and developed high standards for fire prevention and fire protection. It originally operated in Texas, Oklahoma, and Kansas, but gradually expanded into other Midwestern and Rocky Mountain states. This was an important insurance market for A&A. The OIA's member companies originally intended to limit underwriting to the central United States, but A&A and other brokers kept pressing for expansion. A&A was highly influential because it handled more petroleum-related business than any other broker and serviced several large petroleum clients.[16]

W. F. Alexander and Roy Jenkins were close to executives in several OIA member companies, among them Springfield Fire & Marine, Hartford Fire, and Crum & Forster. The two men complained bitterly to those companies about the difficulty in placing oil risks on western properties. In 1926, Union Oil Company of California sustained the largest insurance industry loss to that time on American oil properties—a $7 million loss when lightning destroyed various types of oils in earthen reservoirs. Shortly after, the Pacific Coast insurer executives invited the OIA to extend its operation to the coast. A&A's influential role in this extension marked its rise as a national brokerage.

[16] Marsh & McLennan did not write a major petroleum account until the Sinclair Oil Company in 1921. Frank B. Hall handled the insurance requirements for the Texas Company, later to be named Texaco.

The last notable innovation of the 1920s was aviation insurance, which began in the United States with a single Travelers policy in 1919 and was flourishing by 1929. Its impressive growth—rather like the "mighty oak from a tiny acorn"—resembled the development of aviation itself. In 1903, when the Wright brothers opened a new chapter in history, the *Boston Herald* ran a one-paragraph account of it on page 10 reporting that "a successful trial of a flying machine had been made at Kitty Hawk by Wilbur and Orville Wright. The machine flew three miles[17] in the face of a 21 mile an hour wind and then gracefully descended to earth."

[17] In fact, the first flight of the *Flyer* lasted 12 seconds and covered 120 feet.

In 1908, Lt. Thomas W. Selfride became the first person to die in an airplane accident when he flew in a plane piloted by Orville Wright; a propeller broke, and the craft crashed from 150 feet. Three years later, G. B. Rogers completed the first crossing of North America by air—from New York to Pasadena, California (with many intervening stops); air time: eighty-two hours, four minutes.

Although Lloyd's wrote the first aviation insurance policy in 1912, few others were written before World War I. Those covered only persons and property because the aircraft itself was considered unsafe. After the war, planes became reliable enough to be insurable, and on May 1, 1919, the Travelers Insurance Company offered a comprehensive policy. It provided aircraft insurance that included public liability protection, life insurance, workers compensation, and trip accident coverage. This marked the true beginning of U.S. aviation insurance. Basic airplane policies followed marine insurance language, with the aircraft referred to as a "hull." Many early Lloyd's policies for American planes were handled by Barber & Baldwin, Inc., a New York underwriting agency established in 1922.

In 1925, the *Eastern Underwriter* noted that lack of insurance restricted the growth of commercial flying. Underwriters were convinced that all pilots would die in crashes if they flew long enough, and new planes cost $20,000 to $50,000 each. A year later, demand for aviation insurance took off as more flying companies were formed to compete for U.S. mail contracts.

Three pools of underwriters were started to underwrite aviation insurance in 1928 and 1929.[18] Aero Insurance Underwriters succeeded Barber & Baldwin and wrote business for Lloyd's. The United States Aviation Insurance Group and Associated Aviation Underwriters were made up of U.S. insurers.

[18] Marsh & McLennan had formed an aircraft insurance unit in 1920 within its New York casualty department.

A&A established a New York aviation department in 1929. The firm's first aviation account probably covered the eleven planes owned by Standard Oil of New Jersey. Coverage was just for liability insurance, at a premium of $280 per plane. Another early account was Southwest Air Fast Express, headquartered in Tulsa, which carried passengers in a fleet of twelve Ford Tri-Motors on no-frills flights connecting St. Louis, Tulsa, and Dallas.[19] The account was apparently written in Tulsa during 1928 and was certainly A&A's first commercial airline business.[20]

Southwest Air Fast Express was anxious to expand under its aggressive leader, Erle Halliburton. U.S. Postmaster General Walter Folger Brown had different ideas. In 1930, he set out to consolidate the industry into a few strong carriers, using his power to award mail contracts. When Southwest Air was eliminated from consideration, it sold out to American Airways, which became American Airlines in 1934.[21]

W. F. Alexander, meanwhile, realized that airlines would take passenger traffic from railroads, and he began acquiring airline business. In 1932, the firm wrote Shell Petroleum's aircraft fleet insurance, but W. F.'s goal was to win one of the four major airline accounts. Two stories are told about A&A becoming American Airlines' insurance broker. The first, possibly apocryphal, was always cited as typical of W. F.'s ability to make a cold call, sweet-talk a secretary into introducing her boss, and sell a contract. It was said that C. R. Smith was at lunch when W. F. came to call. True to form, W. F. talked his way past the secretary and into the boss's office. When Smith returned from lunch, W. F. was sitting on the edge of his desk—snoozing!

A less exotic version suggests that W. F.'s son, Fontaine, set up an introduction between the two executives. When W. F. arrived, he noticed numerous and varied clocks in C. R.'s office. A long conversation about clocks ensued, and C. R. was impressed with W.F.'s interest and knowledge. Whichever account is correct, there is no mistaking that the two men shared a strong bond until W. F.'s death in 1947. Although the date American Airlines became an A&A client can't be pinpointed, the best guess is 1935. By 1939, Amer-

[19] During the 1950s, American Airlines restored a model of Southwest's tri-motored Ford plane based on A&A's record of detailed plane data, including pictures of the interior.

[20] For the several years A&A had the account, no passenger injuries were reported.

[21] The origins of American Airlines date to 1929, when Averell Harriman and Robert Lehman launched Aviation Corporation. They raised $35 million through a stock sale to form this multipurpose aviation company. Appointed managers purchased five airline companies, which represented the merger of twelve original airmail routes. The conglomeration took the name American Airways. President Roosevelt considered aviation holding companies to be monopolies and decreed their end in 1934. Aviation Corporation then sold its American Airways stock, which resulted in independence and a name change to American Airlines. C. R. Smith, the savvy financial executive of South Air Transport, one of American Airways' airlines, was named the president of American Airlines. Almost immediately, he stunned the aviation business by his aggressive action in ordering a new plane, the DC3, which came into service in 1936 and still flies in many parts of the world.

ican was the nation's foremost air carrier in terms of passenger miles and remained one of A&A's most important clients, its signature airline account.[22]

W. F. never tired of trying new things in aviation insurance. In the 1930s, he made a strong effort to obtain United Airlines business. He and Rodney Piersol proposed on behalf of Chubb, an insurance company manager, to furnish passenger trip insurance of $5,000 for a twenty-five-cent premium. Such coverage demonstrated the airline industry's belief in the safety of air travel. While A&A did not get this business, Chubb later offered the coverage, which was very popular as well as extremely profitable.

While there is no record of A&A handling a dirigible account, the Detroit Insurance Agency, which joined A&A in 1970, provided insurance in 1929 on the first metal-clad dirigible. It covered the maiden voyage from Detroit to Lakehurst, New Jersey. The metal dirigible was a short-lived phenomenon. It was insured on a standard aviation policy that excluded losses incurred "while flying between one hour after sunset and one hour before sunrise." Also excluded were losses from "upside-down flying, looping-the-loop, spinning, rolling, hedge hopping or other aerial acrobatics."

Except for the Clarksburg and Tulsa offices, which maintained separate books, A&A's annual premium volume (excluding Chrysler's) ranged between $4 million and $5 million from 1920 to 1927. Although new business was abundant, most of it related to fire risks, and fire rates were under constant pressure. Automobile insurance continued making only a small contribution; although car sales were mushrooming, Americans generally chose not to insure their cars.[23]

In 1929, A&A's premium volume jumped to $5.8 million. The New York office staff numbered twenty-two, and business was booming—until the stock market crashed in October and billions of dollars of paper value were wiped out virtually overnight. Any insurer with large stock investments watched assets disappear in a flash; some never

[22] A&A also wrote insurance for Chicago-Southern Airlines in 1938, Mid-Continent Airlines and Canadian Colonial Airways in 1939, and National Airlines in 1940. The Beech Aircraft Corporation became a client in 1939.

[23] The state of Massachusetts started a new trend by experimenting with compulsory auto insurance.

recovered. Most brokers felt the impact by 1931. A&A's premium volume dropped from $5.8 million in 1930 to $4.5 million in 1931. Most businesses slashed salaries and personnel rosters. Pay cuts of 25 to 50 percent were common.

On November 1, 1931, C. B. imposed a 10 percent pay cut for employees who were paid by the week and most senior employees who were paid by the month. The only exception was the office boy. This was a precautionary move, and no employee was discharged. The cuts were restored over a three-year period, one-third each year. These actions were probably the least punitive among the major brokers. At Frank B. Hall, Cecil Stewart took a 10 percent salary cut and other key employees hit the street to canvass for business, as their only compensation was a share of profits.[24]

A&A continued hiring during the Depression and made other expansion moves. Its first marine insurance department began in New York in 1930. Marine insurance became an increasingly important adjunct to property and casualty lines. Also in 1930, Roswell Dunn was transferred from New York to operate a full-service office in St. Louis. The city was a vital railroad center and especially important to A&A. That office later designed one of the first excess public liability and employer liability insurance covers. It also was instrumental in developing insurance for large gas transmission lines laid in major river beds.

Thus, the decade that began so vibrantly for the insurance industry and much of America wound down into the depression. Yet wherever economic activity continued, there were risks to guard against and insurers to cover these risks.

[24] Marsh & McLennan imposed one 10 percent cut on all employees in early 1933 and another at the end of the year. While expenses were reduced, travel was almost eliminated, and employees started contributing to their group life insurance plan. The cuts were later restored. Johnson & Higgins also imposed two cuts, one of 10 percent and another of 20 percent. One was restored in 1934 and the other, a year later.

CHAPTER 10

The Nineteen-Thirties: Internal Conflicts and Other Challenges

Early in 1930, an unexpected development caused new friction between W. F. and Roy Jenkins. W. F. received word that Franklin D. Roosevelt, then governor of New York, wanted to see him about his son, James Roosevelt. "Jimmy" was working in Boston as an insurance agent for a flamboyant Russian with a spotty reputation, and FDR wanted him to find a new position. W. F. immediately saw potential in combining Roosevelt contacts with A&A's insurance marketing expertise. But Roy Jenkins demurred.

Perhaps Roy saw Jimmy as a potential threat to his own status. He also realized that having a Roosevelt on the letterhead would be a two-edged sword. He did agree to go with W. F. to meet FDR, and they journeyed to New Hyde Park, where FDR requested that A&A hire Jimmy as a senior partner. W. F. wanted to oblige, but Jenkins remained adamant. Roy felt so strongly that he approached one of the largest insurance companies and was offered a job. Faced with losing Jenkins, W. F. backed off, and the matter never resurfaced. W. F. may also have been influenced, in part, by his declining health due to tuberculosis, which would plague him for the rest of his life.[1]

President Hoover was voted out of office in November 1932, and the nation languished in the depression, awaiting

[1] Periodically, he would seek treatment at sanitariums in Saranac Lake, New York, and Tucson, Arizona. Although he was slowed by this horrible affliction, he remained effective until after World War II.

President Roosevelt's inauguration. The new president declared America had "nothing to fear but fear itself" while the business community feared that worse was yet to come. To halt the deepening economic spiral, FDR ordered American banks closed on March 6. C. B. anticipated this, and the week before called A&A's offices to make sure that they had emergency cash. A&A might not be able to pay major insurance claims during the "Bank Holiday," but it had ready cash to meet expenses.

During this period of uncertainty and change, 1933 premium revenues sank to $4.1 million, with casualty/surety surpassing fire premiums for the first time. Acquisition of major parts of the Warner Brothers' account lifted spirits, and A&A formally entered the life insurance business as well. W. F. had stubbornly resisted this step because of his deep distrust of life insurance salesmen, but a client request commanded his attention.

The financial vice president of the Missouri Pacific Railroad inquired about a pension program for certain employees. Since A&A had no life, group, or pension insurance capability, a Prudential Insurance Company actuary was called in. The actuary counseled that A&A needed a benefits department such as Marsh & McLennan had established ten years earlier.[2] W. F. held out a little longer and changed his mind when the president of Standard Oil of Ohio, an A&A client, sang the praises of a competitor's life insurance representative. He recalled Roswell Dunn from St. Louis to establish a life insurance capability in the New York office, although Ros had no previous life insurance experience.[3]

Later in 1933, C. B. became A&A's chairman, with W. F. assuming the presidency. Reflecting his status as A&A's third-ranking executive, Jenkins became the firm's first executive vice president as well as a director. C. B. also continued as the tightfisted financial controller. Ever wary of extravagance, he sent a message to the Tulsa office about corporate frugality and cost control.

Tulsa was considered an innovative office. Among its achievements in the 1920s was origination of the first workable concept for insuring oil wells against fire. In 1930, the

[2] From 1935, Johnson & Higgins also maintained a group insurance department, which was segregated as a satellite office.

[3] It was not unusual in the brokerage business for senior managers to be given responsibilities in areas where they had no previous experience.

office designed the first business interruption insurance on oil refineries. Although the office was not making money in 1933, it had acquired several company automobiles, and C. B. reacted by calling for an audit of the Oklahoma corporation's books. Nothing untoward was uncovered, but the message was clear: expenses were being monitored.

A significant A&A bylaw change resulted from an embarrassing lawsuit against W. F. involving a woman's million-dollar suit for breach of promise. The matter in dispute related rather specifically to a promise of marriage. W. F. was required to deposit his A&A stock with the court, guaranteeing that it would not be transferred before disposition of the case. Although he lost, the financial agreement permitted him to retain the stock. The case itself highlighted the vulnerability of controlling company stock. This led to modifications in A&A's charter and bylaws, enabling the

America might spiral deeper into the Great Depression in the mid-1930s, but air travel was still on the rise as American Airlines launched its Condor Sleeper service, taking advantage of improved navigation that took some risk out of night flying. A&A executives themselves would be spending more time in the air after 1936, as the firm opened offices in Chicago that year and in Los Angeles the next.

firm to repurchase shares in the event of the death, retirement, or termination of any current shareholder employee.

In 1933, recordkeeping was labor intensive, as all records were handwritten. The Baltimore office, with thirty-eight employees, had an electric adding machine on a heavy rolling stand, which was used when an itemized tape was required. Multiplications and divisions were calculated by hand. All accounting procedures were performed manually; records were balanced and books closed monthly. Working under sixteen-foot ceilings and electric lights called "miniature suns" that shed less than five-foot candlepower, bookkeepers often felt overwhelmed. More adding machines and a file clerk eventually reduced their stress.

Starting in 1934, C. B. became obsessed with keeping company control within the Alexander family. He had extensive discussions and correspondence with W. F. from 1937 to 1939. C. B. wanted to ensure that upon his and W. F.'s deaths or retirements, their sons would receive a good share of their stock at a fixed price. W. F. resisted, however, on the basis that C. B.'s son, as a solicitor, was not entitled to stock.

C. B. ultimately proposed that Roy Jenkins's son also receive shares. Finally, out of frustration, he asked Fred Drake to change W. F.'s mind. W. F. responded with a blistering telegram advising Drake to mind his own business, and the subject was dropped. W. F. wanted his sons to have appropriate positions and titles rather than stock. Although both sons had considerable skills, A&A probably would not have reached the heights it did if control had remained within the family.

Two key hires were made in the Baltimore office during 1934. Hugh Long, a graduate of the Virginia Military Institute, was a popular and a remarkably unselfish person. He supported promising young employees throughout his career and promoted their ascendancy within the organization. Elected an A&A director in 1958, Long managed the St. Louis, Tulsa, and Chicago offices at various times.

The other notable newcomer, Phillip Ness, was a rarity— a natural instigator, innovator, and A&A's first trained life insurance employee. After his graduation from Johns Hopkins University in 1929, he sold life insurance very successfully for Sun Life of Canada. He was then hired by A&A on commission to develop life, pension, accident and health, and hospitalization insurance. He was so productive that A&A quickly made him a salaried employee. Ness was elected vice president in 1939, when only four others held that title. He was available to assist all offices and traveled extensively—particularly to New York, where he eventually relocated.[4] His interests were in sales and new business—identified as particularly crucial areas once W. F. would no longer be the engine driving the company.

A&A opened new offices in Chicago and Los Angeles in 1936 and 1937 respectively. A New York claims specialist was sent to manage the Chicago office in 1936, a move lasting only a year and doomed from the start. It was highly unlikely that a claims specialist would have the experience and knowledge to successfully open a distant office. For much of the twentieth century, broking was a sales activity as well as a business service, and office managers needed a thorough understanding of sales and customer relations.

In 1937, Latimer Stewart obtained the casualty insurance business of RKO Radio Pictures on the understanding that a Los Angeles office would open to handle the account. W. F.'s son, Richard, moved from Baltimore to manage the office. Although Dick had much of his father's charm and strong company support, he would have been happier in another occupation. A painter by avocation, and a good one, he performed quite adequately, but his heart was not in it. He lacked his father's drive and intense ambition.

Dick Alexander's baptism of fire began when he arrived in Los Angeles and learned that because of a premium quoting error there would be no commission on the RKO account during its first year. The office did not become profitable until Warner Brothers' West Coast business was acquired a few years later. Most new accounts were movie-related, but other types of businesses supported the office

[4] Possessing an exuberant personality and keen intellect, Phil Ness was interested in people and what was taking place around him. His curiosity was pervasive and enabled him to converse on a wide variety of subjects. Over the years, he was instrumental in influencing the company to adopt various practices that kept it competitive.

even when the expansion of television threatened many movie studios.

This situation illustrates a major opportunity and challenge. Unfortunately, A&A did not respond effectively. By the mid-1930s, it was too late to establish a formidable West Coast presence. M&M and J&H already had strong foundations and were building on them. Lacking financial resources and relying on W. F.'s son to develop a West Coast strategy, A&A relegated itself to a secondary role that it never overcame. By the time the company could offer stock for acquisitions, few attractive candidates were available, and F. B. Hall won most of them.

In 1937, A&A's premium volume reached $6.4 million and four decades of sustained growth followed. W. F. Alexander's productivity began to decline, and junior members of the firm stepped forward.

As A&A became more successful, senior staff members were required to work very long hours. The heavy workload took a toll on some, particularly those with no interests outside of their work. C. B. Alexander was an exception. He had a long-standing interest in Democratic Party politics. When asked why he became involved, C. B. responded that he was raised in a small town where everyone got involved in politics, since the fire department offered the only other excitement. C. B. said he was an old fire horse, and when the bell rang he was ready to go. In 1924, he became chairman of Maryland's Democratic campaign finance committee and supported the presidential candidacy of John W. Davis, a boyhood companion.

In succeeding years, C. B. held similar posts in support of Maryland governors and U.S. Senate nominees. He was named treasurer of the Maryland Democratic Party in the fall of 1938, when President Roosevelt unsuccessfully tried to purge Senator Millard Tydings. Late in 1940, after having faithfully served the Democrats for years, he denounced Roosevelt as lacking sincerity and statesmanship and threw his support behind the Republican presidential candidate, Wendell Willkie. However, by 1944, C. B. was back in the Democratic fold, helping Senator Tydings.

In September 1939, Germany invaded Poland and World War II began. The conflict had little effect on A&A until Japan attacked Pearl Harbor on December 7, 1941, and America declared war. With a modest marine insurance account and insignificant international involvement (other than insurance placements at Lloyd's), domestic retail business consumed the firm's attention. Healthy growth continued. Revenues for 1940 were $728,000 on a premium volume of $8.5 million; the company was growing, and the staff now numbered about ninety.

On the eve of the war, A&A remained primarily a property and casualty insurance brokerage, although it had modest capability in most other lines of insurance. Although progress was satisfactory, Marsh & McLennan and Johnson & Higgins continued moving rapidly ahead. A real impediment to A&A's growth was the lack of meaningful contacts with large corporations. Perhaps a dozen executives had potential entrée, but only a few knew how to use relationships to develop new business.

With the emphasis on learning the technical side of the business, opportunities opened for a diverse group of employees to excel. For A&A and other brokers, possibilities expanded for those without social or professional contacts. Joseph Barr was an early beneficiary of this egalitarian reality. Hired as a New York office boy in 1941, he rose through the ranks. Barr became head of the aviation department, key liaison with insurance company executives, a developer of international insurance and reinsurance, and head of the New York office. He eventually became a director. Louis Bonar, who started in 1932 as an office boy, traveled a similar route to become executive vice president.

Even with a talented group of employees, A&A was handicapped by modest financial resources. This disadvantage contributed to its limited expansion in actuarial consulting, marine insurance, and reinsurance broking. A&A's shortcomings were highlighted by the passage of the Social Security Act in 1937.

Social Security ushered in opportunities for actuarial consulting. Marsh & McLennan promptly hired two actuaries and quickly gained preeminence in the pension field by consulting with banks for their clients' trustee plans. It wasn't until 1949 that A&A employed its first consulting actuary.

With marine insurance, A&A chose a defensive posture and invested little. M&M, meanwhile, had been a serious player in this area after acquiring Parsons & Egbert in 1919. During much of the 1930s, M&M's marine department acted almost as a separate company. J&H's position was well established, and its marine directors controlled the company from New York. F. B. Hall remained primarily a marine broker until much later.

At A&A, reinsurance broking slipped through the cracks—a major strategic mistake. The firm was small in 1941, and probably it would have taken more than vision to devote scarce resources to a field in its infancy. With Sedgwick's assistance, A&A placed some reinsurance for Aero Insurance Underwriters and Royal Insurance Com-pany. Later, Mutual Fire and Marine Insurance Company became a reinsurance client. A&A's first reinsurance technician was hired in 1941, and it would be another forty years before the company became a major player in that field.

In the early 1960s, A&A invested in a reinsurance brokerage unit, Ream Wrightson. Other investors were London broker Matthews Wrightson and a significant U.S. broker, Flynn, Harrison & Conroy (later acquired by M&M). By 1967, A&A had a 65 percent interest in Ream Wrightson; by 1973, this became 100 percent and the name was then changed to Tower Treaty. Unfortunately, A&A's effort was modest. Among brokers, only Marsh & McLennan continued to identify reinsurance broking as worthy of significant commitment.

Management style also contrasted among the three leading brokerages, reflecting their respective sizes and degrees of specialization. While J&H was marine dominated, M&M was the most decentralized—its two large offices, New York and Chicago, operated quite independently and competed against each other. Even within the New York office, each major department ran its own show for a number of years. Within A&A, Roy Jenkins was directly involved in every aspect of the New York operation and C. B. Alexander was equally involved in Baltimore. Gradually, however, a rivalry also developed between these two offices.

CHAPTER 11

Competitive Pressures: World War II and W. F. Alexander's Passing

The United States entered World War II after Japan attacked Pearl Harbor on December 7, 1941, "the date which shall live in infamy," and twenty-five Alexander & Alexander employees joined the armed services. In keeping with the country's mood, C. B. Alexander wanted to do something special for A&A's servicemen. He established a trust to give each veteran a year's salary when he returned from service, a substantial cushion for easing financial pressures of civilian life.[1]

The trust was funded with $40,000; veterans would receive monthly payments. The firm's lawyers doubted the Internal Revenue Service would allow a tax deduction, and an advance ruling was requested. Surprisingly, the IRS approved the plan, provided that any unused principal was donated to charity.[2] When the concept became widely discussed, the IRS forbade A&A to talk about it. Ultimately their decision on deductibility was reversed, but A&A and one other company were grandfathered.

Americans on the home front—A&A personnel among them—endured many hardships, especially shortages of services and commodities. Civilian railroad travel was arduous and uncertain as military and government personnel got priority treatment. Hotel rooms became scarce; gasoline and tires were rationed. Censorship of overseas cables presented particular difficulties. In one instance,

[1] The widow or next of kin would receive this benefit in the event of a serviceman's death.

[2] The Red Cross subsequently received some $10,000 of A&A's excess funding.

A&A wanted to send flowers to a Shell Oil Company official in London named T. D. Peace, and as brevity was essential, the dispatch to A&A's London correspondent read: "SEND PEACE FLOWERS." The company was subsequently investigated to determine whether anyone knew about peace negotiations.

The war created new problems for clients such as Sun Shipbuilding and Dry Dock Company, a prime candidate for sabotage. Though no salesman, C. B. Alexander decided to handle this situation himself. He obtained an attractive rate for a policy covering sabotage, labor strikes, riots, and civil commotion. The policy also carried a provision requiring a triple premium if a strike claim occurred within fifteen days of policy inception. Sun's treasurer agreed on the necessity for the protection. C. B. had to study the myriad policy details and persuade the CEO, J. Howard Pew, to accept them, which he succeeded in doing. But the next week there were reports of strikes in Maine and Boston shipyards. When C. B. was asked whether he had told Mr. Pew about the strike condition, he turned pale and acknowledged he had completely forgotten to discuss this. Fortunately, Sun's workers did not walk.

In 1939, C. B. Alexander Jr. started holding office Christmas parties for employees and their spouses—dressy, formal affairs that became very popular. C. B. Sr. and his wife participated and would depart soon after dinner. Everyone was on their best behavior, and the occasion was a genuine morale booster. Although the Baltimore social environment was conducive to such a function, New York's was not. Because of sprawling suburbs, it was difficult for spouses to attend. Consequently, the New York Christmas party was for employees only. The results were predictably unfortunate, with excessive drinking and embarrassing behavior. After a drunken safety engineer berated a senior manager, the New York Christmas party was discontinued.[3]

In 1942, the Baltimore office hired its first black employee, Ambrose Smith, the son of C. B.'s butler. He was hired as

[3] Liquor was served extensively, particularly at lunch when entertaining clients and prospects. This practice was increasingly discouraged by the 1970s because of occasional reprehensible episodes inside and outside the office.

an office boy, and his position and duties reflected the racial segregation of the period. Smith was a jazz musician, but despite his success as a pianist at civic and social functions, the low pay forced him to seek more reliable work with A&A.[4]

War-related activities fueled the economy in 1942 and 1943. A&A's revenue exceeded $1 million, and premium volume topped $16 million. But in 1944, the year's gross premiums decreased for the first time since 1936. A drop in revenue extended through 1945 as many industries foundered. A&A's new business development lagged because of W. F.'s failing health and the temporary loss of several key personnel to the military. Most other brokerages faced similar wartime revenue patterns. Marsh & McLennan, however, benefited by placing large amounts of war risk insurance backed by the federal government.

Revenue patterns changed abruptly in 1946, as almost all wartime wage and price controls were lifted, launching a period of unprecedented economic prosperity and activity. It was a tumultuous year, with premiums and net income rising to record levels. The New York office ended 1945 with seventy-five employees, and in 1946, A&A offices hired many new employees.

One young man, Larry Lassus, became the epitome of an outstanding account executive. Able to master the intricacies of his job, he seemingly spent all his waking hours thinking and planning on his clients' behalf. Lassus began his employment in the New York property engineering department and mastered the art of obtaining favorable rate reductions for clients. His knowledge broadened to other forms of insurance, and he handled several large accounts. Lassus produced significant new business from clients who were loyal to him, and thus to A&A. Unlike some, he never considered them "his clients"; rather, they were the firm's.[5]

The professionalism exemplified by Larry Lassus and others was critical to A&A's success after World War II. Such account executives were essential for a successful brokerage, as they generally oversaw all aspects of an account and met

[4] Smith played with the first all-black jazz orchestra to perform in London, a group so celebrated that they played a command performance before the king and queen.

[5] Larry Lassus retired at the end of 1991 after forty-five years of outstanding service. It is unlikely that he ever lost an account except through the client's acquisition by another company.

with clients. In addition to knowing their clients and their risks, the account executives' complex role required flexibility and tact. It was necessary to earn the insured's respect and, ideally, his or her friendship. This meant understanding the client's likes and dislikes. It might also entail ongoing entertaining, and sometimes questionable demands, which in turn required knowing where to draw the line. On rare occasions, a client's unreasonable behavior (such as calling at all hours of the night) left no alternative but to resign the account.[6] In the 1980s, A&A management dropped an account producing over $1 million in annual commissions because of the client's abusive treatment of A&A employees.

With all the new hires, the New York office required more space, but the planned move was supposed to be cloaked in great secrecy. A secretary mentioned the move to the office manager, indicating that she had heard about it from an impeccable source. When pressed to divulge the informant, she said, "The window washer of course!"[7]

In the fall of 1946, W. F.'s health problems worsened, as he suffered from heart, hernia, and prostate ailments as well as tuberculosis. He wrote to C. B. about positioning Roy Jenkins to succeed him as president, although he intended to retain his director title. Apparently this contact ended a ten-year period of limited communication between the brothers. After this, there was frequent correspondence between them and with Roy Jenkins. Surviving letters demonstrate that the brothers shared a strong underlying affection and a powerful sense of family solidarity.

C. B. and Roy vainly attempted to delay W. F.'s retirement. During 1946 and 1947, Dick Alexander taped telephone conversations with his father. W. F. made clear that in his lifetime he wanted Roy Jenkins to become A&A's president. W. F. also wanted both of his sons to become corporate vice presidents, as well as Lou Bonar, whom he singled out for special praise.

W. F. prevailed. At a directors meeting on October 17, 1946, Roy Jenkins was elected A&A's president. At the railroad station on his way home, Roy dictated a telegram to

[6] One client requested that we rent an apartment in Manhattan for him. We decided to get along without his business.

[7] This informal network of "corporate intelligence" was exemplified by Mario, a marvelous shoeshine man, who became the most reliable contributor to the rumor mill. Taking great pride in his work, he carried his shine equipment from office to office, serving a clientele daily that included the company's senior officers, so his information was almost always accurate. Mario was also well known for observing, "The more senior the officer, the lower the tip!"

W. F. in Tucson, Arizona: "Officially made President here today in Balta. While this is most gratifying to me personally, nevertheless, I have a certain feeling of emptiness without you at my side. Thirty-five years of intimate association with you makes me feel a sense of loneliness without you. Best wishes for a speedy recovery. Roy."

W. F. died on October 4, 1947. Protecting family interests, he had arranged for Dick Alexander to become a director earlier in the year. Presumably with W. F.'s sanction, six new directors were elected after his death. The company purchased his 910 shares of stock for approximately $430,000. These and the additional shares from Fred Drake's retirement were offered to other directors. C. B. and his wife were careful to retain voting control of the company.

W. F.'s death left a void that could never be filled, even by several people. A&A would have remained a local West Virginia agency without his vision and drive. Whereas other firms accomplished expansion through several or many leaders, A&A had but one. While other individuals made significant contributions, it was W. F.'s unique achievements that were essential to A&A's first three and a half decades.

The full measure of W. F. Alexander extended beyond his sales ability. He was also a sensitive and thoughtful man. When he learned that Bert Chin, who inspected the Missouri Pacific Railroad properties, had not had a salary increase in ten years, he was aghast. W. F. invited him to lunch and later said that the most difficult sale he had ever encountered was trying to get Chin to ask for a raise. He would not ask, and W. F. had to initiate the subject. Chin praised W. F. for taking time to invite a "little man" to lunch and give him a raise.[8]

After World War II, A&A was underpaying its clerical employees, many of whom were threatening to resign for jobs elsewhere. Significant raises were needed to remain competitive, and Roy Jenkins referred the matter to the Alexanders. W. F.'s sensitivity and common sense were evident in his response: C. B. turned down the request for across-the-board raises but W. F. insisted on further review.

[8] Chin was humble but no "little man." During World War I, he was a runner with the American Expeditionary Forces in France. During the Meuse-Argonne offensive, he won a citation for "Gallantry in Action . . . by carrying messages from Battalion Headquarters to Regimental and Company Headquarters most of the time under heavy shell and machine gun fire. . . ."

The economic pendulum swings back as war looms and crippled industries retool to make military hardware. Here M-4 tanks roll off the assembly line of a factory that dominated Hammond, Indiana, for generations. First built to make railroad cars, the plant had been modernized just in time to fold after the 1929 crash. (After World War II, it would switch back to railroad cars and stay open for 35 years.) The insurance industry must evolve in similar ways as new coverages developed, and as the government assumed some "war risk" coverage while, generally speaking, losses caused by "acts of war" remained as policy exclusions.

After a compromise raise was agreed to, only one secretary was lost.

Premium volume grew to $25 million during 1947, W. F.'s last year of life—a 40 percent increase over the preceding year. This was partially attributable to the cancellation and rewriting of some large policies to avoid possible tax problems in 1948 with the expiration of Public Law 15. This law, passed by Congress in 1945, provided for continued state regulation of insurance. A&A feared that federal insurance regulation might result in new taxes on premiums. Nevertheless, this rise in premium volume represented a healthy increase and demonstrated that new business could be developed by individuals other than W. F. London– based premiums were also becoming important. Of the firm's $29 million premium volume in 1948, almost $1.5 million was brokered by Sedgwick in London, and most of that was placed at Lloyd's.

Throughout the 1940s and more so after the war, A&A's Baltimore and New York offices hired many fine technical professionals as well as inexperienced people to be trained. Staff expansion reflected exponential client growth. Most of these employees spent the rest of their careers with A&A. Many rose to positions of importance and visibility; some started new departments. However, few ever professed to be originators of new business.

The firm's inadequate sales capability had become a serious concern. Neither C. B. nor Roy Jenkins ever acknowledged this problem; meanwhile, continued revenue growth masked the absence of new clients. Perhaps they also felt that those hired in the 1930s could generate new business. The question of the future went begging.

The company was at a continual disadvantage with leading competitors that were replete with well-connected, sales-oriented employees. To be well connected meant having access to corporate decision makers. They, in turn, determined what agent or broker handled corporate insurance. To be well connected also meant knowing individuals of influence in industries such as banking—individuals who could provide introductions to decision makers.

A&A's principal competitor, Marsh & McLennan, continued moving ahead rapidly.[9] Henry Marsh, inactive for many years, died in 1943 and Don McLennan, who owned 45 percent of the stock, passed away unexpectedly a year later at age seventy-two. Charles W. ("Ward") Seabury became the next CEO and the sole voting trustee of the company's stock. In 1945, M&M's revenues exceeded $9 million, with a net profit before taxes of approximately $2.5 million. By comparison, A&A's figures were $1.1 million and $330,000.

M&M's internal growth slowed after Don McLennan's death. New initiatives were needed. Ward Seabury was reluctant to accept the targeting of industries other than railroads. In 1946, when urged to authorize a study on aviation business, he agreed but insisted, "Remember, first and

[9] One of Marsh & McLennan's many 1945 hires was Jack Regan, who became CEO in 1973 and led the brokerage through some of its most productive years in the 1970s and early 1980s.

always, that railroads are our bread and butter." That strategy notwithstanding, the firm did target the "Big Three" automobile manufacturers, and in 1947 acquired the Ford account. This was the first new major account since McLennan's death. By 1948, M&M employed 1,688 men and women, and the New York office surpassed Chicago's in size.

To remain competitive, A&A had to invest in sales. The firm needed some of its new hires to be young college graduates who, in time, were expected to produce significant business. Others had to be seasoned producers. To better compete with other brokers, the company needed to beef up areas of untapped potential such as actuarial consulting and group life. C. B. and Roy Jenkins were reluctant converts to the idea of expanding the staff, but the younger directors, led by Ros Dunn and Phil Ness, finally persuaded them.

The prototype for sales trainees was Kenneth Soubry; in hiring him, the firm hit the jackpot. Born and raised in England and a Cambridge University graduate, Soubry had served as an Indian Cavalry officer during World War II. He had been taken prisoner by the Japanese in Burma, near an area immortalized in the film *Bridge on the River Kwai.* Soubry spent nearly four years in a prisoner of war camp—one of relatively few survivors out of 80,000. After the war, he came to the United States to recover his health. After spending time at an Arkansas insurance agency, he joined A&A at the end of 1949 and worked his way up through our ranks to become CEO. No one played a more vital role in A&A's period of extraordinary growth and prosperity. His intelligence, warmth, and infectious personality were model traits to seek in future trainees.

Hugo Standing, another Englishman, and I were hired in 1950. We started as business producers and subsequently held a variety of management jobs. Other promising salespeople came on board during the 1950s.

The new emphasis on sales—"production" in industry parlance—was controversial because recruiting was costly and

the results were uncertain, but no one denied its necessity. Some resented that inexperienced recruits received special treatment before they made measurable contributions. This attitude toward young salespeople was difficult to eradicate, though it was readily understandable. For the first real sales program to succeed at A&A, we had to offer a sales career path with potential for above-average compensation.

Tension between sales and technical people is difficult to manage. Sales is almost never a one-person effort. Others contribute strategic or technical advice or have special expertise—for example, knowing which are the best insurance companies to be offered particular risks. Salespeople often receive direct compensation for business production while others who assist may get little or no recognition. When compensation is directly linked to sales, a salesperson can earn more than the firm's top executives in a given year. Some feel that there is no justification for this. Marsh & McLennan ceased paying producer commissions during the

The upheaval of World War II had some unexpected and positive consequences on the homefront. America's economy recovered as unemployment shrunk to the vanishing point and women filled jobs previously held by men. "Rosie the Riveter" became the poster girl for women who joined the war effort, such as here at a Chrysler plant in St. Louis. Typically, the risks involved in manufacturing munitions would be covered by private insurance, though doubtless the cost indexes for workmen's compensation coverage would rise to reflect the dangers of a particular work site.

mid-1950s because it couldn't make a profit by giving producers 37.5 percent of the commissions the firm received on their accounts.

That salespeople frequently have flexible schedules is another chronic irritant, as it requires time away from the office and includes entertaining clients and prospects. From management's standpoint, there is also the challenge of evaluating accounts. Should the same commission be paid to salespeople irrespective of account profitability? Compounding the challenge, it can often be difficult to analyze account profitability.

Over time, there were fewer pure producers. More employees combined new business development with responsibilities for servicing accounts. A&A promoted the idea that a career in some technical specialty area, or in management or staff work, was just as important and rewarding as sales. To varying degrees, employees accepted this philosophy, but many believed that sales offered disproportionate financial rewards.

In 1950, A&A had approximately 200 employees. Its net premium volume, excluding life and group insurance, was $25 million and net income was $2.3 million. These were modest numbers compared to those of Marsh & McLennan and Johnson & Higgins. J&H, for example, had a staff of approximately 1,000, of whom more than 300 were in New York. M&M had upwards of 2,000 employees. These brokers enjoyed compelling geographic breadth, and their staffs were skilled in a broad range of specialties. To compete, A&A had to be bold, imaginative, and willing to take risks. And we had to spend money.

To broaden our range of services, a few experienced life and group benefits specialists were hired after the war. In 1949, the first actuary was employed to establish a pension and actuarial division. A common joke about actuaries is that they wanted to become accountants but lacked the personality. Geoffrey Calvert, a New Zealander by birth, was a dynamic contradiction to that perception. With an ebullient personality, he resembled the stereotypical life insurance salesman. He was a busy traveler, writer, and speaker.[10] Of remarkable intelligence, Calvert was highly innovative and spent much time evaluating the future of Social Security and other government programs. He immediately put A&A on the map in the pension consulting field and also installed the company's first pension plan.[11]

Eccentric employees were commonplace in brokerages, and they were often quite uncontrollable. Charles Brenemann, A&A's chief engineer in Baltimore, was a free spirit. Highly respected by clients, he came and went as he pleased, sometimes on extended trips, without telling superiors. The job of keeping track of him was given to the Baltimore office manager, who requested the authority to fire the maverick if he didn't conform. C. B. demurred, leading the office manager to observe that if A&A's chairman couldn't handle Brenemann, he, the manager, had no chance at all. The subject was never again raised.

Hiring Geoff Calvert helped stimulate an awareness among younger A&A directors that a formal strategy was needed to focus on geographic expansion; this in turn required acquisitions. During the 1950s, agencies were purchased in Atlanta, Pittsburgh, San Francisco, Miami, and Philadelphia—all new locations. In addition, a Tulsa merger enlarged that office.

The Atlanta acquisition was particularly significant. Adams, Holmes & Tharpe was a model agency. Fort Adams, its leader, was a pillar in the community, and his employees offered a balance of production and technical strength. For instance, Frank Asbury epitomized the best qualities of an A&A account executive/producer for more than forty years, and Tinsley ("T.") Irvin would become A&A's CEO years later.

While A&A was finally in a position to expand through acquisition, Marsh & McLennan had begun this strategic approach years earlier. During 1957, in a considerable coup, M&M purchased the California agency Cosgrove & Co., which handled accounts such as Crown Zellerback, Hilton Hotels, Howard Hughes's interests, Lockheed, Rayonier,

[10] Calvert had a healthy regard for his abilities. When I once asked him to explain the string of letters after his name on his business card, he replied "All you need to remember is 'B.A.O.E.,' which stands for 'Best Actuary on Earth.'"

[11] A health buff long before it was in fashion, Calvert didn't smoke or drink and was a strict vegetarian. His eccentricities were numerous and occasionally bizarre. A voracious reader with insatiable curiosity, he often awakened his young daughters at 5 A.M. to read them Shakespeare. Since he distrusted banks, it was rumored that he buried large sums of cash around his home. His investment prowess was such that many stories circulated concerning his "buried treasures."

and Shell Oil. Its leader, Willard Keith, was a dominant personality among brokers and an exceptional producer. This successful merger encouraged M&M to become a publicly owned company several years later.

F. B. Hall's growth was also fueled by acquisitions. It entered 1955 with about 120 employees. Between 1955 and 1961, the firm purchased three mid-sized brokerages in New York City and built up its nonmarine business. It rapidly established itself as the country's fourth largest brokerage.

All major brokerages were interested in Canada. F. B. Hall entered the country in 1920 through a joint venture with a local insurance executive, forming Hall-Ormiston & Company, Ltd. M&M started serious international expansion in 1949 by purchasing Canadian broker Irish & Maulson in Toronto and Montreal. M&M had first entered Canada in 1914, when it opened an office for servicing the Canadian Pacific Railroad account—its first international account.

Before establishing a Montreal office in 1906, J&H handled Canadian business from its New York headquarters. Between 1906 and 1930, J&H and Willis Faber shared equally in the profits from all new Canadian business even though they operated from separate offices. In 1919, they were named joint brokers by the Canadian government for the prestigious merchant marine account. At the end of 1929, the pooling arrangement was discontinued. J&H purchased two Toronto agencies—in 1942 Romeyn & Company, Ltd., specializing in marine insurance, and in 1944 E. L. McLean, Ltd., which handled mostly nonmarine coverages.

As part of A&A's geographic expansion, Roy Jenkins and Ralph Henderson were authorized to form a Canadian subsidiary. But Canada's restrictive insurance regulations in the 1950s precluded establishing either a new retail or reinsurance brokerage entity, while A&A's principal competitors were grandfathered. A&A's inability to function independently in Canada's property/casualty business caused constant frustration and inconvenience for three decades. In hindsight, A&A missed the boat by recognizing Canada's importance too late. While limited financial resources prevented other strategic moves, a Canadian brokerage office would have required only a minimal initial investment.

With domestic expansion in focus, the firm's younger directors turned their attention to public relations. An advertising committee was formed and a $4,000 expenditure authorized for an initial company brochure. The first draft did not fare well. It contained an unfortunate if accurate statement that Richard Alexander had been in the insurance and manure business. When C. B. read this, his face turned crimson. He slammed the proposal down, announcing, "There'll be no brochure!" It was the kind of dictatorial pronouncement that suited a nineteenth-century environment of rolltop desks and eyeshades. However, it was out of touch with the increasingly egalitarian postwar era. Times were changing—and A&A's challenge would be to respond in kind.

CHAPTER 12

The Postwar Period: A Changing of the Guard

In 1953, C. B. Alexander began retiring from day-to-day operations, although he maintained a tight rein on the firm's finances. By distributing additional shares to six executives, he permitted voting control of A&A to pass out of his family's hands. Then, on July 9, 1955, C. B. retired from active management, accepting the honorific title of "Founder." Roy Jenkins became board chairman and R. S. Henderson, president.

Although premium volume could be volatile, business in general was excellent during the third quarter of the twentieth century, a period of enormous growth and technological breakthroughs on many fronts, including electronics, communications, transportation, medicine, and others. [1] Future historians may look upon this period as revolutionary, with the growth of television; advent of jet travel; invention of the microchip, transistor, and microcomputer; conquering of diseases from smallpox to polio; forays into space—the list goes on, with each item representing new challenges for insurance companies.

[1] With the exception of 1949, A&A's net income increased every year until the 1980s.

Responding to new technologies was no honeymoon, witness computers. By the late 1940s, A&A was experiencing serious difficulty with its accounting records. Balancing accounts receivable was particularly cumbersome, with twenty receivable ledgers under a general ledger control.

There was no way to divide control by ledger or even groups of ledgers. C. B. authorized an IBM study to determine whether its equipment could solve the problem, only to learn that IBM apparently had no likely application for A&A.

About a year later, Phil Ness was in Baltimore and asked why IBM had not been explored. He was shown a copy of the earlier report, and he expressed amazement that they could not help. He arranged for a new IBM review, and this resulted in the use of IBM's equipment, phased in over eighteen months. Except for one manual procedure, this solved the problem. A&A could claim to have introduced the first successful IBM application to a brokerage operation.[2]

With computers, user education became an immediate necessity and patience was required. By today's standards, early computers were primitive, even laughable; but they permitted additional business without a comparable increase in accounting employees.

Another challenge for expanding companies was office space. In New York, the Continental Insurance Company owned the building at 80 Maiden Lane and needed more space. A&A was the last major tenant in the building. On September 12, 1953, A&A relocated to the Transportation Building at 225 Broadway, near City Hall, where we remained for almost twenty years. In 1955, the Baltimore office moved from the Standard Oil Building to 225 North Charles Street, housing all employees on one floor for the first time in many years.

Incentive pay was another difficult issue. A plan was devised for senior employees to receive a small percentage of the company's monthly profit. Over time, this became the largest part of an executive's total remuneration. Employees considered that they had "arrived" when awarded these "units of participation." From time to time, the formula was revised, and the number of participants constantly grew. During the busy agency acquisition period, the formula could not be revised frequently enough to keep distributions in proper balance, so the program was dropped in the early 1970s.

[2] One of A&A's competitors had installed an IBM system four months earlier but had encountered such serious problems that it was considered a false start.

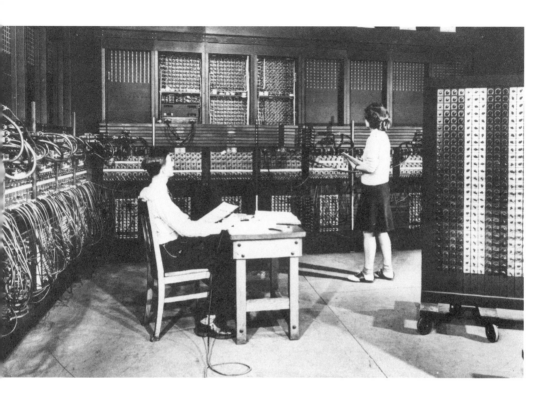

In 1953, a year-end bonus plan, known as the "king's list," was implemented with initial funding of $75,000. A special committee—usually comprising board members—used its judgment to assign bonuses. This was intended to reward outstanding performance; in practice, the employees on the list soon viewed the plan as an expected component of pay. It became increasingly subject to divisiveness and was finally abandoned.

When the firm struggled in areas such as compensation without the benefit of an in-house specialist, management consultants were usually proposed. C. B. Alexander, however, did not believe in them. Their use came primarily after his death. At first, they were hired in finance and administration to promote efficiency and reduce costs. Later, consultants were employed in the technology era with greater frequency and with mixed results. Whether or not their advice was heeded, consultants' recommendations could be problematic, even insidious—especially when they were

The demands of war prompt leaps of technology that change society and enrich the coming peace. Two years before Pearl Harbor, the U.S. Army Ordnance Department foresaw the need for fast and complex mathematical computations to improve the accuracy of our artillery and bombers. A $61,700 research contract led to the first "electronic numerical integrator and computer" (a.k.a. ENIAC) which became operational only after war's end. It could make a calculation in 30 seconds that previously had taken 20 hours. Driven by 19,000 vacuum tubes, ENIAC filled a room but had only a fraction of the power of laptop computers carried by agents and brokers today.

hired at a senior director's urging to reinforce his perceived need for a pet project.

Arthur Wooddy retired in 1957. He was a respected and highly professional insurance broker who had spent nearly forty years in Baltimore with C. B. At times Wooddy was C. B.'s pawn in the subtle (and sometimes not-so-subtle) rivalry between W. F. and C. B. He was to C. B. what Roy Jenkins was to W. F. Fortunately, the brothers' rivalry usually simmered just below the surface and motivated each to excel.

As the New York office gradually dwarfed Baltimore in size, competitiveness remained Baltimore's preoccupation. Unquestionably, it contributed to Baltimore's constant push for perfection. Its profit margins were always among A&A's highest. No office offered better client service. Under the guidance of Sam Shriver and Lat Stewart, the Baltimore office continued to produce highly qualified candidates for senior positions. Occasionally, however, fate intervened. One man, John Grasty, was transferred from Baltimore to run the Chicago office. He then went to New York in a similar capacity, where his work was superb. Grasty had all the talent to become a future CEO and was on that track when cancer killed him at age forty-six.

With C. B. Alexander's death on September 25, 1958, senior management changes occurred more frequently; new initiatives developed that would not have been possible under his command. Directors meetings became more open. Previously, little information was shared in advance, and minutes were not regularly distributed. With changed procedures, agendas were sent out seven days before a meeting, and each director received board minutes. A personnel committee was formed for the first time, and a new public relations study was authorized.

Prior to C. B.'s passing, there had been $70,000 in life insurance policies naming the firm as beneficiary. Some policies had lapsed, but most were in force when C. B. instructed that no further premiums be paid and converted the policies to extended term insurance. C. B. reasoned that he would die before the end of this period, but he misjudged his own demise by a few months. Consequently, the term insurance lapsed, and no life insurance was in force at his death.

As 1958 drew to a close, new milestones highlighted commercial aviation travel. In October, the British Overseas Airways Corporation (BOAC) introduced the first jetliner service across the Atlantic. On December 10, National Airlines began the first domestic U.S. jet service between New York and Miami.[3]

Lou Bonar became, like Phil Ness, executive vice president in 1959, a move that strained their already fragile relationship. By virtue of their titles, one of them normally would have been in line to become A&A's CEO. Unfortunately, they had totally different personalities and did not hide their disapproval of each other. Each was extremely talented and made considerable contributions, but their mutual antipathy became a difficult problem. In the end, it was a standoff; neither got the top job.

The 1950s closed with A&A in sound shape. Its net premium volume for 1959 was $55 million, more than double the figure ten years earlier. Net income of $5.5 million represented an increase of 162 percent over 1949. It was commonly acknowledged that A&A was the country's third largest brokerage, after M&M and J&H. There appeared to be no impediment to continued growth and success.

Of course, new problems arose. One was the increase in lawsuits against agents and brokers, which caused them to buy higher limits of professional liability insurance. This became ever more expensive and put increased pressure on brokers to manage their costs. Over the years, the expense became formidable, and internal reserves required frequent upward revisions.

In the 1960s, huge changes took place in many areas. Issuance of a new class of corporate stock allowed more employees to become shareholders. The expanded opportunity to own A&A stock was highly motivating for them.

Selection of new senior management became a dicey matter.[4] Sometimes this is a simple process, especially if

[3] America had placed its first satellite in orbit with the launching of Explorer I on January 31, 1958. The Soviet Union launched Sputnik I to open the era of space exploration on October 4, 1957.

[4] Senior employees were quite conscious of their position within the company. When the threat of nuclear war became a national concern in the 1960s, the company's response was to adopt a disaster plan, which included ranking thirty-four executives in order of their ascendancy to lead A&A if those above them were incapacitated. Many assumed that this was management's determination of their current position; the ranking, however, involved a geographic dispersion factor and had no relevance under nonemergency circumstances.

succession has been publicly established. However, there was no obvious candidate to succeed Ralph Henderson as president upon his January 1, 1961, retirement. He had been Roy Jenkins's closest confidant, although he didn't leave lasting impressions or any particular legacy. Jenkins, who was then chairman, did not support any of the most logical candidates to replace Henderson. A compromise selection was inevitable. Sam Shriver was chosen and agreed to move from Baltimore to New York. Shriver was within several years of retirement—an important element in his election.

A&A's fortieth annual meeting, on April 30, 1962, was epochal. Sam Shriver was elected CEO, and Roy Jenkins announced his intention to retire within a year. The board was informed that an investment banker had approached A&A about selling out to a larger competitor, obviously Marsh & McLennan. This was perhaps the first effort by investment bankers to arrange insurance brokerage combinations, and it triggered considerable panic within A&A. Immediately, a resolution was adopted opposing such a sale. In addition, the board took action to protect Roy Jenkins's shareholding from any acquisition that might otherwise take place while the firm was redeeming his shares. Nothing further materialized on this "merger," which apparently was prompted by M&M's announcement that it was becoming publicly owned.

After fifty-two years of service, Roy Jenkins retired at the end of 1962. It would be an injustice to describe his reign as merely building on W. F.'s production success. The two men were true partners to a far greater extent than were the Alexander brothers. While C. B. was capably monitoring the finances and guiding the Baltimore office, Jenkins was building the rest of the organization. He oversaw the employment of capable technical insurance brokers; and, while questioning the need, he did agree to build up both a production team and account executives. Roy was a good leader. He left the company solidly established as the

Effective manager and communicator, Roy Jenkins was W. F. Alexander's right-hand man for 35 years. He led A&A as it become the third largest insurance brokerage in the United States.

nation's third largest insurance broker—one with a bright future. Premium volume for 1962 skyrocketed and the year's $10 million increase was a fitting tribute to Roy's tenure.

His retirement paved the way for Ken Soubry to join the board in 1962. Soubry and Geoff Calvert were the only directors who joined the firm after 1934. New blood and new ideas were needed. Joe Barr and I were elected to the board in 1963. At that point, the board majority made new business development a top priority, and the company prepared to take appropriate action. There was also a greater urgency to make quality acquisitions.

Acquiring Bartholomay and Clarkson in 1963 reflected the new generation's influence. A&A's Chicago office, with nine employees, had been principally a service office for local business produced by W. F. Alexander. Its six largest accounts were transportation related, headed by the Chicago, Rock Island & Pacific Railroad and the Chicago & East Illinois Railroad. Virtually no new accounts were being developed. A&A's board felt that acquiring a high-quality and aggressive Chicago agency was essential. Thus, the chief financial officer, Robert Borg, and I were dispatched to Chicago to identify a candidate. We visited a number of local insurance company offices, as well as banks and other financial institutions. We identified and prioritized about a dozen prospects. Bartholomay and Clarkson, founded in 1906, headed the list, and an introduction was arranged. Our timing was propitious because the younger partners felt they needed a national service capability. The senior executives of both firms mixed well, and an acquisition was subsequently concluded.

Significant organizational changes occurred in October 1963, when Sam Shriver was elected chairman of the board and CEO. Phil Ness became A&A's first vice chairman of the board, and Ken Soubry was elected president. Geoff Calvert's new title was executive vice president–personnel coverages. Shareholder employees were encouraged to attend annual meetings. (Previously, little information was distributed, and most shareholders considered attendance a waste of time.)

Acquisitions became ever more important as we observed Marsh & McLennan's rapid growth. Not all merger activity involved insurance agencies. During 1964, a joint venture with Comptronics was approved. A 51 percent interest was acquired, followed by total ownership. Its name was changed to Alextronics and finally to Benefacts. The company had developed a revolutionary concept in employee communications.

Utilizing a computer, Benefacts prepared customized reports for individual employees. The reports explained benefits and retirement programs provided by the government and the employer. Employees generally received their personalized statements once a year (usually showing the dollar value of the various benefits). The service was extremely well received.

Although it took several years for Benefacts to become profitable, many large companies that had never done business with A&A became clients. Major competitors were forced to develop similar services. Although A&A did not originate the concept, Benefacts was one of several services in which we became a leader. A&A was generally successful in analyzing concepts and services to determine whether they applied to our market. We had to determine: Was the project adaptable? Did it have potential for above-average profit? Once we had agreed that an idea had commercial merit, senior personnel and adequate funding were usually made available.

Either through acquisitions or start-up operations, most large brokerages experimented with noncore services. Their degree of success ranged from disastrous (e.g., ownership of insurance companies, particularly those owned by A&A and F. B. Hall) to spectacular (e.g., M&M's purchase of an investment management group, Putnam Investments, LLC). With the exception of the Putnam acquisition, most of the brokers' experimental endeavors were divested by the mid-1990s.

At the July 1966 annual meeting, Ken Soubry was elected CEO. When the year ended, Sam Shriver announced that he would retire; the board subsequently elected Phil Ness chairman. These were profound changes because the next ten years would prove by far the most important and complex A&A had yet seen.

Phil Ness presented a positive image during his six-year chairmanship. Ken Soubry's election as CEO surprised many people who expected a more senior executive, but it was a brilliant decision. Although factions existed among A&A directors, Soubry was a master at preventing personal animosities from seriously damaging the company.[5]

Strategic actions were to play an ever greater role in acquisitions. In large cities, it became increasingly important to achieve critical mass. This was reflected in A&A's 1967 acquisition of Lukens, Savage and Washburn (LS&W) in Philadelphia. LS&W was a venerable agency founded in 1923; it had eighteen technically sound and well-connected active partners.[6] Merck & Co., a prestigious client, had a long and close business relationship with LS&W dating back to 1927. Services to Merck were on a fee basis and were one of the earliest uses of this practice. As a bonus of acquiring LS&W, Alexander & Alexander also got small offices in Boston and Paris.

[5] Dick Alexander and Rodney Piersol, key players in A&A's development, retired in 1966. Roswell Dunn retired in February 1968. He had been instrumental in hiring two future CEOs, Ken Soubry and me. Ros Dunn was a new business advocate and fortified Phil Ness's efforts to redirect focus toward production. In addition to his keen sense of humor, Dunn was a perceptive judge of people and their motives.

[6] In 1939, LS&W's New York office was the first to arrange with the British government an open war risk policy—this on behalf of Cunard Lines.

As new employees came to A&A through acquisitions, company management meetings became essential. The first was held in New York City during 1965. Then, commencing with a Miami conference in January 1967, management meetings were conducted annually. The goal was for senior employees to mingle in a relaxed setting. Such meetings also offered corporate management an opportunity to communicate simultaneously with many senior employees.

In April 1968, the gathering was at the Arizona Biltmore Hotel in Phoenix and called a "heads of office meeting." [7] Forty-one people attended out of a total workforce of approximately 1,100. Fourteen of the attendees had joined A&A when their agencies were acquired. M&M, by contrast, conducted its first national meeting at the Greenbrier Hotel in White Sulphur Springs, West Virginia, in 1972 with 120 attendees. For some years, its conferences were held at three-year intervals.

A week after the A&A gathering in Arizona, W. F. Alexander Jr. was killed in an airplane crash while flying from Houston to Dallas.[8] Fontaine was highly respected in Dallas, and his excellent contacts were invaluable to A&A. At his funeral, the large church overflowed with the many people whose lives he had touched. Losing an outstanding person is difficult for any firm to absorb; it was especially difficult for us at this vital stage, when employees of Fontaine's caliber were already too few.

[7] For a number of years, the meeting shifted to Clearwater, Florida, before returning to Arizona.

[8] Booked on a later flight, he arrived at the airport in time to be the last stand-by taken aboard the ill-fated plane As a marketing gimmick, the airline was offering to pay each passenger a silver dollar if a flight was more than five minutes late. The pilot of Fontaine's plane elected to fly through a fierce thunderstorm rather than skirt it, and the aircraft was torn apart.

PART III

GOING PUBLIC AND GROWING GLOBAL:
The 1960s to the Early 1980s

CHAPTER 13

Brokers Go Public: The Era of Acquisitions Begins

Marsh & McLennan's transformation to public ownership permanently changed the insurance brokerage industry. Seven years elapsed before another firm would offer shares to the public, but the die was cast. Eventually, most brokers and agents of sufficient size offered public shares. In retrospect, M&M's move foreshadowed the dominance of several giant brokerages, which would ultimately serve most of the large insurance buyers in the United States and the world.

M&M was forthright in citing its reasons for an ownership change. It needed to overcome the financial burden of buying out employee shareholders when employees turned seventy, died, or ceased to be officers, directors, or employees. The formula for redeeming shares required paying out 50 percent of the shares' book value, plus 50 percent of each share's net earnings for the next ten years. This liability severely constrained the firm's financial resources. A second reason for public ownership was M&M's need for acquisitions. Most agencies could be acquired at a multiple of seven or eight times earnings. M&M's public sale was set at twenty-three times its 1961 earnings. Moreover, publicly traded stock was an acceptable vehicle for acquiring privately held agencies.

M&M first prepared for a public offering back in 1959. However, in 1961, two members of the executive committee, Willard Keith and Walter Schwindt, favored the action and two others, John Holbrook and Pete Kelsey, opposed it. Despite uneasiness, President Herman Smith ultimately cast the deciding vote in favor. The announcement surprised many employees and caused much consternation. Some employees felt outraged, even betrayed, when M&M shareholders were identified and the size of their holdings revealed.

M&M's revenues for 1962 were $52 million or seven-and-a-half times A&A's. It had thirty-nine offices, including eight abroad, compared with A&A's total of fourteen. A&A's international involvement was minimal. M&M provided worldwide facilities through connections, mostly exclusive, with leading brokers in other countries. J&H followed a similar practice, and its international capability was unsurpassed among U.S. brokers.

M&M's public ownership created anxiety within J&H. Its executive committee rarely disagreed on significant matters, but the debate on this issue was highly emotional. J&H's chairman, Elmer Jefferson, felt that the subject was too important to dismiss casually. An investment banking company was engaged to explore the pros and cons of public ownership. The result was a strong preference to remain private, and the subject was shelved.

David Winton, a former senior J&H executive who served for forty-four years, observed that J&H could have been larger than M&M, when it went public, if J&H's focus on marine insurance had not been so dominant. He pointed out that J&H's principal competitors concentrated on property and casualty insurance, which offered greater growth opportunity than marine insurance.

By 1968, as a vice president and director of Alexander & Alexander, I was in charge of our international expansion and national sales effort. During that year, I became increasingly convinced that if A&A continued to represent large buyers, we would have to become publicly owned. Risk and insurance-related matters became more complex

and demanding as clients diversified and expanded internationally. Clients needed special counsel on complex issues such as nuclear exposure, foreign credit, and tort liability changes. To effectively meet these challenges, we required a critical mass to spread the costs of specialized personnel, and we also needed a worldwide physical presence.

In 1968, we were still small compared to our two major competitors. Our ten largest accounts—four petroleum companies, three railroads, two airlines, and a pipe and foundry firm—had been produced by one person. In 1961, the year before Marsh & McLennan went public, its revenues of $49 million exceeded A&A's by $43 million. By the end of 1968, this differential doubled to $86 million; M&M's revenues from international sources represented nearly $2 million of this.

M&M had forty domestic offices and fifty offices or affiliated offices outside the United States. A&A had twenty-two

Accelerating technologies combined with increasing globalization of markets and economies produced more travelers—and accelerated travel too. By 1970, this meant an airplane with more seats than the U.S. House of Representatives; early configurations of the Boeing 747 could carry as many as 490 passengers—a quantum leap in capacity and in possible loss, i.e., risk for insurers.

domestic and six foreign locations. M&M's staff totaled 4,500; ours, 1,100. M&M's staff included more than 900 employee benefit specialists, forty of whom were fully accredited actuaries. Moreover, M&M had acquired fifteen agencies and brokerages between 1957 and 1962, and then rapidly increased its acquisition pace. The 1962 acquisition of J. C. Griswold of New York City, with offices in Los Angeles, San Francisco, and Tampa, Florida, was particularly significant. M&M was rapidly distancing itself in size from all other brokers and threatening to dominate the large commercial lines business.

A&A stood at a crossroads in mid-1968. Internal growth, coupled with an occasional acquisition, would not keep us competitive with M&M. Yet we were large enough and profitable enough to be attractive to the public. I presented my reasoning to the board, which endorsed the concept in principle. Phil Ness, Lou Bonar, and I interviewed three investment banking houses. Smith Barney was ultimately selected to take us public through a secondary offering of stock.

The 300,000 shares offered were held by current A&A employees. They were allocated by a formula based on age and percentage of total shares owned by each shareholder. Lou Bonar, Phil Ness, and Lat Stewart owned the largest holdings. The offering was made on April 22, 1969, at $26 a share and traded in the over-the-counter market.

The prospectus provided a detailed list of shareholders and their holdings, which, as in M&M's experience, was traumatic for many old-time employees. There was particular displeasure (among those not selling shares) over the number of new A&A shareholders who were joining the company through acquisition. The number of shares owned by certain individuals also caused grumbling. Some feeling about inequity was justified. Certain senior managers had employees they championed, and this led to various compromises. If one director pushed for his shareholder choices, another expected equal opportunity to advance his candidates. Complaints about share allocation subsided with time, but there were many hurt feelings.

Becoming a publicly owned company was the most significant event in A&A's history. Its timing was validated when two large competitors, Frank B. Hall and Fred. S. James, went public later that year. F. B. Hall's 1968 revenue was $9 million, and late in 1969 it had 540 employees. James & Co. recorded 1969 revenues of $13.5 million with a staff of approximately 400.[1]

F. B. Hall prepared to go public at a 1967 "Future Planning Meeting" on Long Island, New York. It considered three options: remaining basically a one-office operation, merging with another firm (M&M, J&H, A&A, or James & Co.), or expanding into a multi-office international firm, primarily through acquisition. The third option was chosen, and taking F. B. Hall public began to be explored. This difficult decision was debated extensively by senior executives over many months.

The company was led by Melvin Holmes, as president and CEO, and James Stewart, grandson of Henry Stewart, as chairman. Both of them were outstanding executives and thoughtful students of the insurance business. In early 1969, F. B. Hall prepared to go forward with a public stock offering when the John Hancock Life Insurance Company unexpectedly approached the firm. Hancock planned to merchandise property and casualty insurance nationwide through its 15,000 life insurance agents. It proposed to take a controlling interest in F. B. Hall, which would then oversee the mass merchandising program. F. B. Hall rejected the proposal and went public in late 1969.

Until 1968, F. B. Hall's U.S. operations were concentrated in New York City. During the next four years, the company made a number of acquisitions. Many were among the country's better independent firms, including three California companies: Alexander, Sexton & Carr of California; Brander & Company; and Allen T. Archer & Co.[2] Others included Boit, Dalton & Church of Boston; Byrnes-McCaffrey of Detroit; W. H. Markham & Co. of St. Louis; C. A. Sporl of New Orleans; and Brown, Crosby & Co. Inc. of New York City.

Perhaps the most significant purchase was Parker &

[1] The relationship between revenue and number of employees can vary considerably between brokerages based on the composition of their clients' insurance requirements.

[2] Richard Archer became Hall's CEO in 1973.

Company, International, in 1970. This leading brokerage specialized in aviation insurance and had handled Pan American Airways' needs since 1926. Parker had offices in ten cities, including Caracas and Mexico City. It also had a formidable reinsurance facility. This was the largest brokerage merger to date and propelled Hall to a top position among brokerages handling aviation insurance.

During the 1970s, A&A made nearly 150 acquisitions, which solidified its position as the third largest U.S. broker. The successes and failures in this process mirrored challenges faced by others. A&A's early strategy was extremely focused, and the results were outstanding. Certainly no other firm exceeded the quality of agencies purchased from 1969 through the early 1970s. This was an especially prolific acquisition period for most major U.S. brokerages.

A focal point of the acquisition process was the annual industry meeting at The Greenbrier in White Sulphur Springs, West Virginia.[3] This gathering included senior officials of insurance companies, brokers, and agencies. Traditionally, insurers held cocktail receptions for agents and brokers, while the larger brokerages secured cottages for entertaining insurers and selected agents. What transpired was "acquisition frenzy," with brokers attempting to line up, evaluate, and sometimes get commitments from targeted agencies.

A&A sought to identify and acquire the finest agency in each of the nation's major industrial centers. An ability to issue stock was a key factor in accomplishing the objective. Incentives for agencies included: the opportunity for owners to convert illiquid assets to the liquidity provided by owning publicly-traded stock; advantages of broad national and international representation; specialists in virtually every area of the insurance business; and diverse friendships within a large organization. Disincentives revolved around the loss of independence and concerns about local staffs.

Major brokers had a variety of reasons for seeking particular agencies. They often wanted to enter promising new

[3] The Council of Insurance Agents and Brokers has been meeting at The Greenbrier from its founding in 1913. This tradition was interrupted by World War II—when the resort served as an internment camp for German, Italian, and Japanese diplomats, then as a military hospital—and again by the tragic events of September 11, 2001, when the meeting was cancelled. Council members operate from over 3,000 locations worldwide and place about 80 percent of U.S. commercial business—with premiums well over $90 billion in 2001.

locations. Sometimes they wanted to bring in new services or key individuals. Frequently, the foremost factor was the need to build up an existing office. As brokerages grew, however, questionable logic occasionally drove some acquisitions.

As noted, A&A's acquisition strategy was especially effective during its first few years as a public company. This can be seen by the number of mergers that made significant contributions.

Late in 1969, Hutchinson, Rivinus & Co. of Philadelphia was acquired, adding 110 professionals and staff to A&A's already strong presence. The office was then Philadelphia's largest brokerage; our objective was to hold a dominant position. Hutchinson's John Sienkiewicz made valuable contributions to A&A over the years, serving in several management capacities. He was especially good at maintaining sound client relations and particularly skillful in understanding their risk management needs.

The Philadelphia acquisition was the first in a series of superb mergers. The timing was favorable because of A&A's need to replace senior managers. By then, long-time directors Latimer Stewart, Louis Bonar, and Hugh Long had retired. Recently elected Mark Balis and Waldo Hardell, whose Minneapolis firm Charles W. Sexton Company was purchased in January 1970, followed soon thereafter. The Sexton Company was incorporated in 1894 by Charles Sexton as successor to another agency he had opened in Minneapolis in 1884. Sexton's principal clients dealt in lumber, milling, and grain. It handled more important grain and lumber accounts than any agency in the upper Midwest or Northwest.[4]

The Sexton acquisition never could have occurred if A&A had remained private. Even so, it was one of the two most contentious negotiations A&A ever faced. We approached Sexton at the eleventh hour, when the firm was well into merger discussions with Marsh & McLennan. However, A&A initiated contact because M&M already operated a Minneapolis office, and several Sexton directors preferred an alternative. Sexton was worth battling for. It was not only

[4] Sexton was one of the first U.S. agencies with a Canadian office, and several of its clients had extensive operations in Winnipeg. Charles Sexton himself believed in thoroughly training employees and felt that their commitment should be equivalent to that of a successful physician. Many became recognized specialists in their fields. Employee turnover was exceptionally low and morale very high.

the dominant Minneapolis/St. Paul agency, with more than 150 employees, but it also had an attractive branch office in Portland, Oregon, specializing in lumber accounts.

The struggle to obtain Sexton was intense. The company's board split about evenly on whether to join A&A or M&M. Price is usually a factor with agency principals approaching retirement age; young directors are more interested in future opportunities. At the insistence of John Harrison, one of Sexton's younger directors, A&A was selected. Deliberations caused some bitterness, but the ranks soon closed, and there was no ongoing rancor.

Sexton's annual revenue of $3.2 million placed it among the nation's larger agencies. John Harrison served with distinction as a member of A&A's board of directors. A second 1970 Minneapolis acquisition, Wert Wilson & Company, put us in an even stronger position in the upper Midwest. This firm, established in 1913 by Wert Wilson and Ed Force, was an outgrowth of a bonding agency founded in 1906. In the 1920s, it pioneered the development of a grain storage bond, and during the depression, it originated a depositor's bond that guaranteed checks drawn on different U.S. banks. It also negotiated a contract to automatically handle, on a "bordereau basis" (a list of issued policies providing essential details and sent to the insurer at intervals), insurance on Minneapolis district farms upon which the Federal Land Bank had mortgages.[5]

We had also targeted representation in Detroit. The Detroit Insurance Agency (DIA) was the largest independent firm with 150 employees. Its annual revenue exceeded $4 million, and it had branch offices in Chicago and New York. The acquisition was completed in 1970, and the firm's principal executive, David Marantette, became an A&A director, retiring a year later. DIA was founded by the Gaulker brothers in 1894, the same year as Sexton. Originally named Detroit Insurance Ltd., the agency began to flourish in 1912 when George Carter was hired.[6]

In 1970, A&A purchased Moore, Case, Lyman & Hubbard, Inc.—perhaps Chicago's oldest active agency—whose fine client list was a major attraction. This agency had been

[5] Several accomplished professionals among the agency's thirty-eight employees were also influential members of the community. William Baker, who handled the Honeywell account, became a particularly valuable member of the A&A team.

[6] Carter was born on a North Dakota farm; his formal education ended when he was fourteen and hired as office boy by the Orient Insurance Company. He then gained experience with three Chicago agencies before joining Detroit Insurance. While building a formidable organization in Detroit, Carter became a leader in the Midwest insurance community and played an active role in civic affairs. He retired in 1953 and was replaced by David Marantette, who had been hired as a solicitor in 1930. Marantette continued to expand the operation, specializing in the automobile industry as the principal insurance broker to General Motors. The firm's clients also featured pharmaceutical companies as well as educational, institutional, and church properties.

formed as a partnership by Silas M. Moore in 1859, the year Chicago saw its first horse-drawn streetcar, first Pullman car, and first fire engine.[7] Another superb 1970 acquisition was Harris-Moore & Associates, the largest independent Dallas agency, with ninety-eight employees.[8] Based on its subsequent contributions, which extended far beyond the confines of Texas, Harris-Moore must be considered our finest agency acquisition. Bill Carter, its leader, ultimately served as CEO of A&A. He was a tough Texan with high moral standards who tolerated little nonsense or aberrant behavior.

Carter was also a firm believer in insurance education. He insisted that the agency's professionals attain the demanding professional designation of CPCU (Chartered Property Casualty Underwriter). While he occasionally pounded his fists on a table, he also could display considerable charm and compassion. He always maintained close friendships within insurance circles, often with the owners of other agencies. (He had a legendary short fuse and little tolerance for pranks. This proved an irresistible temptation for his associates. On one occasion in south Texas, the talk turned to the abundance of rattlesnakes in the area. That evening, a fake rattler was placed under his sheets, and the ensuing yells were a source of considerable amusement, to all but Bill.)

Through acquisitions, the A&A employee count rose to 2,000 by the end of 1970. We were expanding on other fronts as well. In conjunction with London broker Matthews Wrightson, we opened small offices in Hong Kong and Tokyo. We also entered the premium finance field instead of providing the service through others. A number of insurance buyers opted to have their premiums financed. When an exceptionally large contract was agreed to by an A&A client, a major U.S. petroleum company, management's interest was stimulated. Research confirmed a place for an additional provider and a good opportunity for profit. The new unit was named BUFCO (Business Finance Company).

After nine 1970 domestic acquisitions, another fifteen were made in 1971. Two of these were of special interest.

[7] In the great fire of 1871, the agency paid every one of its claimants in full; not more than 55 of some 200 insurance companies in the city could meet their claim responsibilities. The agency paid some claims itself. It had continually represented the Hartford Fire Insurance Company since 1864 and the St. Paul Fire and Marine Insurance Company since 1871.

[8] Harris-Moore & Associates was formed by the combination of two partnerships in March 1969. Munger-Moore had been organized in 1931, with the Munger interest sold to Charles Bailey in 1952. Bailey's partner, William Moore, was one of the most widely respected members of the Dallas business community, "the best friend" of countless acquaintances. Felix Harris and Company was Munger-Moore's partner in 1969. Felix Harris had represented the insurance side in the real estate/insurance firm of Collum and Harris. In 1941, Harris broke away and formed his own insurance agency with $10,000 borrowed capital. After World War II, Felix's son-in-law, William Carter, and his eldest son, Benjamin, joined the agency, followed by two other sons. In addition to Bill Carter, several others made significant contributions to A&A. Michael White eventually served as president of A&A. Charlie Bailey and Bob Cline wore many hats as A&A board members. Tom West became the firm's senior liaison with insurance companies. The Patrick brothers, Brooks and Charles, headed other A&A offices. Giles Madray occupied a senior administrative post in Baltimore. The quality of their staff was exceptional.

[9] Field & Cowles was founded in Boston as Foster & Cole in 1867. George E. Foster was active in the firm until his death in 1910, and F. B. Cowles joined during 1897 and died in 1913. George P. Field was active between 1892 and 1897 when the firm was Scull & Field. As early as 1872, the agency operated as general agent for the Royal Insurance Company and two other insurers. By 1926, the agency was one of the largest in the country with 225 employees, and it represented at least eleven insurers as managers or general agents. During the 1950s, it was New England manager for the INA's local marine business as well as the Royal's fire and casualty account. It also managed the Aetna Insurance Company's fire account in the Boston area. For years, Field & Cowles's primary revenue came from this type of activity. During the 1930s and 1940s, only 25 percent of the agency's income was derived from direct agency/brokerage activity. This figure had risen to 88 percent by the time of A&A's purchase.

The first, Field & Cowles, a Boston agency, made its mark as a general agent representing various insurers.[9] This type of representation was popular in several sections of the country and remained important in Boston until about 1960.

And the second—arguably the best managed agency we ever acquired—was Weaver-Minier Company in Lincoln, Nebraska. This acquisition came after a competitive situation in which the two principal partners backed different suitors. Founded in 1942, it joined A&A with a staff of forty and revenue of $1.5 million. One principal, Patrick Minier, a quintessential manager and planner, backed the A&A offer. The other principal, Arthur Weaver, son and grandson of Nebraska governors and a highly respected man, originally favored a merger with Fred. S. James.

Weaver-Minier, an exemplary agency, embodied many characteristics that A&A sought in its acquisitions:

• It was the dominant insurance agency in the area it served.

• It had outstanding leadership and management discipline.

• There was a broad age range among employees.

• There was a successor plan in place for each professional, with several highly promising candidates for top management succession.

• It had a tradition of growth and promotion from within.

• Its professionals signed noncompete contracts, preventing them from taking Weaver-Minier business if they left the firm.

• Its personnel were heavily involved in community affairs.

• Professionals pursued formal training and educational courses pointing toward earning CPCU designation.

• There was virtually no turnover of personnel.

• The office targeted prospective new clients and assigned a team to the production effort.

Weaver-Minier's emphasis on business development was exemplary. It conducted meticulous background research; presentations left no stone unturned. Its success ratio was 80 percent on new business, and price was rarely the determining factor. The quality of engineering reports and the detail of underwriting reports were lavishly praised by the insurance companies.

As these various acquisitions suggest, geographic spread was an important goal. It was also important to identify unusually attractive agencies in smaller market areas such as Lincoln, Nebraska, and Green Bay, Wisconsin. In addition, we sought agencies that specialized in handling business for certain industries. For example, bonding requirements for construction companies were often complex, and it was imperative that they be handled with expertise. A&A initially obtained this specialization by purchasing surety-type agencies in Atlanta, Nashville, and San Jose, California.

With early acquisitions, there tended to be a dominant senior manager whose personality set the tone. In Nashville, William Geny fit this description. He owned a third of McKee, Geny & Thornton, which traced its start to 1892. More than half of its business was with contractors. Geny, once a college football star, was a born salesman. People enjoyed associating and doing business with him. He was a leader, however, rather than a manager, and A&A needed

The imposing facade of The Greenbrier Hotel conceals a history with many facets: luxury resort, internment camp, nuclear age bunker. Famous as a royal and presidential playground, it was taken over by the government in World War II and used to house interned Fascist diplomats. During the Cold War, it acquired a super-secret underground facility, which was built to house Congress in case nuclear war forced the legislature to flee Washington. Since 1913 it has hosted almost annually one of the world's premier gatherings of commercial insurance leaders.

top managers. The challenge in this and similar situations was introducing a new manager without destroying office vitality. A&A was only partly successful in such endeavors.

Superior leaders were not necessarily similar types. Walter Jensen of Fisher-Jensen Insurance in San Jose was his agency's driving force. He was a leader and manager. Both he and Willie Geny were the essence of integrity and totally professional in demeanor. Although unlike Geny in personality and style, Jensen also ran a superb operation. Discipline was important to him, and the office was organized and run to reflect this principle. No coffee drinking was allowed in the office because he felt it created an internal distraction!

As new U.S. offices were established, international expansion finally became a high priority. The goal was to have equity in operations within various countries, which would allow A&A to respond to clients' global needs. In early 1971, Phil Ness went to Europe with a small team of A&A's international and financial specialists to identify local brokers with whom we might establish joint ventures.

Unfortunately, A&A was a latecomer. Twenty years earlier, J&H had formed UNISON, a similar network of exclusive international correspondents. Marsh & McLennan International also had correspondent relationships—or in a few instances, subsidiaries—in more than fifty countries. One of its strategic goals was to abandon correspondents and emphasize equity interests and control where possible. In 1966, Frank B. Hall had arranged extensive correspondent relationships throughout Europe and Latin America. Two years later, it implemented important joint ventures in Australia and Hong Kong.

A&A wanted to set up local companies, 75 percent owned by A&A and 25 percent by the indigenous partner. The partner's staff would service accounts we referred. As of July 1, 1971, new offices were in place in Belgium, France, Germany, the Netherlands, Ireland, and Italy. The joint venture partners, with the exception of those in Germany, were well known and highly thought of within A&A. This gave us access to thirty offices with 1,400 employees. Subsequently, it led to similar agreements with six brokers in Central and South America as well as Australia and other European countries.

By the early 1970s, A&A had a formal international network that appeared to address our needs. However, it soon became apparent that we should have as much control as possible over international facilities. Without 100 percent or a majority control, we had difficulty ensuring adequate client service. And, in the years ahead, high quality global services would be indispensable for large U.S. brokers.

CHAPTER 14

The Chaotic Seventies: More Mergers

Between 1968 and 1972, A&A's revenue rose from $21 million to $61 million, with almost all of it generated from U.S. business. Coping with this growth required frequent reorganization, and in 1971, domestic regions were created to decentralize day-to-day decision making. Each of our seven regions, with few exceptions, had the ability to provide full service. Canada, with activity restricted to benefits consulting, was also defined as a region.

In 1972, seventeen agencies joined A&A, six representing new locations, while the others augmented existing offices. Some of the smaller agencies acquired then were outstanding. The Murphy Insurance Agency, Inc., in Green Bay, Wisconsin, was very well managed and our Green Bay office produced superior results through the 1990s.[1] The agencies of Robert Gielow and Horace Holcomb gave A&A two men whose subsequent national activities were indispensable.

The same was true of William Mayo in Dallas, a born salesman who needed A&A's technical insurance capability. Bill Mayo's infectious personality caused people to laugh with him as well as at him. Almost immediately, he became one of our top ten new business producers. In Greenwich, Connecticut, the acquisition of Peter Pauley's agency set in motion a rapid business expansion in lower Connecticut, as he was another top producer. With the acquisition of Lionel Goldberg's firm, A&A gained an employee so widely

[1] Many felt its excellence stemmed from a client role model, the Green Bay Packers, coached by the legendary Vince Lombardi. The team was a paradigm for football fans everywhere.

respected that his presence greatly enhanced the prestige of A&A's large Long Island office. In a few instances, the incentive for acquisition related to a particular client. Such was the case with San Francisco's R. E. Kelley agency, which handled the World Airways account and bolstered A&A's airline business.[2] The success of most small acquisitions depended on the agency's head remaining actively and effectively involved.[3]

After 1972, mergers were under the direction of a new management team as the "old guard" moved on.[4] With the retirement of Phil Ness, Ken Soubry became chairman of the board while remaining CEO. Bill Carter was elected president and chief operating officer. These were sound moves, as the two men complemented one another extremely well.

Ken Soubry's calm manner contrasted with Carter's more volatile personality, yet they respected each other and meshed without conflict. Both were men of great integrity and outgoing personalities conducive to a service business; also, both were highly intelligent. Moreover, neither flinched at tough decisions. During his administration, Soubry especially had to initiate difficult personnel changes at senior levels. They had different management styles, each effective in his own way. Soubry was a delegator, while Carter, who operated by tight control, was a consummate communicator and motivator in one-on-one and small group situations.

During 1972, the New York office left the financial district, where it had been located since its inception in 1918. The move to 1185 Avenue of the Americas preceded by a few weeks Marsh & McLennan's relocation a few blocks farther north. These decisions belied traditional wisdom that insurance brokers needed to be within walking distance of insurance companies where they placed business. In fact, the relocations recognized that most clients had moved from the financial district to midtown or to the suburbs as they sought to lower overhead and raise the quality of life. Although Johnson & Higgins remained downtown, most major brokers followed our lead and moved elsewhere.

[2] World Airways, which had clandestine U.S. government contracts, became more widely known at the end of the Vietnam War when it flew the last American rescue mission out of Saigon.

[3] For sentimental reasons, A&A's first office, in Clarksburg, West Virginia, had been retained much longer than the area's depressed economy justified. Despite the nostalgia of oldtimers, it was finally sold to a respected local agency, Chamberlaine & Flowers, and our excellent local manager, Marty Root, joined them.

[4] Phil Ness departed at the end of 1971 at the age of 65. Dave Marantette and Geoff Calvert retired in 1972. With the exception of Doug Kincaid of the Baltimore office, all of the new directors joined A&A with the acquisition of their agencies. These men were Chicago-based Henry Bartholomay, George Clark, and Bob Gielow; John Gray, who succeeded Dave Marantette in Detroit; John Harrison from Minneapolis; and John Sienkiewicz from Philadelphia. At the end of 1972, eight of the fourteen board members had joined A&A by way of merger and were part of the "new management."

Such decisions also reflected the principle that it was more important to be close to clients than to insurers.

Competition among insurance brokerage companies had been fierce for two decades. A&A management was always looking for a new service that offered a competitive advantage. Simultaneously, the business world was changing dramatically, and change seemed to be accelerating during the 1950s and 1960s. Our perennial watchfulness and the evolution of the business prepared us to make a great leap in 1972.

Technological developments, especially in computers and related fields, suddenly rendered much business equipment and many traditional practices obsolete; thus, corporate analysis of risk received greater management attention.[5] Buying insurance became only one element in a complex strategy of how best to deal with an entire array of corporate risks.

One landmark in risk management came in 1963 with the pioneering text *Risk Management in the Business Enterprise* by Robert J. Mehr and Bob A. Hedges, insurance professors at the University of Illinois. In 1966, a Canadian company, Massey Ferguson, formalized the position of risk manager. Thereafter, most companies with departments headed by insurance managers converted to risk management departments led by individuals who became known as risk managers. Depending on individual circumstances, these individuals considered self-insurance, or perhaps no insurance for some risks, as part of corporate business strategy.

In response to marketplace changes, A&A hired Joseph Destein and James Paulding in 1972. These two innovators developed a methodology called Anistics (an acronym for "analytical statistics"), which applied quantitative methods, computer science, and financial planning to risk management and insurance. We formed an Anistics division and staffed it with professional consultants who held advanced degrees in such specialties as economics, finance, account-

[5] Apropos, the National Association of Insurance Buyers had changed its name to the American Society of Insurance Management (ASIM) in 1955, and in 1975 would become the Risk and Insurance Management Society (RIMS). These name changes reflected the altered realities of our business as methods of protecting a company's assets underwent a dramatic evolution.

ing, computer science, engineering, statistics, mathematics, and physics.

A 1980s study in a prominent trade journal identified our Anistics division as the nation's leading consultant for computer-based systems in risk management. We exported Anistics concepts globally, and its success encouraged many imitators. Over the years, Anistics opened hundreds of doors for A&A and was responsible for generating many new business opportunities. It was one of our most significant contributions to risk management development.

Among fifteen 1973 acquisitions, two small ones had far-reaching consequences: Bronson, Donnehy & Ulseth in Chicago and E. D. English & Co. in St. Louis. Both specialized in administrative and claims service to companies with self-insured workers compensation programs. By identifying the potential for offering claims and loss control expertise to a rapidly expanding number of self-insurers, A&A became the leading broker in this field and one of the nation's top two firms. The business became national in 1975 under the name of Alexsis (Alexander Self-Insured Services).[6]

Since the company frequently provided services outside traditional brokerage activities, a holding company, Alexander & Alexander Services Inc., was formed in January 1973. Alexander & Alexander Inc. became a wholly owned subsidiary. This structure provided greater flexibility for offering a broader range of services.

Two states, Ohio and North Carolina, made out-of-state ownership of local insurance agencies very difficult. In 1973, Ohio's insurance regulations changed, and we responded by acquiring two old-line Cleveland agencies. North Carolina, unlike other states, permitted local banks to function as insurance agents, and they were the major players. This became increasingly controversial because of possible conflicts of interest. By the end of 1980, banks had to divest themselves of insurance agencies, and A&A purchased Wachovia Bank's agency. Dating from 1893, the agency was a powerful presence, maintaining fourteen North Carolina offices. A&A closed the smaller offices,

[6] A larger acquisition, Bleichroeder, Bing & Co. Inc., was an initial success and met our need to bolster marine insurance expertise. This was a venerable marine brokerage agency that traced its origins to 1859 in Hamburg, Germany. Most of its nearly $3 million annual revenue derived from marine accounts, 90 percent of them ocean hull and cargo insurance. Also of interest were some foreign-based treaty reinsurance accounts. For several years, Bleichroeder, Bing managers supervised A&A's fledgling reinsurance broking operation under their name. Although it was a potentially sound acquisition, when the agency's leaders retired, A&A was unable to retain much of the business.

*Kenneth W. S. Soubry, a personification of the coming global-
ization of the insurance industry, joined A&A as a trainee in
1949 and stepped down as CEO in 1977. A Briton born and
bred, he had come to America to recover his health after surviving a Japanese POW camp.*

which were not a strategic fit, and established a firm foundation in the state.

In 1973, we also bought May, Potter, Murphy & Carter
Inc. of Hartford, Connecticut. This fine agency was led by
Edward May, who had been a congressman, candidate for
governor, and U.S. Senate hopeful. Several additional agencies were acquired in Hartford, with highly qualified personnel in property/casualty and group life insurance.

A&A dominated the Hartford brokerage scene. The
momentum slowed, however, with Ed May's retirement.
Experienced managers had to be moved in from other
offices, but no one was up to the job. If ever a situation
called for a dynamic and disciplined leader to pull an office
together, this was it. Regrettably, such an individual was not
forthcoming, and the office languished. Other national brokerages experienced similar concerns.

This illustrates a critical challenge that any business faces
in periods of rapid expansion. If management positions
open, the temptation is to fill them with "the best available
person" irrespective of that person's location. If this temptation is institutionalized as policy, it tends to boost morale
among potential managers with promise and ambition. Yet
even with a sophisticated management training program

(which A&A did not have), it is very difficult to move managers from office to office. Local knowledge and contacts take considerable time to develop. Only an exceptional individual fits into the new locale smoothly. In retrospect, it appears that A&A moved senior managers too frequently.

A 1974 acquisition exemplified why J&H as a private brokerage was disadvantaged when competing with public brokers in acquiring agencies. Hamlin & Co. Brokers Inc., a small New York City brokerage with attractive business and outstanding principals, was about to join J&H when A&A entered the picture. J&H couldn't match our financial offer, which included stock.

In the early 1970s, A&A had established a Canadian presence in the field of benefit consulting. Dissatisfied with our progress, we formed a partnership in 1972 with the Canadian broker Tomenson Saunders Whitehead Ltd. (later Tomenson, Inc.) to provide benefits services. Five Canadian offices were operating in 1974 with mixed results.

As for our expansion overseas, particularly in the U.K., A&A began seeking opportunities in the 1970s. Thus began an adventure of epic dimensions and unhappy ramifications that warrants subsequent chapters in this narrative.

A&A's rapid growth resulted in senior managers assuming new responsibilities, which required on-the-job training. In 1974, the Human Resource Management Group (HRM) was formed to oversee all aspects of our employee benefits work. Actuarial, estate and financial planning, employee information systems, and benefit plan communications all came under the HRM umbrella and accounted for 18 percent of A&A's revenues in 1974. A year later, that statistic rose to 22 percent on revenues of $22 million. HRM executive responsibility was assigned to T. Irvin, one of the company's top property/casualty executives.

Similarly, John Sienkiewicz was tapped to head the international retail operation, which required full-time leadership. Despite little or no previous international involvement, Sienkiewicz elevated these operations to a level where they significantly contributed to the company's image and profits. For A&A and other large brokers, on-the-job training was commonplace.

Entering 1974, A&A had 3,100 employees, with offices in forty-four U.S. cities and various international arrangements. Eight regional U.S. directors and four heads of special staff services reported directly to Bill Carter as chief operating officer in January 1975.

At Carter's direction and encouragement, the U.S. offices adopted a management-by-objective program. As the year began, each employee was to negotiate with his or her supervisor a specific list of objectives. These written objectives would be formally agreed to by both parties. This allowed supervisors to better evaluate performance over the course of a year.[7]

Almost all of A&A's special services were particularly vulnerable to marketplace vagaries and unexpected challenges. The economic climate in 1974 had not been favorable for the premium finance business. Profits could be significantly affected by cyclical interest rate swings, and increasing rates in 1974 squeezed premium finance providers. In addition to BUFCO (Business Finance Company), which was formed to serve A&A clients, TIFCO (The Insurance Finance Company) was started in early 1974 to offer premium financing to other brokers and independent insurance agents. After a slow start, business accelerated late that year and early in 1975. Tight money made premium financing attractive, and agent clients swelled from 159 during September to 411 in March.

Maintaining quality control of the agent clients was a challenge. In March 1975, while A&A's executive committee was having dinner in Atlanta, Bill Carter took an urgent call: A notorious financial felon had perpetrated a substantial fraud in Florida involving TIFCO. Happily, a sharp-eyed employee in a Florida bank recognized the man, who was detained and arrested. Without this timely action, the loss could have amounted to millions of dollars. Fort-

[7] Unfortunately, introducing such a totally new concept to thousands of people is not simple. Results were inconsistent, and gradually the system, in its formal state, was abandoned. Nonetheless, many benefits were derived. Constructive dialogue was promoted among employees, and manager subjectivity was frequently reduced. Managers, supervisors, and employees began to focus more constructively on clear and timely communications.

unately, the loss was limited to approximately $500,000, which was covered by insurance.

Among the eleven 1975 acquisitions, Shand, Morahan & Company, Inc., (Shand) represented a different thrust in an area not overpopulated by other brokerages. Shand was a leading surplus lines broker and managing general agent that handled hard-to-place lines not generally written in the U.S. market. Shand acted as underwriting manager for five insurers. It also owned two insurance subsidiaries, which reinsured most of their portfolio, leaving Shand with little exposure. Professional liability was a particular specialty for the firm, and Shand's business became inextricably linked to the underwriting disasters created by America's litigious society.[8]

When dealing with groups such as lawyers, it became almost impossible to increase liability premiums at a pace and level sufficient to offset escalating losses. Two problems resulted. First, loss experience deteriorated rapidly for insurers on whose behalf Shand underwrote. Second, Shand had to retain more business in its own insurers because adequate reinsurance could not be obtained.

The most serious problem Shand faced was with the Mutual Fire Insurance Company, which was placed in rehabilitation by the Pennsylvania courts in December 1986. In February 1991, the rehabilitator began an action seeking compensatory and punitive damages of approximately $234 million. He alleged that Shand had contributed to Mutual Fire's insolvency through negligent underwriting. On its merits, this case should have been won by A&A. But because of huge legal expenses and the uncertainty of defending a highly technical case before a jury, the prudent move was to seek a settlement. A structured settlement was arrived at in early 1995 for approximately $50 million. Another 1995 payment, in excess of $30 million, was made to the firm that acquired Shand in 1987. This payment involved contract contingencies.

[8] Shand's clients were agents and brokers. As such, A&A had to be especially careful not to exert influence that might create a conflict of interest for Shand. As it turned out, A&A's own brokers sometimes felt discriminated against by Shand employees, who bent over backwards to assure objectivity. For many years, Shand was a material contributor to A&A's profits, before becoming a liability in the mid-1980s.

In the evolutionary process of providing clients with non-traditional services, A&A established a Risk Analysis and Management Group directed by Bob Gielow. The group included Alexander International Ltd., a Bermuda-based facility specializing in the management of client-owned captive insurance companies; Alexsis, A&A's self-insurance services group; and Anistics, our risk management statistical analysis operation.

This group's activities were bolstered by an abrupt change in the insurance market. Brokerages and their clients frequently contended with rapid market shifts. During 1974, a very soft U.S. insurance market persisted for the second year. Property and liability insurers suffered their greatest financial setbacks since the Depression. Underwriting losses exceeded $2 billion, with a combined loss ratio exceeding 104 percent after dividends. This was the highest ratio since 1932. Policyholder surplus dropped 29 percent, the largest year-to-year decline on record. The premium-to-surplus ratio stood at 2.6:1, compared with a historical average of 1.4:1. The industry had never been more leveraged.

In a complete turnaround, from late 1975 until April 1978, insurance prices skyrocketed, especially those for liability risks. Demand quickly overwhelmed a shrinking supply. Except for a brief period in 1985 and 1986, this would be the last hard market of the twentieth century. Many buyers were forced to reexamine their risk management programs. Alternatives to insurance were routinely considered and frequently adopted. Various operations of the Risk Analysis and Management Group benefited from the difficult environment. Broking operations, however, encountered the unfamiliar challenge of sharply increased demand with limited supply. In addition to increased profits, such conditions allow the most talented brokers to excel because their innovative skills are essential for placing risks.

During the mid-1970s, acquisitions continued at a rapid pace—perhaps too rapid. Because of A&A's size, more reliance had to be placed on regional management to identify appropriate acquisition candidates. These managers were concentrating on growth, and agency purchases were obvious vehicles for growth. Although the basic due diligence process was conducted, sometimes new locations proved far less promising than anticipated.

Upstate New York provides a melancholy example. A&A was not represented there, and in 1974 an opportunity arose to acquire Utica Mutual Associates Inc. We negotiated a deal, and overnight A&A had seven offices in upstate New York, including Buffalo, Rochester, and Syracuse. On paper, this represented a coup, but in practice it was a mistake. None of the offices became a significant profit center, and they consumed considerable management time. Eventually, the offices were consolidated or sold.

Small agencies with one key employee presented other problems. We generally expected the key employee to stay aboard as a productive professional when A&A acquired the agency. But some did not live up to expectations. Agencies with one key account or a specialized service also posed problems, as these situations called for extensive analysis of the viability of the account or product. One of the most difficult evaluations involves an agency with a single very large client. Was this client a likely candidate for acquisition? When the answer was yes, it obviously was more prudent not to acquire the agency. On other occasions, the key client was unexpectedly acquired by another firm, and the merger backfired.

Despite problems with some U.S. mergers, we clicked on all cylinders in Puerto Rico with Barros & Carrión, which dominated the insurance agency business on the island. Started in 1963 by Pepe Carrión, the scion of a distinguished local family, and his partner, Justo Barros, a widely respected industry professional, the office consistently turned in superior performance. The only problem was Barros's morbid fear of flying, a malady that required creative methods to get him aboard a plane.

A number of acquisitions involved local property tax organizations as A&A became the only nationwide consult-

Acquisition of a local California agency led A&A to venture into show business and Hollywood's terra incognita. Here dress codes favored leisure suits over serge, while six- or seven-digit policies covered such unique risks as comic Jimmy Durante's nose and the famous "gams" of Betty Grable, once America's most popular pinup girl.

ing firm advising on ad valorem taxes. We were introduced to the business when we acquired Weaver-Minier in Lincoln, Nebraska, which had a specialist in property tax consulting.

Ken Soubry stepped down as A&A's chairman and CEO to become chairman of the executive committee in April 1977. During his twelve-year tenure, the company's growth had been phenomenal. A&A was recognized as the world's second largest insurance brokerage, consulting, and actuarial firm; only M&M exceeded us. Soubry was respected throughout the industry, and his presence was crucial in attracting many merger candidates. His personality and demeanor captivated people at all levels. He was as natural and effective with risk managers as with CEOs.

Bill Carter succeeded Ken Soubry as chairman and CEO in 1977. I was elected president and chief operating officer, and T. Irvin became the executive vice president. When the year ended, we operated with ten regions. National committees were formed to share information with the offices and coordinate marketing strategy. The committees consisted of specialists in aviation, boiler and machinery, human resource management, loss control, marine, marketing, railroad, surety, and utilities. Such specialization was becoming common among brokerages.

Specialty areas, such as Benefacts, enhanced A&A's reputation with major corporations. By the late 1970s, Benefacts serviced more than 20 percent of Fortune 500 companies. It was a single source for employee communication services and information systems. Benefacts designed and produced cost-effective programs in areas such as recruitment materials, employee orientation aids, personal annual benefits reports, and government reports mandated by ERISA, EEO, and OSHA—viz. the Employee Retirement Income Security Act, Equal Employment Opportunity programs, and the Occupational Safety and Health Administration.

The Human Resource Management Group also was expanding its consulting capability to include defined contribution plans, flexible benefits, and interactive communications. Additionally, HRM designed and maintained up-to-date record keeping services for thrift, profit sharing, and other capital accumulation plans. The group established an off-site support office for research and training purposes in 1977, which also became an information resource in areas such as analyzing government regulations. The importance of consulting to brokers was highlighted in 1975 when Marsh & McLennan globally consolidated its life insurance and benefit consulting under the independent name, Mercer.

A&A had a particularly successful year in 1978. Of the fifteen agency acquisitions that year, Albert G. Ruben & Co. was our largest to date. Ruben was an intriguing enterprise and placed A&A in a dominant position within its industry segment. Its Beverly Hills entertainment division handled 75 percent of the entertainment industry's U.S. property/ casualty insurance. It placed entertainment-type insurance for other agents and brokers as well as for its own accounts. As a new A&A office, it was certainly atypical.

The private office of Scott Milne, the division manager, was adorned with an old nickelodeon and a slot machine. The dress code for men was a leisure suit, and neckties were reluctantly produced only on rare occasions. An inside dining room for employees and clients was dimly lit and resembled a nightclub. W. F. Alexander would have loved it; his brother, C. B., would have been aghast. Nonetheless, business was serious and the results outstanding. Joint ventures and other close connections were formed in London, the European continent, and Australia.

Cast and negative insurance were two especially important coverages. Cast insurance covers actors as well as any animals that producers consider irreplaceable.[9] Negative insurance covers exposed film until prints are made. Protection is provided against defective film, processing, even stolen film, and the cost of reshooting damaged or lost reels. Another Ruben operation was devoted to the construction industry.[10]

In 1978, A&A initiated discussions with the public brokerage R. B. Jones Corporation, headquartered in Kansas City, Missouri. R. B. Jones had offices in fifteen American cities, with revenues of approximately $30 million and 700 employees. It had become publicly owned in 1970 and was considered the ninth largest U.S. broker.

Richard Bacon (R. B.) Jones founded the firm. A Kentuckian who had headed west in 1889, he never got beyond Kansas City, where he lost all his belongings in a fire. He subsequently opened an insurance agency, whose first customer bought a policy with an annual premium of $12.80. Between 1889 and 1912, R. B.'s four sons joined him in the

[9] For example, the dog Benji in the 1980 movie *Oh, Heavenly Dog!* had cast insurance of over $1 million.

[10] By 1993, however, the loss experience on entertainment risks was horrendous. It had become difficult to find insurance companies that were willing to provide a stable market. Consequently, A&A decided to sell the entertainment division.

business. After the second son, Cliff, joined the agency, it moved to larger space measuring nine by fourteen feet.

By 1914, annual premium volume had reached $250,000. A year later, R. B. Jones became the first agency in that area of the Midwest to have a fire insurance engineering department. In 1923, it originated the personal property floater, which became a staple in the inland marine insurance field. In 1928, R. B. Jones became a pioneer in providing group insurance for employees. During the next year, it founded the Kansas City Fire and Marine Insurance Company. Small acquisitions, which commenced in 1922, contributed to its record premium volume of $5 million by 1943. This was approximately a third of A&A's premium volume for that year. In 1953, R. B. Jones opened a travel insurance desk in the Kansas City airport, the world's third such endeavor. Stimulated by additional acquisitions, the premium volume increased to $10 million in 1954, $15 million in 1958, and $20 million in 1960.

When Cliff Jones Sr. died in 1960, R. B.'s youngest son, Morton, became president, and Cliff Jones Jr. became chairman. Cliff added the title of president two years later, upon Morton's death, and branch offices were established through acquisition. Robert Braddock was elected president in 1964, and he, more than anyone else, was responsible for the firm's expansion and growth. He developed a master plan for revenue enhancement through mergers and then by becoming a public company. Braddock's plan was successful and was still being implemented in 1969, when he died suddenly. The company went public in 1970; its revenues were almost $11 million. During that year, it acquired an old Brooklyn, New York, agency, Benedict & Benedict, giving it a visible New York presence. Several St. Louis acquisitions were also combined to create a sizeable office.

In 1974, John Tucker became R. B. Jones's president and CEO. Cliff Jones remained chairman for a year and then retired. When A&A acquired Jones in January 1979, its customer base represented a broad cross section of industrial and transportation concerns, public utilities, and contractors. Its strength lay in geographic areas where A&A either had no office or needed beefing up. Itself the product of more than twenty acquisitions, R. B. Jones typified broker growth during the second half of the twentieth century.

During the R. B. Jones negotiations, tragedy struck when A&A's CEO, Bill Carter, died on October 21, 1978, at age fifty-eight. Bill was recuperating from an apparently successful heart bypass operation when he suffered a fatal heart attack. This occurred at a critical juncture for A&A. The decade of the 1970s, a period of intense concentration on domestic growth, was drawing to a close. Global expansion was looming as the focus of the 1980s.

Bill Carter's untimely death led to further management changes. I became CEO and T. Irvin was elected chief operating officer. Ken Soubry reassumed the office of chairman, and Bob Gielow joined the executive committee as its fourth member.

One of Bill Carter's last actions was to establish an office of Government and Industry Affairs (GIA) in Washington, D.C. Dr. Robert Moore, a former university professor and congressional consultant, developed and managed GIA.[11] Initially, the office analyzed the impact of federal legislation and regulation on the financial exposures and risk management problems of clients. In the mid-1980s, GIA's operations, expanded to include long-range planning, public relations, and a broad range of communications initiatives.[12] Subsequently, the office pioneered using new technology for computer-assisted research and analysis of clients' emerging risks. GIA eventually became highly visible inside and outside A&A.

The company finished the 1970s with two strong years. In 1978, revenues increased 20 percent and net income almost 25 percent. More than 2,000 employees were added. However, a soft insurance market returned, becoming progressively softer for six years. During this period, brokers' income was largely derived from commissions based on a percentage of premium—an income stream that is severely

[11] Robert Moore is the author's collaborator in this volume. Having joined the company in 1977, he became senior vice president for corporate relations in 1985 with added responsibility for New York–based corporate communications. He was elected president of the National Association of Insurance Brokers for 1985–86 and subsequently served four terms as chairman of NAIB's Past President's Council. In 1998, NAIB merged with the Council of Insurance Agents and Brokers in Washington, D.C.

[12] GIA was put to the ultimate test after 1982, when developments in London turned global eyes on Alexander & Alexander.

affected by market conditions. It is usually difficult to make up for this loss through new business and other activities. In spite of this, 1979 was another very successful year.

For A&A, the year's highlight was the award of a highly competitive contract by the Kingdom of Saudi Arabia's Royal Commission. In concert with its Saudi partner, A&A arranged insurance coverage on $35 billion worth of public facilities construction. The focus was on the development of two new cities, Jubail and Yanbu. This was the first time an insurance and risk management program had been devised for an entire municipal complex. It was probably the largest insurance broking services contract ever written. Two years later, A&A's Saudi office employed twenty-three employees, representing eight nationalities and many different languages.

The Saudi contract concluded an active decade. In the 1970s, A&A was the only public insurance broker that did not experience flat or reduced quarterly earnings from the preceding year. We completed some 150 mergers and acquisitions in this decade. The company operated in eighty-three U.S. cities and forty-three countries, with 7,200 employees.

We were satisfied with our U.S. expansion. A&A was represented in every area of the country. In many major cities, our property/casualty retail office was the dominant agency or brokerage force. Anistics and Alexsis were leaders in their fields, and Anistics was spreading abroad. The Risk Analysis and Management Group introduced ARIS, the first fully integrated broker–client information system specifically designed to help risk managers measure exposures, analyze losses, and control costs. HRM's benefits and related consulting services were moving ahead, and the life insurance department changed its name to the Executive Planning Services Division to better reflect its activities.

Our organizational culture had changed significantly since going public in 1969. The people who followed the Alexander brothers and built on their creation were mostly gone. By 1980, a large number of the professional staff and managers had joined A&A through acquisitions. They were usually well connected and highly visible in their communities, accustomed to being fully involved in the business. They produced accounts, often placed risks with insurers, and maintained close relationships with clients' senior management.

We had made a conscious decision to build our company through acquisitions. A key objective was to develop the range of services needed by large commercial clients. More than its major competitors, A&A relied on acquisitions to do this. On the one hand, this blueprint proved a considerable strength. It gave us people with vitality, enthusiasm, and willingness to take risk. These individuals formed a diverse and entrepreneurial group that was largely responsible for our achieving a leadership position among global brokers.

On the other hand, this strength also brought daunting challenges. Leaders of independent agencies were not easy to integrate into a large multinational organization. Many were outstanding business producers and centers of influence, but they frequently lacked management and administrative skills. Others simply did not have the necessary discipline or interest to run a large office and work for organizational goals.

Many did adapt and became fine managers. Frequently, a solution was for the new people to serve in managerial positions other than office head. They were given senior titles, ample financial rewards, and high recognition. Our approach was successfully implemented in many cases; in others, it failed. When it failed, an office could deteriorate—a difficult problem to rectify. Despite such challenges, A&A would not have become a top global broker without the change of culture and the contributions of these new leaders. The growth we experienced would be crucial to our handling of the enormous challenges that lay ahead.

CHAPTER 15

Innocents Abroad:
A&A Goes to Britain

Although A&A concentrated during the 1970s on building a first-class domestic organization, international development was by no means ignored. With a satisfactory group of international correspondents in place, the search continued for ways to acquire a London broker. Historically, a number of U.K. brokerages differed from their American counterparts. Either they did not initially broker insurance or insurance played a minor role in their business. This anomaly was present in the development of the three largest firms—C. T. Bowring and its competitors, Willis Faber & Company, Limited, and Sedgwick, Collins & Company (Sedgwick).

C. T. Bowring had the longest history. As Godfrey Hodgson has noted, Benjamin Bowring began work as a watchmaker, but he was prospering in the shipping business by the early 1820s. "By the 1850s, the Bowrings owned a large fleet of fast trading schooners," he wrote. Later, they sailed the faster clippers, and from the 1860s until 1912, they were also important players in shipping oil. Hodgson reports that, "Individual Bowrings had written marine insurance in Liverpool early in the nineteenth century, but it was not until 1876 that the first of them became a member of Lloyd's." By the end of the century, the company was broking marine and nonmarine coverages. Although its insurance brokerage business became increasingly significant, the company remained active in banking and shipping until the 1970s.

Henry Willis and Company was formed in 1828; and, according to Hodgson, it combined insurance brokerage and a larger business of selling diverse commodities. Fifty years later, Henry Willis "sold his commission merchants business in order to concentrate on marine insurance." During 1898, to diversify its insurance book, Willis merged with a Lloyd's specialist firm, Faber Brothers, to become Willis Faber & Company, Limited. Another old marine specialist, Dumas & Wylie Limited, was added in 1929, and the company became Willis, Faber & Dumas Limited (Willis Faber).[1]

[1] Hodgson reported that, "Until 1950, Bowring, Willis Faber, and Matthews Wrightson maintained offices in the same building and, by tradition, did not compete for one another's business."

Most of the firms that became part of the Sedgwick Group were started by men whose primary business was insurance. Frank L. H. Collins actually started in warehousing but soon left to open an insurance agency in 1846. His firm, Frank L. H. Collins & Sons, became fire insurance specialists of the first order. Henry B. Sedgwick's first insurance experience was with Alexander Howden & Co. (Howden), circa 1877. He then established a marine insurance brokerage, eventually merging with G. H. B. Moger, forming Sedgwick, Moger & Co.

In 1912, the Sedgwick (then H. B. Sedgwick & Co.) and Collins firms combined to become Sedgwick, Collins & Co. Ltd. (Sedgwick). Later, Price, Forbes & Co. Ltd. and Bland Payne Holdings Ltd. joined the group to produce one of the world's most formidable brokerages. T. W. Forbes had begun broking marine insurance in 1825 at the old Lloyd's room at the Royal Exchange, and Charles Price had been a non-marine pioneer. Their merger created Price, Forbes & Co.

In turn, Bland Payne traced its origins to Alexander Maclean, who had started in marine insurance in 1830 and whose firm combined with broker Bland Welch in 1890. Bland Welch was a major player in placing insurance on drilling rigs through its association with and later acquisition of Southern Marine & Aviation Underwriters Inc., a New Orleans specialty brokerage. E. W. Payne & Co. was founded in 1919 by Ernest William Payne. It specialized in

reinsurance and merged with Bland Welch to form Bland
Payne.

By the end of 1973, Alexander & Alexander had grown substantially at home. The London insurance market, particularly Lloyd's, had become increasingly significant to A&A.
Our premium volume placed through Lloyd's had reached
$22.5 million annually, with two-thirds handled by Sedg-
wick and the remainder spread among several other brokers. Most Lloyd's placements were for marine and aviation
risks, a mix that changed radically as clients' liability exposures escalated.

It became critical for us to examine all of our traditional relationships. Were they still valid? What obstacles might
be encountered, for example, by shifting business to other
London brokers? Since certain clients had allegiances to
particular London intermediaries, perhaps only half of our
London premium volume could be easily transferred. To
provide optimum client service, brokers had to control the
ultimate source of their insurance placements—yet only a
Lloyd's broker could place Lloyd's business. Although these
brokers were eminently qualified, a non-Lloyd's broker
such as A&A could never be certain about the information
given to the underwriters. This lack of control became an
increasing source of frustration for "foreign brokerages."

Bill Carter felt strongly about these control issues. As a
result, in December 1973, he, along with Ken Soubry and
John Gray, who was an A&A director and future executive
vice president, initiated merger discussions with the
Matthews Wrightson Group Ltd. (MWG) and with
Alexander Howden Swann (Howden) in London.[2] Both
firms had strengths and weaknesses, as we would soon dis-
cover.

MWG's managing director, E. Gordon Henry, was a marvelous Scot with a keen wit and practical mind. His firm was
highly regarded. It had a sound U.K. retail broking business
and had also made inroads in the Asian market. However, a
major constraint for A&A was MWG's ownership of Stewart

[2] S. G. Warburg, a merchant
banking firm, held a 27
percent interest in MWG and
had a representative at the
meeting with A&A.

Smith (later renamed Stewart Wrightson Holdings plc), a large U.S. surplus lines broker specializing in the aviation field.[3] It also handled a considerable volume of directors' and officers' liability insurance and other coverages. A large share of Stewart Smith's business came from U.S. brokers who could adopt alternative avenues for their placements rather than do business with an A&A subsidiary. There was no solution to the dilemma, even if British insurance and tax complications could be overcome.

[3] A surplus lines broker handles specialized property and casualty coverages not available from licensed insurers.

Howden presented different challenges. Similar in size to MWG, its strength was in reinsurance broking and underwriting. Although reinsurance broking was an A&A priority, more comprehensive international retail broking facilities were an even greater need. Howden had a modest retail network, but it was contemplating an offer for C. E. Heath & Co. Ltd. With Heath's significant retail broking presence as well as its strong Lloyd's broking capability, a Howden and Heath combination was attractive to A&A.

Although neither MWG nor Howden matched the overall appeal of Sedgwick, Howden's disadvantages seemed more manageable. A&A agreed to maintain contact with Ken Grob, Howden's chairman. In 1974, serious acquisition negotiations began at an Arizona hideaway. Detailed information was exchanged and a pro forma analysis providing financial figures for a combined organization was prepared. Major hurdles were identified in accounting, exchange control, and legal and tax issues. To circumvent these problems, a profit sharing arrangement was considered. However, it was discarded when ownership percentages could not be agreed upon. Finally, our only agreement was to establish a small Bermuda joint venture that would facilitate reinsurance business for clients with captive insurance companies.

During 1975, meetings were held with Reed Shaw Osler Ltd. (renamed Reed Stenhouse Companies Ltd. in 1978) in New York, Chicago, London, and Glasgow. Reed Stenhouse's dual strength in Canada and the U.K. had much appeal, but it would be another ten years before an acquisition would be arranged. There was no solution for the Canadian prohibition against U.S. ownership of a Canadi-

Bill Carter, A&A's president and chief executive officer, helped to lead the firm's early efforts to find a British partner. A dynamic personality, he previously ran the Dallas agency of Harris-Moore & Associates which produced many of A&A's leaders.

an insurance broker until the Canadian government altered its position in 1985.

In short, Alexander & Alexander was in a quandary. We wanted a London partner and identified several prospects—each of them attractive in some aspects and unappealing in others. As the merger process unfolded, I was reminded of Dr. Johnson's dictum, "I stopped looking for the perfect wife when I admitted I would not be the perfect husband."

One of the many issues we needed to resolve was the U.K. law precluding foreign brokers from taking more than a 20 percent equity interest in a Lloyd's broker. By 1977, this regulation appeared destined for revision, and visits with potential partners seemed worthwhile. At the end of that year, A&A was placing business with twenty-nine London brokers. This unwieldy situation in part reflected the London relationships of A&A's acquisitions. While Sedgwick remained the primary wholesaler for A&A in the U.K., a number of others also commanded respectable accounts: Howden; C. T. Bowring; Chandler, Hargreaves Whittal;

Hartley Cooper; C. E. Heath; Hogg Robinson; Ropner; and Wigham Poland.

In the fall of 1977, A&A executives visited Sedgwick, Howden, Bland Payne, C. T. Bowring, and Wigham Poland. Contact with Reed Stenhouse also continued. Sedgwick was an obvious choice as a partner, even though most of the closest personal relationships between the two firms had been lost through retirements. Sedgwick was reluctant to consider an exclusive arrangement. It depended on various U.S. sources for business, and those relationships would be jeopardized. Since the early 1930s, Sedgwick had close ties to F. B. Hall and Swett & Crawford, a well-established surplus lines broker. As we shall see, Sedgwick's reluctance to enter into a merger would be challenged by events beyond its control.

Early in 1978, F. B. Hall bid for London broker Leslie & Godwin Limited. Undaunted by Lloyd's threats and restrictions, F. B. Hall purchased Leslie & Godwin in August and placed its Lloyd's broking segment into an independent trust. After F. B. Hall's action, Lloyd's finally acquiesced and other combinations of U.S. and U.K. brokers appeared on the horizon. With that in mind, Bill Carter, Ken Soubry, and I headed to London for talks in September.

We participated in several intense meetings, one with Sedgwick (which had become Sedgwick Forbes Holdings LTD after merging with Price Forbes). Another was with all the senior officers of Howden. Yet another was at an elaborate dinner hosted by eight of C. T. Bowring's most senior executives and their wives. This gracious affair was pulled off without a hint of the following day's announcement that C. T. Bowring and Marsh & McLennan intended to enter into a profit-pooling arrangement.

A luncheon was also held with Chairman Neil Mills and his executive team at Bland Payne. A&A's executive committee was particularly impressed with Mills and his colleagues. We vowed to become better acquainted, and we didn't have to wait long. Events moved rapidly.

Despite Bill Carter's death in October 1978, we returned to England in November for a clandestine three-day conference in an isolated location northeast of London with the top officers of Sedgwick Forbes and Bland Payne. There was exceptional camaraderie; enthusiasm was electric and contagious as plans unfolded.[4] Our potential as a combined organization seemed limitless.

Optimistic about resolving various complex issues, we announced in November 1978 that talks were in progress among the three entities. We hoped and expected to reach an agreement for coordinating our worldwide operations. Our announcement stunned the insurance world, which was still absorbing the disclosure of M&M's pursuit of C. T. Bowring.

Business Insurance reported from London that "the proposed link-up of Alexander & Alexander with merged London brokers Sedgwick Forbes and Bland Payne is the biggest surprise to hit the insurance industry here in two centuries." Endless speculation circulated about the intentions of the world's major insurance brokerages.

The most practical way to begin our U.K. linkage was for Sedgwick and Bland Payne to merge. This goal was met on February 12, 1979, by creating Sedgwick Forbes Bland Payne Ltd. (Sedgwick). The next step proved overwhelmingly complex. Although legal and tax obstacles remained, in December 1980 Sedgwick and A&A announced an agreement in principle to merge. Unfortunately, these legal and tax obstacles eventually proved impossible to overcome, despite the unflagging efforts of top lawyers on both sides. Merger talks were terminated in July 1981.

Meanwhile, other U.S. brokers were moving forward with U.K. mergers. In Marsh & McLennan's case, although it was offered an opportunity in early 1978 to buy Wigham Poland Holdings Limited, it had been seeking a permanent relationship with C. T. Bowring since 1973. However, it was not until mid-1978 that the prospects with C. T. Bowring appeared promising.

Serious negotiations were conducted from June 1978 to May 1979. Despite its strong negotiating position, M&M was frustrated by its failure to arrange a profit-sharing arrangement. Not only did M&M supply about half of C. T.

[4] During short periods of relaxation, the Americans were almost able to hold their own in games of darts. A Sedgwick host became so relaxed in his bath one evening that he dozed off with the taps running and was only discovered when water leaked into the dining room below.

Bowring's U.S. business, it also held a 20 percent interest in C. T. Bowring's competitor, Bland Payne. M&M subsequently sold this interest and, at the end of 1979, made a tender offer. Within C. T. Bowring, the tender was met with considerable resistance, and the matter was not resolved in M&M's favor until May 1980.

Meanwhile, Lloyd's objection to such acquisitions had crumbled during the summer of 1979, and Fred. S. James had gained control of Wigham Poland.

By summer 1981, A&A's frustration and disappointment over its failure to merge with Sedgwick was intense. We urgently needed a U.K. brokerage partner. Our U.S. competitors were creating alignments, and the number of suitable unaffiliated candidates was dwindling. No remaining prospects met the criteria previously established: a strong Lloyd's wholesale staff, an extensive international retail insurance presence, and a competitive reinsurance broking capability. However, Howden came closest.

Howden's history shared many similarities with other major British brokerages. During its early years, insurance broking took a back seat to other endeavors. Howden had a proud history that spanned many decades, and the acquisition of other agencies and brokerages played an important role in its growth.

The founder, Alexander Howden, was born in Leith, the port of Edinburgh, in 1800. His father, a corn merchant, had links to London through the shipping business. As an apprentice in his father's firm, young Howden encountered shipbrokers and insurance brokers—often the same people. At twenty-one, he moved to London and with a partner founded Howden and Balleny, shipbrokers and agents. Intrigued by insurance, the partners became subscribers to Lloyd's in 1823. A year later, they purchased their first ship, *The Competitor*, an above-average-sized sailing vessel of 425 tons plying trade between England and the United States.[5]

Despite setbacks, from 1825 to 1839, the firm, by then known as Howden & Gardner, prospered as shipowners,

[5] On its maiden voyage, a storm forced it into Plymouth, England where the crew deserted and was replaced.

ship agents and brokers—and insurance brokers. Being a shipowner was precarious, as ships of the period were notoriously unsafe.[6] In 1833 alone, more than 800 British vessels sank in storms at sea. Pirates also were a constant menace.

Howden & Gardner experienced a period of consolidation from 1840 to 1865. Alexander Howden Jr. entered the business as a seventeen-year-old clerk in 1842, and two years later, his father became a member of Lloyd's. Insurance was still secondary to various shipping activities, and the firm's vessels began frequent trade with India. In 1861, insurance began to gain in importance, reflecting the requirements of extensive South American trade.

After the senior Alexander Howden died in 1866, the businesses continued to flourish as new trading routes opened. Gavin Ewart in his history of Howden reports that the firm "had an interest in the ships of the new Colonial Line, clippers sailing to Australia. During the '70s, sail began to give way to steam, and Colonial Line steamers set new records for the Australia run. One of them, the *Rotomahana*, was the first ocean steamship ever to be built of steel. At the same time, the second Alexander Howden . . . founded the Union Lighterage Company . . . which by 1905 had a fleet of 370 barges and was associated with the development of 'flat irons'—the shallow-draught steamships designed specially to transport coal. . . ."

Between 1882 and 1890, the firm found success with the Argentine meat trade, which thrived with the improvement of refrigerating plants. Participation in the formation of the International Line led to a contract to carry British emigrants to South Africa.

By 1890, the second Alexander Howden was a leading businessman in the city of London, actively engaged in almost every shipping development. As the deputy chairman of the London Shipping Exchange when it was founded in 1891, he was known as "the father of the shipbrokers." He died in 1901 at age seventy-six.

The founder's grandson, the third and last Alexander Howden (1864–1914), worked with two others (including another Howden, David Alexander Howden) to develop the

[6] Most had wooden hulls that were seldom more than three inches thick, while Royal Navy ships' planking, for example, was fifteen inches thick.

insurance business. Under their management, insurance became as significant as shipping. Old family firms, however, had problems raising capital to buy the new large ships, and limited liability companies replaced them. When David Alexander Howden became senior partner in 1901, the insurance department contributed about 31 percent of the firm's revenues. By 1908, it had increased to 43 percent; and by 1914, after an acquisition of Mackinnon & Co., it reached 64 percent.[7]

After the third Alexander Howden died in 1914, the firm ceased to be a family business. Howden had forty-five employees at the outbreak of World War I. At the time, A&A had eight employees in Clarksburg, West Virginia. In 1914, David Tweddle, who led Howden's nonmarine business, became its first employee to visit the United States. He returned with a few orders, and thus Howden's U.S. reinsurance presence was launched.

Business grew slowly between the world wars. The London office moved to Leigh, in Surrey, during World War II. This proved to be providential when, during the Blitz, fire destroyed the Lime Street office in London. After the war, a London headquarters was reestablished at Bankside House in Leadenhall Street. Slow growth resumed between 1945 and 1960. By 1961, when Howden's stock first became listed on the London Stock Exchange, the staff had increased to 400. The initial market capitalization was £3.5 million, with profits derived primarily from reinsurance broking. As underwriting agents for Lloyd's and other insurers, Howden focused on writing excess-of-loss reinsurance.

With increased visibility as progressive brokers and with a publicly traded stock, acquisitions were a viable option for growth. Underwriting began with a 20 percent share in Sphere Insurance Company in 1963. This was followed by the purchase of Groves, John & Westrup Ltd., insurance brokers and consultants in Liverpool. This firm also acted as specialists in the Scandinavian insurance market. In 1964, two Lloyd's underwriting agents were added: T. L. C. J. Davies and J. Arpel Ltd., which was also a reinsurance specialist in London and continental Europe.

[7] While most of the insurance was marine, Howden became an expert in bloodstock insurance through its Argentinean connections who were importers of Thoroughbreds. The importance of such coverage is illustrated by a very large canceled check displayed on a Buenos Aires client's office wall, which represented the claim settlement on a famous racehorse, Botafogo, who died from swallowing a needle.

Howden's most significant acquisition, Swann & Everett Holdings, Ltd., occurred at the end of 1966. Formed in 1921, its antecedents dated to the late nineteenth century. It was basically a reinsurance broker with a small supporting retail insurance account involving both life and nonlife insurance coverages. Swann & Everett Underwriting Ltd. was formed in 1949, and among its shareholders were its chairman, Kenneth Mark, and a director, Edward Cathie. Two notable additions were Kenneth V. Grob, who had joined Swann & Everett in 1937 at age sixteen, and Jack H. Carpenter, who joined in 1938.

Swann & Everett ran into considerable difficulties in the 1950s. An alleged 1956 scandal resulted in the dismissal of Mark and Cathie as Lloyd's brokers. It seems that a marine underwriter at a major insurance company had opened an account into which only "safe" business was placed. Illegal payments from the account were then given to Mark, Cathie, and the underwriter.[8]

Lloyd's assigned an auditor—from the firm that had investigated them earlier—to supervise Swann & Everett. The supervisor oversaw the operations for eighteen months, arriving every morning and again in the evening to inspect outgoing letters. As senior underwriter, Ken Grob was named the new chairman in 1956. Subsequently, Grob hired Ronald C. Comery in 1956 and Allan J. Page in 1973, both of whom would figure prominently in later developments. With Carpenter, Comery, and Page, Ken Grob had a group in place that would eventually control Swann & Everett and Howden and produce one of Lloyd's most incredible scandals. These four men constituted a rather odd lot. Their responsibilities were individually delineated, but they functioned as a team. As we and the rest of the world would eventually learn, this team played by a private set of rules and in a league of their own.

Ken Grob was suave, smooth, and charismatic. His calm demeanor belied an active and creative mind as well as considerable ambition. He was accustomed to and enjoyed the

[8] Mark also enjoyed a substantial expense account. One of his more "notable" expenses turned out to be his wife's fur coat.

good life. In contrast, Grob's right-hand man, Ron Comery, was the rough-edged son of a policeman. Although large and indifferent to his appearance, Comery embraced the good life as if he had been born to it and took a special interest in horse racing. As bright as Grob, although perhaps not as creative, Comery could expand on Grob's concepts and extend them to remarkable dimensions. Grob could not have devised his various schemes without Comery's input. Additionally, when things began unraveling, Comery was the most unflappable of the group.

Jack Carpenter was a tall, handsome man and another stylish dresser. His debonair appearance contributed to the group's aura, and from Grob he learned to appreciate the high life and to speculate in fine art and Spanish real estate. However, Carpenter lacked leadership skills and was used exclusively to arrange insurance and reinsurance at Grob and Comery's direction. He was primarily an "order taker."

Allan Page, the financial man, had a modest demeanor. He handled the group's accounting and financial arrangements. Upon instructions from Grob and Comery, Page orchestrated intricate methods to cover up the location and ownership of huge amounts of Howden assets. Although intelligent, he probably did not play a significant role in devising these schemes.

Under Grob's management, Swann & Everett prospered and became a highly successful reinsurance broker, in part by pioneering special relationships with state-owned insurance companies behind the Iron Curtain. In 1967, it also established a U.S. presence by purchasing Wohlreich & Anderson, a managing general agent and surplus lines broker. While marine insurance was Swann & Everett's particular expertise, it also promoted nonmarine as well as life and pension business.

Most people considered Howden's acquisition of Swann & Everett in 1967 a "reverse takeover." Grob and Comery's influence as Howden board members was immediately apparent. At Grob's urging, Howden by 1967 had acquired

Symbol of tradition, the fabled "Lutine Bell" hangs today at One Lime Street, headquarters of Lloyd's, the world's most storied insurance market. For over a century the bell was rung to herald announcements— one peal for bad news, two for good. It had been forged for a French frigate that was captured in 1793, then sank six years later flying British colors and with a fortune in bullion aboard, a cargo insured and fully paid by Lloyd's underwriters. The bell was recovered in 1858 and hung in the Underwriting Room. It last rang out the loss of an overdue ship in 1979 and last pealed a safe arrival in 1981. Now it rings to mark memorial occasions—on November 11 for U.K.'s Armistice Day, on September 11 to toll the tragedy of the terrorist attacks on America.

100 percent of the Sphere Insurance Company and 36 percent of the Drake Insurance Company (increased to 100 percent in 1972). Sphere Drake Underwriting was formed to administer the underwriting of these two companies, as well as several others.

In 1970, Ken Grob was elected chairman of Howden. With Swiss and U.K. passports, he was an internationalist at heart. He viewed insurance broking and underwriting as complementary in nature and set about to strengthen both areas simultaneously.

An opportunity arose in 1971 to purchase an interest in I. R. Posgate & Company, which later became a highly visible and successful Lloyd's underwriting agency managed by Ian Posgate. A marine underwriter, Posgate was renowned for successfully underwriting risks shunned by others. Frequently, his judgments and instincts were correct. He made above-average returns for his syndicates, earning notoriety in the media as "Goldfinger." Dignitaries from many walks of life joined his syndicates, and for many years, they were well rewarded.

Posgate undoubtedly was the most controversial figure in Lloyd's history, a man of many contrasts. Of average appearance, he was often seen with papers bulging from his pockets. He could be exceedingly charming, cooperative, and helpful when it served him. He was also flamboyant, with a quick and often acid wit. He taunted and mocked his perceived adversaries, but his bluster masked personal insecurities.

Posgate could be his own worst enemy. He was an unusually able and imaginative man with undeniable charisma. With his intelligence and verve, he might well have become a brilliant leader at Lloyd's, perhaps even its chairman. Instead, he opted for the role of iconoclast and gadfly, never far removed from controversy. Posgate was totally self-absorbed, and his insatiable craving for the limelight, along with his striking underwriting successes and personal anomalies, made him an international media celebrity. Unfortunately, he ended up squandering talent that few possessed.

In retrospect, hints of eccentric personality traits and trouble ahead were evident by 1970. Posgate had let stand the general perception that he was a Cambridge University graduate and Army officer. But a *Barron's* article reported that officials at Cambridge's Gonville and Caius College said Posgate had withdrawn from Cambridge after one year, and the Army could not confirm that he was ever an officer. He joined Lloyd's in 1953 and became an underwriting member in 1957 while employed by the F. C. Davey syndicate. He was appointed its underwriter in 1963. That same year, he formed I. R. Posgate Agencies Ltd. to manage a marine and incidental nonmarine syndicate.

In 1970, amid indications that he was exceeding Lloyd's prescribed underwriting limits, the Committee of Lloyd's requested an outside audit of Posgate's books. This revealed premium overwriting, incorrect reporting of premium income, undisclosed reinsurance with a Bermuda company he controlled, and use of syndicate funds for a personal interest-free loan to purchase a house.[9]

Posgate was "posted" by Lloyd's in 1970, indicating to the market that he was guilty of serious transgressions. The Committee also barred him from serving as a director or shareholder of any company acting as a Lloyd's underwriting agent. Further, his underwriting was limited to acting for a single Lloyd's-approved agent. How ironic that when Ken Grob purchased Posgate's agency, Lloyd's sanctioned the sale with the understanding that Grob would oversee Posgate's conduct.

Over a four-year period, Posgate did well and the investors in his syndicates (i.e., Names) grew to over 500. He consistently overwrote his premium limits, however, which put him increasingly at odds with the Lloyd's establishment, including the chairman. His caustic tongue often exacerbated a fragile situation, and Grob did not effectively supervise him. Grob was called before the Lloyd's Committee in late 1974 and threatened with Howden's delisting as an owner of approved underwriting agencies unless Posgate stayed within premium underwriting limits.

Subsequently a love-hate relationship developed between Grob and Posgate. Although Posgate was impossible to manage, he provided an increasingly vital source of Howden's business and profits. Grob temporarily solved the problem by hiring Leonard Hart, a Halford, Shead (Holdings) Limited agency underwriter, to keep track of Posgate's underwriting volume and report back on a frequent basis. This solution worked effectively until Hart became ill in 1981.

In 1971, Posgate was given a very favorable five-year contract by Howden. His annual salary was set at £100 for every different Name in each Lloyd's syndicate for which he was the underwriter. His contract was ultimately extended for two five-year terms. At his peak, before Howden's acquisition by A&A, he underwrote for more than 6,000 Names

[9] This and other excesses were subsequently documented in a 1990 report from Britain's Department of Trade and Industry.

(including those who were in more than one Posgate syndicate), and he was responsible for some 7.5 percent of
Lloyd's total business.

Posgate's income was considered among the top earned
incomes in Britain. This did not go unnoticed by Howden's
competitors. In 1977, Posgate was wooed by the underwriting agency of Willis Faber and almost moved there. The
Committee of Lloyd's refused to permit him to go, but they
did allow him to assume a 35 percent interest in a new
agency, Posgate & Denby (Agencies) Ltd., which would
underwrite a similar albeit smaller line than his Howden
syndicates.

Posgate was appointed to Howden's board in February
1978. His heightened visibility attracted ever more Names
to his syndicates, including figures from the entertainment
world, politics, and sports. His "Goldfinger" nickname
added a certain allure and mystique. Much of his success as
an underwriter came from writing business that other
underwriters avoided. Posgate was at his best during periods of war-threat crises, first undercutting war risk premiums and then raising them as competitors withdrew from
the market. He also profited handsomely from kidnap and
ransom insurance.

By 1972, the Howden firm, led by Ken Grob, was moving
aggressively. Grob took a one-third ownership position in
The Manor Insurance Company Limited (The Manor), the
Bermuda-based subsidiary of the Sentry Insurance Company. Sentry was headquartered in Wisconsin, and Grob was
anxious to establish Howden roots in the United States.

In 1973, reinsurance broking accounted for 37 percent of
profit. The staff was roaming the world, making 386 trips to
seventy-three countries. In addition to establishing strong
Russian and Polish relationships, Howden had reinsurance
accounts in France, Italy, Norway, Switzerland, Israel, and
Latin America.

The acquisition of the Sterling Offices' reinsurance
broking business in 1974 opened important links to Aus-

tralia and Canada, as well as adding 140 employees to Howden's London reinsurance group. In 1975, Howden and Sentry concluded an arrangement, with Sentry becoming the sole owner of The Manor in return for Howden becoming owner of the Banque du Rhône et de la Tamise S.A. (Banque du Rhône) in Geneva and The Manor's insurance and reinsurance brokerage operations in Australia and the Far East. Along with Sterling Offices' Australian business, Howden now had a sound foothold in that area.

Howden continued to target the United States as the principal area for future growth. Both Wohlreich & Anderson and its underwriting operation were expanding. By the end of the 1970s, Howden had majority interests in three U.S. insurers, the primary one being the Atlanta International Insurance Inc. (formerly the Drake Insurance Company), in which it held approximately 90 percent ownership. Also, Bermuda insurer subsidiaries were established in 1974–75. In January 1978, Howden acquired South Eastern Aviation Underwriters Inc. (S.E.A.U.), a U.S. underwriting agency and surplus lines broker. S.E.A.U. controlled a substantial segment of aviation insurance premiums as well as a growing volume of nonmarine business. Howden was S.E.A.U.'s principal Lloyd's broker, and the relationship between the organizations was very close.

Howden's retail insurance effort was bolstered in 1976 by the purchase of two old-line and respected British brokerages: Morice, Tozer and Beck (Holdings) Limited and Halford, Shead (Holdings) Limited. A&A was particularly attracted to Howden's growing emphasis on retail broking. However, Howden's jewel was its reinsurance broking operation, which enjoyed worldwide respect. The managing agency business was sound, serving fifteen syndicates involving over 4,000 individual members of Lloyd's, but would soon have to be divested. The Lloyd's broking capability, while competent, required bolstering.

In 1981, Lloyd's viewed Howden's management as nonconformist and eccentric. The managers were far removed from Lloyd's inner circle, a circumstance A&A had to accept. It also had to reconcile its insurance underwriting, an activity in which A&A had no interest. Ken Grob downplayed Howden's underwriting position by emphasizing how little risk its insurance companies retained. There was no apparent reason to doubt him. A&A and Howden's relationship had always been excellent. Nothing untoward had ever surfaced, nor had questionable evidence appeared during the due diligence process.

Inexorably, A&A's acquisition of Howden made it more intimately involved with Lloyd's. The new relationships would decisively affect our future. As we shall see, Lloyd's impending crisis would bring that venerable if flawed institution to the brink of collapse and threaten worldwide insurance industry stability.

CHAPTER 16

Chicanery and Conflict: The Howden Affair

Serious problems surfaced almost immediately after Alexander and Alexander acquired Howden in January 1982. Even then, no one anticipated that the merger would eventually cost A&A hundreds of millions of dollars over a period of ten years and consume thousands of hours of executive management time every quarter for years. Questions arose, with hindsight, about why A&A had not carried out a full audit in England before the acquisition. Yet, even if A&A had pressed for such disclosures, the rules of the U.K. Stock Exchange would not have permitted audit findings to be given to A&A as a potential buyer.[1]

Some aspects of the "Howden Affair" remain enigmatic and shielded by the deaths of its principal perpetrators. However, most of the story is known, and although my perspective is inevitably subjective, I believe the events may be pieced together with a high degree of certainty.

At the time that A&A acquired Howden, seven employees held key positions. Ian Posgate was the most highly visible, albeit controversial, underwriter at Lloyd's. Michael Glover, an aviation brokerage specialist, had been appointed Howden's CEO the previous September, although he had little of a CEO's conventional authority. Ron Iles chaired the brokerage operations and was a top reinsurance specialist. The real management of Howden resided in four men who constituted an informal executive committee.

[1] As it was, A&A did recover $24 million from auditors who failed to identify improper financial dealings.

213

Ken Grob was chairman; he and Ron Comery called all the shots. Their instructions were implemented by Allan Page, as chief financial officer, and Jack Carpenter, overseer of the in-house insurance companies. These four men would shortly become known in the media as "the Gang of Four," or just "The Four."

Within three weeks of the acquisition, A&A received news of a large insurance claim submitted on behalf of a Posgate syndicate to Howden's Sphere Drake (Underwriting) Limited. A&A was surprised by the absence of sufficient reinsurance protection. Ken Grob and his associates offered lame explanations. Grob maintained that Posgate had assured him of the profitability of that business.

A&A subsequently requested its auditors, Deloitte Haskins & Sells (Deloitte), to perform a fair value audit of Howden. Its purpose was to allocate the purchase price to the tangible net assets acquired, a fairly routine exercise after acquiring a publicly-owned company. Deloitte also reviewed Howden's previous auditor's work and examined the adequacy of its insurance subsidiaries' funds. Almost from the start, Deloitte was frustrated by various obstacles. The Four evaded direct questions, and delayed their responses to requests for the previous auditor's working papers.

Despite no definitive evidence of dishonesty, A&A's concerns mounted. As uncooperativeness bordered on stonewalling, our suspicions increased. We were particularly frustrated by an inability to learn details about a purported Panamanian insurance company that was being used to reinsure Howden-owned insurance companies and Posgate's syndicates. A Deloitte investigation revealed the Southern International RE Company S.A.—or "SIR," as it was commonly called—was not licensed for reinsurance. Rather, it was incorporated to trade in goods, real estate, and other merchandise.

During May and June of 1982, Deloitte and the A&A financial staff worked virtually around the clock to unravel the growing number of perplexing questions and dead-end trails. New entities were identified in Howden's records. Some were obviously companies; others were referenced by code words such as "Bloomers," "Blissful," "Karoli," and "Skyair." The Gang of Four claimed to be mystified by these codes—which subsequently were shown to stand for themselves.

The Four insisted that SIR was a bona fide insurance company owned by a Swiss syndicate whose identity was protected under Swiss banking laws. A letter from Howden's Banque du Rhône declared that no Howden employees were owners of SIR.

By July, although there was no absolute proof of malfeasance on anyone's part, aggressive action had to be taken. On July 9, Ken Soubry and I met Ken Grob in his London home. We gave him one last opportunity to answer the many pressing questions. He refused. We then told him to instruct Carpenter, Page, and another Howden employee to leave their offices immediately, taking only personal belongings. They left after their briefcases were searched and considerable Howden-related materials removed. The newly acquired documents heightened suspicions, and the audit committee of A&A's board of directors assumed control of the investigation. Ken Grob resigned from A&A's board on July 21.

On July 27, we publicly announced that A&A was reviewing Howden's accounting practices and business transactions prior to the January 1982 acquisition. On August 6, The Four agreed to full disclosure. Documents were turned over that clarified the ownership of various Panamanian companies as well as Liechtenstein trusts and settlements. With new information, our accountants quantified a $35 million impairment to A&A's balance sheet.

We then attempted to hold the Gang of Four accountable for the deficits. As loathsome as making a deal with the culprits might seem, it represented a one-time chance to recoup Howden funds that had been diverted for The Four's personal benefit. Although questioned by some, it was clearly in the interests of A&A's stockholders to seek restitution. An agreement was signed in the wee hours of August 14. A&A was to receive $26 million in cash, stock, real estate, and works of art.

From August 17 to the end of the month, new information revealed additional liabilities. Moreover, the value of some assets turned over by The Four was less than represented. Thus, we abrogated the August 14 agreement. On August 24, Grob and Page resigned from Howden's board. On August 25, I assumed chairmanship; and on August 31, we sent dismissal notices to Grob, Comery, Page, and Carpenter.

On September 1, we announced that assets received from the Gang of Four were lower than expected. We also reported on Howden reinsurance transactions with companies owned and controlled by four persons no longer employed, and that Sphere Drake's insurance reserve required a $25 million infusion. We declared that we would honor the obligations of Sphere Drake and other Howden insurance companies. This announcement brought great relief to Lloyd's; a number of working members had feared that A&A might walk away from its Howden obligations.

We soon learned that Posgate was one of the owners of the Banque du Rhône, which had been purchased from Howden with Posgate syndicate funds. Posgate hotly denied these allegations. Although we had suspicions about Posgate's involvement, we had no proof. However, there were bizarre incidents in that connection. For example, private investigators spotted a fire on Posgate's residential property late one rainy night. Papers were being burned, but their contents could never be determined.

In the early weeks of the "Howden Affair," Posgate was something of a Jekyll and Hyde. He appeared friendly and helpful for an extended period, then suddenly repudiated earlier positive actions and comments. Because of the bad blood between them, it seemed possible that Grob had falsely implicated Posgate. In addition to Posgate's huge Sphere Drake claim, which he had wrongly assured Grob would be profitable business, Posgate infuriated Grob in other ways. Back in 1981, he had told an A&A executive that we should make a bid for Howden and that he (Posgate) and Michael Glover would run it for A&A.

Perhaps most egregious to Grob were Posgate's machinations during the debate in Parliament over insurance brokerage divestitures of managing agencies. At issue was a potential conflict of interest. Since Howden's managing agencies were very profitable, Grob and Comery spent considerable time and money working aggressively against divestiture, while Posgate ardently supported it. He claimed his position was based on principle. Grob was certain that Posgate wanted to run his own underwriting agency at a bargain price. Posgate's comments received prominent media attention, which enraged Grob and other Howden senior executives. The relationship between the two men was never the same.

For his part, Posgate was angry with Grob for excluding him from acquisition negotiations with Alexander & Alexander. Although not involved in Howden's day-to-day management, Posgate felt that he should have been included in merger discussions.

Most of Posgate's peers acknowledged his intellect, but they were unimpressed with him as an individual. A 1982 *Barron's* interview with Paul Dixey, a former Lloyd's chairman, reflected many working members' opinion. Dixey observed, "[Posgate] may be a man of courage, single-minded and completely self-reliant. He has a wonderful memory and terrific head for figures. But I would say that he has a complete lack of moral scruples." Dixey added, "I think he is a ruthless bully who has constantly and deliberately broken the rules."

Dixey also commented on Posgate's election to the Committee of Lloyd's by a narrow margin in January 1982. Posgate had received considerable support from external Names who were demonstrating a newly found independence. Dixey noted, "Very often rogue elephants have been tamed to responsibility. It's not unknown for a poacher to become a successful gamekeeper. I think many people voted for Mr. Posgate because they felt putting him on the Committee might make him responsible. I think they were wrong. . . . I don't think it's a good idea to put someone who's had trouble with the choirboys in charge of the boy scouts."

Not surprisingly, Posgate returned such sentiments. He stoked the fire, referring to the majority of underwriters as "paid clerks." He told *The Guardian*, "I've taken a lot of underwriting business deliberately. I believe in the survival of the fittest." He added, "Most underwriters here are cowardly, cosseted and cozy and there is an establishment Mafia that doesn't like me." The media welcomed controversial copy and prominently reported his comments.

As late as early September, Posgate continued to put up a brave front. He said A&A could have any share he might unknowingly own in Banque du Rhône. Unfortunately, he was bluffing. By mid-September, an A&A representative had irrefutable proof in Posgate's own hand that he was fully aware of his bank connection and had journeyed to Geneva to collect dividends.

By September 20, 1982, A&A had sufficient factual information to terminate Posgate as a director and underwriter of its managing agency, Alexander Howden Underwriting Limited (AHUL). Lloyd's chairman, Peter Green, had been kept abreast of events. The Committee of Lloyd's also required that Posgate be suspended from AHUL and his own Posgate & Denby (Agencies) Ltd. In September, A&A's board began legal action against Grob, Comery, Page, and Carpenter based on breach of fiduciary duty, misrepresentation, and breach of the settlement agreement. Posgate was included for breach of fiduciary duty and misrepresentation.

Posgate was accused but found not guilty by Lloyd's Disciplinary Committee of misappropriating funds, plundering a reinsurance company for his own benefit, and falsifying group accounts. However, the Committee found him guilty of accepting a Pissarro painting to influence his underwriting and not declaring his Banque du Rhône stake. It recommended his expulsion from Lloyd's for life. Subsequently, the appeals judge, the Right Honorable Lord Wilberforce, overturned the verdict. He found that the Committee of Lloyd's was not empowered to effect the suspension. However, through a series of five- or six-month suspensions, Lloyd's was able to continue to bar Posgate from both underwriting and as a Committee of Lloyd's member. These administrative suspensions were issued by a Council of Lloyd's subcommittee and extended through 1984.

Along the way, Posgate received a severe reprimand and censure from the Disciplinary Committee on another matter related to Lloyd's broker Wigham Poland. At the end of 1984, the Disciplinary Committee gave Posgate a six-month suspension from Lloyd's on one count and expulsion on another (the Banque du Rhône). This was appealed in February 1985 and overturned in May by the Appeal Tribunal, which confirmed another six-month suspension and expulsion from Lloyd's. The Council declared the expulsion on July 8, 1985.

In October 1985, R. L. Glover & Co. (Underwriting Agents) Ltd. applied to become managing agents and proposed Ian Posgate as a director and underwriter. The Council of Lloyd's refused the application in February 1986 because Posgate "was not a fit and proper person" to be a director and/or underwriter of a managing agency. Posgate appealed this ruling to the Appeal Tribunal. On July 9, Lord Wilberforce issued a decision that the tribunal could not find reason to overrule the Council's decision and therefore dismissed the appeal. This was Posgate's swan song in his efforts to be reaccepted at Lloyd's.

How did Grob, Comery, Carpenter, and Page pull off such massive chicanery? Essentially, they used overseas personal accounts to divert funds for private use. In the late 1960s, Grob and Comery first established numbered accounts as repositories for personal assets. By parking funds outside Britain, they avoided some British income taxes. Subsequently, The Four each formed an *anstalt* to hold overseas assets.[2] Then Grob and Comery secretly traded Howden shares. This enabled them to fund Carpenter and Page's *anstalts*. During 1979, four Liechtenstein *settlements* replaced the *anstalts*, which allowed the beneficiaries greater flexibility in using the funds.[3]

[2] An *anstalt* was a legal Liechtenstein entity with some of the characteristics of a trust in British law. One could use it to conceal ownership, and there was no tax on income.

[3] A *settlement* was similar to a trust but less costly to maintain.

From 1975 to 1979, The Four formed an exclusive management group, which set them apart from other Howden directors. During 1975–76, they formed two Liechtenstein overseas companies owned equally by their *anstalts*. Southern Reinsurance A.G. (SRAG) was nominally a reinsurance company. The Four centralized funds in this company and then dispersed them for various purposes.[4] For example, payments were made to certain Howden executives and key employees, presumably to buy loyalty when competition for personnel was high. Of course, The Four took good care of themselves. They used *anstalt* withdrawals to collect art and real estate. Grob bought a large villa overlooking the Mediterranean in southern France. By the end of 1979, they also sought to manipulate Howden's profits through companies they owned or controlled.

Secrecy was paramount in facilitating The Four's schemes. In addition to SRAG, three companies—S.N.A. Re (Bermuda) Limited (SNA), New Southern Reinsurance Company, S.A. (NSR), and SIR—were used to hide their activities.

Howden owned about 20 percent of SNA and was authorized to underwrite policies for which SNA acted merely as a fronting reinsurer. The Four transferred premiums from such policies to Banque du Rhône accounts they controlled. Other SNA shareholders were unaware of this practice.

NSR was formed in late 1979; it was an illegally registered Panamanian company that was not authorized as an insurer. Its purpose was to acquire a 51 percent interest in Banque du Rhône on behalf of a syndicate set up by Grob. The Four, plus Posgate and the two top Banque du Rhône officials, each held 10 percent of NSR; employees, friends, and business associates of Grob held the other 30 percent. Except for this 30 percent, funds to purchase the Banque du Rhône came from Howden syndicates. The first installment of funds to purchase the remaining 49 percent came from a Banque Paribas loan on normal commercial terms. These transactions involving five Howden directors required disclosure to the full Howden board, but disclosure was not

[4] Zepher Reinsurance Brokers Limited S.A. was the second company established for transferring funds.

made. A&A's acquisition of Howden led to our obtaining the 84 percent interest in the Banque du Rhône controlled by The Four, and that interest was subsequently sold.

In March 1980, The Four established SIR to support SRAG. From April, SIR was the principal vehicle through which Howden's results were distorted. Bogus reinsurance was used to cover up Howden's underwriting losses. By August 1982, SIR had a $56 million deficit.

Funds used to perpetrate the machinations came from various sources. Howden supplied some as "contingency premiums." These were intended to cover "unforeseen problems." Profit-stripping policies were used to take credit for anticipated profits on policies whose results would not be known until a future date. Such profits never materialized. Considerable cash flow was generated by reinsuring Posgate syndicates through the "Southern companies."

The Department of Trade and Industry (DTI) estimated in a 1990 report that The Four had transferred $7 million to their individually controlled *anstalts* and personal companies. In addition, The Four and others acquired their interest in Banque du Rhône using more than $7 million of Lloyd's syndicate funds.

Like scribes in Dickens' novels, clerks at Lloyd's in the early 20th century write entries by hand in "casualty books" to record specifics of ships lost or damaged around the world. Financial losses would escalate in the decades ahead. By the late 1970s calamitous marine disasters such as the wreck of the Amoco Cadiz *and the explosion of the oil tanker* Betelgeuse *would cost underwriters, many of them at Lloyd's, billions of dollars.*

With the possible exception of A&A's internal research, the DTI's report was by far the most extensive investigation of the "Howden Affair." Its investigation commenced in November 1982 and covered every aspect of the affair. It was completed in late 1985 but not released until 1990 so that it would not interfere with a criminal case and other ongoing investigations. Although the time lag seemed appropriate to authorities, it delayed the Crown's criminal case against Posgate and Grob and quite likely affected the result.

The DTI report was widely considered thorough and objective. Significantly, it stated that key elements of Posgate's testimony were thought not to be true. For example, on the matter of the funding source for the Banque du Rhône purchase from Howden, the report observed:

> . . . When taken together with Posgate's evidence about an interest-free loan from the Banque (which is unsupported either by documentation or by the evidence of other witnesses) . . . [this] leads us on balance to conclude that Posgate knew about the sources of funds, which were used to acquire the Banque; namely his syndicates quota shares. . . . We have formed the opinion that Posgate did know where the money came from.

Referring again to the Banque du Rhône purchase, the report notes: "The Four and Posgate, knowing their responsibilities, failed to disclose their interests in the transaction to either the Howden board or to shareholders." In what amounted to a summary statement, DTI opined:

> When a number of intelligent and ingenious individuals in the most senior positions, but bereft of commercial morality and intent on personal gain, set out to rob and deceive, it is extremely difficult to ensure that they will be deterred or exposed before too much damage is caused.

After "How?" the question most frequently posed regarding the Gang of Four is "Why?" Why would four men, three with superior intellect, perpetrate the greatest scandal in Lloyd's 300-year history? The question is especially perplexing because they were capable of rewarding and legitimate brokerage careers.

I believe they were initially seeking to avoid taxes and circumvent exchange control. To these illegal activities they added unreported dealing in Howden shares. They believed they could beat the "inconveniences" imposed by legal authorities. No doubt greed was also a factor. Except for Grob, they came from modest backgrounds, and the prospect of great riches must have been extremely appealing. None of them, not even Grob, could have enjoyed such grand lifestyles without the ill-gotten gains.

Grob's appreciation of the good life became the norm for all four. His love of art also rubbed off, and the others purchased paintings by celebrated French artists. Real estate in exotic locations was also an attraction. They all enjoyed the horse races, and at least one bet heavily. Grand restaurants were always the order of the day, and, even in their offices, they served the finest champagne in silver goblets.

I also believe the insurance schemes emerged, in part, because Grob and Comery felt intellectually superior to the Lloyd's establishment. Outwitting Lloyd's was a challenge and eventually a game. They also had a cash cow in Posgate, whose syndicates generated an ever greater premium flow. Their most aggressive initiatives probably developed when initial plans met insurmountable obstacles. For a while, they believed that profits, mainly generated by Posgate, would enable them to pay back money diverted for personal use. About the time A&A acquired Howden, they realized that their schemes were doomed as anticipated profits failed to materialize. Their collective brilliance was put to the ultimate test as they worked to cover their tracks.

Perpetrators of alleged fraud on so grand a scale may revel in feelings of power and invulnerability, but they usually have a fatal flaw. In The Four's case, it proved to be the formation of SIR in Panama without a license to write reinsurance, an egregious error that remains an enigma. It is my belief that after a planned retirement in 1982, The Four intended to leave England permanently to avoid prosecution.

Unquestionably Grob, Comery, and Page were willing conspirators in all phases of the plans. Carpenter's understanding of the big picture is unclear. He was caught in a whirlpool and in over his head, but he was a willing participant. As the last living member of The Four, Carpenter apparently withdrew from society and lived as a recluse.

During the accountants' investigation of Howden, they discovered that two well-known Lloyd's members, Peter Cameron-Webb and Peter Dixon of PCW Underwriting Agencies, operated a scheme that was in many ways similar to Howden's. Indeed, Howden insurance companies were among the entities used to facilitate their activities. By mid-September 1982, Deloitte presented evidence of wrongdoing to Lloyd's. By the end of October, A&A gave the Lloyd's chairman further details, prompting an investigation.

This scandal rivaled Howden in its sordidness. In 1968, Cameron-Webb and Dixon had founded a Lloyd's managing agency, PCW, as the chairman and managing director, respectively. In 1974, another managing agency, WMD, was formed under common administrative supervision with PCW. Over the years, PCW prospered and became one of Lloyd's largest and most highly visible agencies. Peter Cameron-Webb was considered among Lloyd's most talented underwriters.

From 1970 to 1982, many brokers placed PCW reinsurances. Howden and Housley Heath & Company Limited were used most extensively, but the list also included Sedgwick. More than 150 companies and trusts in various overseas locations played some role in handling nearly £40 million of premiums from PCW-managed Lloyd's syndicates. Almost all of these overseas entities were controlled by or associated with Cameron-Webb and Dixon. In excess of £25 million was stashed—primarily in Gibraltar, as well as in Guernsey, Isle of Man, and Switzerland.

Seven others were illegal beneficiaries of syndicate funds. Most were PCW syndicate underwriters, but John Wallrock, chairman of the large British broker J. H. Minet (Minet), was also involved. Cameron-Webb and Dixon each received many millions of dollars, which they invested in such properties as the Banque du Rhône; a French orange juice company; U.S. oil, gas, and bloodstock syndicates; and even a pornographic film. As with the "Howden Affair," schemes were intricate, with money passing through multiple entities so that it could not be traced to its origin.

Lloyd's Disciplinary Committee ultimately punished the scheme's perpetrators. Peter Dixon was found guilty on six of eight charges, expelled from Lloyd's, fined £1 million, and required to pay court costs. The committee reported:

> Mr. Dixon together with Mr. Cameron-Webb was the brains behind most if not all of the off-shore reinsurance schemes . . . we are absolutely sure that Mr. Dixon is a clever, dishonest, greedy and unscrupulous individual who for a period of over ten years conducted the affairs of PCW and subsequently WMD in a manner which represents a complete negation of those standards of professional honesty, good faith and rectitude upon which the world-wide reputation of Lloyd's and through Lloyd's of the whole of the London insurance market has been founded for over two hundred and fifty years. No other dealings at Lloyd's of which we are aware—including those which have come to light since late 1982—equal in the magnitude of the sums misappropriated through the depredations of Mr. Dixon and Mr. Cameron-Webb. Their conduct represents a disgrace to the London insurance market.

Cameron-Webb resigned from Lloyd's early in 1982 and therefore escaped the Disciplinary Committee's jurisdiction. He and Dixon moved to the United States. Then, unbelievably, for a time Cameron-Webb participated as a marine underwriter in launching the Florida Insurance Exchange. Other defendants also were found guilty and received penalties ranging from reprimand and notice of censure to expulsion from Lloyd's.

In June 1984, A&A and Minet made a joint offer to the Names. When added to funds recovered in Gibraltar, this would restore the approximately £40 million in diverted syndicate funds. The offer was accepted by more than 1,500 Names representing virtually all of those affected. Releases by the Names were a settlement condition.

Other problems soon arose, compounding the damage of these schemes. Huge nonmarine losses, projected to reach £700 million gross and £235 million net, were forecast for PCW Names. Those affected were outraged; many faced financial ruin and personal bankruptcy. Lloyd's and other entities were threatened with lawsuits. Lloyd's set out to preside over a "market solution," which took until June 1987 to arrange.

The settlement offer to the Names was £137 million; £48 million would come from Lloyd's Central Fund, which contained more than £300 million to protect the interests of Lloyd's policyholders. The 1,537 Names most affected were called on to pay £34 million. The remaining £55 million was allocated among several sources, including insurance brokers, members' agencies, accountants, and a law firm. A&A, while maintaining it was free of any liability, contributed. The twenty-four Names who refused the offer included some of the wealthiest. Eventually they negotiated individual settlements.

Lloyd's chairman, Peter Miller, summing up the widespread feeling about the "PCW Affair," said that it was "one of the most shameful episodes in the history of Lloyd's." The final negotiation would never have occurred without Miller's herculean efforts in bringing all participants to the table. It was the chairman's finest hour.

American A&A employees working in London also played key roles. They provided essential information and invaluable counsel to Miller. Three men stood out: Daniel Osterhout, A&A's chief negotiator; Richard Page, Howden's CEO; and Ronald Berardi, Howden's treasurer. These individuals worked tirelessly and were indispensable to a successful resolution.

This should have ended a most sordid chapter in A&A's proud and productive association with Lloyd's of London. Unfortunately, this was not to be.

In 1984, the Securities and Exchange Commission initiated an inquiry into the timeliness and accuracy of A&A's

disclosures during the first phases of the Howden scandal. Accounting issues also were raised. Although A&A had worked meticulously with accountants and lawyers to conform with all legal and regulatory requirements, the complexities involved here led to extra SEC scrutiny.

Though we felt we had performed in accordance with the spirit and the letter of the law, we were compelled to marshal top managers and outside legal counsel in order to defend ourselves. Thousands of executive hours and millions of dollars in legal expenses were consumed. This inquiry became more costly in terms of management focus than any other aspect of the Howden matter. Given the severity of possible charges and their ramifications, we had to take the SEC's advisory very seriously—though we believed it was incorrect. In 1987, we were exonerated when the SEC notified A&A that it had completed a three-year probe and found no cause for further action.

In addition to the time loss and financial burden brought on by this investigation, A&A had to contend with the financial impact of one Howden-related disaster after another. Steady deterioration of Howden insurance companies' reserves was a primary problem, and it soon became apparent that it was a problem without a viable remedy.

CHAPTER 17

Earlier Troubles at Lloyd's: A Long Unraveling

To better understand the devastating turn of events that afflicted A&A and its shareholders, we must reflect back on Lloyd's earlier history. Lloyd's was well known internationally and enjoyed a sound reputation for much of the twentieth century. But, as the world discovered in the 1960s, the Society of Lloyd's had problems.

Part of Lloyd's historic mystique—and its Achilles' heel—involved its unique organizational structure based on its underwriting members, i.e., Names, and the system that had evolved around this distinct class of investors. Every Name enjoyed near anonymity while participating in a traditionally highly profitable enterprise; and every Name accepted unlimited liability—repeat *unlimited liability*—in each syndicate that he or she joined.

Almost all Names had a members' agent responsible for their Lloyd's affairs. As the representative of numerous Names, the members' agent placed its clients in various syndicates, very much as a mutual fund manager invests the shareholders' pooled investment in appropriate stocks. In addition, each Name had a managing agent who was responsible for a syndicate's underwriting and handled its operational affairs. The managing agency and the members' agency were often under the same ownership.[1]

[1] Names paid an annual fee to each syndicate they joined, along with a commission on any profit the syndicate earned. Those contributions were divided on a prearranged basis between the two agencies.

When A&A acquired Howden in 1982, its managing agency had twelve underwriters writing for fifteen syndicates with more than 4,000 individual Names participating. Howden believed that it was Lloyd's largest managing agency in terms of underwriting capacity.

Lloyd's system of accounting is on a three-year basis, meaning that an account is normally held open for three years. This allows time for premiums to be received and for claims and expenses to be settled for the relevant years. Typically, outstanding liabilities are then reinsured into a subsequent account for an appropriate premium so that profit or loss can be determined. New Names inherit liabilities with respect to business written before their memberships commenced.

Lloyd's series of crises actually began in the United States in 1965 with Hurricane Betsy, which wreaked havoc on oil rigs and vessels in the Gulf of Mexico. For the first time in decades, the battering caused by Betsy and other hurricanes caused Lloyd's underwriters to lose money for three consecutive years, from the year before Betsy through 1966.

Although the average loss was modest, it caused a reduction in the number of members for 1966–67. Shock waves rippled through the market. Simultaneously, the value of oil refineries and oil rigs was skyrocketing. More underwriting capacity, not less, was needed for Lloyd's to sustain its competitive position.

Lord Cromer, a former governor of the Bank of England, led a study group to examine the problem. Recommendations were implemented, including a lowered "minimum wealth standard" for becoming a Name. It was reduced from £75,000 to £50,000, but subsequently increased to £100,000 in 1979. Another change opened membership to women and foreigners.[2] Changes in eligibility for Lloyd's membership, together with a period of favorable underwriting results, spawned dramatic membership growth during the 1970s.

The number of Names almost doubled between 1974

[2] When the first three female brokers, sent by Alexander Howden Swann, entered Lloyd's room, they were egregiously and promptly dubbed "Howden's Hookers."

and 1978. When the decade ended, Lloyd's had nearly 17,000 members. In part, the push for new Names reflected that some underwriters had overwritten their premium limits in 1976. Unfortunately, many Names joined just in time for a terrible year in 1978. The newcomers represented a broad cross section of the population, rather than the traditional moneyed elite. They ranged from business professionals to sports and entertainment celebrities. Others had very limited means, and they met the membership test through bank guarantees based on modest homes. These people were in over their heads and should not have been allowed to become Names.

Although this flood of cash temporarily solved Lloyd's need for new capital, it also sowed the seeds of an eventual revolution. While the old Names were far more complacent and unquestioning, many new Names were more demanding. They were skeptical of the superficial information Lloyd's gave about their investment. Managing agencies argued that more detailed advice would only confuse the new Names. Such tactics guaranteed that the situation would escalate from confrontation to open revolt.

During the 1960s and 1970s, while Lloyd's underwriting capacity was expanding rapidly, the U.S. judicial system was undergoing a major transformation. With courts more often rendering idiosyncratic interpretations of tort law, contract principles became less relevant. This resulted in an avalanche of rulings that held insurers responsible for consequences they often had never intended to insure. Asbestosis, environmental pollution, professional malpractice, and product liability produced billions of dollars of losses.

The culpability of underwriters in general and Lloyd's in particular has been widely debated. It is a very complex issue, and many insurance experts have contended that the role of underwriting misjudgment is exaggerated. However, little doubt exists that inept underwriting did occur, notably from 1974 until 1977. Some underwriters failed to stay abreast of rapidly changing global technology.

An especially noteworthy transaction involved more

than fifty Lloyd's underwriters of computer leases. Underwriters offered insurance for rental income losses in cases where computer leases were canceled as they became obsolete. IBM was the dominant computer manufacturer at the time, but leasing companies were undercutting IBM's rental pricing. These companies required insurance to secure bank loans. The largest of these was Itel.

Lloyd's underwriters wrote a number of leasing policies during 1974. They tightened policy conditions and then wrote many additional policies in 1976 and 1977. Approximately 14,000 separate computer risks were underwritten for seventeen insureds. All but two were for American firms. Coverage was for potential claims exceeding $1 billion. During the spring of 1977, IBM introduced a more cost-effective, top-of-the-line computer with significant improvements. This did not deter underwriters, because most machines they covered were smaller and performed more routine functions.

The underwriters' complacency was short-lived. In the fall of 1977, IBM announced plans to release two new computers in the spring, the 3031 to replace the 370/148, and the 3032 to replace the 370/158. The new models were two to three times faster and would cost about half as much as the older ones. An avalanche of claims followed as customers canceled leases and ordered new computers. The rental income shortfall caused by lease cancellations produced losses of some £450 million.

Although Lloyd's underwriters could not keep abreast of every technological development, common sense should have dictated that it was a matter of time before IBM would produce cheaper, more effective machines. Perhaps pressure for Lloyd's growth precluded the due diligence required for sound underwriting.

The first six years of the 1970s produced relative calm and very acceptable profits, but Lloyd's had become a time bomb. Remedial action on a broad range of significant matters was urgently needed, but not forthcoming. Change,

Called by some the first "billion-dollar storm," erratic Hurricane Betsy hit southern Florida and then flooded New Orleans in 1965. It caused over $1.4 billion in insured losses and claimed 75 lives. It was the worst in a disastrous series of storms that battered ships and oil rigs in the Gulf of Mexico; when skies cleared and books were balanced, the Lloyd's market operated in the red for three years running.

whether social, technological, or economic, was occurring too rapidly for Lloyd's to hide behind arcane practices.

If there was a single year after which Lloyd's would never be the same, it was 1978. From 1978 through 1979, calamitous marine disasters interrupted the underwriting calm. The *Amoco Cadiz*, wrecked in history's worst spill, dumped 230,000 tons of crude oil along the Brittany coast. Then in early 1979, the French oil tanker *Betelgeuse* exploded while discharging cargo in Ireland, with a loss of fifty lives. These two catastrophes each cost underwriters over $2 billion; these were among thirty supertankers lost in a fifteen-month period.

As Godfrey Hodgson has noted, between January 1979 and March 1980, "There were thirty-five cases of fire or explosions on board tankers or combined oil-and-bulk carriers of over 100,000 tons deadweight." According to Lloyd's records, 156 vessels, each with a value exceeding $750,000, were total losses during 1979. Underwriters contended with a rash of losses: scuttlings, marine frauds, piracy in the Mediterranean, and the beginning of the 1990 Iraq-Iran conflict in the Persian Gulf. Insurance rates should have been rising but were held down by overcapacity and competition. The Lloyd's market was responsible for a healthy share of marine claims, including huge liabilities in addition to those associated with hulls and cargoes. Ominously, these claims coincided with the payouts from computer leasing claims.

Simultaneously two scandals, whose origins were public knowledge several years earlier, became headline news.

At the end of 1974, an Italian vessel, *Savonita*, allegedly sustained a fire shortly after leaving port. Its cargo included many new Fiat automobiles. Approximately 300 were declared a "constructive total loss" by marine surveyors and sold for a fraction of their new car value. The insurer then submitted a reinsurance claim to Lloyd's through Malcolm Pearson, its Lloyd's broker. Pearson refused to process the claim, believing it was fraudulent. His investigation indicated that the cars had not been damaged and were being sold as new vehicles.

The case dragged on with many twists and turns. The original insurer, Società Italiana Assicurazioni Transporti (SIAT), unable to collect its reinsurance claim, replaced Pearson's firm with Willis Faber, who had a close business relationship with SIAT. Willis Faber applied pressure on Lloyd's underwriters, who finally honored almost the entire SIAT claim. A huge public outcry arose and reached the floor of Parliament, where Pearson was well connected. Lloyd's was roundly criticized for denouncing Pearson and backing Willis Faber.

Lloyd's critics were increasing; they had a field day questioning whether Lloyd's was honoring its most cherished motto, *Uberimma Fides* (always behaving in utmost good faith). The *Sunday Telegraph* observed that "the way in which Lloyd's has mishandled the *Savonita* affair has dealt its reputation the worst blow in living memory . . . not to put too fine a point on it, Lloyd's had succeeded in making itself appear both incompetent and cowardly."

The "Sasse Affair" was even more alarming. F. H. (Tim) Sasse, a rising Lloyd's underwriter, gave his syndicate's underwriting authority to an unscrupulous Florida insurance agency. The agency placed a large volume of property insurance on substandard housing in New York City's South Bronx slums and similar areas elsewhere in the United States and Canada. The business was supplied by John V. Goepfert, who had previous involvements in insurance frauds. Goepfert subsequently received a ten-year federal prison sentence in this case. A number of the insured properties burned, causing about $40 million in losses. Arson appeared to be a likely cause.

The scheme's perpetrators pocketed several million dollars, and Sasse's Brazilian reinsurers refused to pay, leaving Sasse holding the bag. This was a classic illustration of the dangers in carelessly granting underwriting authority. It became the first of many scandals, leading a number of Names to unite and refuse to pay their calls. Instead, they sued Lloyd's, among other parties, alleging that Sasse or his agents had acted fraudulently and that Lloyd's had breached its duty to oversee its managing agencies.

Lloyd's had suffered considerable damage. Like the lion in *The Wizard of Oz*, it had a mighty roar but no resolve and, regrettably, did not respond quickly or efficiently. The Sasse fraud began in early March 1976, but it was not until late 1977 that Lloyd's finally suspended Sasse, and mid-1980 before it reached a compromise settlement with the Names.

Lloyd's contributed some £9 million to the settlement, largely raised by a levy on all 18,000 Names. The Sasse Names were also responsible for a considerable sum. Unfortunately, the Committee of Lloyd's had little flexibility or real authority. It was only empowered to expel or suspend a miscreant, and such actions could only be taken after a lengthy appeals process. The Sasse scandal was poorly managed, in part because oversight responsibility rotated among Lloyd's deputy chairmen.

Sasse and *Savonita* hit the headlines in the spring of 1978, but Lloyd's soon faced other distractions and again responded inadequately—such as in its failure to accept the reality that insurance business had become global. British and American brokers would have to develop international combinations to remain competitive and serve their clients.

As has been noted, this Lloyd's position backfired. It became a catalyst for bringing Lloyd's and U.S. brokers together and heightened the focus on mergers and acquisitions, profit pooling, and joint ventures—discussions that had been underway throughout the 1970s. The Committee's action also gave impetus to the formation of the New York Insurance Exchange, which would soon become a Lloyd's competitor.

With the Sasse scandal, Lloyd's became the subject of in-depth media scrutiny for the first time. Previously, close media ties had always given Lloyd's the benefit of any doubt. This relationship had changed, and the press relentlessly challenged Lloyd's motives and actions and criticized its resistance to change. Increasingly, questions were posed about the efficacy of self-regulation—a matter Lloyd's viewed as sacrosanct.

The media aggressively focused on the growing issue of divesting brokers' ownership of managing agencies. Brokers controlled 70 percent of the agencies, and potential conflict of interest was apparent. When Lloyd's brokers owned managing agencies, for example, their allegiance to clients could conflict with their underwriters' responsibilities to

On his way to acquittal, in a rare photograph Kenneth Grob (right) smiles in the London sun. Although a court acquitted him of criminal charges, the U.K. Department of Trade and Industry report on the "Howden Affair" declared that Grob was responsible for serious transgressions while at Howden, causing problems that threatened the stability of the Lloyd's market.

Names. Underwriting activity supposedly was independent, but pressure from an owner-broker could be difficult for an underwriter to resist.

Ian Findley, Lloyd's chairman and a former broker, and his committee dealt with the emerging crisis of confidence by calling for a new working party. This group was to be chaired by Sir Henry Fisher, a former High Court judge as well as a bank and university head. In early 1979, the committee was formed. It was charged with examining and recommending changes to Lloyd's constitution.

In May 1980, the Fisher report focused on a basic anomaly within Lloyd's, namely that the Committee of Lloyd's was expected to control the institution, yet it lacked relevant constitutional authority. While the General Meeting of the members of Lloyd's theoretically had such control, it lacked the will and mechanisms to be effective.

Sir Henry Fisher's committee proposed establishing a council of Lloyd's. Of its twenty-eight members, sixteen would be elected by Lloyd's working members; they would form an executive committee and handle the executive functions. The other council members, eight elected by nonworking members and four nominated by the council, with Bank of England approval, could act as a standing disciplinary committee to handle disciplinary matters.

Citing the potential for abuse, the report also called for brokers to divest themselves of underwriting agency ownership and management. Further, it recommended that Lloyd's formally eliminate the 20 percent foreign-ownership rules. These changes were incorporated into an Act of Parliament, which, after considerable debate on the divestiture issue, was passed on July 23, 1982.

Critics complained about a clause granting Lloyd's ruling members immunity from liability. Such members were covered for actions taken in discharging their regulatory duties. There was also criticism that self-regulation was not addressed. On balance, Lloyd's had a more effective regulatory structure. However, the structure would be sorely tested by the events taking place at Howden.

The two-year period between A&A's first public disclosure of Howden-related problems and the June 1984 financial offer to the PCW Names was a nightmare for Lloyd's. The media fed on one sensational revelation after another. Simultaneously, the Bank of England and other government regulatory authorities, as well as Names themselves, spoke out with increasing frequency. From the Names, the tone was more and more belligerent. Fortunately for Lloyd's, its chairmen, Peter Green and Peter Miller, dealt relatively effectively with the Howden and PCW scandals that emerged during their respective tenures.

In 1982, Chairman Green lamented that alleged violations occurred almost entirely outside of Lloyd's jurisdiction. Nonetheless, he was strong in dealing with the Howden situation. Once the crisis broke, the chairman and the Committee of Lloyd's immediately responded to protect Names and policyholders. After Posgate was suspended from underwriting in September 1982, Lloyd's insisted on a committee dominated by non-Howden people to oversee Posgate's syndicates and ensure that diverted syndicate funds were returned. Additionally, two-person teams of accountants and Queen's Counsels were appointed to investigate the Howden and PCW scandals, as well as a third of lesser magnitude, Brooks & Dooley.

Unfortunately, Peter Green faced his own Lloyd's-related problems. As lead underwriter for the prestigious Jason Green syndicate, he had personal dealings involving risks placed with a Cayman Island insurer, the Imperial Insurance Company. He held a 7.59 percent interest in Imperial and had accepted undisclosed interest payments from the company. Green also admitted his intention to create a "roll-over" catastrophe fund in a tax haven—where money in the form of "premiums" was parked, to be returned at a future date—often an illegal scheme when no true insurance transaction was involved.

Peter Green resigned as chairman of Lloyd's in September 1983. Four years later, he was officially censured and found guilty of "discreditable and detrimental conduct" for accepting interest on Imperial Company funds to which he was not entitled. This event overshadowed some of his many Lloyd's accomplishments.

Peter Miller was especially decisive and persuasive when leadership was essential during the PCW scandal. After the scandal became public in November 1982, the pressure became so intense that the Bank of England urged Lloyd's to appoint an outside CEO. This request was reluctantly accepted. In February 1983, Ian Hay Davison, the past U.K. managing partner of the Arthur Andersen accounting firm, was appointed as Lloyd's first chief executive.

The relationship between Lloyd's and Hay Davison was not a harmonious one, and the man's austere demeanor undoubtedly made his task more challenging. The real obstacle, however, was Lloyd's resistance to appointing an outsider. Nevertheless, as a man of energy and considerable intellect, Hay Davison implemented much needed reforms. He observed, "With the approval of the Chairman and the Council, I set myself three principal objectives: to bring to book those in the Lloyd's community who had misbehaved themselves; to establish a new regulatory framework for Lloyd's based upon higher standards of disclosure, accounting, and auditing; and to improve the staffing, organization, and management of the Corporation." Hay Davison felt that his mission was to educate the Lloyd's market on practices that were acceptable and those that were unacceptable. As he often said, "Sunshine drives away the mists."

Reforms advanced by Hay Davison and adopted by Lloyd's included the following: required filing of syndicate accounts on a central and public register available for inspection; mandatory auditing of syndicate accounts; the outlawing of insurance transactions between underwriting syndicates and their agents-owned offshore companies; and disclosure of material transactions among underwriting member companies in which agents have a personal interest. In addition, other new rules were adopted for the use of binding authorities and for the abolition of baby syndicates.[3]

[3] These small syndicates, usually comprising "special" Names, frequently underwrote "cream" business.

Despite these constructive changes, many in Lloyd's objected to Hay Davison's presence. Matters reached a climax when his independent role and his authority were challenged by an internal Lloyd's inquiry. Believing his effectiveness was compromised, he submitted his resignation late in 1985, to take effect in May 1986. Fortunately, Hay Davison ultimately saw his commitment to sound principles pay off. His resignation and advocacy to diminish the working Names' role in governing Lloyd's helped prompt a government inquiry into Lloyd's regulations.

Chaired by Sir Patrick Neill, warden of All Souls College, Oxford, and the former chairman of the Council for the Securities Industry, the inquiry was led by objective outsiders. The Neill report, published in January 1987, contained numerous critical observations that others, especially Hay Davison, had been expressing for many months. The report noted that "our task has been to consider whether the regulatory arrangements at Lloyd's provide protection for Names comparable to that proposed for investors under the Financial Services Acts of 1986."

It found that:

> We have detected a number of shortcomings in particular areas of regulation at Lloyd's. . . . More fundamentally, the constitution of Lloyd's does not currently provide for that degree of involvement of outsiders. . . . The checks and balances at Lloyd's are not, in our view, so firmly in place. The balance of initiative rests too much with the working members. . . . Our solution involves reducing the number of working members on the Council so that they cease to have a majority. . . . Many members of the Lloyd's community in senior positions were not even vaguely aware of the legal obligations of agents to act at all times in the best interests of their principals, not to make secret profits at their principal's expense and to disclose fully all matters affecting their relationship with their principals.

Owing to the Neill recommendations, the makeup of Lloyd's supervisory body, the Council of Lloyd's, was altered. Four nominated members replaced working members. Nominated and external members then outnumbered working Names sixteen to twelve. Nominated members were to chair committees, including Disciplinary, Investigations and Rules, and Names Interests. Control of public information shifted to outsiders and provided more extensive protection to the Names.

After the "PCW Affair" wound down in 1987, daily reporting on Lloyd's scandals subsided. Interest was reactivated, however, in the summer of 1989 with the criminal trials of Grob and Posgate, who had been arrested by the Fraud Squad in 1987 on fraud charges. Grob was the only member of the Gang of Four to be indicted. Comery died in an auto accident in 1986; Page was diagnosed as terminally ill in 1988; and Carpenter was relieved from trial for medical reasons. The trial lasted fifteen weeks, making it one of the longest and most complex fraud trials in British history. Lloyd's maintained a low profile during the proceedings.

The presentation of the Crown's case was a fiasco, argued in highly technical terms to a jury of lay people, five women and seven men. The prosecution's line of evidence was so convoluted that it was difficult for even highly skilled insurance specialists to follow. Jurors frequently dozed off during the government's presentations, while the defendant's barrister had the jury focused and relaxed. He effectively developed a subtle theme of the British versus the Americans. Sequestered in a hotel for three nights, the jury deliberated for twenty hours and forty-three minutes. When the "not guilty" verdict was announced, few were surprised.

Because of the Crown's presentation, that finding was a certainty. Nevertheless, it was an outrageous travesty of justice, duly confirmed by Grob when he told the *Independent* in 1990, "The case against me was very good. I'm the man about whom they say, 'He got away with it.'" Grob died on December 28, 1991, at age seventy, without having paid his debt to society.

CHAPTER 18

A Rocky Recovery: Lloyd's Revisited

Examining some of the more serious Lloyd's crises from the 1960s through the 1980s is instructive, but it does not fully account for how Lloyd's lost its way. In actuality, mischief had been building behind the scenes for years. By the early 1980s, Lloyd's had become hospitable to malfeasance; this led even men of high repute and visibility into temptation and disgrace. To understand the genesis of these problems, it is useful to revisit segments of Lloyd's volatile history between 1945 and 1982.

For two decades after World War II, while the United Kingdom and much of the rest of the world experienced unprecedented change, Lloyd's remained its old self—an insular and private enclave. Tradition was inviolate, and there was little motivation for anything but business as usual. Lloyd's was profitable for its Names, whose numbers tripled to 6,000 in the decades after the war. A homogeneous group, Lloyd's members were predominantly its underwriters and brokers and their relatives. Another group of Names came from financial, shipping, and industrial circles, while scions of old monied families represented a third group. Members of Lloyd's were British men. They could be counted on to be supportive and noninterfering.

Lloyd's resembled a fraternal order. Members working within Lloyd's marketplace knew and generally liked each other. When a disciplinary matter occasionally arose, it was handled informally and privately. In 1954, for instance, when it was discovered that Lloyd's underwriter Alec Wilcox and his auditor had manipulated their syndicates' books for years, the Committee of Lloyd's stepped in and relieved the syndicate Names of any liability for fraudulent claims. The event passed with little fanfare. The Lloyd's principle of self-regulation seemed to work well and was fiercely championed. Unlike in the United States, self-regulation within the U.K. financial community had apparently stood tests of time, and few people questioned its suitability.

Lloyd's enjoyed a revered status in Britain. With a preponderance of international business, it was a principal generator of foreign exchange within the City of London. Next to the Bank of England, Lloyd's was the country's leading financial institution. Its name was recognized universally and was synonymous with respectability and integrity.[1] In retrospect, however, it appears that many of its traditions were deeply rooted, as were the seeds of calamity.

How can we best understand what went wrong? Among other things, Lloyd's was not structured to cope with multiple challenges. Portents of impending calamity appeared but were usually ignored. Chronic myopia prevailed, along with a classic attitude of "if it ain't broke, don't fix it."

Reasonable foresight by Lloyd's leaders should have identified many areas for careful monitoring and prompt remedial action: underwriting, administration, logistics, and competition, as well as legal, societal, and governmental matters. All of this was complicated by the dramatic changes in international business. The most essential matters that Lloyd's should have examined more wisely include the following:

• *The need to expand underwriting capacity.* Increased competition was everywhere, particularly on the Continent and in the United States. To keep pace, membership restrictions should have been liberalized much earlier than 1967.

• *The need for additional underwriting expertise.* Traditionally,

[1] From insuring Betty Grable's legs or Jimmy Durante's nose to originating an insurance policy to provide medical malpractice protection, the Society of Lloyd's had earned its unrivaled reputation for innovation and underwriting flexibility.

Lloyd's underwriters received little formal training. On-the-job learning was the preferred method. Many underwriters and their deputies had no university background and limited exposure to finance, taxation, or corporate and agency law.

• *Maintenance of an updated and user-friendly electronic data processing system.* Lloyd's was among early computer users, establishing an IBM system in 1960. However, the system was not adequately upgraded to meet new needs. Underwriters had limited ability to monitor cash flow and limited access to current claims status. Lloyd's did not ensure that underwriting agents' and brokers' systems were compatible with theirs; this caused enormous inefficiencies.

• *The need to provide Names with adequate information on their investment.* An attitude of "don't confuse them with the facts" predominated. The annual accounting audit did little more than confirm a Name's solvency compliance.

• *Troublesome tax issues.* British tax rates on earned income rose to 75 percent—and on unearned income, as much as 98 percent—between 1945 and the late 1970s. Underwriters tried to help Names minimize tax exposure. Efforts to avoid taxes led to some illegal and fraudulent schemes. Lloyd's leaders mostly ignored this incendiary situation.

• *Exchange control.* Regulations radically limited the amount of capital British residents could export between 1945 and 1978. Commencing in the 1950s, brokers and underwriters increasingly operated in offshore tax havens. This reflected client activity, and also afforded additional freedom from regulation and interference. Again, Lloyd's overlooked the potential for abuse.

• *Binding authorities.* Some Lloyd's underwriters authorized non-Lloyd's brokers and agents to bind coverages on their behalf. This seemed to be a painless and inexpensive way to write additional business. Unless the authority was carefully structured and supervised, however, it became a prescription for disaster. In the United States, this practice was sometimes badly, even fraudulently, abused. Although binding authority was not widespread, it should have been severely curtailed.

• *Use of baby syndicates.* These syndicates typically consisted of a small number of Names who were insiders close to the underwriter or managing agency. The underwriter generally placed only the "cream" business in such a syndicate. The intent was to provide members with preferential business. When employed in this manner, the use of baby syndicates was blatant insider dealing.

• *The use of "rollers."* These were funding policies subject to being rolled over for additional periods of time. Typically, "premiums" were paid to reinsurers domiciled in offshore tax havens. The reinsurers bore no risk because policy conditions stated that claims could not exceed the premium plus interest, less a commission. No transfer of risk occurred. These "policies" were generally placed during the profitable 1970s, when favorable tax deductions could be taken. The scheme was then to repatriate the profits during the 1980s, when taxes and underwriting profits were lower.

The use of "rollers" proved catastrophic; Names were left with undisclosed tax liabilities owing to undeclared syndicate profits. To the extent that rollers were used to equalize syndicate results over multiple years, some Names unjustly benefited and others were unfairly penalized. Often, the reinsurance "premiums" were neither audited nor accounted for and were used to circumvent Lloyd's premium writing limits. In addition, including or excluding these policies in syndicate assets significantly influenced the reserves established to pay future claims.

At worst, the premiums were placed, undisclosed, in companies where underwriters or brokers had financial interest. Such premiums could be easily diverted for personal gain. Those in responsible positions at Lloyd's were almost certainly aware of rollers. Although most nonmarket Names did not know about rollers, the practice was accepted as being in the Names' best interest. The incalculable damage of rollers was readily apparent by the early 1980s.

If Lloyd's had been divinely blessed, leaders of exceptional vision and persuasive powers might have emerged to address its festering problems, but this was not to be, and realistically it was too much to expect. While corruption existed in some quarters, day-to-day operations seemed to run smoothly, and the Names were content. Members of the Committee of Lloyd's had their own businesses to look after. Future threats to the market seemed remote.

Unfortunately, potential problems became disastrous

realities. Lloyd's executives rarely addressed underlying causes until it was too late and "Band-Aid" remedies could not suffice. Remedial action was taken only after extreme outside pressure from external (nonworking) Names, the government, the Bank of England, and the media. Lloyd's managers were seen as so entrenched in old habits that they lost public backing and, in the process, severely threatened their institution's future. On the whole, during the crisis years Lloyd's was accurately perceived as suffering from insularity and indecision at a time when bold corrective action was required.

In 1986, Lloyd's settled into its new headquarters, a building equally modern and architecturally controversial—especially for an organization that prized tradition and prided itself on its conservative values. By 1987, the society had almost 32,000 Names, of whom 82 percent were external. Women constituted 22 percent of membership, and foreigners represented 17 percent. The number of underwriting syndicates approached 370, of which more than 75 percent were marine and nonmarine (fire and liability); the remainder underwrote aviation, motor, and, in a few cases, life insurance. Lloyd's capacity was approximately £11 billion, and more than 250 Lloyd's brokers fed it business. Directly or indirectly, Lloyd's employed more than 80,000 people.

By the late 1980s, Lloyd's capacity and costs were soaring out of control. Ironically, the influx of new Names generated too much capacity while there was not enough demand to accommodate it. Consequently, cutthroat competition drove prices lower. By the end of the decade, underwriters utilized only two-thirds of market capacity. Exacerbating the situation, marine underwriters vied with their non-marine brethren to write excess liability reinsurance. Meanwhile, Lloyd's administrative costs escalated.

Lloyd's was reduced to a state of disarray after a series of natural and man-made catastrophes, dramatic increase in U.S. asbestos and environmental claims, and a rebellion by most Names. Outside intervention would be required for Lloyd's survival.

Although 1987 produced underwriting profits of £510 million, a string of crippling losses began in 1988. During 1989 and 1990, insured losses were about $30 billion, compared with $39 billion from 1981 to 1988. In 1989, Hurricane Hugo alone caused roughly $5 billion in insured losses.[2] Additional U.S. losses exceeding $1 billion each included: the October 17, 1989, Loma Prieta, California, earthquake (7.1 on the Richter scale), which killed sixty-three people; the *Exxon Valdez* oil spill; and a Phillips Petroleum oil refinery explosion.

Lloyd's £2.1 billion loss for 1989 was by far the worst in its history. The following year produced an even greater loss—£2.9 billion.[3] Escalating U.S. liability claims and devastating European windstorms in 1990 caused $11 billion in claims. While catastrophic losses during this period and in the following years were not insured only at Lloyd's, the venerable institution's exposure was considerable. These events coincided with very soft insurance pricing, driven by supply/demand imbalance and many insurers' high investment returns.

By early 1989, the total number of Names peaked at over 32,000. U.S. Names had peaked a year earlier at 2,620. These figures dropped dramatically as terrified investors bailed out. By mid-1992, the total number had eroded to 22,300. Only 63 new Names joined Lloyd's in that year and 67 the following year. Various syndicates could not close a year when their normal three-year open period ended because they had been unable to establish realistic reserves. If this had not been the case, many more Names would have defected. Before 1980, it was rare for syndicates to remain open. By 1988, 57 were left open, and that was only the tip of the iceberg. Although Lloyd's capacity remained relatively stable between 1988 and 1993, the number of syndicates actively underwriting dropped from 380 to 228. Sixty-two percent of syndicates reported losses in 1989, then 70 percent in 1990, followed by 68 percent in 1991, and 55 percent in 1992.

[2] Before that, no hurricane-insured loss had exceeded $1.6 billion.

[3] Lloyd's results are approximate, depending on the method used to calculate them.

The period from 1990 to 1996 was the most turbulent in Lloyd's history as it struggled to survive the revolt by its Names, many of whom faced financial ruin. The underlying cause was unprecedented underwriting losses and huge calls on Names to pay for them. Although these losses resulted from many causes, the worst minefield was the London Market Excess (LMX) sector. This excess reinsurance market received an avalanche of U.S. asbestos and environmental pollution claims.

The gamble within the LMX market was that catastrophes rarely occurred, but this was wishful thinking. Unfortunately for the Names, some underwriters heavily involved with LMX business during the 1980s failed to secure adequate reinsurance. This was inexcusable and left many syndicates disastrously exposed.

Names who joined Lloyd's in the early and mid-1980s, many Americans among them, suffered heavy losses from American asbestos and pollution claims. More than 2,000 Names were subject to calls of over £500,000. For many, Lloyd's exposure became the pervasive reality in their lives. A few became so desperate that suicide was their solution. The media recounted the tragic financial plight of others. Many sold homes and farms that had been in their families for generations. A great number took their children from private schools. Retirees saw savings vanish.

The Names had few alternatives. They could pay their calls. They could plead hardship, which meant penalties that severely handicapped family finances. Or they could join an action group and sue those they held responsible. Targets included managing agents; members' agents; and occasionally insurance brokers, auditors, and Lloyd's itself. Individual Names were powerless to attack, but collectively they were formidable. Many joined action groups, usually to seek retribution from one or several syndicates run by the same agency. They employed different tactics to win settlements, and after some initial setbacks, they proved quite successful.

Syndicates specializing in LMX business were principal objects of attack. Four syndicates dealing with excess-of-loss reinsurance illustrate the focus that led some underwriters, management agencies, and members' agencies to disaster. Their stories reflect incredible professional failings.[4]

[4] These activities also resulted in the financial ruin of several thousand Lloyd's Names.

Richard Outhwaite was one of Lloyd's most successful and experienced underwriters. His specialty was dealing with ships, their cargoes, and oil rigs. He also underwrote run-off reinsurances on an unlimited basis. These protected other syndicates from losses (above specified amounts) on prior year results. This business was loaded with asbestos and environmental pollution risks because the most prescient underwriters foresaw the need to eliminate such risks from their books. Outhwaite wrote many run-off reinsurances, including thirty-one between July 1981 and March 1982. His reasoning reflected normal underwriting strategy—namely, to estimate the timing and amount of claims, then charge an appropriate premium that, when investment income was figured in, would result in decent profits. He would also take out the necessary reinsurance protection. Outhwaite's oversight was that he hadn't done his homework on asbestos and its terrible health hazards. As claims poured in, Outhwaite's reinsurance was hopelessly inadequate.

Stephen Merrett was among the most influential men in the Lloyd's market, and his father was a market leader before him. The Merrett Group also underwrote run-off reinsurance and was heavily involved with American asbestos and pollution risks, which produced horrendous losses for Merrett's syndicate Names. As a result, Merrett resigned from the Council of Lloyd's and as deputy chairman of Lloyd's in September 1993. His syndicates were transferred to other agencies.

The Gooda Walker and Feltrim agencies experienced disasters similar to Merrett's. Both brought in many new members in the 1980s because they appeared to be profitable, which in Gooda Walker's case was illusory. By concentrating underwriting on LMX business, they grew dra-

matically, while their Names remained ignorant of the riskiness undertaken on their behalf. Adequate reinsurance protection was nonexistent. One ominous sign was that working professional Names were not joining these agencies' syndicates.

As the 1990s began, ramifications of the previous decade's underwriting became evident. For example, in 1991, three Feltrim syndicates with a total of 2,000 Names faced losses of £320 million for underwriting years 1987 to 1989. To put this in perspective, a Name who committed £32,000 to underwriting faced a loss of £160,000. Adam Raphael reports in *Ultimate Risk* that as losses grew the numbers increased significantly. During this same period, 4,500 Gooda Walker Names lost £900 million. Raphael notes, "By the end of 1993, the average losses of the 250 Names who had joined Lloyd's directly through the Gooda Walker members' agency amounted to more than £500,000."

Through action groups, most Names on the Outhwaite, Merrett, Gooda Walker, and Feltrim syndicates sued their agents for negligence and other transgressions. They

Grounded by human error after striking Bligh Reef in Alaska's Prince William Sound, the supertanker Exxon Valdez lies at anchor within a ring of booms that could not contain 11 million gallons of crude spilling from her tanks. Oil spread across 10,000 square miles of coastal seas, reaching 600 miles from the wreck, poisoning 1,500 miles of shore, and fouling wildlife and fisheries for years after the 1989 disaster. It was a landmark event in terms of environmental damage, and a jury eventually assessed Exxon $5 billion in punitive damages.

recouped varying amounts through court decisions, but few, if any, were made whole. Outhwaite continued to underwrite. Merrett made a deal with Lloyd's, paid a large fine, and never worked there again. The responsible underwriters at Gooda Walker and Feltrim left Lloyd's.

Many other syndicates and underwriting agencies had similar horror stories. The author Jonathan Mantle notes that one Spicer and White syndicate cost its 200 Names approximately £13 million. The underwriter was a favorite with brokers for his willingness to take almost any risk. Often referred to as the "Nodding Donkey," he was considered a soft touch.

By the early 1990s, Lloyd's survival was precarious enough to compel decisive action. A sixteen-person task force toiled throughout 1991 to develop possible solutions. David Rowland, CEO of Sedgwick, was a sound choice as committee chairman, and the other members had extensive insurance experience. In their January 1992 report, they advanced sixty-five recommendations to reform and revitalize Lloyd's. The resulting restructuring transferred Lloyd's governing control from working members to outsiders who had no personal financial interest in the Lloyd's market. Self-regulation, however, continued.

The former head of the British Securities and Investment Board, Sir David Walker, was asked to examine Lloyd's working members' practices with respect to their use of insider information in choosing syndicates. While exonerating Lloyd's members of malpractice and fraud, the Walker committee observed that some Lloyd's underwriters' judgment was "seriously flawed." The Walker report also acknowledged "serious deficiencies" in the performance of some members' agents relative to their Names.

In addition to restructuring, the Rowland task force addressed the need to expand Lloyd's capital base. For the first time, acceptance of corporate capital and limited liability received serious consideration and were ultimately adopted. The Central Fund was also increased by £500 million through a levy on 1990–92 Names.[5] Generally, Names are permitted to retain modest incomes and houses, but in theory they or their estate eventually must repay the fund. Hardship cases were tedious to resolve. Some Names applied for hardship to buy time, but relatively few completed the entire process.

At midyear 1993, Lloyd's capacity dropped below £9 billion. The number of Names was fewer than 20,000, and 80 percent were external. Also, active syndicates diminished to 235. There were 478 open years, and Names remained responsible for their results.

In 1993, Lloyd's finally started facing the depth of its problems. Chairman David Rowland began implementing his task force's wide-ranging business plan. Most significantly, in the 1994 underwriting year, Lloyd's membership opened to incorporated investors whose liability was limited to their pledged funds. Twenty-five corporate entities joined and provided £1.6 billion of new capacity. Twelve early "corporate" participants were U.K. life, unit trust, and listed pension fund investors.

To attract corporate investors, Lloyd's decided to form a central limited liability reinsurance company to reinsure pre-1986 syndicate liabilities. Reserves and liabilities, estimated at £4 billion to £5 billion, would transfer to the new company. Scheduled to open at the end of 1995, the timing was delayed, and the original plan was modified many times.

The concept of attracting corporate capital had many advantages: enhanced investment returns, improved liability management, and economies of scale. Attracting this capital required Lloyd's commitment to reform. Substantial overhead cutting was a necessity. Early casualties were the chairman's "waiters," who, resplendent in bright blue-and-red tailcoats with silver buttons, controlled access to the chairman's office.[6] Lloyd's bloated management layers were drastically reduced, and a performance pay and staff appraisal system was instituted.

[5] The Central Fund steps in if a Name cannot or does not pay his or her debt to Lloyd's. A civil claim is pursued against the defaulting individual, who may then appeal to the Hardship Fund.

[6] The traditional Rolls-Royce for the chairman also disappeared.

Picture-perfect waters are closed to swimmers at Marina del Rey, California, in 1988. New methods of scientific monitoring augment concern for natural resources and for human health—all part of the emerging social concern, "environmentalism." Together, these trends contribute to a rising tide of new vulnerabilities for industries and an increasingly complex array of risks for agents and brokers to assess and insure against.

Other initiatives focused on underwriting changes and improved communications with Names. A more effective database permitted fuller disclosure of claims and cash flow information. Professional training for underwriters, rigid audit standards, and centralized back-office functions for members' agents created a more business-oriented structure.

In 1994, Lloyd's introduced Members' Agents Pooling Arrangements (MAPAs), a form of membership designed to spread risks among many syndicates and lessen risks for individual Names. Some £5.2 billion of Lloyd's total 1994 capacity of £10.9 billion came from this source. The total capacity represented an increase of more than £2 billion over 1993. Lloyd's also set up a specialized claims unit to deal with asbestos, environmental pollution, and health hazards.

By April 1994, more than thirty action groups representing 17,000 Lloyd's Names were suing Lloyd's and/or their managing and members' agents for negligence and mismanagement. They sought £3 billion in restitution. The suits were not confined to Britain. In the United States, 400 Names sued Lloyd's in federal court in California.

By April 1995, an estimated 9,000 Names were insolvent and owed Lloyd's around £1.3 billion. British newspapers frequently speculated that the institution was on the brink of collapse. The *Sunday Times* concluded that "the professionals at Lloyd's are not fit to regulate a flea circus, never mind a multi-billion [pound] market." A financial journalist charged that Lloyd's in the 1980s "resembled a garden in which the rabbits were in charge of the lettuce." Lloyd's debt collection unit, formed in late 1994, met almost total resistance from external Names.

Lloyd's pressed for compromise solutions. It proposed an improved litigation settlement offer to Names of £2.8 billion, a considerable increase over the original £900 million. Of the new offer, £2 billion was to be treated as debt credit for the Names' unpaid losses. The other £800 million would be raised from members' agents, their errors and omissions underwriters, and third parties such as auditors who were implicated in an earlier ruling. Although it came closer to a solution, the new offer was not accepted.

In March 1996, the British government finally gave conditional approval to a Lloyd's proposal for transferring the firm's old liabilities to a new reinsurance company, Equitas. It would assume outstanding liabilities from 1992 and earlier instead of 1985 as originally planned. Equitas would have about £13.5 billion in assets. These came from existing reserves, a levy on Names underwriting from 1993 to 1995, and a levy on managing agencies. Overall members' cost to reinsure their liabilities into Equitas was about £1.1 billion.

The restructuring vote was set for August 1996, but it became clear that a favorable vote would not be forthcoming. In a final effort for approval, the settlement was increased by £300 million in May 1996, bringing the total to £3.1 billion. This reduced by half the average additional amount Names would pay to cover past losses.

In addition to resistance at home, Lloyd's was coping with recalcitrant U.S. Names. They were aided by securities commissioners in thirty-eight states, who filed lawsuits accusing

Lloyd's of securities fraud and selling unregistered investments.

The American Names wanted to avoid their contractual obligation with Lloyd's, which required that suits by U.S. Names be tried in British courts. The U.S. Postal Service, the Department of Justice, and the Securities and Exchange Commission also launched investigations. State insurance commissioners did not join these investigations because they feared that Lloyd's might fail and leave U.S. policyholders vulnerable.

Lloyd's negotiated a deal with the state securities commissioners to relieve U.S. Names of 20 percent of their obligations in return for the commissioners' dropping their legal claims. Some $248 million still was allegedly owed to Lloyd's. Individuals had to agree not to sue Lloyd's for fraud, and many declined the proposal. One hundred American Names sought their rights under U.S. securities laws to force Lloyd's to divulge more information about how it calculated claims against them and how their money would be used in the restructuring.

Several days before the restructing vote by the Names, a U.S. District Court judge in Richmond, Virginia, required Lloyd's to postpone voting for thirty days and provide more information about Equitas. Lloyd's petitioned a U.S. Court of Appeals, and a three-judge panel reversed the lower court's decision. They upheld Lloyd's contention that 2,700 American Names fell under British law and were not entitled to further financial disclosures.

The recovery plan was approved resoundingly in 1996— ultimately by more than 94 percent of the Names worldwide. Yet 1,800 Names, including many Americans, initially refused the offer. Many later changed their minds and paid when Lloyd's exerted legal pressure.

In 1998, the U.S. Supreme Court rejected an appeal by hundreds of American Names seeking to proceed with a U.S. securities fraud lawsuit. In November 1999, a New York State Supreme Court ruled against two plaintiffs who asserted that they had been fraudulently induced to participate in Lloyd's. This strengthened Lloyd's recovery from the 246 American Names who had not yet paid, and it appeared to conclude the principal American litigation issues. Lloyd's also began to reestablish its identity as the world's premier marketplace of concentrated underwriting skill, albeit with a much altered structure.

In May 1997, the Council of Lloyd's endorsed a working party recommendation that the Council retain primary responsibility for daily market regulation but be subject to oversight by Britain's Securities and Investments Board and the Department of Trade and Industry. This virtually ended Lloyd's cherished privilege of self-regulation.

Early in 2000, Lloyd's faced another ominous court battle, potentially its most serious. A fraud case, *Jaffrey* v. *Lloyd's*, was filed in London on behalf of 216 Names who collectively owed Lloyd's some £50 million. The trial dragged on for five months. As anxieties mounted, plaintiffs contended that between 1978 and 1988 Lloyd's senior officials were increasingly aware of asbestos dangers but intentionally withheld information from Names and potential Names. Allegedly, this was done to prevent existing names from resigning and to induce others to join Lloyd's to help pay future asbestos claims.

Witness testimony appeared extremely damaging to Lloyd's. Consequently, many were surprised when the judge, while agreeing there was widespread incompetence among some underwriters and managing agents, ruled in Lloyd's favor. He also expressed hope that his ruling would be the end of Lloyd's legal woes with Names. A final appeal was denied.

Despite these positive developments, Lloyd's future prospects are uncertain. Profits exceeded £1 billion for the 1994 underwriting year and reached a record £1.15 billion for 1995. The next year produced a profit of only £600 million, which included the release of £268 million from prior year reserves. However, 1997 resulted in a loss of £176 million, and 1998 reported a loss of £1.06 billion.[7] Compared to the rest of the market, corporate-owned syndicates

[7] In April 2002, reporting for the first time on an annual basis, Lloyd's disclosed a record £3.11 billion loss for 2001. Losses for 1999 and 2000 were £1.95 billion and £1.20 billion, respectively.

[8] While other corporations were continuing to join, some were pulling out of syndicates. It was expected that corporate-backed syndicates would underperform the Lloyd's market at least through underwriting year 2000.

[9] Included in the 668 members are 512 "conversion vehicles." Names use these vehicles to convert to limited liability status.

underperformed mostly because they started underwriting in 1997, an unfavorable time.[8]

HSBC Investment Bank plc reported, in its volume *Lloyd's—Destroying the Myths*, "The primary vehicle through which new entrants have sought to invest in Lloyd's is the Integrated Lloyd's Vehicle (ILV). Under the ILV structure, a single corporate entity controls a managing agent and at the same time owns a corporate member that provides capacity to the managing agent's syndicate(s). The stated intention…is to provide 100 percent of the capacity, making the ILV to all intents and purposes an insurance company operating at Lloyd's." By 1994, there were sixteen ILVs controlling £666 million, or about 7 percent of the total market. Approximately two-thirds of market capacity is moving in this direction.

Between 1994 and 1999, corporate membership grew from 95 members controlling 15 percent of the market to 668 controlling 73 percent.[9] By 2002, individual members (those with unlimited liability) had declined to 2,480. For the 2001 year of account, the market's capacity was about £11 billion. Limited liability capital provided 80 percent of this amount. There were 108 Lloyd's syndicates.

As Names dwindle and corporate entities dominate membership, some believe that the presence of corporate investors might overshadow Lloyd's identity. Thus, it could become just another insurance market, with little of its former allure. Others wonder whether Lloyd's can survive. In 2001, for example, Equitas experienced much higher than expected asbestos claims, forcing it to strengthen reserves. At midyear its gross undiscounted asbestos reserves were £8 billion. If this continues, run-off reinsurers may be in trouble. Nevertheless by 2002 the "New Lloyd's" functioned as an important international market; however, additional uncertainties were created by the September 11, 2001, shockwave, an event that will apparently cost Lloyd's a net loss of at least £2 billion, an estimate that continues to rise.

PART IV

PREPARING FOR
A NEW MILLENNIUM:
The 1980s and After

CHAPTER 19

The Eighties:
Some Strategic
Acquisitions

Notwithstanding events at Lloyd's and related Howden difficulties, the 1980s were years of substantial growth and success for Alexander & Alexander and of dramatic change for the industry. A & A had acquired eighteen U.S. firms in 1980 alone; two years later, we merged with Howden, and three years after that, we made our largest acquisition.

Most of the 1980 acquisitions were new locations for A&A, with many in midsized industrial areas. Our intent was to target medium and smaller accounts in places with less competition. However, as business costs rose, it became harder to earn adequate profits on small accounts. Consequently, many of these offices were later relinquished; often they were sold to their employees.

With some trepidation, a speculative new venture was launched in the early 1980s. We bought Montag & Caldwell, a small regional investment counseling firm in Atlanta. Although both companies offered consulting services, there was no special synergy between the insurance brokerage and investment counseling businesses. However, some diversification seemed prudent because of the insurance cycle's unpredictability. Montag & Caldwell had an impeccable reputation and a fine track record. The firm managed assets of $500 million through mutual funds and institutional and personal advisory accounts.[1]

[1] We eventually recognized that we would need to make a more significant financial commitment to realize a better return. Consequently, Montag & Caldwell was sold to its employees in 1985.

261

In 1980, we started preparing for A&A stock to be traded on the New York Stock Exchange, and we began recruiting board members from outside the company. The need for nonexecutive board members coincided with our interest in independent outside counsel at the board level, and we identified areas of expertise to be represented. A highly respected banker was one need, and James D. Berry, chairman and CEO of Republic of Texas Corporation, admirably fit that bill. We wanted a top lawyer experienced in dealing with government agencies; that role was accepted by Roderick M. Hills, a partner in the Washington, D.C., firm of Latham, Watkins & Hills, former White House counsel to President Ford and, for two years, chairman of the SEC. The third new director was a senior financial and planning officer; Vincent R. McLean, executive vice president of finance and planning for NL Industries, Inc., gave A&A a third able director.[2]

The insurance market was extremely soft in 1980. This reflected excess reinsurance capacity and a large infusion of foreign capital to underwriters. A&A's growth slowed as the year progressed. The 1981 first quarter failed to exceed prior year earnings after increases for forty-seven consecutive quarters. Nevertheless, the *Forbes Annual Report on American Industry* measured the management performance of the largest 1,041 U.S. public companies and placed A&A tenth in profitability based on a five-year return on equity. M&M, by comparison, ranked twenty-fourth. In the consumer finance category, A&A placed second and M&M third.

For the rest of the decade and beyond, it became ever more difficult for brokers to maintain their historic profit margins. A soft insurance market was just one of the problems. The insurance-buying public was changing, reflecting a fundamental economic shift. Twenty-five years earlier, four out of five Americans worked in manufacturing and natural resource industries, while only 17 percent worked in service industries. By 1980, those in service industries

[2] The timing of the selections was fortuitous. In early 1980, no one could have foreseen the challenges that lay ahead for the board. There would be inordinate demands on the time of nonexecutive directors, and they would respond with dedication and skill. Their counsel was to be invaluable.

Red letter day: On January 25, 1982, Alexander & Alexander is listed on the New York Stock Exchange for the first time. The author (center), then president and CEO of A&A, eyes the initial appearance of the firm's symbol, AAS, on the ticker board with Richard Grasso (left), senior vice president of the exchange, and Ken Soubry, chairman of Alexander & Alexander (right).

had grown to 58 percent, substantially changing our markets and clients. (In 2002, the estimate was 80 percent.) Commercial insurance needs permanently decreased, reflecting their changing exposures and use of alternative risk-financing techniques.

Increasingly, clients preferred fees to commissions. This trend, first publicized in 1950 with M&M's handling of the American Can account, had pros and cons for brokers. Although the trend stabilized brokers' income, it was difficult to readjust fees to recognize increased expenses. Over time, most brokers agreed to work on a fee basis, although Johnson & Higgins resisted longer than most. This inevitable change dramatically cut brokers' incomes.

Of course, new types of risks developed and generated additional revenues for brokers. After the Lindbergh kidnapping in 1932, Lloyd's had pioneered kidnap and ransom insurance. By the early 1970s, as world terrorism began to accelerate, kidnap and ransom insurance was widely purchased by corporations. Professional liability and product liability exposures were other areas where Lloyd's policies met a growing need. Insurance responded to new exposures arising in several fields including nuclear activities, ERISA changes, foreign credit, and environmental impairment liability. Despite these and other new coverages, it was difficult for brokers to increase profits through traditional business segments.

A&A marginally improved its net income during 1981. We acquired twenty-one firms, nearly equally divided between agencies in new cities and those meant to bolster our existing offices. A&A ended the year with revenues of $458 million, a substantial and encouraging figure. In 1982, acquisitions continued at a fast pace. International expansion was a particular focus. We secured a 21 percent interest in our French correspondent, Européenne de Courtage d'Assurances et de Réassurance (CECAR). Also, 20 percent equity was negotiated with our German affiliate, Industrie-Assekuranz, and 40 percent with Bekouw Mendes B.V. in the Netherlands.[3] In Canada, we teamed up with Sedgwick to form Sedgwick-Alexander Canada.[4]

Two major U.S. purchases were also concluded, NTVL in Louisville, Kentucky, and Clifton and Company in San Francisco, two of the country's most professional independent insurance agencies.[5] NTVL's management group, with its president, Baylor Landrum, ran a sophisticated organization.[6] It had formed a subsidiary to help clients implement self-insurance programs—a most unusual and forward-looking service for an agency of its size. Clifton and Company, formed by Fred Clifton in 1964, offered a broad range of services usually associated with larger firms.

We had opened 1982 by acquiring Howden on January 23, and three days later we were listed on the New York Stock Exchange. After twelve years of over-the-counter trading, the new listing gave A&A invaluable domestic and international exposure. The March board of directors' meeting was held in London—the first outside the United States. I became chairman and CEO of A&A; Ken Soubry was elected vice chairman; and T. Irvin, president and chief operating officer.[7]

[3] A fine firm, Bekouw Mendes was the third largest Dutch insurance broker, with 275 employees headquartered in Amsterdam.

[4] Canadian law still precluded us from establishing a wholly-owned office.

[5] These acquisitions were of the same quality as those made in the early 1970s.

[6] Formed by a 1970 merger of Vaughan & Landrum, Inc. (founded in 1922), and Nahm & Turner (1934), NTVL had become Kentucky's largest agency, with more than 2,000 commercial clients.

[7] Six employee board members were repositioned on the internal boards of one of three operating subsidiaries. Directors George Clark, Robert Gielow, and John Tucker subsequently retired during 1982, each having played a prominent role in A&A's growth. In the United States, new group leaders were Bobby Cline, Richard Page, and Michael White. White headed the U.S. subsidiary, Alexander & Alexander Inc., and Page moved to London during 1983, replacing me as head of Howden. Subsequently, he was recruited as CEO of Fred. S. James.

In 1983, we acquired OBrion, Russell & Co. of Boston. Formed in 1876, this firm had become one of New England's top independent agencies. With over 100 employees, it was a leader in broking public utilities, guided by its able CEO, J. Deane Sommerville.

Later in 1983, we made our final attempt at a merger agreement with Sedgwick. We almost succeeded, in part because Sedgwick accepted the challenges we acquired with Howden. For technical reasons, the arrangement was for Sedgwick to acquire A&A. In mid-July, meeting with their bankers in New York, we agreed to a deal. Suddenly—at the eleventh hour—Sedgwick's lead banker announced that he needed to walk around the block. He returned with the startling statement that he could not support the price, and the agreement was dead.

The media speculated that the deal had fallen through because Sedgwick's leader, Neil Mills, and I had not been able to agree on who would run the combined firm. This was never an issue. In fact, we had agreed that I would be responsible for the United States and he would be responsible for business in the rest of the world. This combination would almost certainly have changed industry dynamics by the century's end. There would have been four major global firms instead of three.

Competitors such as Johnson & Higgins and Marsh & McLennan were relentless in their pursuit of international partners. In 1983, J&H—through UNISON, its group of affiliated international brokers—had seventy-one offices in thirty-six countries. J&H also handled in excess of 125 captive insurance companies, more than any other brokerage. M&M focused on global expansion, as did Sedgwick. In April 1985, Sedgwick agreed to acquire Fred. S. James from the Transamerica Group.[8]

[8] Transamerica would then own 39 percent of Sedgwick, although only 29 percent of the voting rights. This was a formidable global combination. James had a staff of some 6,000 in more than 120 offices. Its principal activities were located in North America, and it had recently purchased Canada's third largest broker, Tomenson, Inc. It also had a large reinsurance broking arm, John F. Sullivan Co. Including the recent Tomenson acquisition, James's annual revenues exceeded $300 million. From a competitive standpoint, this merger would make A&A's acquisition of Reed Stenhouse all the more timely and significant.

Despite our inability to join with Sedgwick, in 1985, we were able to merge with the large international brokerage firm of Reed Stenhouse, the one remaining viable candidate with superior international credentials.

When William M. Wilson, CEO of Reed Stenhouse, contacted me in September 1984 to discuss merging, we had a new element to consider. Unlike the prospects at six previous meetings dating back to 1975, there was now real hope that the new Canadian government would allow our combining. Our organizations were complementary and an excellent fit—if the legal obstacles could be removed.

At year's end, Reed Stenhouse was the world's sixth largest broker, with 6,100 employees and more than 180 offices. It dominated Canada's retail brokerage business, which generated 35 percent of its revenues. U.S. business accounted for 22 percent of revenues, and the United Kingdom and Ireland produced 24 percent. The brokerage also had significant French and Australian operations. Consolidation of U.S. offices offered a good opportunity for expense savings, as all but one of Reed Stenhouse's twenty offices were in locations where A&A operated.[9]

[9] There were similar duplications in the United Kingdom. Reed Stenhouse was unique because it was the only non-U.S. broker with a global business that included a large American operation.

Bill Wilson's approach to A&A was fortuitous. The combination directly eliminated weaknesses in each organization's geographic spread and in areas of specialization such as reinsurance. Stock market analysts applauded the December 1984 merger announcement as a sound strategic move. Some in the media projected financial improvement overnight, though that rarely occurs with significant restructuring.

Management teams faced delicate challenges in balancing analysts' and shareholders' short-term focus with the need to build longer-term value. Producing positive short-term results can be accomplished by slashing expenses. But when such a strategy undermines company strength, disastrous consequences follow.[10]

[10] The corollary occurs when management rationalizes poor operating results by invoking long-term objectives.

Major obstacles precluded the efficient and prompt implementation of a merger with Reed Stenhouse. Various complex tax and accounting issues needed resolution—the most difficult involved the Canadian government's Foreign Investment Review Agency. Personal contact with the Minister of Industry, Trade and Commerce, who supervised the Review Agency, was essential for approval. It was not an easy sale. The minister, Sinclair Stevens, met with Bill Wil-

son and his attorney and separately with me. The minister was negative about our merger prospects, and his meeting with Bill Wilson did not go well. I received a draft memorandum rejecting the merger. The government argued that Reed Stenhouse contributed substantially to Canada's financial service business and that A&A's acquisition was not in the best national interest.

Minister Stevens, part of a new Conservative government, seemed proud that this would be the first merger turned down by his administration. I then spent a half-hour explaining the nature of the global insurance brokerage business. I emphasized the role of our merger in securing Reed Stenhouse's future. The minister aggressively probed what representations A&A could make to ensure Reed Stenhouse's prominent role in the merged company. After our meeting, subsequent negotiations continued to our satisfaction. Six months later, in July 1985, the acquisition took effect.

Americans had high hopes for generating cheap electricity with nuclear power—until the 1979 accident at Three Mile Island, near Harrisburg, Pennsylvania. Murphy's Law played out in a combination of technical failure, human error, and bad luck when a small valve malfunctioned, cooling stopped, and core temperature rose to 4300°. The plant was sealed off in the first general nuclear emergency in the U.S., and officials weighed awful options like whether to evacuate 500,000 people. A robot camera later confirmed that a partial meltdown had come close to poisoning a huge region— perhaps including Philadelphia and Washington—at incalculable cost.

Reed Stenhouse's organizational history was comparable to other major insurance brokerages. Founded by an entrepreneur who selected complementary partners, the firm relied on numerous acquisitions and strong internal growth. As with other global brokers, its original location did not determine success; rather, success depended on the founder and subsequent quality of the staff.

Alexander R. Stenhouse, who founded the company, had an upbringing in Glasgow, Scotland, that was reminiscent of W. F. and C. B. Alexander's in West Virginia. When Stenhouse was two, his father died; money was always scarce, and he had to leave school at age twelve to help support the family. In 1897, at twenty-one, he came to the United States and worked six years as a clerk at the Hartford Fire Insurance Company. There he became fascinated by the automatic sprinkler, a relatively new innovation, and he became a strong advocate of the new safety device.

Returning to the United Kingdom, he worked briefly for the National Insurance Company of Great Britain, then returned to Glasgow and opened an insurance brokerage office in 1904. His passion for the automatic sprinkler paid off; from the start, it enabled lower premiums and attracted more and better-satisfied customers.

Alexander Stenhouse had a friendly, outgoing personality and an amazing ability to instantly recall names and faces. He was also kind, unflappable, and ideally suited for his profession. In addition, he had a keen ability to select excellent associates. A most successful early hire was his partner, James Hope, all five-feet-four-inches of him. Hope had a radiant personality and a genuine fondness for clothes, particularly his huge assortment of hats. He traveled 50,000 miles yearly in his chauffeur-driven car, and could engage anyone in conversation. Another hire, William P. Blyth, was the balancing factor in the partnership for over thirty years. A no-nonsense man with a charming smile, Blyth had a knack for defusing arguments and negotiating acceptable solutions to disagreements.

In 1911, the firm became A. R. Stenhouse, Hope and Blyth (nicknamed "Faith, Hope and Charity"); eight years later, it was Scotland's largest insurance brokerage. In the mid-1920s, James Hope left for several years to head a family confectionery company, and Alexander Stenhouse took up the new business slack. Sought after as a financial and management consultant, Stenhouse would not accept fees for such counsel. Instead, he created opportunities to become insurance broker for those with whom he consulted.[11] Alexander Stenhouse opened his first London office in 1930. Hope rejoined the partnership, and the company name changed to A. R. Stenhouse & Partners.

In 1931, the firm endured a major challenge. Stenhouse and fifteen local businessmen were arrested for fraud. The charges related to the Glasgow Financial Trust and a defunct company that the trust had brought public. Stenhouse was dropped as a defendant in February 1932. Fortunately, the loyalty of clients and staff was not seriously eroded, rapid expansion resumed, and, in 1938, the firm changed from a partnership to a private limited company. Hugh Stenhouse, Alexander's son, joined as an outside inspector of client properties.[12]

When a highly regarded twenty-eight-year-old employee accepted a position elsewhere because there was no opportunity to acquire equity in the firm, Hope and Blyth decided to broaden ownership. Despite the founder's resistance, the other partners prevailed; Stenhouse's share of the restructured firm was reduced to 20 percent.

Almost the entire male staff served in World War II. The government controlled most war risk insurance but permitted brokers a meaningful role in processing it. Stenhouse's remaining staff, while severely taxed, coped with war demands and normal activities. Still, a major loss occurred in 1944 with the sudden death of William Blyth. After Blyth's death and the disruption of war, new business became a top priority in 1946, and a new business group was reorganized by Hope and Hugh Stenhouse. In 1952, Alexander Stenhouse died at age seventy-six. James Hope, the last surviving partner, passed away two years later at

[11] Few insurance brokers operated in Scotland then, and there was little distinction between brokers and agents. Insurance companies attended to most firms' needs. Their branch managers were powerful and very protective of client relationships. Thus, brokers walked tightropes to convince the insurance buyers and the insurance companies of the need for broker services. To enhance broker status, Stenhouse became active in forming broker and agent associations.

[12] Hugh, born in Scotland in 1915, entered the insurance business at age seventeen, served with the Caledonian Insurance Company in Glasgow, and joined Stenhouse in 1938 as an outside inspector. An officer in the Territorial Army, he entered the service in 1939 and narrowly escaped capture at Dunkirk. He later served in North Africa, Italy, and Austria and returned to Stenhouse in 1946 with considerable maturity. In 1949, he became managing director of the firm's London branch, which was established as a separate company to facilitate visibility in the London market.

seventy-four. Upon Alexander Stenhouse's death, Gwylim Edmunds, and after him Charles Kelly, served as temporary chairmen before Hugh Stenhouse assumed the reins in 1955.[13]

Stenhouse had always been seen as a "company broker." The vast majority of the firm's business was placed with insurance companies rather than Lloyd's. Because the firm had no direct Lloyd's representation, Lloyd's placements were made through other brokers. Hugh Stenhouse set out to change this.

In early 1958, H. E. Fincham and two of his senior staff of Lloyd's brokers joined Stenhouse, forming Stenhouse Fincham & Co. Ltd. Other small firms of Lloyd's brokers were acquired, including a Lloyd's underwriting agency with an automobile syndicate. In 1962, Stenhouse purchased Cockshoots Holdings Ltd., a substantial brokerage with a London office that did significant Lloyd's and reinsurance business. A strategic acquisition, J. D. Frew & Co., Ltd., opened the door to American business.[14]

Hugh Stenhouse's vision included expanding the company overseas, starting in the Commonwealth countries. Australia seemed to offer the best potential.[15] By November 1969, various acquisitions made it possible to list the company's share capital on the stock exchange. A year later, amid threats of nationalization, diversification was accomplished by purchasing John Wallace & Sons Ltd., a highly profitable industrial holding company.[16] On November 25, 1971, tragedy struck when Hugh Stenhouse was killed in an automobile accident. This calamity left a void that was never completely filled.

He was succeeded by Gavin Boyd, a Stenhouse director. During his tenure, Stenhouse made an important acquisition in Sir William Garthwaite (Holdings) Ltd., a Lloyd's brokerage engaged principally in the marine and general reinsurance business. This acquisition included a New York subsidiary, Great Eastern Associates Inc., marine brokers and average adjusters. This was Stenhouse's first North American venture.[17]

[13] Until the Blyth and Hope families agreed to sell him controlling shares, Hugh Stenhouse felt stymied in the decision-making process. Once that issue was resolved, he moved full steam ahead.

[14] Frew concentrated on handling the British facilities of American companies, particularly after World War II.

[15] Small firms were acquired in Melbourne and Sydney in May 1961. In 1962, the two largest brokerages in Queensland, Chas. A. Clarke & Son and Noble Hall & Co., Pty Ltd., both of Brisbane, were added. Another important addition was Taddington's Insurance Pty Ltd. in Newcastle, a coal-producing area and large industrial center. John C. Lloyd & Co. Pty Ltd. of Melbourne was an even more significant purchase. A small Adelaide acquisition and the opening of a Perth office gave coverage over the entire continent. Progressively, New Zealand and South Africa were entered. Then came France, where controlling interest in three brokerages was negotiated; a European headquarters office was established in Paris in 1964.

[16] This operation expanded and became ever more successful. It was divested to the public in early 1979 so that Stenhouse could concentrate on the core insurance business.

[17] Other investments included a minority stake, which grew to almost 50 percent, in the French brokerage Société Générale de Crotage d'Assurances. Founded in 1839, it arranged insurance on the Eiffel Tower's construction. A century later, it became the broker for Palais de Chaillot construction.

By 1972, Stenhouse had over sixty offices in the United Kingdom, Ireland, Australia, New Zealand, South Africa, Southeast Asia, the United States, and France. It coveted a strong presence in Canada. Reed Shaw Osler Ltd. was Canada's largest brokerage, and a combination of the firms would create a significant global force. Although a 1968 meeting was unproductive, Judd Whittall, Reed Shaw's chairman, and Hugh Stenhouse met in Britain in 1970, setting in motion a chain of events that resulted in a merger in 1973.

Stenhouse's assets represented 61 percent of the combined total, but it agreed to a 55 percent interest in the new firm. Stenhouse believed its considerable management responsibility offset this equity sacrifice.

Reed Shaw Osler Ltd. had begun as three old, well-established insurance broking firms: Reed Shaw & McNaught; Osler, Hammond and Nanton Insurance Ltd.; and Cronyn, Pocock and Robinson Ltd. It is instructive to briefly review the early history of each of these three firms.

Samuel Shaw opened a Toronto office in 1872. In the early 1890s, his son, George, joined the agency, which became Shaw & Son. Samuel Shaw died in 1899. In 1903, Charles B. McNaught, who formed a Toronto agency in 1901, became George Shaw's new partner. Together they became Shaw & McNaught.

Joseph Reed established his business in 1874 as Stadacona Fire Insurance Company's Toronto agent. The prestigious Liverpool & London & Globe made Reed its agent in 1877. When his sons joined in 1892, the agency became Joseph B. Reed & Sons. Joseph Reed died in 1905. In 1906, the firm merged with Shaw & McNaught and was renamed Joseph B. Reed & Sons, Shaw & McNaught; this was shortened to Reed Shaw & McNaught in 1908.

The firm grew steadily throughout the 1920s. It expanded more rapidly with the 1959 acquisition of B. L. Johnson Walton Ltd. in Vancouver, a marine agency started in 1920.[18] By 1936, an insurance man, Arthur Law, managed Johnson Walton. Subsequently, a young man just out of

[18] One of the principals was Captain Barney Johnson, a glamorous World War I hero. Captain Johnson had no insurance background when the agency was opened, but he was a prolific salesman.

school, James (Judd) Whittall, was hired. He was shrewd and forceful, with a compelling personality. Before World War II, Whittall and Law purchased Johnson's interest. The "new" organization became a total brokerage. Loss prevention and other premium reduction techniques were introduced, and the agency dominated western Canada.[19] The merger with Reed Shaw & McNaught brought both agencies the broad Canadian representation they needed.

[19] During the war, Whittall won a Distinguished Service Cross in the Sicily invasion; later, he returned to Johnson Walton as a senior partner.

Osler and Hammond Ltd., a Toronto mortgage and finance firm, sent a young man named Augustus Nanton to western Canada to develop business in about 1881. By 1883, his rapid success had led to the firm's new name, Osler Hammond & Nanton Ltd. Soon insurance was added to other services. The insurance sector prospered, opening branches in Calgary, Vancouver, and six other major cities. In 1964, the insurance brokerage separated from the firm, incorporating as Osler Hammond & Nanton Insurance Ltd. It wanted to go public but required a broader base.

Marsh & McLennan sought to acquire Reed Shaw & McNaught in 1967. The approach was rejected but fortified the belief that it was time for Reed Shaw & McNaught to become a public company. Osler Hammond & Nanton, with its strength in western Canada, was a natural partner. By accident, this turned into a three-way deal. Both agencies had barely concluded merger terms and were celebrating in Toronto when George McEvenue, the president of the Cronyn, Pocock and Robinson Ltd. insurance agency, arrived. When he learned the reason for the celebration, McEvenue instantly asked to be included. After a week's due diligence, he was. After the three-firm merger, stock shares were offered to the public. Reed Shaw Osler Ltd. became Canada's largest insurance broker.[20]

[20] Ontario-based Cronyn, Pocock and Robinson Ltd. was established in 1930 as the successor to the Beddom Brown Insurance Agencies, which had been founded in 1850. By 1968, the firm was highly regarded with branches in Toronto, Winnipeg, and Montreal.

For five years after the Stenhouse merger, the merged company used the Reed Shaw Osler Ltd. name, although each former entity operated independently. In 1978, global identity became an issue; thus, the name was changed to Reed Stenhouse Companies Ltd. Toronto remained its base.

Judd Whittall effectively managed the firm, melding together its parts and forming a strong and cohesive organization. In 1979, William Wilson succeeded him as CEO. Born and bred near Glasgow, Wilson became a chartered accountant at the Deloitte accounting firm and then joined Stenhouse Holdings in 1961 as group accountant. In 1966, he became a board member and the financial director. Wilson helped negotiate the 1973 Stenhouse–Reed Shaw Osler merger and became vice president for finance and chief financial officer of the combined enterprise. Energetic, intelligent, and pragmatic, and with a keen sense of humor, Wilson built on Judd Whittall's strategy of solidifying Reed Stenhouse's global operations.

Bill Wilson was willing to forgo short-term success to develop a profitable U.S. subsidiary. If Stenhouse and Reed Shaw Osler had merged several years earlier, this goal might have been realized, because premier U.S. acquisitions were still available. Unfortunately, without a strong U.S. base in place before the mid-1970s, it was nearly impossible to build a first-rate U.S. brokerage organization. By the end of the decade, it was impossible. Efforts to build a strong U.S. base drained Reed Stenhouse's management and financial resources that might have been better used elsewhere. However, the firm was able to acquire several large U.S. agencies.

In 1974, it purchased Insurance Consultants, Inc. (ICI), of St. Louis. S. Lee Kling, an influential national Democratic Party fund raiser, had formed this seven-office operation in 1964. In 1977, Underwriters Service, Inc., of San Francisco was acquired. This agency originated in 1920 as Contractors Insurance Agency of California, an insurance brokerage and manager of Contractors Indemnity Exchange of California. Large contractors such as W. A. Bechtel sponsored this exchange to insure their workmen's compensation exposure, which traditionally was placed in the State Fund at exorbitant cost. More or less, the agency became a captive broker for W. A. Bechtel and Henry J. Kaiser until it merged with Reed Stenhouse. Shiff Terhune, an old, well-respected New York City agency with 250 employees, was added in 1982 and became Reed Stenhouse's largest U.S. office.

[21] They included Bill Wilson, the new chairman and CEO of Alexander & Alexander International Inc.; John Devine, David French, and Cedric Gyles, who were responsible for Reed Stenhouse's three major geographic regions; and two nonexecutive Reed Stenhouse directors—Douglas Gardner, the nonexecutive chairman of Reed Stenhouse companies, and Angus Grossart, chairman of Noble Grossart Limited in Edinburgh. New directors from A&A were Ronald Iles, the deputy chairman of Alexander Howden Holdings in London; Bobby Cline and James McCormick, responsible for U.S. geographic areas; and Rolf Towe, chief financial officer. In May, a fourth external director was added—Kenneth Black Jr., Regents' Professor of Insurance at Georgia State University and a nationally recognized scholar.

After acquiring Reed Stenhouse, A&A had offices in ninety-two American, twenty-three Canadian, and thirty British locations. At that time, A&A was probably the largest retail insurance broker in the United States, Canada, Australia, and New Zealand. When Reed Stenhouse joined A&A, the board expanded to eighteen with the addition of ten new board directors, six of whom were associated with Reed Stenhouse.[21]

Its complementary nature aside, the merger's size and geographic scope was difficult to digest. Some aspects—unit name changes, for instance—were not fully implemented until 1993. Problems were anticipated, but their severity was not. Strong individual cultures had to be blended and incompatible electronic data processing systems synthesized. Reed Stenhouse's reinsurance group dissolved because the principals no longer controlled the unit. Additionally, there were the inevitable difficulties of combining Reed Stenhouse and A&A offices in twenty American cities.

Satisfactory integration throughout the company's global system was also a significant challenge. We needed a sophisticated plan with clearly defined objectives, but planning and execution were not always successful. Administrative costs were initially higher than anticipated and only slowly came under control. Despite our difficulties, the combination was a positive move.

We promptly realized one reward when, competing with six other brokers, our new U.K. operation won the prestigious British Gas account. The combined expertise of Reed Stenhouse and Howden personnel in financial analysis, loss control, and other risk management skills was decisive. Likewise, Canadian and U.S. teamwork won a significant part of Toyota's North American account.

Later in 1985, complying with Lloyd's requirement that brokers divest themselves of managing agencies, A&A sold most of Alexander Howden Underwriting Limited (AHUL) to the newly formed A. J. Archer & Partners. The larger

AHUL syndicates were in this group. Devonshire Under-writing Agencies Limited purchased remaining portions. The members' agency was temporarily retained and from January 1, 1986 was renamed Alexander Howden & Beck Limited. It looked after the affairs of 560 Names, with a total capacity of about £106 million, and it supported more than 150 Lloyd's syndicates.

In 1986, for the first time, A&A's operating revenues topped $1 billion. The general consensus was that A&A then had the world's largest retail brokerage operation. We made several small acquisitions in the late 1980s.[22] Most enhanced our existing operations, but we also added agencies specializing in the mass marketing of insurance products and conducting surveys.

Insurance market pricing had been tight for two years, but then it started to moderate and remained soft and highly competitive for the balance of the century. In light of insurers' uncertain and extraordinary liabilities, it was mystifying that so many succumbed to aggressive price competition. For many, maintaining or increasing market share was an overriding goal, irrespective of potential financial impact.

As the decade of the 1980s approached its end, other developments were setting the stage for a decade during which the structure of the industry would be fundamentally changed.

[22] While U.S. acquisitions had pretty well dried up by 1987, we did acquire Kientz & Company in Columbus, Ohio, one of the country's finer small agencies. Its head, William D. Kientz, left no stone unturned to ensure that each of his employees was fully trained in his or her specialty. Training to this degree was seldom seen elsewhere.

CHAPTER 20

A Cataclysm of Torts:
Risks Run Amok

During the 1980s and 1990s, the most troublesome development for the global insurance industry was the specter of gargantuan liabilities that derived primarily from asbestos, environmental pollution, and medical malpractice claims. Changes in U.S. tort law grew dramatically during this period. Courts assumed a decisive role as final arbiters of safety. There are thousands of trial courts in the United States: fifty state courts of final appeal (most of them supreme courts); hundreds of trial courts in the federal judiciary (district courts), then federal courts of appeal, and, finally, the U. S. Supreme Court. For many companies and organizations, America's court system was an endless maze of threats, particularly in interpreting the wording of insurance policies.

Insurance companies were stunned by the magnitude of what they faced. The combination of the rapid expansion of various judges' definitions of liability and the astronomical sums awarded by juries (especially for punitive damages) had devastating effects on insurers and other defendants. As one executive observed, "Unguided juries, like bolts of lightning, wreak retribution on wrongdoers in amounts determined primarily by instinct, passion and the chemistry of a particular wholly unique case." Although the language of insurance may often be ambiguous, judgments frequently ignored policies' specific provisions. In 1999, the ten largest jury verdicts for individuals and families totaled $8.86 billion, with punitive damages accounting for 88 percent.

Many judges, juries, and politicians saw insurers as having deep and accessible pockets. When court decisions mandated penalties exceeding economic loss or gave compensation for unforeseeable events, insurers understandably priced their product accordingly. Higher prices for many products and coverages resulted. For example, roughly a third of a stepladder's price was insurance related, as was a similar portion of the cost of a ski lift ticket. The medical field suffered especially serious repercussions. When a neurologist in Dade County, Florida, paid $250,000 a year for professional liability insurance, or when obstetricians and gynecologists paid nearly $200,000 for protection, they and their patients bore an unreasonable economic burden.

The overall costs of America's legal system were staggering. The actuarial firm Tillinghast reported that, from 1933 to 1950, tort costs generally rose in line with the overall economy. After 1950, they rose at a compounded yearly rate of 12 percent. This increased to about 16 percent in the early 1980s, and then dropped to a single digit later in the decade. The growth rate of tort costs was four times greater than the rate of economic output for the same period. America's tort system was by far the most expensive in the industrial world.

The Institute of Civil Justice, a nonprofit research group, estimated that in 1985 our legal system spent $16 billion to $19 billion in transaction costs to deliver $14 billion to $16 billion in net compensation to plaintiffs. Tillinghast found that tort claims expenses that year—based on lawyers' fees, claimants' payouts, and insurers' administrative costs— were $80 billion. For 1987, Tillinghast calculated that tort claims cost the country $117 billion. This included payments to resolve all the potential lawsuits that never reached the courts, as well as insurer costs to process claims and defend suits.

Huge jury awards favoring plaintiffs seemed to mirror a public mindset. A 1987 *Wall Street Journal* account of a law professor's experience was symptomatic. She had tripped on her untied shoelace while running through an airport and injured her leg. Witnesses said not to worry because they would testify when she sued. She later recounted this experience to her law class; the consensus among the law students was to sue the shoe manufacturer and the contractor who poured the concrete.

Judge Richard Neely of the West Virginia Supreme Court, a well-informed appraiser of the system, wryly remarked in his book, *The Product Liability Mess: How Business Can Be Rescued from the Politics of the State Courts,* "As long as I am allowed to redistribute wealth from out-of-state companies to injured in-the-state plaintiffs, I shall continue to do so. Not only is my sleep enhanced when I give someone else's money away, but so is my job security because in-state plaintiffs, their family and friends will reelect me. My micro-problem as a judge who wants to sleep at night has begun to create a macro-problem for the entire economy."

In the politicized context, advertising became a frequent means of soliciting clients. In the late 1970s, lawyers began placing advertisements in the popular media to attract persons who felt they were experiencing pressure, stress, or mistreatment on their jobs—in other words, seeking clients with the object of suing.

Indirect costs were impossible to quantify. When insurance prices rose to prohibitive levels, manufacturers ceased making certain products. Once there were fourteen U.S. manufacturers of football helmets; then, for a time, there were none. One top builder of privately owned airplanes withdrew from the market. Of greater concern, the manufacturer of whooping cough vaccine ceased production until the government intervened. This led to a 1986 federal law shielding vaccine producers from all liability unrelated to manufacturing error. As Peter W. Huber, a prominent attorney and engineer, noted in 1987, "The legal system's current message to scientists and engineers is: don't innovate; don't experiment; don't be venturesome; don't go out on a limb." He reported that product liability cases in federal courts rose from 1,579 in 1975 to 13,554 in 1985.

In trying to protect itself, the fragmented insurer community was no match for well-organized consumer groups and trial lawyers. The media often fomented public resentment of insurers by highlighting increased insurance costs without exploring the reasons. Few people accepted the insurers' plea that they were the victims and not the cause for the frequent absence of affordable insurance. A Texas attorney general captured the public mood when he noted, "Two things people hate are lawyers and insurance companies!"

Some relief came in the late 1980s from individual states as one by one they examined the issues. Remedies generally focused on particular aspects and varied widely by state. Any federal-level approach that carried the potential of adopting uniform standards was doomed from the start. With many lawyers in Congress closely aligned with trial lawyers, and with a public unsympathetic to insurers' solvency, restructuring the tort system was not realistic.

Although one can sympathize with insurance companies that had to pay claims for situations where no coverage was intended, in many instances insurers wrote liability policies that covered any risk not specifically excluded. Asbestos and the diseases it caused (asbestosis, lung cancer, and more), were the most costly problems from such policies. The claims they engendered were enormous. While asbestos adversely affected most liability insurance markets, Lloyd's was particularly vulnerable because of its huge reinsurance exposure.

Warnings about potential health hazards associated with asbestos were issued periodically after World War I in the United States and the United Kingdom. Life insurance companies were concerned, as were government agencies and medical groups. Liability underwriters should have been aware of these concerns, but they were not reflected in their underwriting decisions. For years, no asbestosis claims materialized; it was not until the mid-1970s that they started to proliferate. By then, it was too late.

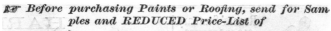

☞ *Before purchasing Paints or Roofing, send for Samples and REDUCED Price-List of*

H.W. JOHNS' **ASBESTOS** PATENT

MATERIALS

ASBESTOS IS A FIBROUS STONE, INDESTRUCTIBLE BY FIRE OR ACIDS.

ASBESTOS ROOFING.

This article is now well known in all parts of this country as the only reliable standard, low-priced Roofing. It is furnished in rolls ready for nailing to the roof, weighs only about 60 pounds to 100 square feet, and when finished with the **Fire-Proof** Asbestos Coating, presents a handsome white or light-gray surface. It is adapted for steep and flat Roofs in all climates, costs about half as much as Tin, and can be readily applied by any one.

☞ Do not be deceived by worthless materials which are represented by unscrupulous parties as genuine ASBESTOS ROOFING. *THERE IS NO OTHER RELIABLE PORTABLE ROOFING IN THE MARKET.* The cheap, tarred felts, petroleum oil paints, &c., which are sold as Roofings under various names, and warranted by irresponsible venders to be more durable than the standard articles, are a source of constant annoyance and expense, while a reliable Roofing from reputable manufacturers can be purchased at about the same price asked for these worthless articles.

ASBESTOS ROOF PAINT.

Cheap and versatile, in the late 19th century asbestos seems a miracle product, the perfect material to waterproof, fireproof, and insulate the roofs of buildings in burgeoning cities. The ancient Greeks used asbestos in their cloth, and the Romans in their building materials. American use of asbestos peaked during World War II and into the 1970s until evidence began to show that it causes health problems, many of them lethal.

If underwriters had heeded the warnings, they could have saved billions of dollars. However, excluding a specific product such as asbestos from insurance coverage would have required the backing of the full insurance market. For competitive reasons, such cooperation was not to be.

As Adam Raphael has noted, for underwriters, the gravity was compounded by U.S. court interpretations of insurance policy conditions. Policies were originally written on an "occurrence basis"; this provided coverage for exposure to conditions that caused bodily injury at any time during the policy period. With respect to asbestos, the U.S. courts ruled that claims could be made at any time in the future for exposure that occurred in the past. Thus, a claimant could contend that coverage existed with any policy written during the latent period. Most underwriters argued for the manifestation theory; namely, that coverage should be restricted to policies in force when the disease was first diagnosed. Alternatively, asbestos manufacturers argued for the exposure theory—that associated diseases were covered by all policies in force during the entire period of exposure.

Raphael graphically described the plight of the Keene Corporation, which in 1968 purchased for $8 million Baldwin Ehret Hill, a firm that made a product containing about 10 percent asbestos. Between 1968 and 1972, Baldwin sold $15 million worth of asbestos-containing products out of total sales of more than $500 million. In 1972, Keene eliminated its use of asbestos and closed Baldwin in 1975.

Twenty years later, Keene's founder, Glenn Bailey, reported that the company had paid out $400 million to resolve asbestosis claims stemming from Baldwin products. Approximately two-thirds had gone to lawyers, and there was no end in sight. The company was spending $800,000 a week on asbestos-related litigation. Bailey noted that Keene had done nothing illegal or improper. In response to contemporary medical research, the company's cartons bore caution labels and instructions on how to handle its products.

The courts were not sympathetic to Keene's position. They backed the exposure theory and went even further on appeal. A court of appeals ruled as relevant both the exposure theory and the manifestation theory. It ruled that all policies were valid from the very first exposure to asbestos inhalation to the outbreak of the disease decades later. In 1982, the U.S. Supreme Court declined further appeal. Bailey reported that sixteen of its codefendants had been bankrupted. Under the "joint-and-several responsibility rule," remaining defendants shouldered the burden. Insurance coverage offered inadequate protection for such huge awards, and litigation consumed most of Glenn Bailey's time. In essence, the company was almost ruined by an $8 million investment.

The following is text visible on the signs in the photograph: A CANCER EPID[EMIC]; WE NEED A HEALTH SCREENING PROGRAM; CLOTHING CONTAMINATED WITH ASBESTOS HAS AFFECTED THE HEALTH OF ASBESTOS WORKERS FAMILIES; AM I KILLING MY FAMILY WITH ASBESTOS?; COMPANY COMPANY PHYSICALS not adequate; TO MANY FELLOW WORKERS DEAD!; I HOPE I DONT GET IT; ASBESTOS IS HARMFUL TO YOUR HEALTH ICWU LOCAL 146 Lompoc C[A]; COMPANY PHYSICAL KILLING US; WE ARE ALSO DYING IN J.M.'S PLANT! LOMPOC. I.C.W.U. LOCAL 146; RECENT DEATHS ALVIN ADLER- Fred Aguilar Bob Yeager- Tom Mills Leland Pinney - Ed Knapp Alfred Jalbert- Joe Core Earl Kerlin - Rich Pfeifer

By January 1989, more than 60,000 bodily injury claims were pending against twenty-one asbestos manufacturers, with up to 2,000 new claims monthly. Lloyd's syndicate Names were just beginning to realize that they were subject to risks about which they had little knowledge or understanding.

The quandary for insurers was demonstrated by a case involving Fiberboard Corporation. In 1993, a global settlement, subject to court review, was entered into by insurers owned by The Chubb Corporation and CNA Financial Corporation, together with Fiberboard and attorneys representing claimants against Fiberboard. The amount of the settlement was approximately $1.5 billion and was approved by a Texas district court. It was upheld by an appellate court but returned to that court by the U.S. Supreme Court for further review. The U.S. Court of

Employees of a California plant that used asbestos in its products demonstrate for new, augmented health benefits to cover asbestos-related illnesses in 1976. Late in the century, asbestos was seen as a sinister material that lies dormant, often causing lung diseases and cancers 30 years after exposure. Liability suits became common—and financially devastating—as companies that had once used asbestos were held culpable decades after the fact. Informed estimates of potential liability now exceed $200 billion.

Appeals for the Fifth Circuit reaffirmed its decision, but a further appeal sent the case back to the Supreme Court. In June 1999, the Supreme Court threw out the settlement as being unfair to potential litigants. Meanwhile, the insurers and claimants lived with uncertainty for years. At the end of 2001, nearly 2,000 companies with potential asbestos liability operated under similar uncertainties.

If asbestos was an 800-pound gorilla for insurers, environmental pollution was also showing signs of becoming a very weighty issue. In 1980, Congress passed the Comprehensive Environmental Response, Compensation and Liability Act, which mandated the cleanup of pollution sites irrespective of cost. The legislation was retroactive and included joint-and-several liability

Again, insurers were targeted as the deep pockets. And again they had not excluded the peril in their liability policies nor factored in premiums for its inclusion. Moreover, there were no aggregate liability or time limits restricting loss exposure. During the 1950s and 1960s, Lloyd's underwriters wrote broadly inclusive general liability policies that contained no exclusion for environmental pollution. By 1973, U.S. underwriters began to add pollution exclusions but continued providing relevant coverage if the event was "sudden and accidental." Most U.S. underwriters ceased writing pollution coverage in 1985, except on a specific basis. U.K. underwriters, on the other hand, waited until 1990 to restrict their policies. As with asbestos, many U.S. courts expanded policy coverage—this time by deeming almost any pollution claim as sudden and accidental. With pollution, however, there was less unanimity among the courts, with some backing the insurers' position. Uncertainty was the order of the day.

A. M. Best Co., the highly respected organization that rates insurance companies, estimated in 1995 that asbestos and pollution claims could ultimately cost $132 billion. The unnerving question was what portion of this enormous sum would be the insurers' responsibility.

In its 1998 *Annual Report*, Chubb summarized the insurers' frustration, noting:

. . . judicial decisions and legislative actions continue to broaden liability and policy definitions and to increase the severity of claim payments. As a result of this and other societal and economic developments, the uncertainties inherent in estimating ultimate claim costs on the basis of past experience continue to further complicate the already complex loss reserving process.

The uncertainties relating to asbestos and toxic waste claims on insurance policies written many years ago are exacerbated by inconsistent court decisions and judicial and legislative interpretations of coverage that in some cases have tended to erode the clear and express intent of such policies and in others have expanded theories of liability. The industry is engaged in extensive litigation over these coverage and liability issues and is thus confronted with a continuing uncertainty in its efforts to quantify these exposures.

Chubb's 2000 *Annual Report* updated the gravity of the asbestos situation for insurers, reporting:

Asbestos remains the most significant and difficult mass tort for the insurance industry in terms of claims volume and dollar exposure. . . . Our other asbestos exposures are mostly peripheral defendants, including a mix of manufacturers, distributors and installers of certain products that contain asbestos as well as premises owners. . . . As the financial resources of traditional asbestos defendants have been depleted, plaintiffs are targeting these peripheral parties with greater frequency and in many cases for larger awards. In addition, the plaintiffs bar continues to solicit new claimants through extensive advertising. . . . Class actions are then initiated even though many of the claimants have not manifested evidence of serious injury. Thus new asbestos claims and new exposures on existing claims have continued unabated despite the fact that practically all manufacturing and usage of asbestos ended nearly two decades ago.

Adding credibility to Chubb's warning in 2001, A. M. Best Co. reported that property/casualty companies' ultimate asbestos liabilities alone could be $65 billion—or 63 percent higher than estimated four years earlier.

It is regrettable that underwriters were not more discriminating in taking on huge liabilities, but they could not have known that policies would be variously construed by different courts. Sometimes the underwriter's judgment is good, and other times it is flawed. As for Lloyd's underwriters, their remuneration is partly dependent on underwriting results, and no one can question their intent to make a profit. However, when they compound potential underwriting liabilities by faulty reinsurance, the financial fallout can be catastrophic.

Insurance brokerages also were subject to U.S. tort system vagaries. Suits against them for various errors or omissions were increasingly common. In many cases, brokers were at the mercy of unpredictable jury deliberations over extremely complex issues. Verdicts were often confusing and resulted in an expensive appeal process. Brokers' professional liability exposures were huge—and because of the prohibitive cost of their own professional coverage, they were increasingly self-insured except for high excess limits.

Clearly, as an anthem of an earlier generation had it, the times they were a-changin'.

CHAPTER 21

Riding the Roller Coaster: Upheavals of the Eighties and Nineties

The late 1980s seemed merely a preparation for what was to follow—a frenetic decade in which technological influence, proliferation of alternative risk-funding techniques, and unimaginably large acquisitions changed the business of insurance.

In February 1987, I announced that I would relinquish my responsibilities as CEO of Alexander & Alexander in May and retire a year later. I would continue as a director. The board elected Tinsley (T.) Irvin to replace me, and he chose Mike White and Bill Wilson to become executive vice presidents.

Irvin, the logical and correct choice, was well prepared. Commanding a thorough knowledge of the business, he was excellent at dealing with clients and people in general. His task was enormous, since A&A's resources were severely depleted by the personal and financial costs of events in London. Many problems posed open-ended financial threats and were both expensive and difficult to resolve. Some resulted in major setbacks, but T. addressed them vigorously.

Before retiring, I spoke out on two issues that were especially troubling. As my first concern, I pointed out that some senior insurers appeared apathetic about the steady erosion of their market share by new methods of handling risk. These included captive insurance companies, risk

1 Signs of change began
appearing as early as the
1950s, but most insurers
minimized the trend.

retention groups, self-insurance, and other risk-financing techniques.[1]

Captive insurance companies underwrite their parent company's own risks.[2] They appeared in the mid-1800s but took over a century to gain prominence. The first significant captive was British Petroleum's Tanker Insurance, formed in 1919. Today, most of the *Fortune* 500 companies and many other organizations around the world use a captive in some form.[3] The advantages of a captive include the following: opportunities to share underwriting profits normally retained by conventional insurers; options of having a formalized means for self-insuring high-frequency risks with a fairly predictable loss ratio; uses as a means to insure some low-frequency, high-severity risks where coverage is unavailable in the traditional market; methods for providing direct access to reinsurers; and a method to permit the parent company to retain control.

In 1986, the Federal Liability Risk Retention Act introduced two alternative programs to facilitate access to liability coverage, "risk retention groups" and "purchasing groups." Risk retention groups are organizations with similar risk exposures who join together to provide their members with most types of liability insurance. They must be chartered or licensed under the laws of a state. Purchasing groups are organizations within the same industry that join together to buy liability coverage for common risks.

Lloyd's diminishing capacity in the early 1980s resulted in sharp price increases by mid-decade. U.S. brokerages, concerned about Lloyd's future, sought additional capacity elsewhere. Marsh & McLennan acted decisively when it decided that alternative insurance facilities were urgently required. The firm was instrumental in forming American Casualty Excess Insurance Company (ACE Ltd.) in 1985 and EXEL Ltd. (later XL Capital Ltd.) in 1986.[4]

M&M acted on another opportunity in 1992. After Hurricane Andrew forced catastrophe reinsurance rates to rise by 40 percent, M&M and J. P. Morgan & Co. organized Mid-Ocean Reinsurance Company, a property catastrophe reinsurer that immediately became highly profitable. Other

[2] A captive insurer is an insurance company that is wholly owned by a noninsurance organization, usually a large company or group of companies in the same business. The captive insurer's purpose is to insure or reinsure the risks of the parent organization, though captives can also cover risks of nonrelated parties.

[3] Captives were usually formed in tax havens, Bermuda being the favored site. Other preferred locations were the Cayman Islands, Guernsey, Luxembourg, and Barbados. Vermont was the preferred state in which to operate a U.S. captive.

[4] Both of these were established in Bermuda as liability insurers pooling client risks. ACE, for example, was formed with the financial backing of thirty-four large corporations and other investors including J. P. Morgan and M&M. ACE specialized in excess liability coverage at limits in excess of $100 million. Both facilities were very successful, and many major corporations insured with them. They were eventually listed on the New York Stock Exchange and grew in part by acquiring other Bermuda reinsurers.

catastrophe reinsurers quickly followed in Bermuda; almost all partnered with insurers or insurance brokerages joining with investment bankers.

Self-insurance increasingly was used for cost-effective risk management. This was particularly effective with workers compensation insurance, where U.S. companies assumed high deductibles.

For many years, traditional insurers had not seemed concerned about alternative risk funding. They felt that there was adequate business available for future growth. But by 1995, their market share stood at only 56.4 percent and was dropping steadily. This trend was finally taken seriously by some American and European insurers, as well as reinsurers who started investing in new Bermuda reinsurers.

Insurer solvency was the second issue I addressed as I prepared to pass the torch. Solvency was threatened by inept underwriting, changing legal concepts of liability, abrupt economic swings, and an inability to keep abreast of increasingly sophisticated technological and scientific change. Most underwriting organizations dealt successfully with these challenges and remained financially sound. But others, primarily small reinsurers headquartered outside the United States, fought to stay alive. Some companies' inability to meet their obligations led them to delay or resist paying legitimate claims.[5]

Among A&A's ongoing successes was the development of three subsidiaries that were not engaged in its core business. Although all three were eventually to be spun off, because it was difficult for us to monitor their operations or in order to raise needed capital, each became a leader in its field under our management.

TIFCO, the premium finance organization created in 1972, had grown to become the second largest in its industry, with assets of $400 million. Its 190 employees serviced 70,000 individual accounts, and they operated from eleven U.S. offices and one in Canada. Thanks to TIFCO's reputation, it was utilized by more than 2,000 other insurance

[5] Unfortunately, such behavior was not always confined to financially troubled companies. To the extent that American insurers tried to evade claims, their actions threatened their campaign for civil justice reform and further eroded the concept of intent in insurance contracts.

brokerages and agents. Although profitable, results were strongly influenced by the insurance cycle. The operation struggled along with A&A's retail insurance unit when insurance pricing was soft. Consequently, we decided to sell TIFCO, and entered into a definitive agreement with Transamerica Financial Corporation in September 1988. The year before, Transamerica had purchased Borg Warner Acceptance Corporation, which owned the fourth largest premium finance company.

Strategis was the A&A facility serving corporations' special tax consulting needs. Started in Lincoln, Nebraska, in 1975, it counseled on ad valorem taxes and performed related services. By late 1987, sixteen Strategis offices with 250 employees were generating the largest revenue in the independent tax consulting industry.[6] A&A's challenge was to help Strategis become profitable, as this was a stand-alone operation having no synergy with other A&A services. Our senior management had inadequate time to assist in plotting a future course or to give the subsidiary the attention it deserved. Strategis was sold in 1992 to its employees.

Alexsis was a third-party administrator that handled claims for companies that self-insured their workers compensation exposure. With about 1,000 clients, it offered claims administration, telereporting, litigation management, managed care services, adjuster services, administrative services for associations, and excess insurance placement.[7]

Alexsis was a complicated enterprise to oversee, with potential accounting and control problems that made it vulnerable to litigation. It also had limited synergy with A&A's core business. Moreover, competing brokers frequently directed their clients to other providers, thereby eliminating a potential revenue source. Most important, a new state-of-the-art (and very expensive) computer was required for increased profitability and efficient claims handling. Consequently, we sold Alexsis to CNA Financial Corporation in 1995.

[6] The company expanded to include real estate appraisals and corporate valuation services, and it was equipped to handle complicated tax assignments in each of the fifty states, including a wide variety of taxing jurisdictions. Specialists were also knowledgeable in IRS and SEC regulations. Strategis represented a sound business addressing a real need. It experienced rapid growth, internally and externally, and made a number of acquisitions.

[7] Some 70 percent of the claims related to workers compensation and 20 percent to general liability. Headquartered in Northville, Michigan, Alexsis operated from some sixty offices in thirty-seven states. Revenues over the years grew to approximately $100 million, and it became the country's second-largest property/casualty third-party claims administrator.

In July 1988, Lloyd's held a formal dinner for me in London, hosted by its chairman, Murray Lawrence, and attended by three of his predecessors. The chairman wrote a generous letter that, although addressed to me, was intended for A&A employees and outside directors who had responded to the calamitous London events of the early 1980s. In part the letter read:

I would particularly highlight the Lloyd's aspects of your distinguished career and especially the great contribution you made to helping to resolve some of the most difficult problems that affected the Lloyd's market in the early 1980s. Your integrity and tireless commitment to resolving these problems at whatever costs in terms of demands and strains on yourself, your family and your colleagues was outstanding.

As the 1980s came to a close, little business had been lost because of the furor surrounding the Howden acquisition. This was testimony to the extraordinary efforts of loyal

Within years of the first "billion dollar" hurricane, that level of loss occurred more frequently. For example, the loss in boats alone topped $500 million in 1992 when Hurricane Andrew hit southern Florida. Causing 65 deaths and $16 billion in insured losses, the storm contributed to a terrible year for insurers; they paid out $1.16 for every $1.00 of premium.

employees who faced month after month of hardship and frustration. Ron Iles merited special recognition for holding his staff together and leading Howden's outstanding London-based reinsurance operation. The adage that people can pull together in adverse times was never more poignantly demonstrated than by A&A employees during that tumultuous decade.[8]

[8] In 1989, Douglas Gardner retired as an A&A director and new directors were named: Robert Boni, a former CEO of Armco, Inc., and Peter Godsoe, the future CEO of the Bank of Nova Scotia. Doug Gardner had been an asset to the firm. A straightforward thinker, he was supportive of management, yet he could be very firm with constructive criticism. He epitomized the director who was sensitive to shareholder interests while not being oppressive to company management.

From the late 1980s, insurance companies, agencies, and brokerages expanded through acquisitions. This historic pattern set the stage for the 1990s, when global brokerage behemoths were created, and it was becoming evident that the insurance brokerage industry was experiencing a sea change. On a slightly lesser scale, similar conditions existed for U.S. insurers. Meanwhile, in Europe, banks were emerging as cores of enormous financial service conglomerates, which included many of the continent's largest insurance companies.

Based on 1989 year-end revenue, the ten largest global brokerages were Marsh & McLennan, Alexander & Alexander, Sedgwick Group, Johnson & Higgins, Willis Faber, Corroon & Black, Frank B. Hall (controlled by Reliance Group Holdings, Inc. [Reliance]), Rollins Burdick Hunter (owned by Aon), Minet, and C. E. Heath. Except for Marsh & McLennan, Rollins Burdick Hunter, and Heath, all faced serious challenges in the 1990s. Some issues, notably the insurance marketplace, were common to all brokerages. On the other hand, each had its own set of problems.

M&M's only highly visible snafu occurred in 1984. Its treasury department accumulated $2 billion in government securities on credit, transferred funds to brokers when prices declined, and made other unauthorized investments. A loss of $155 million, plus $10 million in legal fees, illustrated one of the most challenging responsibilities facing a brokerage: the importance of internal controls. M&M subsequently formed an ad hoc committee headed by Frank Tasco, which mandated a "return to basics." His work earned high marks within the company and contributed to his election as CEO in 1986. Tasco gave M&M many years of steady and wise leadership.

In 1990, Corroon & Black and Willis Faber negotiated a merger that startled the insurance world. The new firm, Willis Corroon plc became the world's fourth largest brokerage and gave Willis Faber a strong U.S. market presence. Corroon & Black now had top Lloyd's representation and entrenched positions in the United Kingdom and other overseas locations. Unfortunately, the new company ran into complications. A previous Corroon & Black acquisition, Synercon, was a fine organization, but the two brokerages' senior executives did not mesh well. This caused internal problems, and the Synercon team gradually became dominant. Meanwhile, their growth in the United States faltered. Internationally, Willis Faber continued its policy of working through correspondents. Curiously, it extended this practice even as other major brokerages built global organizations that gained control of local operations.

Eventually, Willis Corroon's competitive position deteriorated, and by 1995, the firm was in trouble. In early 1995, *Lloyd's List* commented, "Willis Corroon still looks like a very sick company. Crisis management has been necessary to cut the vast cost base which management has progressively built up since 1991 . . . it has set some ludicrous targets for returns in all five of its key areas. Given the severe problems in U.S. retail broking, these targets of a minimum of 15 percent returns after investment and brokerage/fee income are a joke. Hell probably stands a greater chance of freezing over." The *Sunday Times* was equally critical, observing, "Results last week from Willis Corroon, the insurance broker, showed just how troubled the company has become." Barclays de Zoete Wedd research made the most incisive observation, "The Willis Corroon Group has failed to outline a coherent strategy since the 1990 merger of Willis Faber and Corroon & Black and has been hampered by a confused chain of command." Despite obvious problems, Willis Corroon remained a major force and a tough competitor.

The 1990 Willis Corroon merger had sent shock waves through Johnson & Higgins. To lose an invaluable partner of over ninety years is distressing, but to have the rug pulled out from under your international organization is devastating. Over the years, J&H and Willis Faber had worked diligently to sort out their respective futures. In 1985, Willis Faber proposed a merger that might have produced an international powerhouse. Not consummating this merger contributed to J&H's later decision not to remain independent.

Sedgwick's challenge in 1990 continued to be the integration of its 1985 Fred. S. James acquisition. The merger was not working out as expected, and U.S. growth was lagging. In part, this was caused by James Co.'s acquisitions, which were not as profitable as expected. [9] Another obstacle was that Sedgwick and James maintained separate retail and wholesale broking operations. Additionally, as major competitors expanded substantially, Sedgwick did not.

[9] These included the 1986 purchase of the E. H. Crump Cos., Inc. in Memphis, Tennessee.

In the case of Minet, by 1990, revenue growth could not keep it viable. Its acquisition by the St. Paul Companies, Inc., offered financial support, but nothing else. It was only a matter of time before St. Paul would sell Minet to a large brokerage.

As the decade began, Frank B. Hall and Alexander & Alexander were extremely vulnerable. [10] Hall defended itself against a potential raider and contended with the curse of owning insurance companies. It did neither well. In 1981, the Ryder System, a truck and car leasing firm, acquired a 9.2 percent stock position in F. B. Hall. Hall reacted to this unwanted investment by purchasing a Ryder competitor, Jartran, Inc. Ryder subsequently sold its F. B. Hall shares to Reliance Group Holdings, Inc., but Jartran went bankrupt and incurred $110 million in pretax losses.

[10] In May 1987, A&A learned that the Fireman's Fund Corporation, a major insurance underwriter, had purchased 9.2 percent of its stock. Many observers were convinced that large insurers would eventually acquire agents and brokers, and they expected a takeover. This purchase, however, was purely an investment, and nothing further came from it.

Frank B. Hall and its insurance subsidiaries were targets of litigation throughout the 1980s. Several cases were particularly damaging, including those related to a devastating 1980 fire that killed eighty-five people and injured 591 at the Las Vegas hotel owned by MGM Grand Hotels, Inc. (MGM). F. B. Hall placed backdated liability coverage for the hotel. Rapid settlement of claims triggered a coverage dispute. In 1983, MGM sued F. B. Hall and its underwriting unit, Union International Insurance Company, as well as other insurers. The 1985 settlement cost F. B. Hall $36 million in addition to the $11.4 million that Union had already paid MGM.

Another F. B. Hall subsidiary acted as a managing general agent for the Protective National Insurance Co. Protective sued F. B. Hall for breaching its duties as managing general agent. In a 1986 settlement, F. B. Hall agreed to pay $45 million.

A third case involved another F. B. Hall underwriting subsidiary, the Union Indemnity Insurance Company of New York. The subsidiary was declared insolvent in 1985 by $138 million. Two years later, the New York Insurance Superintendent, as liquidator of Union Indemnity, sued F. B. Hall, its auditors, and certain former officers and directors of the insurer. He asked for damages of not less than $140 million, and the suit was settled in 1989 for $48 million, together with some shareholder and insurer suits.[11]

Following these losses, F. B. Hall's board authorized discontinuance of direct underwriting operations. It also disposed of reinsurance underwriting in 1985 and sold Jartran, Inc., the same year. Al Tahmoush, F. B. Hall's flamboyant chairman, president, and CEO, was forced to resign. By 1985, Saul Steinberg, chairman of Reliance Insurance Company, had accumulated 100 percent of F. B. Hall's preferred stock and 30.8 percent of Reliance's common shares. In 1987, Steinberg had full control of F. B. Hall and served as its chairman and CEO. F. B. Hall's results, however, continued to disappoint.

From 1984 until Aon purchased it in 1992, F. B. Hall showed only one year of modest profit; its net loss from discontinued operations totaled $353 million through 1989. This was a sad decline for an organization that once had been one of the world's finest brokerages. Almost all brokerages with underwriting operations ended up very seriously damaged.

Even Aon ran into difficulties at the end of the 1990s. It

[11] The sum of $19 million was paid immediately, with $29 million paid over a ten-year period; $20 million of the total was paid by F. B. Hall's directors & officers liability insurers.

recorded a $150 million pretax charge against 1999 fourth-quarter earnings. This primarily reflected payments to U.K. customers who had bought pension plans based on allegedly improper sales advice in the late 1980s. The pretax charge also reflected litigation costs on a reinsurance contract placed through Aon.

In the early 1990s, A&A and its competitors confronted a dramatically changing marketplace. U.S. business no longer could be counted on to generate automatic and above-average growth. For the first time, the insurance sector was growing at a slower rate than the economy, and the outlook was not promising. Opportunities seemed more attractive in other parts of the world as uncertainties prevailed in the United States.

Within this environment, A&A was a stark contrast of enviable strengths and debilitating weaknesses. Most of the challenges, such as the devastating financial impact of our Howden acquisition, were internal. (Howden-related write-offs and legal fees during the 1980s and early 1990s totaled well over $300 million.) Additionally, tens of thousands of employee hours were consumed yearly in damage control. External events such as advances in technology were also challenging, particularly since we did not have the financial resources to make strategic investments.

Although the media and security analysts frequently focused on the negatives, A&A maintained an extremely powerful global presence. Our retail broking strength was compelling, with offices in 105 U.S. cities employing over 4,500 people. We continued as the market leader in Canada, with nineteen offices and more than 1,200 employees. Our Asia-Pacific region's network was by far the most extensive of any brokerage, with over forty offices in fourteen countries.

The Europe/Middle East sector contained sixty-four offices employing more than 2,000, and our ranking in these countries varied between first and seventh. In the United Kingdom, clients included 20 percent of the coun-

try's largest companies. Prestigious accounts such as the Eurotunnel were added. Amid fierce competition, the company also remained the Middle East's largest insurance brokerage and provider of risk management services. In 1992, we enhanced this position by winning the business of Saudi Arabian Basic Industries Corporation, the largest industrial enterprise in the Middle East. More than 150 insurers had bid to participate in underwriting the program.

Reinsurance broking remained A&A's "crown jewel," making us one of the three largest reinsurance brokerages in the world—and the fastest growing. While Alexander Howden Reinsurance Brokers (AHRB) revenues represented only slightly more than 10 percent of A&A's total, its profits were much more significant. The worldwide reinsurance operation was consolidated under Ron Iles's direction, and the U.S. unit changed its name to Alexander Re.

Reinsurance was also responsible for A&A's strong position in eastern Europe, where fundamental transformations

As luck had it, the Loma Prieta earthquake struck San Francisco during evening rush hour and as 62,000 baseball fans were filling Candlestick Park for the 1989 World Series. The stadium was spared but a stretch of elevated interstate highway collapsed, pancaking cars—as this row of houses crushed a vehicle in the Marina district. Damages in the San Francisco Bay area were over $6 billion and although at least 3,700 people were injured, only 62 died.

were underway. Traditionally, insurance companies there were state-owned monopolies and closely supervised by their finance ministers. Dealings with the West were principally in reinsurance. After years of cultivation, Alexander Howden Reinsurance Brokers handled a substantial share of reinsurance transactions in Eastern Europe (except in Czechoslovakia). It had productive twenty- to thirty-year-old relationships with Bulgaria, Hungary, Poland, Romania, and the Soviet Union. AHRB also handled nonmarine reinsurance in Yugoslavia.

By 1990, state monopolies were breaking up. In Hungary, the monopoly had ended four years earlier with the creation of two new insurers, which, in turn, formed small specialty insurance companies. Many state insurers entered into partnerships and joint ventures with Western insurance companies. British and American brokers moved quickly to secure a local presence.[12]

Another A&A winner was Alexander Howden Intermediaries, which merged three geographic areas into one operating entity. Our significant investments in this operation during the 1980s were paying off. The wholesale brokerage's London-based team of over 300 employees was led by one of the industry's most outstanding managers, Dennis Mahoney. Its contribution of 6 percent of our revenues belied its importance.

The Alexander Consulting Group (ACG) was growing rapidly, with 1991 revenues topping $230 million. Like its competitors, ACG kept adding new services. In 1990, it established an Operational Effectiveness Practice, headquartered in London. This unit provided services in strategic planning and communications, organizational restructuring, change management, management training and development, and diagnostic research. A previously separate unit, Executive Planning Services, which provided individual life insurance, estate planning, and other services, became part of ACG in 1991.

The composition of A&A's revenues and profits was

[12] In a developing situation such as this, where there had been no brokerages before, the Western broker's challenge is to develop an investment strategy. Profit opportunities usually lie further into the future than initially anticipated. Alternatively, relationships must be cultivated and nurtured over time. In this case, leading competitors were starting to locate in various former Iron Curtain countries. The Eastern European market potential was considerable, with more than 400 million consumers.

shifting rapidly. A decade earlier, 98 percent of our income had been derived from U.S. sources. At the end of 1990, that figure had shrunk to approximately 42 percent. During this period, property, casualty, and marine insurance revenue decreased from 95 percent to 73 percent of the total. Recognizing these changes, U.S. employees increasingly thought in terms of global rather than domestic business.[13] Opportunities beckoned almost everywhere outside the United States.

[13] "Global" was applied to any client with multicountry facilities irrespective of its headquarter's domicile.

CHAPTER 22

O Brave New World: New Risks and Initiatives

For many employees, the changing business dynamics were becoming more perplexing, even bewildering. As personal computers became commonplace, the new technology challenged work practices and produced more rapid transmission of information. Client needs frequently became more complex, and clients explored new risk management techniques. Employees also faced the reality that the industry's traditional growth was slowing. The 1997 *Annual Report* of General Reinsurance Corporation (Gen Re) provides a useful overview of the 1990s.

Gen Re observed that favorable 1997 insurer results masked continued deterioration in the industry's basic business conditions:

• an intensely competitive environment fueled by excess capital, deregulation of certain markets, and slowing insurance demand in mature markets;

• loss reserves coming under pressure owing in part to provisions for latent injury and other mass tort losses;

• weak and, in some cases, negative underwriting cash flow;

• increasing expense ratios, which pressured underwriting margins and earnings;

• declining interest rates, which reduced investment income.

Directly or indirectly, all these trends affected brokers; other trouble spots affected both brokers and insurers. One challenge was a by-product of general business consolidations. After most mergers, the combined operation paid less to brokers and insurers than they had before the union. One reason was the larger enterprise's frequent decision that it could handle more risk internally through self-insurance or other risk-financing techniques. This trend caused a significant loss of income to insurers and brokers.

Another specter loomed during the mid-1990s: new initiatives in "alternate risk transfer" (ART). This concept referred to risk transfer methods other than traditional insurance vehicles. Many firms' initial exposure to ART came when they established captive insurance companies or joined either risk retention or purchasing groups.

By the end of 2001, *Business Insurance* estimated that there were approximately 4,000 captive insurers globally. Over 2,000 were U.S.-owned and 600 U.K.-owned. Bermuda continued as the domicile of choice, with more than 1,100 captives. The Cayman Islands ranked second, and the United States was becoming an ever more attractive headquarters site. For medium-sized companies, "rent-a-captives," which are capitalized and owned by a third-party sponsor who performs administrative functions, also gained favor. Although captive growth had slowed, partly because of more attractive risk transfer options, captives handled an estimated $28 billion worth of net written premiums by 2000. Meanwhile, at the end of 1998, risk retention groups had stabilized at around 70, while purchasing groups had mushroomed to almost 670. None of these statistics pleased traditional insurers.

During the early 1990s, insurers started to underwrite multiyear contracts for multiline property and casualty policies. This spread policyholder risks over a longer period. Integrated multiline, multiyear products then evolved, allowing clients to bundle property and casualty exposures with financial and operational risks. These included currency exchange rates and commodity price fluctuations normally protected by banks, as well as political and certain business risks previously considered uninsurable.

Traditionally, insurance products addressed "pure risks," i.e., risks that might result in loss while offering no oppor-

Priding itself on a diverse clientele, A&A claimed clients as unique as Harley-Davidson—which became the sole U.S. maker of motorcycles while boasting many female riders, like the woman above. Challenges were often highly original, from placing coverage on priceless Rembrandt paintings and Moscow's first McDonald's to Israel's El Al Airlines, which A&A began serving in 1948.

tunity for gain. "Speculative risks" that could result in a loss or a gain—e.g., new product introduction and investment decisions—now were considered for coverage.

Looking at risk from commercial clients' viewpoints eventually blurred the distinction between "pure" and "speculative" risks. Transferring uncorrelated risks decreased the likelihood that they would all cause losses in a specified period. This gave companies risk diversification, enabling them to increase self-retention and save overall costs. It also reduced the potential for overinsuring and closed possible coverage gaps in uncoordinated policies.

Obtaining underwriting information to process these instruments is particularly complex. Within most large corporations, disparate units such as insurance, risk management, treasury, and individual credit and commodities departments usually are responsible for various risks. Nevertheless, interest in the concept is increasing. Russ Banham, in the journal *ReActions*, cited two examples. Honeywell Corporation added foreign exchange exposures to its multiyear policies in 1997. More recently, a large paper manufacturer opted for a single insurance policy that included property/casualty risks as well as those on foreign exchange translation; interest rates; and commodities pricing of old corrugated cardboard, pulp, natural gas, fuel oil, and coal. The company expected a cost savings of 20 percent.

During the mid-1990s, transferring insurance risks directly to capital market investors became more popular. This involves the securitization of risks with bonds or derivative transactions. The bond's yield and/or principal is linked to insurance-related losses, with investors servicing claims out of the bond principal. The most common securitized product is a catastrophe bond; most deals to date cover U.S. earthquake and storm exposure. Investors tend to be banks, mutual funds, life insurance companies, and reinsurers. Such vehicles generate additional insurance capacity through capital markets.

Another financial instrument is an insurance derivative, whose value is determined by an insurance index's performance. For example, a business that is vulnerable to unusual weather patterns can buy and sell weather options tied to climate indices.

Since 1997, issuers of capital market transactions have primarily been U.S. insurers and reinsurers. Intermediaries include investment bankers, reinsurers, and, occasionally, insurance brokerages. Brokers obviously must develop increasingly sophisticated skills to participate in future offerings. By 2001, insurance and capital markets coverage was gaining momentum.

These new trends, in concert with momentous technological changes, increased employee insecurity. Unlike in the past, few could count on spending their entire careers with one employer. Employee loyalty frequently gave way to seeking the best deal. For those with talent who developed their skills, rewarding personal and professional challenges remained. However, the days of merely being a client's insurance buyer were long gone, and some people could not adapt to the new environment.

As the millennium approached, understanding the Internet became increasingly indispensable in client service. In 1996, A&A began implementing Access A&A, a custom Web-based service for our clients. Clients had electronic links to account service teams and could access their insurance portfolios, industry information, proprietary A&A research, insurance products, and alternative solutions in real time. A partially implemented intranet version of Access A&A was designed to link all of our computers, software, and databases around the world to a single server system.

By the late 1990s, the Internet was just one area requiring mastery. Insurance brokers had to gear up to compete in an entirely new environment. In May 1999, an Aon publication discussed the many sophisticated services major insurance brokerages now offered. For example, it reported that Aon's Risk Analysis Management Group:

. . . Provides a broad range of high-level analytical and financial consulting services to support client risk management needs. Services include loss forecasting, risk analysis, retention level analysis, reserve analysis for financial accrual purposes, premium allocations, cash flow analysis of risk financing plans, self-insurance studies, captive feasibility studies, finite risk modeling, loss portfolio transfers . . . designing the most cost effective insurance funding vehicles for major casualty, property and marine accounts.

To illustrate the intricacies of modern risk analysis, the report noted the need to:

. . . Evaluate the client's financial condition and outlook, taking into account not only key financial parameters such as revenues, earnings, operating margins, equity, cash flow, debt leverage and stockholder dividends, but also considering the economic and business issues the client faces. Examples are increasing competition, penetration of global markets, pricing outlook for specific commodities, capital investment requirements, environmental compliance issues, pending legislation, asset sales, acquisition strategies, research and development programs.

Such analysis determines a client's risk-bearing capacity.

In the last half of America's 20th century, interest in fine art rose, market values of art soared and insurance prices followed suit. Museums such as Washington's National Gallery of Art (above) and New York's Metropolitan mounted "blockbuster" exhibitions—unique and temporary arrays of irreplaceable paintings whose normal insurance costs would be prohibitive. Thus the Indemnity Act of 1975 made the federal government a sort of back-up underwriter, as it became committed to partially indemnify owners of art loaned to institutions mounting international exhibitions if their works were lost or damaged.

Brokerages also use loss probability distribution and computer simulations to forecast losses and potential variability for various self-insured retentions. The most appropriate and cost-effective retention levels are identified. Insurance programs then are arranged to transfer the risk's unwanted portion to risk transfer markets.

In addition to competence in such services, insurance professionals must deal with hundreds of clients in a broad cross section of industries. Amid keen competition, innovation is increasingly what distinguishes the winners from the losers.

For insurance brokers, the unusual is routine. Business challenges frequently require extensive research and analysis. When Cook Inlet, Alaska, was first being considered for oil exploration, an A&A underwriter quickly learned that it had one of the highest tide ranges in the world. He traveled there to observe the phenomenon and appraise how tidal variations might affect an insurer's terms.

Around the world, thousands of interesting insurance placements occur every week. For example, A&A placed $1.5 billion of insurance protection for the most comprehensive exhibition ever compiled of paintings by Rembrandt and his students. The 1991 exhibition opened in Berlin's Altes Museum and moved to London's National Gallery. Many of the works, borrowed from private collections, had never been publicly shown and would not have been loaned without insurance. A&A units in Amsterdam and London teamed up to tackle this complex placement. The entire Dutch insurance market and nearly 80 percent of Lloyd's syndicates were used to complete the insurance package.

In another case, our Toronto office had a unique opportunity when a client, McDonald's of Canada, opened its first restaurant in Moscow. As the fast food chain's largest and most ambitious facility, it had a seating capacity of 900 and utilized twenty-seven cash registers. On opening day, 30,000 meals were served, and the queue of customers frequently exceeded the line waiting to visit Lenin's tomb.[1] Sometimes, just the inclusion of an unusual peril in a policy made the placement special. This occurred with the reconstruction of Shakespeare's Globe Theatre in London. Insurance was required for potential damage from unexploded World War II bombs.

Another satisfaction of our business is celebrating long-standing and unique client relationships. Harley-Davidson, which produced its first motorcycle in 1903, combined both of these characteristics. Out of 150 American motorcycle manufacturers that once existed, Harley-Davidson became the sole survivor. The inability to purchase affordable liability insurance was a leading cause of the others' demise.

By 1991, A&A's Detroit office had handled the insurance requirements of the Family Motor Coach Association for twenty-five years. Before its formation in 1963, most "homes on wheels" were converted buses. In 1991, we

[1] The McDonald's restaurant was virtually the only place in Moscow where the average Russian citizen could obtain beef on demand in the early 1990s.

served 17,000 motor home clients. Their special insurance needs included unique policy features, such as a premium reduction for part-time use.

Two years earlier, A&A's New York office celebrated a forty-year relationship with El Al Israel Airlines. We had handled its risk management requirements almost since the airline's founding in 1948. Although forty-year business connections are not rare, we were particularly close to El Al. Our focus was on the overriding issue of security and the need for underwriters to appreciate that the airline's efforts and success with security were second to none.

In a service business, employees are a company's principal asset, and recognizing their contributions is essential. For years, we formally feted employees who excelled the previous year in such areas as new business development, client service, and technical achievement. Outstanding offices were also celebrated. At a meeting in the early 1990s, over 400 individuals earned awards, including 108 women. The latter number represented a significant increase over previous years and reflected A&A's commitment to greater diversity within its ranks. Working in a technical insurance position was becoming a wide-open field for women as well as ethnic minorities. Sales also offered considerable potential as male clients and prospects more readily accepted women in that capacity—and an increasing number of women were becoming clients and prospects.

Some remarkable women trailblazers paved the way for those who followed at A&A. For example, in the 1980s Kathy Mitzel, a young Columbus, Ohio employee, produced several hundred new commercial accounts in one year through her activities with the Chamber of Commerce. Although most of these accounts were small, no one else ever came close to duplicating her feat. In Dallas, Mary Laughlin, a top producer for years, sold mainly to construction companies. Kay Hartlieb's professional acumen with the hospital industry, and her ability to convert that knowledge into large insurance sales, became legendary. After establishing herself as a top A&A producer, Ms. Hartlieb took time out to explore a possible religious vocation as a nun, before returning to A&A's Chicago office and resuming her successful insurance career.

Unfortunately, opportunities were not as forthcoming for women to become senior managers and office heads. This reflected male skepticism and the inevitable corollary of women's lack of management experience. This bias would change only gradually.

Despite such attitudes, the company took gender issues seriously, and our Chicago office was exemplary in its efforts at the local level. The office held regular meetings with women on the professional staff to discuss career advancement. A psychologist specializing in office dynamics conducted seminars for women and men on interpersonal work relationships. This improved morale and business development. Fortunately, by 2002, women's escalating progress and achievement in all facets of the business have eclipsed such modest activities.

CHAPTER 23

Decline and Fall: Acquisition Frenzy

Alexander & Alexander, along with much of the insurance world, was almost totally reconstituted in the 1990s. While many A&A operations performed well, several situations cast ominous shadows. Among them was the continuing fallout from the Howden acquisition. Howden-related problems plagued management and impaired our finances.

A&A had disengaged from underwriting but it was burdened by deteriorating reserves resulting from payment obligations for future claims and uncollectible reinsurance from companies Howden formerly owned. Predicting the ultimate cost of asbestos-related claims was actuarially impossible because no valid statistical base existed. A string of disappointments ensued, and setting aside more reserves was a chronic challenge. To cap this exposure, we had to buy additional insurance, available only at very high rates and with very high deductibles. These contingencies cost A&A hundreds of millions of dollars.

We were especially frustrated by adverse U.K. court rulings. The bitterest blow was a two-to-one appeals court ruling upholding a decision against Howden-owned Sphere Drake Insurance Company plc with respect to contracts with Orion Insurance Company plc, which Sphere Drake contended had been legally terminated in the mid-1970s. An underwriting exposure existed from 1953 to 1967;

A&A's position was clearly correct, and we should have won the case. An arbitrary ruling extended our losses in gray-area cases and cost Sphere Drake $145 million in 1992. Surprisingly, the case resurfaced in the late 1990s with an appeal based on 1989 fraudulent testimony by a senior executive of the defendant. The appeal was sustained in 2000 and went before the House of Lords.[1] (Any recovery will inure to the current owners of Sphere Drake.) A&A's legal counsel in London, it must be said, was highly regarded but was unable to win a verdict in our most important cases. More favorable outcomes would have profoundly improved A&A's financial health and greatly increased our ability to remain independent.

The U.S. retail property/casualty business also caused problems. This had always been the engine driving A&A's success, but revenues began faltering and we lost more and more accounts. New business, while adequate, wasn't enough to overcome lost business and price erosion on renewal policies. Although insurance pricing and interest rate fluctuations were beyond management's control, we could not blame lost business on others.

Insurance pricing often seems arcane and confusing. Although the broker's job is to negotiate the best price appropriate for a risk, logic dictated that premium increases were imperative for insurers' financial health. However, except for reinsurance, this was not the pattern in the late 1980s and throughout the 1990s. Our industry faced many uncertainties during this period: a U.S. tort system run amok, recurring and sizable catastrophes, the need to increase reserves for potential liability claims, increased incidence of uncollectible reinsurance, a generally hostile regulatory environment, and new competition from insurers forming in various tax havens. Paradoxically, a chronic soft insurance market persisted. Insurers' behavior was driven by a mix of forces: fear of losing market share; their own strong investment returns; regulatory price restraints; and, in some cases, weak management.

[1] It is pending at this writing.

Insurers faced major uncertainties. Who were the responsible parties for paying the cleanup costs for pollutants? The answer was far from clear, but insurers knew that they could end up paying a huge portion.[2] As for liability claims, insurers constantly had to increase reserves, with dire consequences for their annual bottom lines. For instance, A. M. Best Co. stated that PRUPAC, the Prudential Insurance Company's property/casualty unit, was technically insolvent before its parent provided a $900 million reserve injection.

Not the least of insurer problems was reinsurance. In 1990, reinsurance rates on some classes of business hardened to all-time highs. Insurers couldn't complete their own retrocession (reinsurance) protection programs. Primary insurance companies often assumed more risk than they wanted, creating even greater vulnerability. In 1991, London's excess-of-loss market virtually ceased to exist. Oil and gas companies were affected most. Many had difficulty purchasing adequate property and casualty insurance at any price. At reinsurers' insistence, nonmarine and liability risks were excluded from marine-driven policies, and this required energy companies to buy separate programs for offshore, onshore, and liability risks. The result was price increases and sometimes less protection.

Catastrophic losses also became a major problem for insurers. The disasters of 1989 were followed by the second worst year on record for catastrophes in 1990. Hurricane Bob, a Denver hailstorm, and a fire in Oakland Hills, California, resulted in a combined $2.5 billion in insured losses. But 1992 was even worse and will be remembered for Hurricane Andrew's devastation of southern Florida. Uniquely destructive, its damage exceeded $25 billion, with approximately $16 billion of that insured. Two direct-writing insurance companies, Allstate and State Farm, paid a total of over $6 billion.[3] The storm significantly contributed to U.S. property/casualty insurers' net pretax loss of $36.5 billion that year. Insurers paid $1.16 in 1992 for every $1.00 of premium.

Subsequently, insurers reevaluated their Florida expo-

[2] One highly respected consultant estimated that total costs to insurers from inactive U.S. waste sites could fall between $41 billion and $1.06 trillion. This disparity reflected uncertainty over which insurance policies, if any, might be designated by a court to provide coverage.

[3] Despite those losses, Applied Insurance Research, Inc., estimated that the hurricane could have caused over $50 billion in losses had it hit land only twenty miles farther north.

sure and many took corrective measures despite the rigid scrutiny of the state's insurance commissioner. At least fifty-nine property/casualty companies failed in 1992; some of them also were hurt by Hurricane Iniki, which caused $1.6 billion in insured losses in Hawaii. More insurers would have failed if their investment portfolios had not experienced robust gains.[4]

[4] The conservative portfolios of most insurers contain at least 60 percent of their assets in bonds.

Ferocious East Coast winter storms affected underwriters in 1993. A series of March tempests cost them nearly $2 billion and became the fourth costliest catastrophe in American history. Fifty tornadoes devastated Florida alone, and 230 lives were lost. In California, the 1994 Northridge earthquake caused about $12.5 billion in insured losses.

The insurance market continued in turmoil, and the high cost or unavailability of reinsurance again forced primary underwriters to accept greater exposure. To address this supply deficiency, various financial professionals, including investment bankers, kept forming Bermuda-based reinsurance companies focusing on specific specialty markets. For example, Johnson & Higgins and Goldman, Sachs & Co. sponsored Global Capital Reinsurance Limited, which specialized in property catastrophe coverage.[5]

[5] This Bermuda company was subsequently sold to XL Capital Ltd.

An uncertain market was just one of the problems confronting A&A management. Because of limited financial resources, we had to consider controlling expenses, aggressively increasing new business, stemming the loss of existing business, raising funds through sale of nonessential units, and tapping financial markets. Some options, such as the sale of units, were straightforward. Others were more difficult to implement and eroded already-fragile employee morale.

Expense controls were addressed through restructuring efforts from 1990 until early 1994. Many initiatives were right on target and effectively implemented. Others, however painstakingly thought out, were misdirected. In a period of rapid change, some restructuring is always required.

It becomes more problematic, however, when management is under constant pressure to improve financial results—as was our case between 1990 and 1994.

During 1990, we faced an important operational challenge of linking our global retail broking operations under the Alexander & Alexander name. There was considerable uncertainty about client reaction outside the United States. Bill Wilson was instrumental in convincing his former Stenhouse associates that the plan was in everyone's best interest, and the conversion was essentially accomplished over a three-year period.

In September 1990, Wilson and Mike White were elected deputy chairmen and joined T. Irvin in forming an Office of the Chairman. Both assumed additional management

A benchmark tempest, Hurricane Andrew destroyed 25,524 homes and damaged 101,241 others in southern Florida. In the city of Homestead, more than 99 percent (1167 of 1176) of all mobile homes were completely destroyed, leading insurers to reexamine how much Florida exposure they could handle. Some homeowners wrote claim numbers on buildings before leaving (above), expecting their losses to be handled by the armies of adjusters who flocked to the region.

responsibilities, and coordination of the company's operating units was enhanced. Over the next three years, radical restructuring was undertaken. The measures were intended to service clients more efficiently and economically, but results were mixed.

More than thirty global business units were established in our principal offices. They serviced multinational accounts where risk management consulting skills were imperative. Within the United States, national marketing teams were formed to serve specific industries such as aviation, construction, energy, financial services, health and medical care, public entities, railroads, and utilities. These measures facilitated large clients' access to A&A's most knowledgeable professionals.

Other initiatives were more questionable. A "matrix management" structure, for instance, while logical in concept, can be chaotic in practice. Our plan identified broad global categories of client service, sales, and marketing as well as global specialties such as Anistics. Each area was to be supervised by a senior executive who was relieved from his previous job. For such an arrangement to work, supervisors' responsibilities must be clearly delineated, understood, and accepted throughout the company. Otherwise, the result is difficult to measure and its impact questionable. The new positions can be meaningless. We were not successful in meeting such criteria. Many employees did not see the value of the new structure, and the time of key executives was subsequently misdirected.

At the beginning of 1994, a Risk Management Division (RMD) was formed in the United States to offer a consultative approach to clients with national or global operations. Each RMD office was located in a large city and led by a managing director. More significantly, an Insurance Service Division was established to manage middle-market accounts through seven centers. Offices were based on industry segments rather than geographic areas. One specialized in construction risks, another in trucking risks, and so forth.

For the sake of efficiency and cost containment, smaller

commercial accounts were consolidated in specialized offices. Since most clients expected local service, A&A lost accounts when their handling was moved to new locations. It was difficult to make profits on such accounts; on average, they had to generate at least $10,000 in annual revenues to provide a fair return. On the other hand, this class of business generally was profitable for insurers who needed it to balance their portfolios. Moreover, brokers often had profit-sharing arrangements with insurers. Sometimes these were enough to make this business profitable.

At the end of 1994, A&A sold its personal lines business (insurance for individuals) to raise capital. Personal lines business is in general highly desirable for insurers, and the company frequently benefited through profit sharing, so selling it was questionable. Furthermore, many corporate clients' employees used A&A to handle their personal insurance needs, and some account executives felt that this move could jeopardize the corporate accounts. Others believed it was positive because it eliminated the possibility of making mistakes on an executive's personal coverage.

In any event, restructuring eliminated local profit centers. The traditional position of an office managing vice president was also eliminated, and an office principal was designated to oversee routine procedures. Many employees resisted restructuring, finding it radical and unwieldy. This adversely affected morale and contributed to further loss of staff.

Meanwhile, A&A's bottom line took a beating. For 1991, the firm took a one-time charge of $75.6 million, which included restructuring as well as an increase in reserves for various contingencies. Our net loss for the year was $12.6 million. The following year's $90.1 million loss included the $145 million indemnity payment on behalf of the Sphere Drake Insurance Company to its purchasers.

An urgent need to raise capital required various initiatives. We concentrated on our core business and sold units that did not fit the strategy. Under different circumstances, this might have been questionable, but in the early 1990s there was no alternative. We sold the U.S. tax consulting subsidiary and a British pension fund management operation.[6] A&A also divested a Netherlands nonbrokerage facility and a Florida administrator of workers compensation funds. Sales proceeds totaled $77 million, representing about a $44 million gain. The following year, to bolster the company's capital base and improve its debt-to-capital ratio, a private placement of 2.3 million shares of convertible preferred stock brought net proceeds of approximately $111 million. This provided some temporary financial stability.

In the early 1990s, several key executives and a director retired. At the end of 1992, Bill Wilson stepped down but remained as a director and consultant. He was an exceptionally stable influence throughout the company, and his performance was exemplary. Jim Berry retired as director at the end of 1993 and died shortly thereafter. He was greatly missed for his irreverent wit and down-to-earth demeanor.[7] Ron Forrest, CEO of Alexander & Alexander, Inc., also retired and was replaced by Lawrence Burke, formerly managing director of global business development.[8]

Murphy's Law doggedly followed A&A in 1993. The fact that revenue growth for the brokerage industry was 2.7 percent, an all-time low, only compounded our problems. The company suffered a stunning reversal in the third quarter of 1993 after an internal investigation revealed improper revenue recognition practices within the Alexander Consulting Group. ACG's revenues had been overstated for 1991, 1992, and the first half of 1993. A&A's earnings for that period were restated, decreasing by approximately $12 million. These developments led to a major management restructuring in 1994.[9]

Constrained by its finances, A&A could not make major acquisitions. However, in 1993 we were able to purchase Clay & Partners, a prestigious actuarial and benefits consulting firm, the United Kingdom's third largest, with more than 250 employees. We also negotiated a minority interest in Asesores Kennedy, a leading Mexican insurance broker and longtime correspondent, as well as controlling interest in M&A Limited, a Colombian brokerage firm. Our per-

[6] This British unit had a record of spectacular results; however, the manager wanted to be independent.

[7] When surrounded by lawyers and seemingly complex situations, Berry often would cut through the "legalese" and demand plain English.

[8] Forrest went on to head a prominent London-based brokerage, the Bain Hogg Group, and would rejoin his former A&A associates within several years.

[9] During the same period, Angelo D'Alessandro, the consulting group's architect and leader, died following an accident on a Mexican business trip, and Donald Seeley, who had been responsible for A&A's financial management and strategic planning, was appointed to succeed him.

centage ownership in A&A Italia went up to 75 percent, and we opened new offices in Poland, the Czech Republic, and Hungary.

Nonetheless, A&A's head count continued to fall. From more than 18,000 employees in 1986, it dropped to 16,000 in 1990 and to under 12,000 in 1995, reflecting the sale of the personal lines business the previous year.

As 1994 began, events were set in motion that would subsequently lead to A&A's loss of independence. In mid-January, the board of directors and T. Irvin agreed that he would retire to accelerate the pace of change and operational improvements. Dr. Robert Boni, a board member, was elected nonexecutive chairman of the board and chairman of its executive committee. This committee immediately took on additional responsibilities for oversight of company policy and management controls and launched an international search for a new CEO.

T. Irvin retired effective April 1. Because of unforeseen corporate developments, he undoubtedly was relieved to step aside. Over the years, as A&A developed into a leading global insurance broker, T. had played several key roles and had been involved in virtually every facet of the organization, while producing excellent results. His "street smarts" and intuitive judgment were indispensable to the success of many operations.

Security analysts and shareholders were understandably frustrated with A&A's performance. Although many of our operations were profitable, the open-ended liabilities flowing from the Howden acquisition continued to devastate A&A's bottom line. Unfortunately, the fragile financial condition created by Howden-related liabilities greatly impaired our flexibility in managing the company.[10] On June 7, 1994, A&A announced that Frank Zarb was joining the company as chairman and CEO. The announcement evoked enthusiastic response from security analysts and hope from employees. Zarb had an impressive career, most recently as Travelers Insurance Inc.'s vice chairman and

[10] It was difficult for the most senior executives to allocate enough time to concentrate on the firm's operations, visit with clients, maintain high public visibility, and help produce new business.

group chief executive. Previously he had served as chairman and CEO of Smith Barney and was credited for its fine performance. During President Gerald Ford's administration, he was national "Energy Czar."

Coinciding with Zarb's appointment, American International Group invested $200 million in a new issue of an A&A Series B convertible preferred stock. Upon converting the preferred shares into A&A common stock, AIG would own approximately 21 percent of the common stock. Both the preferred stock (if converted) and common stock were nonvoting in AIG's hands, and it had no board representation. At the same time, A&A reduced its common stock dividend from one dollar to ten cents a share. These measures were taken to improve the company's precarious financial situation. Frank Zarb promised to move immediately to improve profitability and strengthen A&A's core business.

Initially, Zarb slashed expenses, mostly through staff reductions and consolidations of office space, a fairly common tactic for a new CEO. There was room for considerable savings, but not for the amount targeted. Previous managers had already reduced expenses until the howls from key employees convinced them that they could squeeze no further. A new outside CEO, however, seldom understands previous management actions; Zarb cut deeper and morale eroded further. Office consolidations probably were appropriate, and A&A decided to vacate its elegant midtown Manhattan headquarters, which sent an important message; unfortunately the proposed move to lower Madison Avenue projected a "second-class" image in the eyes of employees, competitors, and clients. The process of cutting costs led to the loss of key personnel and profitable accounts.

Zarb also brought in high profile nonexecutive directors, including former President Gerald Ford and former American Express CEO James Robinson. To make room for new directors, Bill Wilson and I were asked to retire from the board. Although a proper request, it left just one director who had working knowledge of our business—Ron Iles. Zarb obviously believed that financial service businesses were similar in nature, and he evidently felt that he and his team had the necessary experience to successfully manage A&A. Unfortunately, these assumptions proved to be erroneous. Despite similarities, insurance brokerages have unique nuances and characteristics not found in other financial service organizations. To be effective in the insurance broking and consulting business, one must have experience in the field and understand the intricacies of selling and marketing its products and services.

A substantial fourth-quarter restructuring charge led to a $138.7 million net loss for 1994. Some $25 million was earmarked to consolidate space at forty-eight offices, and another $44 million for the early retirement of approximately 1,100 employees, 650 of them in the United States. A $70 million pretax charge was taken to cover indemnifications related to Shand and a settlement with the state of Pennsylvania.

While A&A's new management was preoccupied with internal problems, there was considerable merger activity within the brokerage community. Based on 1995 revenues, each of the top six insurance brokerages were more than twice the size of the seventh. Marsh & McLennan, Sedgwick, Alexander & Alexander, Willis Corroon, and Johnson & Higgins had been the traditional incumbents of the top spots, and Aon, now in second place, was a remarkable newcomer.

Aon was the creation of Patrick G. Ryan. He had entered the insurance business in 1964 and pioneered the sale of life insurance policies that were linked to automobile loans and sold through insurance agents working out of car dealerships. In 1982, Ryan acquired the Combined International Corp., a profitable door-to-door insurance business, and established Aon as a specialty insurer holding company. Aon entered insurance brokerage that same year by purchasing a fine company, Rollins Burdick Hunter. Between 1982 and the end of 1996, Aon made five acquisitions, bringing it closer to Marsh's size.[11]

Another significant development occurred in 1993,

[11] The Aon acquisitions were: in 1989, Bayly Martin & Faye, a large California–based brokerage, which had some significant clients, but which had been on the selling block for some time; in 1991, Hudig-Langeveldt B.V., a highly regarded Netherlands brokerage, the world's fourteenth largest and continental Europe's largest; in 1992, Frank B. Hall, which, despite a troubled history, still had an impressive client list and complemented Aon in many geographic and specialty insurance areas such as aviation; in 1994, Jenner Fenton Slade Ltd., a U.K. energy specialist brokerage; and in 1996, the Bain Hogg Group, which had become the largest U.K. retail brokerage. (Two years before, the Hogg Group had purchased Bain Clarkson, a wholly-owned subsidiary of the U.K. shipping-to-retail group Inchcape, and the firm was renamed Bain Hogg.)

when Willis Corroon lost seventy employees to Aon from its very successful U.S. risk management division. This group serviced construction clients, and they brought many accounts with them. Aon gained an outstanding team of professionals in a highly profitable industry segment. Poaching groups of employees from competitors, once frowned upon, had become a common practice.

At the start of 1996, Pat Ryan was determined to raise the acquisition stakes. Early in the year, he sold two life insurance units—The Life Insurance Company of Virginia and Union Fidelity Life Insurance Company—to General Electric Capital Corporation for approximately $1.2 billion. He dedicated the proceeds to building his brokerage business.

Meanwhile, M&M actively fortified its European operation. In 1990, it acquired the large German insurance broker, Gradmann & Holler. A year later, the Swiss firm of EWI S.A. was added to the fold, followed in 1992 by the purchase of Faugère & Jutheau, an important French insurance brokerage. All were strategic additions.

Sedgwick had not made a large acquisition after Fred. S. James in 1985. Before merging with U.S. brokerage Corroon & Black, Willis Faber bought the U.K. brokerage Stewart Wrightson in 1987. A&A's activity was confined to several small acquisitions.[12]

The second-tier U.S. brokerages (with respect to size) also expanded by acquisition. Among the most active was Acordia, which purchased the American business of Bain Hogg at the end of 1994. Hilb, Rogel & Hamilton Co., another U.S. brokerage, completed 122 acquisitions between 1984 and 1994. By the mid-1990s, with annual revenues of $157 million, it ranked eighth in the world based on U.S.-generated business. Merging was the name of the game during the 1990s. However, all of the activity was merely a prelude to what would occur between 1997 and 2000.

While the number of brokers was shrinking, so was the number of insurance agents. In 1994, there were 45,000 agencies, 20 percent fewer than in 1984 and roughly 50 percent fewer than in the mid-1950s. The Aetna L&C, for example, had decreased its agency force from 8,000 in 1986

[12] J&H, while continuing to rely on its exclusive correspondent partners in UNISON to service international accounts, began taking equity positions in other firms during the early 1990s. It purchased Mees & Zonen in the Netherlands and established subsidiaries in the United Kingdom, Italy, and South Korea. It also purchased half of Gil y Carvajal in Spain and Portugal and set up captive insurance company management facilities in Japan and Sweden.

to 4,445 in 1994 before again adding agents. INA had dropped two-thirds of its agents during the same period.

On the surface, conditions at A&A seemed much improved by the middle of 1995. Several of the most troubling chronic problems had been resolved. The balance sheet was considerably improved, and the cost cutting of approximately $100 million produced improved earnings. The company's stock price reflected security analysts' bullish expectations and, in some circles, Frank Zarb was being hailed as a miracle worker.

Unfortunately, the perception of well-being was illusory. Cost cutting created considerable uncertainty among remaining staff, morale was poor, and many excellent U.S. employees went to competitors. Lost business continued to be a serious problem. In such an environment, even if new business is quite robust, the net results can indicate trouble, and trouble became obvious in 1996.

In 1995, Frank Zarb negotiated the purchase of most of the U.S. business of British-based Jardine Insurance Brokers, Inc., for $60 million. Adding significant business, particularly in the western United States, was attractive and the price was right—but the timing was dubious. A&A was perceived as a fragile company, and all sorts of rumors were circulating about its future. Consequently, many of Jardine's best employees were vulnerable to entreaties from competitors. The situation was further complicated by Zarb's announced intent to buy a number of smaller brokers; fortunately, this never materialized, as it would have been an unwise use of limited resources.

In the 1990s, insurers kept pace with brokerages in acquisition activity. Partly this reflected the deregulation of the European insurance market in 1994. Insurance companies in Europe targeted other insurers for acquisition and some of them, in turn, were gobbled up by large banks.

Acquisition frenzy by Germany's Allianz AG and France's AXA S.A. rendered as ephemeral the designation "Europe's largest insurer." Allianz gained a strong U.S. market position in 1991 by purchasing the Fireman's Fund Insurance Companies' property and casualty operations.[13]

AXA, which bought a 60 percent interest in the Equitable Insurance Company (U.S.) in 1991, was an equally aggressive acquirer. In 1996, it merged with Union des Assurances de Paris, the French market leader, in a $17 billion deal; and in 1999, it purchased Britain's Guardian Royal Exchange plc for $5.6 billion. Now AXA was Britain's third largest property/casualty insurer and placed solidly behind Allianz as Europe's second largest insurance company.

Europe's reinsurers sought representation in the U.S. market, which led to various acquisitions including:

• The Munich Reinsurance Company (Munich Re) solidified its position as the world's largest reinsurer by acquiring American Re-Insurance Co. in 1996 for $3.3 billion. By taking financial positions in various local insurers, it became the second largest German insurer next to Allianz.

• The Hannover Re, another German reinsurer and the world's fifth largest, bought Clarendon Insurance Group, a New York specialty insurer, from Finland's Kansa International Corp. in 1998.

• A third German reinsurer, Gerling Global Reinsurance Corp., purchased U.S.-based Constitution Re.

• The world's second largest reinsurer, Swiss Reinsurance Co., purchased three U.S. reinsurers, Life Re Corporation in 1998 for $1.8 billion, Underwriters Re in 1999 for $725 million, and Lincoln Re in 2001 for $2 billion.

Also in 1997, Crédit Suisse purchased the Winterthur Insurance Group, Switzerland's second largest and Europe's fourth largest insurer, for almost $10 billion. Crédit Suisse then was nearly the size of Deutsche Banc, Europe's largest bank.

Insurance activity was also very lively in the Netherlands. The ING Group NV was Europe's fastest growing and most complete financial services company. Among its insurance portfolio was the country's largest, National-Nederlanden NV. In 1997, the ING Group purchased the life insurer Equitable of Iowa Companies for nearly $3 billion. It also acquired Barings plc, a large U.K. merchant bank, and Furman Selz, a U.S. investment bank.

The United Kingdom was the site of several mega-combinations. These included:

• The 1996 merger of the Royal Insurance Holdings plc and Sun Alliance Insurance Companies in an $8.8 billion transaction.

• A 1998 union of two of the country's largest and oldest insurers, Commercial Union plc and General Accident plc, in a $22.5 billion stock swap, creating Europe's fifth largest insurance company (CGU plc).

• A 1999 transaction in which financial giant Lloyd's TSB group acquired Scottish Widows Fund and Life Assurance Co. in an $11 billion deal. This created the United Kingdom's second largest provider (after Prudential Corp. plc) of life insurance, pensions, and mutual funds.

• In 2000, the CGU plc and Norwich Union plc merger in a $12 billion stock swap created the world's sixth largest insurance company and enabled the new company, CGNU, to better compete with the continental giants.

Deregulation within Japan's financial services opened the door for consolidations rivaling those in Europe and the United States. Massive insurer combinations were announced months or even years before their anticipated completions, and some could not be completed as planned. The most significant included the following:

• Dai-Tokyo Fire & Marine Insurance Co. Ltd. joined Chiyoda Fire & Marine Insurance Co. Ltd. in April 2001, forming Aioi Insurance Co. Ltd.

• Nippon Fire & Marine Insurance Co. and Koa Fire & Marine Insurance Co. merged in April 2001 and were renamed Nipponkoa Insurance Co. Ltd.

• Sumitomo Marine & Fire Insurance Co. and Mitsui Marine & Fire Insurance Co. Ltd. merged in October 2001.

• Tokio Marine & Fire Insurance Co. Ltd. and Nichido Fire & Marine Insurance Co. Ltd. merged in early 2002. They plan to combine their operations with Asahi Mutual Life Insurance Co. in 2004.

• The anticipated April 2002 combination of Yasuda Fire & Marine Insurance Co. Ltd., Nissan Fire & Marine Insurance Co. Ltd., and Taisei Fire & Marine Insurance Co. Ltd. to form Sompo Japan Insurance Inc. had to be postponed due to Taisei's collapse following the September 11 terrorist attacks. It was consummated in July 2002 without Taisei.

Meanwhile, in the United States, insurer acquisition activity was almost as lively. Two venerable New York City companies, Continental Corporation and Home Insurance Company, had fallen victim to mounting liability insurance claims, weakening their competitive positions. In 1991, Home Holdings Inc. became a subsidiary of a consortium led by Sweden's Trygg-Hansa AB. In late 1994, Zurich Insurance Company agreed to purchase a $1 billion selective insurance portfolio from the consortium, essentially sealing Home's demise. In early 1995, CNA Financial Corporation bought Continental Corporation, once one of the country's most respected insurers, for $1.1 billion.

At this point, either through direct purchase or previous acquisition by Continental Corporation, the CNA group of companies included many previously independent and prominent insurers (with shortened names): American Eagle, Buckeye Union, Continental Casualty, Fidelity-Phenix, Fidelity & Casualty, Firemen's of Newark, Glens Falls, Kansas City Fire & Marine, National Fire of Hartford, Niagara Fire, Pacific, Seaboard F&M, Valley Forge, and Yorkshire.

As 1996 drew to a close, Alexander & Alexander was in extremis. Morale was at rock bottom; many outstanding professionals were leaving. Certain significant clients were promising business to competitors when their accounts came up for renewal in 1997. In a 1995 interview, Frank Zarb recalled that when he first arrived he had said, "We are going to have this place turned around in two years or we're going to take a hike." The two years had come and gone.

Nevertheless, many informed insurance people were stunned by the December 1996 news of Aon's tender offer for A&A's shares. Its offer of $17.50 per common share, which was accepted, seemed a bargain for the acquirer and was disappointing for most A&A shareholders. For me, after a forty-five year business career with A&A, its sale was a deep disappointment. I had always envisioned the firm vying with M&M for industry leadership into the twenty-

最近の動き
経平均 11126.92 -26
来高 906.67 百万株

first century. Nonetheless, if the deal had not occurred when it did, matters could have deteriorated even more rapidly.

For Aon and for those A&A employees joining the combined organization, the transaction was superior. The two huge brokerages' strengths and weaknesses were surprisingly complementary. Aon's task was to retain A&A employees who made a difference. In this matter, it was not entirely successful.

In fairness to Frank Zarb, A&A might have been saved when he arrived in mid-1994, but it was problematic. Lingering litigation was daunting, the insurance marketplace was terrible for brokers, and employee morale was constantly undermined by uncertainties. Although promising, his initial strategies were not effectively prioritized. Expense savings were necessary, but many of those implemented were too arbitrary and severe. A&A's new management first needed to mount an all-out effort to retain business and key employees. They should have quickly visited A&A's most valuable employees and largest clients to personally reassure them of their commitment to the compa-

Once a service provided within this feudal state or that principality, insurance has grown as an industry beyond mere "international" dimensions; it is truly global in scope. Given deregulation of financial services in the U.S. and other countries, given emerging entrepreneurship from Europe to China, and given new needs for worldwide coverage, the business of insurance barely knows political boundaries. An explosion in India can shake an American conglomerate, a merger in New York can affect prices on Tokyo's Nikkei Stock Exchange, shown above when trading reached a 17-year low on August 23, 2001.

ny's viability. Such actions could have been indispensable to sustaining A&A's independence beyond 1997.

Aon's acquisition of A&A created the world's largest insurance broker, if only for a moment. On March 12, 1997, Marsh & McLennan announced a $1.8 billion purchase of privately held Johnson & Higgins, its archrival for a century. The news reverberated throughout the insurance world; it was the most astounding merger ever concluded between brokers.

Although the combination created an awesome powerhouse, its parts required several years to integrate, and many challenges arose. One common problem in same-industry mergers involving large companies was the loss of senior executives. In this case, by the middle of 2000, four of the five most senior J&H officers had left M&M. They had financial security, although their new positions may not have offered the satisfaction they had enjoyed as part of a privately owned firm. Another immediate and well-publicized problem was the bitter reaction of many retired J&H partners. They were angry about the allocation of acquisition proceeds among themselves and the active partners. After the retired partners sued for restitution, a compromise was worked out, but it did not satisfy many former partners.

Additionally, in 1993, J&H had been involved in an age-bias lawsuit filed by the Equal Employment Opportunity Commission on behalf of thirteen former J&H employee-directors. That suit was settled in 1999 for $28 million, which M&M paid. Despite such glitches, M&M's revenues catapulted ahead of Aon's. In 1997, M&M also purchased the large French brokerage CECAR and Mexico's largest brokerage, Brockman y Schuh S.A.; both were once A&A correspondents.

Aon's Pat Ryan was also in an aggressive expansion mode. In early April, the firm bought British broker Minet from St. Paul Companies, Inc., which had recently been in serious negotiations to sell Minet to M&M. At first blush, acquiring Minet, which had been encountering financial difficulties, seemed questionable. On a closer look, however, there were many pluses. Minet's $250 million annual revenues included strength in wholesale broking in North America. Aon now had almost twice the revenue of its nearest competitor in this area. More significantly, Minet's reinsurance revenues enabled Aon to replace M&M's Guy Carpenter unit as the world's largest reinsurance broker. In late 1997, Aon also acquired Jauch & Hübener KGaA in Germany, thereby creating the largest German brokerage, with seventeen offices and a staff of more than 1,600.

Aon was competing with M&M to acquire the most important brokerage in each European country. In addition to the German acquisition, during 1998 and 1999, Aon purchased the leading brokerages in Spain and Italy, Gil y Carvajal and Nikols Sedgwick. Nevertheless, for 1996, M&M's annual gross revenues were approximately $5.5 billion, compared with Aon's $4 billion. M&M's retail broking revenues were $2.4 billion, and Aon's were $2 billion.

There were yet more surprises to come. In July 1998, the leveraged buyout group of Kohlberg Kravis Roberts & Co., along with five American and British insurers, purchased the Willis Corroon Group plc for $1.4 billion. KKR & Co. initially took 76 percent, with management holding 5 percent and an option to increase that to 15 percent. The surprise was the involvement of American insurers including Chubb Corporation, Hartford Financial Services Group, and Travelers Property Casualty Corp. With insurance brokerages consolidating, insurers apparently were determined to ensure an opportunity to write business for one of the largest brokerages. KKR & Co. subsequently announced its intention to reduce its ownership to a minority position.

Sedgwick now remained the only unconsolidated player among the large brokerages, but only for a matter of weeks. In another stunning transaction, Marsh & McLennan announced in late August that it would acquire Sedgwick for approximately $2 billion. Since the acquisition came on the heels of the J&H deal, speculation focused on M&M's desire to beat Aon to the punch. There were areas of complementary strengths in an M&M–Sedgwick combination, but once the cost savings were realized, it was difficult to understand how this was a prudent investment. Marsh clearly paid a premium for the removal of J&H and Sedgwick, two of its main competitors. Except for some smaller, albeit important, international insurance brokerages, few logical targets remained for M&M and Aon.

These events totally recast the relative positions of the global insurance brokerages. By 1997, M&M, Aon, Sedgwick, A&A, Willis Corroon, and J&H all had annual revenues at least double those of the next largest brokerage. Within two years, those six firms had become three, with only two remaining independent. One analyst estimated that among the ten largest insurance brokerages in 1998, M&M would hold a 46 percent and Aon a 28 percent share of annual revenues. In 1998, M&M reported approximately $5.9 billion in brokerage and consulting revenues; Aon, $4.4 billion; and Willis Corroon came far behind at $1.2 billion. The 2001 figures were $7.3 billion, $5.6 billion, and $1.4 billion, respectively.

The world of insurance broking had changed irrevocably.

CHAPTER 24

Uncertain Times: Consolidation and Diversification

The late 1990s mega-mergers that captured press and public attention also involved U.S. insurance companies as well as brokers. Their ramifications would affect the entire global insurance industry. Four distinctive types of unions announced between March and July 1998 foretold insurers' midterm future.

St. Paul Companies, Inc., purchased the USF&G Corporation for a $2.8 billion stock swap that highlighted smaller insurers' problems. Before new management turned it around, USF&G had been a troubled company with a bleak future. Although expenses were brought into line and profits returned, expanding the revenue base in an ever tighter competitive environment proved elusive. Consequently, the firm was receptive to merging with a financially strong insurer. Similar conditions led to like results for other insurers.

Although circumstances were not identical, the reinsurance industry also sought additional capital for expansion. For this reason, Gen Re agreed to be taken over by Warren Buffett's Berkshire Hathaway for approximately $22 billion. Gen Re was the number one U.S. reinsurer; after acquiring Cologne Re in 1994 and venerable National Reinsurance Corp. in 1996, it ranked third globally. Earnings were fairly stable, cash flow was positive, and it had a fine underwriting track record. Nonetheless, like USF&G, Gen Re wanted additional capital.

This transaction mirrored consolidations in other insurance segments. With reinsurers, customers increasingly restricted transactions to those firms with large capitalizations. Foreign reinsurers, seeking a more significant U.S. presence, targeted U.S. prospects, as did larger U.S. reinsurers. For example, Employers Reinsurance Group (a unit of GE Capital) purchased Kemper Reinsurance Companies and became the country's second largest reinsurer and the fourth largest globally.

A third and increasingly powerful merger category was Bermuda-based insurers. EXEL Ltd., became XL Capital Ltd. in early 1999, and increased its ownership from 25 to 100 percent in Mid-Ocean Ltd. EXEL was a strong liability insurer; Mid-Ocean was a six-year-old catastrophe property underwriter that had branched into areas including aviation, space (e.g., satellites), and energy. In early 1999, XL Capital also announced it would purchase Nac Re Corp. for more than $1 billion. Nac Re had a strong U.S. market position; insurance and security analysts considered this a positive development.

The real eye opener was ACE Ltd.'s sudden transformation into a global giant. After acquiring Tempest Re in 1996 and Cat Ltd. in 1998, ACE bought Cigna's U.S. property/casualty business and its international operations for $3.45 billion.[1] Cigna's concentration shifted to health insurance. This purchase significantly extended ACE's range of insurance products, and it became a global force, offering virtually all lines of general insurance. ACE diversified further in May 1999 by acquiring Capital Re, a bond reinsurance company, complementing some of its other financial-insurance business.[2]

Experienced observers pointed to the riskiness of ACE's extensive expansion and theorized it might start resembling a little AIG. However, ACE would not soon threaten the skillfully managed AIG.

The fourth type of consolidation, the 1998 union of Citicorp and Travelers Group Inc. to form Citigroup, sent tremors throughout global financial circles. It challenged the future composition of financial organizations and the

[1] Cigna had been formed in 1982 through a combination of INA and the Connecticut General Life Insurance Company. Cigna—like Aetna, whose property/casualty business merged with Travelers in 1996—spun off its nonhealth-related underwriting activity.

[2] After ACE's offer to purchase Capital Re, XL Capital countered with a rival bid but later dropped out of contention.

services they provided. Given Citicorp's international presence, both U.S. and global implications were extraordinary. Travelers had already extended its services to investment banking by purchasing Salomon Brothers. The rationale behind the Citicorp-Travelers unification was that the two companies could offer a wider array of financial services to individuals and corporations.

The Citicorp-Travelers marriage came at a time when barriers between banking, insurance, and stock brokerages were disintegrating. Banks entered the securities business in the late 1980s and found legal loopholes permitting entrance into minor segments of insurance. The Glass-Steagall Act's barriers were overturned in 1999 when Congress permitted integration of banking, insurance, and securities businesses. Whether one-stop shopping or cross selling would work was uncertain. Previous approaches had been disappointing. In the mid-1980s, American Express Company failed to establish a successful supermarket of financial services. Citigroup, however, believed its business mix fit better than earlier experiments. Although its banking and securities sections apparently were profiting from cross introductions, the company announced late in 2001 its intent to spin off Travelers Property Casualty Corp. The reason acknowledged that cross selling had not worked and that the insurer's earnings were too volatile.

Cross selling is difficult; few can competently sell a range of financial services. Additionally, many consumers will not buy from one source, preferring the flexibility to pick-and-choose vendors. With insurance brokers, many of their larger clients prefer working with more than one provider. Despite uncertainties about cross selling, some banks see an opportunity at least to compete in the insurance brokerage sector. A 2001 combination is an example.

Wells Fargo, the country's seventh largest bank, became the first U.S. bank to establish a strong insurance brokerage operation. It purchased Acordia Inc.'s parent, ACO Brokerage Holdings Corp., adding significant strength to its own insurance agency. The combined annual brokerage revenues were approximately $610 million, creating the world's fifth largest brokerage. Later in 2001, Acordia and Britain's Heath Lambert Group formed a worldwide retail insurance network. This provided each firm servicing capability in areas where its own facilities were limited.

Few insurance people were surprised when the country's dominant all-around insurer, American International Group, Inc., declined to passively watch the acquisition activity. In 1998, AIG launched a $16.5 billion blockbuster acquisition of SunAmerica Inc., a leading issuer and seller of variable annuities.[3] By focusing on retirement savings products, AIG was, in part, reacting to the Citicorp-Travelers combination. In 2001, AIG followed up on the SunAmerica purchase, with a $23 billion acquisition of American General, the largest publicly traded life and annuity insurance company in the United States.

[3] Analysts considered the price to be high, but AIG CEO Maurice (Hank) Greenberg seldom miscalculated.

As the new millennium began, speculation was rife about the impact of banks and insurer mergers on insurance brokers. Many believe the financial giants will eventually consume even the largest brokers. There is a more immediate question: What does the future hold for large brokerages as stand-alone entities, particularly given investor pressure for profitable growth?

The short-term outlook is healthy for the few top firms. Recent acquisitions offer opportunity for substantial expense savings and greater efficiencies. But the picture is unclear several years out, because there are few significant acquisition targets and many daunting challenges. Several of these are of recent vintage and reflect the firms' huge size. For example, some risk managers object to choosing from among only a few large brokers. Size doesn't guarantee good service and sometimes is inhibiting.

Although the Internet is proving to be indispensable, problems still arise because of inadequate internal communications. As clients expand and their risks become increasingly complex, brokers draw on specialists from various locations. The more offices involved, however, the less likely senior account representatives are fully informed about account activity. Coordination suffers, and important matters can fall between the cracks. Smaller brokers are less vulnerable to this critical problem.

Diversification is another large broker issue. Because of their consulting expertise on a wide range of business issues, large brokers are already diversified and thus potentially attractive acquisitions. However, despite the Wells Fargo-Acordia combination, it is difficult to envision a positive risk/reward scenario for a financial service firm in purchasing a broker with only a core business portfolio.

Many brokers are continuing to expand their portfolios. Marsh & McLennan has led its counterparts in introducing new services including:

• MMC Enterprise Risk, a risk management unit, combining hazard, financial, operational, and strategic risk categories to advise clients from an integrated perspective.

• MMC Capital, a private equity business with over $2.5 billion in assets management. It seeks investment opportunities in insurance and financial services firms.

• A new consulting group focused on issues of security and terrorism.

In 2002, Aon planned to spin off its five specialty insurers to shareholders. These five will become a new holding company, Combined Specialty Corp. Presumably, this will give Aon greater flexibility to seek strategic diversification. In mid-2001, Willis Group Ltd. (the new name of Willis Corroon) raised approximately $270 million through an initial public offering in a newly established Bermuda-based holding company. The funds will be used to reduce debt and develop new growth initiatives.

The three brokerages are now positioned to seek partnerships with commercial banks or investment banking firms. If not, they may be compelled to hire bankers to develop clients' capital market solutions.

If diversification is not enough to attract merger or partnership alliances, brokers also provide access to top-level executives in broad cross sections of global companies. With emerging opportunities for dealing with multifaceted types of risk, this intangible might become a catalyst for a large financial organization to acquire M&M, Aon, or, more likely, Willis Group.

With changing distribution channels and potential competition from banks and e-commerce, medium-sized brokerages have limited options. Greater market share for most will be hard to achieve. They will develop and sell new insurance products and will have access to experienced talent available from larger brokerages as they consolidate merged companies. But areas such as controlling clients' international exposures will be difficult and costly. Innovative firms with strong niche positions can remain independent and prosper; Arthur J. Gallagher & Co. is one. Gallagher partnered with an e-commerce firm to launch an Internet-based brokerage for small businesses. The objective is to provide on-line full service—giving quotes, binding coverage, servicing clients, and handling claims for all lines of property/casualty and group life and health insurance. Gallagher is also expanding rapidly, with 2001 revenues of $859 million.

The number of insurance agents will be diminished as new technology provides direct public sales. Allstate is selling auto/home insurance over the telephone and the Internet. This approach will be closely watched, in part because some of its 15,000 agents' careers may be jeopardized and also because Allstate was authorized to form a full-service federal savings bank to market banking products to its insurance customers.

For those with careers spanning the last fifty years, three developments stand out.

First, the relative calm from 1950 to 1970 provided ample time to prepare for the merger frenzy, the rapid use of alternative markets, and the technical breakthroughs that transformed our business.

Second, some of our early principles have not endured. For example, the practice that one's word is one's bond can no longer be taken for granted. And employer-employee loyalty has been battered by personal and industry up-

heavals. Nonetheless, we share a unique industry, which offers enormous opportunity for personal growth. Furthermore, our experiences laid permanent foundations. We have the challenge and excitement of competing with talented brokers and we enjoy lasting friendships formed with competitors and insurers.

Third, we are humbled by the unforeseen array of mergers and acquisitions. It is startling how few of the distinguished old-line insurers and brokerages remain independent. For brokers, successful, strategic, and timely acquisitions have determined turn-of-the-century survivors.

Of the acquired firms, Johnson & Higgins, with a solid critical mass and outstanding staff, was in the best position to prosper as an independent. The financial windfall for J&H's employee-shareholders was most likely the primary motivation for joining M&M. As for insurers, many were forced to join others because of underwriting problems or to seek capital for growth. The list of major insurers from

Increasingly advanced technology means new challenges for insurers, witness the objects that communicate with these NASA antennas in Mexico, part of a worldwide array. Satellites in space, which perform all manner of tasks for mankind—communications, weather observation, extra-terrestrial studies, intercontinental snooping and more—are the most expensive moveable objects ever made. Placed atop rockets which are basically tubes full of explosive fuel, satellites are also among the most vulnerable manmade contrivances since a small error in the rocket or its launch can make debris out of a payload that cost a million worker hours and hundreds of millions of dollars to build.

the mid- to late 1900s that are no longer independent rivals that of large brokers.

Although most of the insurance industry's leading companies lost their independence in the twentieth century, history suggests the average life of multinational organizations is about forty-five years. Surveys of corporate births and deaths indicate that one-third of the 1970 Fortune 500 lost their independence by 1993. On the other hand, most large brokers and insurers survived more than a century—some much longer.

The industry's only certainty is uncertainty. Yet reasonable assumptions can be made. For insurers and brokers, large size, while not essential, is here to stay; consolidations will continue. For brokers, imaginative diversification is necessary; whether bankers buy brokers, brokers buy bankers, or whether they form partnerships, they will be in each other's business.

It will continue to be imperative to anticipate clients' ever-changing needs. And, as we have experienced in 2001, insurers will bear a special burden to diligently work at crafting insurance policy language to protect clients and themselves from unforeseen future risks. Technological breakthroughs, skillfully managed, will help determine which firms are dominant. For brokers, their mix of employees will include fewer clerical staff and more professionals. For individuals working in our industry, opportunities can be as significant as ever; however, they will need thorough command of finance and risk management skills to excel.

The dawning of a new age in which global terrorism is such an unpredictable risk will challenge the insurance industry for years to come. Wise and adept management will be essential for leading companies through an ever more perplexing labyrinth. Only the fittest will survive. Those that do could be richly rewarded.

The World Trade Center: Terrorism and Insurance

The unanticipated, enormous losses produced by the terrorist attacks on the Pentagon and World Trade Center on September 11, 2001, rocked the global insurance industry and created an uncertain future for institutions and businesses worldwide. We now know that terrorism can appear in the most unexpected and deadly ways; the future human and economic costs are incalculable.

While insurance is indispensable to economic growth, the industry itself cannot operate effectively without underlying financial stability. Although the full amount of the insured losses from September 11 terrorism is not yet known, by November 2002 estimates ranged from $40 billion to $60 billion. At least a dozen insurers anticipated pretax net losses of $500 million or more. Large reinsurers such as Munich Re and Berkshire Hathaway (particularly its General Re operation) had losses of well over $2 billion each. Lloyd's loss was a staggering $2.9 billion.

Major insurers promptly announced that they would honor claims resulting from September 11 and would not invoke the war exclusion provisions included in most policies. However, knowing that they cannot provide unlimited protection for every possible future terrorist event, they asked the U.S. government to intervene. A study by the General Accounting Office concluded that many insurers and businesses would not survive a major terrorist attack without significant federal aid.

Numerous reinsurance contracts came up for renewal on January 1, 2002, and companies attempting to insure commercial entities began dealing with a new reality. Adequate terrorism coverage was not available without government intervention. A January 16, 2002, article in the *Washington Post* reported:

The market for terrorism insurance has nearly dried up for large or high-profile properties, according to brokers and analysts. Insurance companies have developed lists of potential terrorist targets for every major U.S. city, the brokers said. If a building is on that list, its owners are almost certain to have trouble getting terrorism coverage when its policy expires this year.

The article also noted that a leading New York developer indicated that lack of terrorism coverage was causing significant problems for the real estate industry and could "grind it to a halt."

In the interim, insurers continued to provide coverage, although limited, even for terrorism. Aon quickly developed a program with Lloyd's and London companies offering protection of up to $170 million. AIG and others also offer protection, but their limits are inadequate for buyers like those in commercial real estate.

Airlines in the United States encountered a special problem. Only $50 million of third-party liability coverage was available from private insurers. The government provided excess protection, renewable every sixty days, while the issue was debated. An AIG consortium offered $950 million excess of $50 million, but airlines considered the limits inadequate and the cost excessive.

Although September 11 created much uncertainty for insurers, it also reinforced rising prices in a hardening market. Industry leaders expected the upward trend to continue at least through 2003. The likelihood of a period of higher premiums attracted new capital from investors, and this capital infusion will help cover 2001 losses.

Once again, Marsh & McLennan led the way. It formed a new Bermudan insurer, Axis Specialty Ltd., capitalized at $1.6 billion. Others quickly followed. AIG, Chubb, and

Epochal day, September 11, 2001, opens a new age in the economics of insurance worldwide. Destruction of New York City's World Trade Center in a horribly original act of terrorism is so costly that private industry can no longer provide adequate insurance protection against this kind of unpredictable loss. Thus government may become the insurer of last resort by means of mechanisms that are not yet clear.

Goldman Sachs collaborated to set up Allied World Assurance Co. with $1.5 billion; Aon, Zurich Financial Services, and various investors established Endurance Specialty Insurance Ltd. with $1.2 billion. Smaller Bermudan reinsurers were also formed; and others injected new capital into ongoing operations. Together, ACE and XL Capital raised nearly $2 billion, with Arch Capital Group Ltd. contributing an additional $750 million.

A total of almost $25 billion was invested in various companies, offsetting some of the $50 billion that Swiss Re economist Thomas Holzheu estimated had been lost in underwriting capacity due to September 11 and the stock market decline. Most observers were amazed that substantial new capacity could be raised in such a short time. Additionally, early in 2002, Lloyd's had a record underwriting capacity of £12.3 billion, which may exceed £13 billion by year-end.

The prospect of higher premiums induced some companies to assume more of their own risks by accepting higher deductibles, reducing their liability limits, or establishing new captives. However, if such approaches backfire, limiting their insurance protection could become an imprudent risk and provoke investor litigation.

Although higher prices generally benefit brokers, they were not immune to the volatile business environment. Marsh and Aon suffered significant loss of personnel and facilities at the World Trade Center. Additionally, stock market gyrations negatively affected M&M's investment management business, and the company experienced a decline in profits from its consulting operations. Aon, on the other hand, had to delay divesting its insurance companies and experienced disappointing earnings.

Meanwhile, Willis, free of such problems, aggressively moved ahead. KKR's ownership was reduced to 40 percent and was likely to move lower. Arthur J. Gallagher continued to prosper as the fourth leading broker. Another seven brokerages had 2001 revenues in excess of $300 million and planned to grow through acquisitions and a focus on the middle market.

In the midst of what was, for many, a difficult and unpredicatable economic environment, the U. S. government finally acted on a terrorism insurance bill. In late November 2002, the lame-duck Senate passed and President Bush signed a bill that could provide as much as $100 billion to cover terrorism-related claims.

While the tragic events of September 2001 have heightened awareness of global political and economic risks, insurers are contending with other open-ended liabilities and an increasingly uncertain economy. Many major companies with asbestos-related losses are in bankruptcy. Plaintiffs have expanded efforts and sued corporations that were previously ignored because of minor involvement. IBM, AT&T, and Ford Motor are recent examples. The litigation net has been cast far afield in search of new targets.

Terrorism, asbestos, and environmental pollution represent three well-publicized areas of unforeseen, catastrophic losses. New risks are also emerging in such areas as <u>the</u> Internet, electronic data technology, and employment (bias and harassment). Such exposures have forced insurers to examine even more carefully what they intend to insure as well as what they do not intend to insure.

Insurers may be facing their most daunting challenge since the eighteenth century. Fortunately for the industry and its clients, most leading companies have strong and innovative management teams. Thus, the industry moves into the twenty-first century with both enormous challenges and great possibilities for serving the public good while achieving financial success.

November 2002

Notes on Sources

GENERAL

With respect to eighteenth- and nineteenth-century statistics in the first four chapters, there are often wide variances among sources. This is a particular problem for figures relating to catastrophic losses (i.e., the number of losses, the number of buildings destroyed and whether residential or commercial, the number of insurers involved, the amount of their losses, and the number of those forced out of business).

During this period, record keeping was inexact, and many records were lost. Consequently, estimates are frequently used. I cite either the most credible sources or give an average or range.

For discussions of Frank B. Hall and Reed Stenhouse throughout the narrative, I obtained internally produced typescripts describing their histories. I also made extensive use of Alexander & Alexander archives and various company publications that appeared before 1997.

Authors of books are identified by full name in the first reference, and authors of articles are usually identified by last name only. Because some books and articles have multiple authors, for clarity and consistency I have used a semicolon after sources where appropriate.

CHAPTER 1—
Origins: From the Code of Hammurabi to Lloyd's of London

The principal sources for the seventeenth century and earlier are Vincent T. Covello and Jeryl Mumpower; and Irving Pfeffer. Other sources include Alwin E. Bulau; J. A. Fowler; and William D. Winter (on general average). For Lloyd's material, D. E. W. Gibb is the principal source, followed by Peter L. Bernstein; Bulau; Hugh Cockerall; Godfrey Hodgson; Jonathan Mantle; and Charles Royster. For Cuthbert Heath, the main source is Antony Brown, followed by Gibb and Hodgson.

CHAPTER 2

Insurance in America: The Beginnings

Bernard L. Webb covers much of the material before the American Revolution, including the William Penn quotation on J. Askew (p. 88) and John Copson's ad (p. 89); Bulau is another useful source. For William Penn and colonial America, see Joseph P. Kelley Jr.; and Harry Emerson Wildes.

For Philadelphia insurance, primary sources are Fowler (who provides the Francis Rawle quotation); Marcus James; and Thomas H. Montgomery. Others include Bulau; and William H. A. Carr. For Boston insurance, Edward R. Hardy offers the 1745 and 1748 *Boston Evening Post* ads (p. 32 and p. 34). The quotation on Boston's early fire safety measures is from the *Insurance Index* (p. 29), and the quotation on Boston competition is from Webb (p. 90). On Connecticut insurance, see P. Henry Woodward. The Friendly Society's Articles of Agreement are from Bulau (p. 21).

Some Philadelphia historians believe Anthony Van Dam's ad referred to a local site from which he forwarded risks to New York for underwriting. (Moreover, sources say Van Dam's office adjoined Philadelphia's London Coffee House.) However, Van Dam's ad cites the Merchants' Coffee House (a New York facility with that name was frequented by insurance shipping men). The earliest mention I found of a Philadelphia Merchants' Coffee House indicates a starting date well after 1759. Logic suggests that Van Dam placed the same ad in both cities because he was soliciting Philadelphia business while operating from his New York office.

Primary sources for the period from Independence to 1820 are Ronald W. Vinson and John Cosgrove; and Webb. Ronald Vinson has kindly shared the unpublished Vinson and Cosgrove material, which provides a helpful perspective on the early development of American insurance.

James is the primary source for the Insurance Company of North America. Carr also offers material, including the Universal Tontine Association quotation (p. 41). Both Fowler and Montgomery are additional sources.

On Providence Washington Insurance Company and John Brown's quotation on salaries, see William Greene Roelker and Clarkson A. Collins III; and Bulau (p. 31). *Earthquake History of the United States* provides information for the New Madrid earthquake. For Robert Fulton, see John S. Morgan; and Cynthia Owen Phillip.

CHAPTER 3

Raising the Ante: The American Insurance Industry Comes of Age

Material on the emergence of agents and brokers is found in Fowler; James; Montgomery (the Phoenix Assurance Company quotation, p. 67); Clive Trebilcock; Vinson and Cosgrove (Davis and Reid ad quotation); and Webb. The INA directors' comments on a Charleston agent and their instructions on appointing new agents come from James (pp. 100 and 104, respectively).

The primary source for the Phoenix Assurance Company (London) is Trebilcock; secondary sources are Vinson and Cosgrove; and Webb. For the Hartford Fire Insurance Company, see Richard M. Bissell; Charles W. Burpee; and Hawthorne Daniel. For the Aetna Insurance Company, the main source is Henry R. Gall and William George Jordan, who quote Aetna's letter to Stephen Tillinghast (p. 152) and its advice to agents in the *Book of Instruction* (pp. 154–155). Woodward also is helpful.

The principal source for railroads is John F. Stover. The primary source for the 1835 New York City fire is Edwin G. Burrows and Mike Wallace; followed by Bulau; and James. For inventions in the 1830s and 1840s, John N. Cosgrove; Bulau; and Bernard Grun. On American clipper ships, see Cosgrove; James; and Microsoft's *Encarta Encyclopedia*. For the 1853 New York City fire, see Atlantic Mutual Companies; and Cosgrove.

Adele Hast offers a short history of the Aetna Life and Casualty, the Home, and the St. Paul Fire and Marine insurance companies. Bulau provides information on other new insurers from 1849 to 1853. For insurer regulation, see Bulau; and Vinson and Cosgrove. For the Civil War, Cosgrove; James; Edward W. Powell; and Vinson and Cosgrove (their report on the Hartford Fire's Charleston agent comes from the *Independent Agent*). The *New York Times* report on post-Civil War accidents is from George Malcolm-Smith.

CHAPTER 4—
Phoenix (and Others) Rising: Foundings, Fires, and Finances

Travelers Insurance Company material (including quotations referring to its purpose, the West Coast insurance contract, the Reverend Mr. Perry, the Civil War major, and Mr. Fred W. Rice) is attributable to Malcolm-Smith. For West Coast insurance agents, John Ashmead. Johnson & Higgins information is in *The Story of Johnson & Higgins*. Fred. S. James information comes from the company. On Frank B. Hall, "Joint Venture . . . A History of Frank B. Hall" (hereafter referred to as "Hall–Joint Venture"). The National Board of Fire Underwriters and the *Insurance Chronicle* quotations are from Harry C. Brearley (pp. 13 and 20–21). Also, see James; and Vinson and Cosgrove for related material.

The Peshtigo fire information is from Writers' Program's, *Wisconsin*, in the American Guide Series; Malcolm-Smith. On the Chicago and Boston fires, see Ashmead; Bulau; Burpee; Daniel; Fowler; Gall and Jordan; James (quotation from *Chicago Tribune* p. 163); Springfield Fire & Marine; Hanover Fire Insurance Company; and Vinson and Cosgrove.

Material for the panic of 1873 comes from Vinson and Cosgrove; and James. Hast offers a short history of Fireman's Fund Insurance Company. Information on the yellow fever epidemic, Richmond's trolley line, and the Bessemer steel-I beam is in "Aetna Timeline." See Cosgrove (p. 67) for the quotation on manufactured goods, and Covello and Mumpower (p. 110) for the quotation on changing responsibility for liability.

CHAPTER 5—
Your Car Has Arrived: Agents and Brokers Speed Ahead

On automobiles, see Bulau; James (including Charles Platt quotations, p. 304, and the *Spectator*, p. 304); Malcolm-Smith; McEwen; Vinson and Cosgrove. Vinson and Cosgrove provide the Mrs. Dodds' quotation. See Hewitt Associates on benefit plans. Golf comments are from "Aetna Timeline." Wysocki offers material on the Standard Oil Company. Valued policy information comes from Brearley; James; and Vinson and Cosgrove. See David Schiff for the public's perception of insurance brokers, including the 1868 circular quotation. Charles Platt's quotation about brokers is in James (p. 183).

Information on Thomas Edison comes from Matthew Josephson; and Barbara Krasner-Khait. Primary sources for facts about Marsh & McLennan are Seabury; Thomas; and Souder. Johnson & Higgins material is in *The Story of Johnson & Higgins,* and Frank B. Hall's is in "Hall–Joint Venture." See Brown for Charles Rollins and Cuthbert Heath. For Fred. S. James, the company furnished information. Hast offers a short history of the Continental Insurance Company and the Zurich Insurance Group.

CHAPTER 6—
Alexander & Alexander: West Virginia Origins

For Alexander family background, see Charles B. Alexander; and Herbert L. Alexander. Information on the Vance family is in Atkinson and Gibbens; and Cyrus Vance's letter to Barbara Rosenbaum. Material about A&A's first few years comes from Herbert L. Alexander. On Clarksburg historical data, see the Harrison County Chamber of Commerce; and Morton. Information about Clarksburg in the early 1900s and its needs is in *Clarksburg Daily Telegram* (February 16, 1900; March 9, 1900; and January 18, 1901). Typical Alexander & Alexander newspaper ads are from the *Clarksburg Daily Telegram* (January 5, 1900).

CHAPTER 7—
Alexander & Alexander Comes of Age: Growing Up and Out

An informal company history offers considerable material relating to Alexander & Alexander from 1899 until 1955. Former corporate secretary Jack Pritchard prepared the history on the basis of interviews with many A&A employees, as well as his personal observations. I also conducted various interviews and drew on extensive A&A archival files.

For C. B. Alexander's involvement with the National Association of Local Fire Insurance Agents, the archives contained C. B.'s 1905 (January 25, February 20, and March 20) letters to the association in Boston. Sources for the 1906 San Francisco earthquake include Ashmead; Brown; Burpee; Daniel; Gall and Jordan; Hodgson; James; Malcolm-Smith; Springfield Fire & Marine; and Webb. Hewitt Associates is instructive on employee benefit programs.

CHAPTER 8—
Emerging Personalities: Four Founders

Material on Henry Marsh and Donald McLennan is found in Seabury; Souder; and Thomas (including the *Collier's* quotation, p. 10). For Richard Alexander's early impression of his father's (W. F.'s) business acumen, the son's letters to Jack Bogardus (February 22, 1977; March 24, 1977; and June 1988) were invaluable.

CHAPTER 9—
The Roaring Twenties: New Venues

Covello and Mumpower offer material on the changing doctrine of civil liability.

Information about Johnson & Higgins growth comes from *The Story of Johnson & Higgins.* On Marsh & McLennan and Guy Carpenter, see Seabury; and Thomas. Frank B. Hall material is from "Hall–Joint Venture." *The Insurance Index* is the source for Fred. S. James. For R. A. Corroon, see Corroon & Black *Proxy* (August 27, 1990).

For the start of Alexander & Alexander's relationship with Sedgwick Collins & Co., the letters from Alan Parry to J. H. Swinglehurst (July 10, 1990); and from J. H. Swinglehurst to Jack Bogardus (July 18, 1990). "The Oil Insurance Association" provides a history of the Oil Insurance Association. The aviation discussion is from Oliver E. Allen, *Eastern Underwriter* (August 25, 1925); Malcolm-Smith; and D. Murray Stewart. T. A. Heppenheimer discusses the origin of American Airlines.

CHAPTER 10—
The Nineteen-Thirties: Internal Conflicts and Other Challenges

For the W. F. Alexander and Roy Jenkins tiff over Franklin D. Roosevelt's request, Jack Bogardus's January 26, 1990, interview with Jenkins's son, George. The reference to Johnson & Higgins comes from Winton. The Marsh & McLennan material is in Seabury; and Thomas.

CHAPTER 11—
Competitive Pressures: World War II and W. F. Alexander's Passing

On Marsh & McLennan, see Seabury; and Thomas. The

"Hall–Joint Venture" provides information on Frank B. Hall. Johnson & Higgins in Canada material comes from *The Story of Johnson & Higgins.*

CHAPTER 12—
The Postwar Period: A Changing of the Guard

I have drawn extensively on personal experience and observations for Alexander & Alexander material after 1962. Beginning in 1963, each A&A acquisition was subject to a detailed report, including historical and financial information.

Material about Marsh & McLennan's becoming a publicly owned company comes from the Marsh & McLennan *1962 Annual Report*; and Thomas. The Johnson & Higgins deliberation of the "public" issue is in Winton.

CHAPTER 13—
Brokers Go Public: The Era of Acquisitions Begins

On Alexander & Alexander becoming publicly owned and my role in the process, Geoffrey Calvert letter to Ruth Rose (January 9, 1979) and A&A's *1969 Annual Report.* Information on Frank B. Hall's public offering and the lead-up is in "Hall–Joint Venture;" and Hall's *1969 Annual Report.* The *National Underwriter* (August 5, 1920) provides material about Charles W. Sexton.

CHAPTER 14—
The Chaotic Seventies: More Mergers

Richard M. Miller and H. Wayne Snider helpfully discuss the industry focus on "risk management" and its origins. For William Carter's death, see Alt. On the R. B. Jones acquisition, refer to Fannin (September 18, 1978). Information about A&A's winning the Saudi Arabia Royal Commission contract is in Emmerich; and Key.

CHAPTER 15—
Innocents Abroad: A&A Goes to Britain

Information on the formation of significant British brokerages, including quoted passages, is from Hodgson (pp. 133 and 137–138). Bernard Ross Collins provides an informative history of Sedgwick. For A&A's focus on international expansion, see Zinkewicz. On media reaction to A&A's discussion with Sedgwick Forbes and Bland Payne, refer to Fannin (November 27, 1978); John Miller; and John Moore (November 17, 1978).

Material about U.S. brokers' "invasion of Lloyd's" comes from Asher; Hodgson; Osborn; and Sturm. For the announcement of an A&A and Sedgwick proposed merger, see Jennings (December 26, 1980). The termination of merger discussions is in Coppack; Hodgson; McIntyre; and Tickell.

Quoted material on Alexander Howden's history is in Gavin Ewart's unpaginated booklet. Hodgson also offers information. For Posgate, see Department of Trade and Industry report (Chapter 4, pp. 4.31-4.33); Hodgson; and Robinson (August 30, 1982, pp.19-20).

CHAPTER 16—
Chicanery and Conflict: The Howden Affair

For the Howden acquisition and its aftermath, A&A maintained extensive records. In addition, a Deloitte report on the events and the Department of Trade and Industry report were principal sources. Since U.K. and U.S. newspapers covered the subject on a daily basis, hundreds of articles were available as sources from which a cross-section has been used. These were supplemented by Ian Hay Davison; Hertzberg; Hodgson; John Moore (September 2, 1982); and Adam Raphael.

On rules of the U.K. stock exchange, see Davison. For references to Posgate during the early 1980s, see Brasier; Bunker (July 11, 1986); David; Hilton; and Bourke; Hodgson; Mantle; Marcus; John Moore (September 21, 1982); Raphael; and Robinson (September 20, 1982).

Quotations attributable to Paul Dixey about Posgate are from Robinson (August 30, 1982, pp.19-20). On Posgate's comments about other underwriters, see the *Guardian* (June 26, 1982). For the quotation on Posgate as a source for purchasing the Banque du Rhône, see the DTI's report (Chapter 9, 9.67). For the DTI's summary statement, see the report (Chapter 23, 23.8).

For an editorial commenting on Alexander & Alexander's handling of the problems at Howden, see *Business Insurance* (July 27, l987).

CHAPTER 17—
Earlier Troubles at Lloyd's: A Long Unraveling

Hodgson; Mantle; and Raphael provide helpful background on most of the issues covered in this chapter.

On the structure of Lloyd's, as well as on Hurricane Betsy's impact on Lloyd's, and on the Cromer report and its aftermath, see Raphael; Hodgson; and Mantle. Raphael also has useful remarks on U.S. tort law.

Hodgson and Mantle are helpful on Lloyd's underwriters' challenge with computer risks. For marine catastrophes, see Hodgson (quotation on vessel catastrophes, p. 154). Mantle; Hodgson; and Raphael report on the Sasse and Savonita affairs. Hodgson quotes the *Sunday Telegraph* (p. 218) on Lloyd's ineptness. For Lloyd's chairman Peter Green's problems, Mantle; and Raphael. On Ian Hay Davison, his quotation is from Davison (p. 207). John Moore (August 2, 1984) supplies Davison's quotation on "the mist." Mantle; and Raphael also discuss Davison's challenges at Lloyd's. Davison; Mantle; Raphael; and the *Guardian* (April 8, 1989) have useful comments on the Neill report. Also see Sir Patrick Neill.

For media coverage on the Gang of Four and Posgate's arrest

by the Fraud Squad, see Bunker (July 16, 1987); John Moore (July 16, 1987); Rocca and Chittenden.

For comment on the "not guilty" verdict for Grob and Posgate, see Aldred (August 21, 1989); and Beckett (August 18, 1989). For media observations on Grob's death, see the *Independent* (January 4, 1992); and the *Times* (London) also January 4, 1992.

CHAPTER 18—
A Rocky Recovery: Lloyd's Revisited

Hodgson; Mantle; and Raphael offer useful perspectives for this chapter. On the "Old Lloyd's," see Hodgson; and Raphael. For Lloyd's problems that should have been foreseen, but were not, see Davison; Hodgson; and Raphael. Hodgson; Lapper (September 9, 1991); Mantle; and Raphael discuss catastrophic losses. Raphael provides tables listing the number of Lloyd's names in many of the years from 1771 to 1993 and Lloyd's syndicates, from 1979 to 1993.

From many sources covering Lloyd's from 1990 to 1996 including "revolt of Names," the following represent a cross section: Barnes (including the financial journalist quotation, p. 85); Bray (December 9, 1993); Lapper (May 3, 1991 and June 20, 1992); Luessenhop and Mayer; Mantle; Milbank (April 13, 1995); Raphael; and *The Economist* (February 29, 1992 and May 16, 1992). For a suicide attributed to Lloyd's losses, *The Daily Telegraph* (August 26, 1994). For LMX business, Mantle; and Raphael.

For underwriter Outhwaite, see Bunker (June 14, 1989); Hodgson; Mantle; and Raphael. On underwriter Merrett, refer to Ashworth; Ion (November 30, 1993); Milbank (September 9, 1995); and Raphael. For underwriters Feltrim and Walker, see Atkins and Mason; Mantle; Milbank (September 9, 1995); Raphael (for the Gooda Walker quotation, p. 173); and *The Economist* (May 11, 1991). Mantle comments on the Spicer and White syndicate. For the suit against auditors, Bray (November 1, 1995).

Bray (July 3, 1992) discusses the Walker report. For the Rowland plan and corporate membership, see Bray (January 13, 1992 and November 16, 1993); Jennings (September 27, 1993); Raphael; and *The Economist* (May 1, 1993). For media speculation on Lloyd's survival, Ingrassia and Milbank; Raphael (for *The Sunday Times* quotation, p. 172); *The Independent* on Sunday (April 23, 1995); and Truell. On Lloyd's settlement offers to Names, Bray (December 9, 1993); Milbank (February 15, 1994); and Parker-Pope. For Integrated Lloyd's Vehicle (ILV), "Lloyd's: Destroying the Myths." For U.S. Names' struggle with Lloyd's, Fialka (March 28, 1996 and July 11, 1996); Fields (May 24, 1996); Knight; and Ortega.

On Jaffrey vs. Lloyd's, see Veysey (May 22, 2000; November 6, 2000; January 8, 2001; and April 30, 2001). For Lloyd's uncertain future, see Fuhrmans. *Business Insurance* (January 22, 2001) is instructive on how the early Lloyd's corporate members were faring. For Lloyd's new system of reporting results and the 2001 results, see Veysey (April 15, 2002). On Equitas's struggle with asbestos claims and potential impact, Veysey (September 18, 2000 and September 10, 2001).

CHAPTER 19—
The Eighties: Some Strategic Acquisitions

For A&A's ranking on yardsticks of management performance, see Gissen. On A&A's final attempt to merge with Sedgwick, Hertzberg and Anders. For Sedgwick Group's acquisition of Fred. S. James, see Sedgwick Group's document to shareholders (June 7, 1985). Braidwood's comprehensive history of Reed Stenhouse is illuminating as background on the A&A–Reed Stenhouse merger. See also Hilder and Zehr; *The Business Scottsman*; and Wilson. For A&A's surpassing M&M as the world's largest retail brokerage, McLeod (December 10, 1984).

CHAPTER 20—
A Cataclysm of Torts: Risks Run Amok

Olson offers a detailed discussion on litigation in the United States. For a comprehensive overview of asbestos and environmental liability issues, see Chubb *Annual Reports*; and Raphael.

On general tort matters relating to this chapter, see Angermueller; Brimelow; Broad (for Peter W. Huber quotation, p. C1); Bruce; Chubb *Annual Reports* (1998–2001); Clark; Evans-Pritchard; Fields (March 26, 1992); Robert Moore; Rand; Schut (May 1993); and Truell.

In the 1980s and early 1990s, A&A's Government and Industry Affairs Office documented the breadth and depth of the liability crisis in a series of "Risk Management Surveys." The results were published each spring in association with the Risk & Insurance Management Society meetings and were covered in front-page stories in *Business Insurance* and other industry publications.

Ion (November 25, 1992); and Spencer report Tillinghast estimates on tort claims. For whooping-cough vaccine, see Tanouye. On the Keene Corporation issue, see Raphael; *The Daily Telegraph* (August 3, 1992—reprint from *The Wall Street Journal*). For asbestos in the Fireboard case, Chubb Corp.; Ion (September 7, 1993); and Labaton. On other asbestos sources, McLeod (January 8, 2001); and Oster (May 7, 2001). For environmental sources, see Bunshaft; *Business Week* (August 2, 1993); Chubb Corp.; Schut (October 1994); and Tyerman. On product liability discussions, Bradford (May 1, 2000 and August 20, 2001); and Danforth.

CHAPTER 21—
Riding the Roller Coaster: Upheavals of the Eighties and Nineties

Business Insurance and other trade publications gave extensive coverage to Jack Bogardus's comments about the pattern of insurers losing market share to alternative risk financing techniques, as well as the problems created by reinsurance recoverables. For a representative example of this coverage, see Aldred (March 2, 1987).

On captive insurance companies, see Calise; Kloman; Mulrenan; Swiss Re; and Wojcik. For the Federal Liability Risk Retention Act, see Geisel; Smith Barney Insurance Research report (January 18, 1988); and Swiss Re. On Bermuda's rise as the domicile for alternative insurance markets, see Howard; Ion (June 24, 1993); and Steinmetz. Murphy; and Sheppard report on reinsurance recoverables.

Lloyd's List (May 17, 1984) covers Marsh & McLennan's 1984 bond loss. For the Corroon & Black–Willis Faber merger, see Corroon's September 28, 1990, *Proxy Supplement*. Robert Hatcher's memorandum to employees (June 4, 1990); and Sullivan discuss Johnson & Higgins' reaction to the merger. For Willis Corroon's mid-1990s problems, Barclays de Zoete Wedd Research Report (November 17, 1994); *Lloyd's List* (March 13, 1995); and *The Sunday Times* (March 12, 1995). On Sedgwick's challenges, see *ReActions* (April 1988). For Frank B. Hall's struggles, Gray; Greenwald; and Hall's *Annual Reports* (1980-1992); McLeod (July 27, 1992); and Sherer.

CHAPTER 22—
O Brave New World: New Risks and Initiatives

Business Insurance (February 4, 2002) gives the number and location of captive insurance companies. Swiss Re offers statistics on the numbers of risk retention groups and purchasing groups. For Alternative Risk Transfer (ART), including securitization and derivatives, the following sources are informative: Aldred (July 3, 2000); Goch (January 1999); Jenkins; Kielholz; McGeehan; Niedzielski; Salomon Smith Barney (July 8, 1999); Spiller and Mellman; Swiss Re; *The Economist* (January 16, 1999 and September 4, 1999); Zolkas (May 14, 2001); Zuckerman; Zuckerman and Lohse. On companies using ART, see Banham (January 5, 1999).

CHAPTER 23—
Decline and Fall: Acquisition Frenzy

Murphy and *Business Insurance* (December 25, 2000) explore insurer reactions after Hurricane Andrew and other catastrophes of the period. Woolley and DeGeorge comment on John Snyder's reference to PRUPAC; they also report on insurer results for 1992.

On AIG's investment in A&A and Frank Zarb's hiring, see *Business Insurance* (July 18, 1994 and July 17, 1995); Quint; Scism (June 8, 1994); and Waters (June 8, 1994 and June 9, 1994). For Patrick Ryan, see Fritz. Fox reports on Willis Corroon's loss of seventy executives to Aon. On second-tier brokerages, see Cohen; and Crerar. For the decreasing number of insurance agents, see Conning; and the Council of Insurance Agents and Brokers (winter 1997).

Business Insurance (July 5, 1993) covers Marsh & McLennan's early 1990s European acquisitions. A&A's acquisition of most of Jardine's U.S. operations comes from Gordon Mackenzie. For Europe's acquisition frenzy, see Ascarelli; DuBois; Fuhrmans; Hiday; Rhoads and Studer; Studer and Lohse. On Japanese insurer consolidations, *Business Insurance* (April 9, 2001); Dvorak (April 20, 2000); and Shirouzu. For U.S. insurer consolidations, see Poole; Studer and Scism.

On Aon's acquisition of A&A, see Gjertsen; Shapiro; and Zarb (report to Alexander & Alexander shareholders, December 16, 1996). For J&H considering its future options, see Scism. Lipin and Scism report on M&M's acquisition of J&H.

See Rapoport's discussion of J&H's age-bias lawsuit. For some J&H past directors' reactions to its takeover, *Business Insurance* (October 23, 2000); Jack Bogardus's discussion with an anonymous, former J&H director (2001); and Treaster (December 27, 1997). Roberts (April 14, 1997) reports on Aon's acquisition of J. H. Minet. Goldsmith covers Willis Group's takeover by KK&R and some insurers. Treaster (August 26, 1998) discusses M&M's acquisition of Sedgwick.

CHAPTER 24—
Uncertain Times: Consolidation and Diversification

Treaster (February 19, 1999) reports on XL Capital's purchase of Nac Re. For ACE's purchase of Cigna units, see Lohse (January 13, 1999); and Treaster (January 26, 1999). Chernow; Lipin and Frank cover the Citicorp-Travelers combination, and Nol discusses Citigroup's intention to spin off Travelers Property Casualty Corp. On Wells Fargo's acquisition of Acordia, Roberts (March 12, 2001); and Zolkos (April 2, 2001). For AIG's acquisition of SunAmerica, see Lohse (August 21, 1998).

Banham (July 1999) explores some clients' objection to using only one broker. For the Willis Group IPO, see Roberts (April 23, 2001); and Souter and Roberts. *Business Insurance* (March 27, 2000) reports on Arthur J. Gallagher. For Allstate Insurance Company, Bowers; Lohse (November 11, 1999); and Treaster (November 11, 1999). Flynn discusses a survey of corporate births and deaths.

EPILOGUE—
The World Trade Center: Terrorism and Insurance

Insurer losses from the September 11 attack are covered in Hoffman, McLeod (October 1, 2001); Oster (October 10, 2001); and Veysey (December 3, 2001). Spinner reports on the congressional debate about the U.S. government's assisting insurers in providing more adequate coverage for terrorism.

For the forming of additional underwriter capital and Thomas Holzheu's estimate of lost capital, see Bradford (October 1, 2001); *Business Insurance* (December 10, 2001); McLeod (November 12,

2001); and Souter (December 3, 2001). Oster (August 1, 2002) summarizes the plight of commercial insurance buyers who are being forced to assume more of their risks. On asbestos plaintiffs suing major U.S. companies that have very limited exposure and the resurgence of asbestos claims, McLeod (December 24, 2001). Abelson; Wojcik (June 10, 2002); and The Council of Insurance Agents and Brokers (February 2000) discuss new types of risk that are proving to be a challenge for insurance companies.

Selected Bibliography

As I am not aware of another work that covers the over-two-century development of insurance broking in the United States, I thought it would be useful to readers and future researchers to provide an extensive bibliography. The material is divided into the following sections: books; articles in journals, magazines, and books; articles in newspapers; public and corporate documents; unpublished manuscripts; and unpublished interviews and letters.

Books

Ackerman, S. B. *Insurance.* New York: Ronald Press, 1928.

Aetna Life & Casualty Co. *Historical Highlights, 1853–1992.* Hartford, Conn.: Aetna Life & Casualty Co., 1991.

Allen, Oliver E. and the Editors of Time-Life Books. *The Airline Builders.* Alexandria, Va.: Time-Life Books, 1981.

Aon Corporation. *1999 Insurance Market Overview.* Chicago: Aon Corporation, 1991.

Ashmead, John, ed. and comp. *The Wings of the Phoenix.* Hartford, Conn.: Phoenix Insurance Company, 1954.

Atkinson, George W. and Alvardo F. Gibbens. *Prominent Men of West Virginia.* Wheeling, W.Va.: W. L. Callin, 1890.

Atlantic Mutual Companies. *The Atlantic Log (July 4, 1976).* New York: Atlantic Mutual Companies, 1976.

Barclays de Zoete Wedd. *Willis Corroon: Drinking in the Last Chance Saloon.* Research Report 98. November 17, 1994.

Bernstein, Peter L. *Against the Gods—The Remarkable Story of Risk.* New York: John Wiley & Sons, 1996.

Bissell, Richard M., comp. *Hartford Fire Insurance Company: The Story of Its Beginnings.* Hartford, Conn.: Hartford Fire Insurance Company, 1940.

Brandon, Lawrence G. *Let the Trumpet Resound: The Insurance*

Industry in the 21st Century. Malvern, Pa.: Harry J. Loman Foundation, 1996.

Brearly, Harry C. *Fifty Years of a Civilizing Force.* New York: Frederick A. Stokes Company, 1916. (Historical appendices compiled by Daniel N. Hardy.)

Brown, Antony. *Cuthbert Heath.* London: David & Charles Ltd., 1980.

Bulau, Alwin E. *Footprints of Assurance.* New York: MacMillan Company, 1953.

Burpee, Charles W., comp. *One Hundred Years of Service: History of the Hartford Fire Insurance Company.* Hartford, Conn.: Hartford Fire Insurance Company, 1910.

Burrows, Edwin G. and Mike Wallace. *Gotham: A History of New York City to 1898.* New York: Oxford University Press, 1999.

Carr, William H. A. *Perils, Named and Unnamed; The Story of the Insurance Company of North America.* New York: McGraw-Hill, 1967.

Chubb, Thomas Caldecot. *If There Were No Losses.* New York: John B. Watkins Company, 1957.

Cockerell, Hugh. *Lloyd's of London: A Portrait.* Homewood, Ill.: Dow Jones-Irwin, 1984.

Collins, Bernard Ross. *The History of Sedgwick, Collins & Co. Ltd.* London: 1969.

Conning & Company. *Changing Property-Casualty Distribution Channels.* Hartford, Conn.: Conning & Company, 1996.

———. *The Independent Property-Casualty Agent.* Hartford, Conn.: Conning & Company, 1995.

Cosgrove, John N., ed. and comp. *Gray Days and Gold.* New York: Atlantic Companies, 1967.

Cushman, Allerton Jr. *Insurance Letter from London.* Morgan Stanley Research Report. March 12, 1990.

Daniel, Hawthorne. *The Hartford of Hartford.* New York: Random House, 1960.

Davison, Ian Hay. *Lloyd's: A View of the Room.* London: George Wiedenfeld and Nicolson Limited, 1987.

Ewart, Gavin. *Alexander Howden—150 Years of Shipping and Insurance.* London: W. S. Cowell Ltd., 1971.

Fowler, J. A. *History of Insurance in Philadelphia for Two Centuries (1683–1882).* Philadelphia: Review Publishing and Printing Company, 1888.

Gall, Henry R. and William George Jordan. *One Hundred Years of Fire Insurance.* Hartford, Conn.: Aetna Insurance Company, 1919.

Gibb, D. E. W. *Lloyd's of London—A Study of Individualism.* New York: St. Martin's Press, 1957.

Grun, Bernard. *The Time Tables of History: A Horizontal Linkage of People and Events.* New York: Simon and Schuster, 1991.

Hanover Fire Insurance Company. *The Hanover Fire Insurance Company: Seventy-Five Years of Progress.* New York: Hanover Fire Insurance Company, 1927.

Hardy, Edward R. *Early Insurance Offices in Massachusetts from 1724 to 1801.* Boston: Frank Wood, 1901.

Hast, Adele, ed. *International Directory of Company Histories.* Chicago: St. James Press, 1991.

Heppenheimer, T. A. *Turbulent Skies: A History of Commercial Aviation.* New York: John Wiley & Sons, 1995.

Hodgson, Godfrey. *Lloyd's of London—A Reputation at Risk.* London: Viking Press, 1984.

HSBC Investment Bank plc. *Lloyd's—Destroying the Myths.* London: HSBC Investment Bank plc, 2000.

James, Marquis. *Biography of a Business, 1792–1942.* Indianapolis: Bobbs-Merrill Company, 1942.

Johnson and Higgins. *The Story of Johnson & Higgins: Insurance Brokers and Average Adjusters from 1845 to 1945.* New York: Johnson & Higgins, 1945.

Josephson, Matthew. *Edison: A Biography.* New York: John Wiley & Sons, 1992.

Kelley, Joseph P. Jr. *Life and Times in Colonial Pennsylvania.* Harrisburg, Pa.: Stackpole Books, 1973.

Lloyd's of London. *A Guide to Corporate Membership.* London: The Corporation of Lloyd's, 1993.

———. *Lloyd's Bye-Laws: Under Lloyd's Acts 1871–1951.* London: The Corporation of Lloyd's, 1973.

Luessenhop, Elizabeth, and Martin Mayer. *Risky Business: An Insider's Account of the Disaster at Lloyd's of London.* New York: Scribner, 1995.

Malcolm-Smith, George. *The Travelers 100 Years.* Kansas City: Rigby Printing Company, 1964.

Mantle, Jonathan. *For Whom the Bell Tolls—The Lessons of Lloyd's of London.* London: Sinclair-Stevenson, 1992.

Montgomery, Thomas H. *A History of the Insurance Company of North America of Philadelphia.* Philadelphia: Review Publishing and Printing Company, 1885.

Morgan, John S. *Robert Fulton.* New York: Mason/Charter, 1977.

Morton, Jennifer S., comp. *Historic Downtown District Clarksburg.* Clarksburg, W. Va.: Clarksburg Development Corporation, n.d.

Mowbray, Albert H. *Insurance: Its Theory and Practice in the United States.* New York: McGraw-Hill, 1946.

Neill, Sir Patrick. *Regulatory Arrangements at Lloyd's.* Report of the Committee of Inquiry, chaired by Sir Patrick Neill. London: 1987.

Olson, Walter K. *The Litigation Explosion: What Happened When America Unleashed the Lawsuit*. New York: Truman Talley Books/Dutton, 1991.

Phillip, Cynthia Owen. *Robert Fulton: A Biography*. New York: Frank Watts, 1985.

Powell, Edward W., comp. *Red Skies Morning and Night—A History of the Atlantic Mutual Insurance Companies*. New York: Atlantic Mutual Insurance Company, 1992.

Rand—Institute for Civil Justice. *The Cost of Tort Litigation: How Much and to Whom*. Rand Corporation Research Report. 1986.

Raphael, Adam. *Ultimate Risk: The Inside Story of the Lloyd's Catastrophe*. New York: Four Walls Eight Windows, 1995.

Roelker, William Greene, and Clarkson A Collins III. *One Hundred Fifty Years of Providence Washington Insurance Company, 1799–1949*. Providence, R.I.: Roger Williams Press, 1949.

Royster, Charles. *The Fabulous History of the Dismal Swamp Company*. New York: Vintage Books, 2000.

Springfield Fire and Marine. *Seventy-Five Years of Fire Insurance; An Account of the Origin and Development of the Springfield Fire and Marine Insurance Company*. Springfield, Mass.: Springfield Fire and Marine, 1924.

Stewart, D. Murray. *Aviation Insurance*. New York: The Underwriting Printing and Publishing Company, 1946.

Stover, John F. *The Life and Decline of the American Railroad*. New York: Oxford University Press, 1985.

Sun Company. *Centennial Celebration: The Story of Sun Company*. Philadelphia: The Sun Company, 1986.

Trebilcock, Clive. *Phoenix Assurance and the Development of British Insurance*. Vol. 1, 1782–1870. Cambridge: Cambridge University Press, 1985.

Werner, Walter, and Steven T. Smith. *Wall Street*. New York: Columbia University Press, 1991.

Wildes, Harry Emerson. *William Penn*. New York: Macmillian Publishing Co., 1974.

Winter, Wilham D. *Marine Insurance—Its Principles and Practices*. New York: McGraw-Hill Insurance Series, 1952.

Winton, David Holt. *Recollections of Johnson and Higgins (1935–1979)*. Canaan, N.H.: Phoenix Publishing, 1987.

Writers' Program. Wisconsin. *Wisconsin; a Guide to the Badger State*. (American Guide Series). New York: Hastings House, 1954.

Woodward, P. Henry. *Insurance in Connecticut*. Boston: D. H. Hurd & Co., 1897.

Articles in Journals, Magazines, and Books

Aldred, Carolyn. "Insurers Become Myopic: Brokers." *Business Insurance* (March 2, 1987).

———. "Posgate, Grob Found Not Guilty by London Jury." *Business Insurance* (August 21, 1989).

———. "Weather Risk Hedge to Keep Bars' Business from Drying Up." *Business Insurance* (July 3, 2000).

Alt, Susan. "Carter's Death Shocks A&A; Architect of Aggressive Posture." *Business Insurance* (October 30, 1978).

American Historical Society. "History of West Virginia." American Historical Society 3 (1923).

Angermueller, H. H. "Litigation Is a No-Win Game." *Journal of the Insurance Institute of London* 74 (1986).

Asher, Wayne. "Hands across the Ocean." *ReActions* (November 1983).

Banham, Russ. "The Final Frontier of Risk." *ReActions* (January 5, 1999).

———. "You've Lost That Loving Feeling." *Treasury & Risk Management* (July 1999).

Barnes, Julian. "Letter from London: The Deficit Millionaires." *New Yorker* (September 1993).

Bowers, Barbara. "Allstate Gets Cyper-Active." *Best's Review* (September 2000).

———. "Analysts Share Dim View of Industry." *Best's Review* (January 1999).

Bradford, Michael. "Jury Awards Rising: Study." *Business Insurance* (May 1, 2000).

———. "Marsh Creating Insurer to Ease Capital Crunch." *Business Insurance* (October 1, 2001).

———. "Report Sees More Asbestos-Related Bankruptcies." *Business Insurance* (August 20, 2001).

Brimelow, Peter. "Judicial Imperialism." *Forbes* (June 1, 1987).

Bunshoft, B. L. "Environmental Pollution Claims." *Journal of the Institute of London* 74 (1986).

Business Insurance. "Captive Report." (February 4, 2002).

———. "Corporates Faring Poorly at Lloyd's." (January 22, 2001).

———. "Marsh & McLennan Cos. Inc." (July 5, 1993).

———. "Slow Wheels of Justice." (July 27, l987).

Business Week. "Bermuda: Billions in New Capital Raised." (December 10, 2001).

———. "Bracing for a New Storm of Claims." (August 30, 1993).

———. "Capital Drain to Fuel Premium Growth." (December 10, 2001).

———. "The Hurricane Called Super-Fund." (August 2, 1993).

————. "Reliance: Dismal Management, Stellar Pay." (November 22, 1999).

Calise, Angela K. "Captive Growth Steady Despite Market." *National Underwriter* (March 21, 1994).

Cohen, Jay. "Brokers Caught in Vise Must Adapt to Survive." *Best's Review* (January 1995).

Council of Insurance Agents and Brokers. "CEOs Predict Consolidation Trend Will Continue." *Council Advocate* (Winter 1997).

————. "Employment Practices Liability: Helping Clients with Coverage." *Council Advocate* (February 2000)

————. "The Times They Are a Changin' For the Distribution System." *Council Advocate* (December 1998).

Covello, Vincent T., and Jeryl Mumpower. "Risk Analysis and Risk Management: An Historical Perspective." *Society for Risk Analysis* 5, no. 2 (1985).

Crerar, Ken A. "Darwin in the Details: The Broker Consolidation Trend." *John Liner Review* (Spring 1999).

Dannen, Fredric. "The Incredible Shrinking Insurance Industry." *Institutional Investor* (January 1990).

De Mott, John S. "Rethinking Property-Casualty Coverage." *CFO* (September 1995).

Economist. "Battered Lloyd's." (February 29, 1992).

————. "Capital Punishment." (January 16, 1999).

————. "Liquidity Gap at Lloyd's." (May 16, 1992).

————. "New Financiers." (September 4, 1999).

————. "A Survey of American Insurance: A Question of Balance." (October 27, 1990).

————. "Sweeping Up the Lloyd's Messes." (May 1, 1993).

————. "Uberrima Fides? Losses at Lloyd's Continue." (May 11, 1991).

Emmrich, Stuart. "A&A Wins Saudi Arabian Contract, Gains Prestige." *Business Insurance* (April 30, 1979).

Fannin, Rebecca. "A&A Forges Link with Two Merging Lloyd's Brokers." *Business Insurance* (November 27, 1978).

————. "A&A, Jones Merge Strengths." *Business Insurance* (September 18, 1978).

Flynn, Julia. "The Biology of Business." Review of *The Living Company* by Aried de Geus. *Business Week* (July 14, 1997).

Fritz, Michael. "The Man Who Made Aon a Global Power." *Crain's Chicago Business* (June 2, 1997).

Geisel, Jerry. "Risk Retention Act." *Business Insurance* (October 31, 1988).

Gissen, Jay. "Financial Services." *Forbes* (January 4, 1982).

Gjertsen, Lee Ann. "Aon, A&A to Merge in $1.23 Billion Deal." *National Underwriter* (December 16, 1996).

Goch, Lynna. "1998: The Year in Review—Property-Casualty." *Best's Review* (January 1999).

———. "When Banks Met Brokers." *Best's Review* (January 1999).

Greenwald, Judy. "Hall Acquisition Seen as Victory for Reliance, Aon." *Business Insurance* (August 3, 1992).

Hewitt Associates. "Employee Retirement Systems: How It All Began." *Pension World* (July 1976).

Hoffman, Mark A. "Attacks Loss Tally Grows, May Pass $30 Billion." *Business Insurance* (September 24, 2001).

Howard, Lisa. "Influx of Bermuda Capital Is the Talk of Monte Carlo." *National Underwriter* (September 27, 1993).

———. "J&H to Acquire Stake in Large Mexican Broker." *National Underwriter* (June 21, 1993).

Insurance Index. (November 10, 1923).

Jennings, John P. "A&A, Sedgwick Agree to Merge: Slated for 1982." *National Underwriter* (December 26, 1980).

———. "Corporate Capital Hailed as 'Savior' for Lloyd's." *National Underwriter* (September 27, 1993).

Kloman, Felix. "Captive Insurers in the 'Key of C.'" *Risk Management* (April 1992).

Krasner-Khait, Barbara. "Risky Business." *History Magazine* (August/September 2000).

McIntyre, Kathryn J. "A&A Cancel Their Plan to Join Forces." *Business Insurance* (August 3, 1981).

McLeod, Douglas. "Aon to Acquire Hall in $475 Million Deal." *Business Insurance* (July 27, 1992).

———. "Asbestos Continues to Bite Industry." *Business Insurance* (January 8, 2001).

———. "Asbestos Resurgence." *Business Insurance* (December 24, 2001).

———. "Attacks Prompt Influx of Reinsurance Capacity." *Business Insurance* (November 12, 2001).

———. "Insurers Shaken But Solvent—So Far." *Business Insurance* (October 1, 2001).

———. "New A&A Beat M&M in Retail Broking." *Business Insurance* (December 10, 1984).

Miller, John. "London in Turmoil as News of A&A Link Hits Home." *Business Insurance* (December 11, 1978).

Miller, Richard M. "Satisfying the Changing Needs of Risk Management." *John Liner Review* (Fall 1993).

Moore, Robert H. "A Corporate Perspective: The A&A Experience." In *Business Environment/Public Policy: The Field and Its Future,* edited by Edwin M. Epstein and Lee E. Preston. St. Louis: American Assembly of Collegiate Schools of Business, 1982.

———. "Ethics and Risk Management." *Risk Management* (March 1992).

———. "The Broker's Role." *International Insurance Monitor* (December 1985).

———. "Meeting the Demands of the Workplace of the '90s." *John Liner Review* (Winter 1991).

———. "Planning for Emerging Issues." In *Private Enterprise and Public Purpose,* edited by S. Prakash Sethi and Carl L. Swanson. New York: John Wiley, 1979. Also published in *Public Relations Journal* (November 1979) and *Business Tomorrow* (August 1980).

———. "Regulatory Monitoring: The Corporate Approach." *Enterprise* (September 1983). Excerpted as "Monitoring Government Regulation" in *National Underwriter* (September 23, 1983).

———. "The U.S. Insurance Crisis." *Lloyd's of London Newsletter* (March 1986).

National Underwriter. "Death of C. W. Sexton." (August 5, 1920).

Ortega, Tony. "How Not to Make a Shilling in Insurance." *New Times* (December 18, 1996).

Osborn, Neil. "The American Invasion of Lloyd's." *Institutional Investor* (October 1979).

———. "The Bloody Battle for Bowring." *Institutional Investor* (August 1980).

Pfeffer, Irving. "The Early History of Insurance." *The Annals of the Society of Chartered Property and Casualty Underwriters* 19, no. 2 (Summer 1966).

ReActions. "Sedgwick Profit Down—And Analysts Fear Worse to Come." (April 1988).

Roberts, Sally. "Acordia, Wells Fargo Both Benefit in Deal." *Business Insurance* (March 12, 2001).

———. "Aon Buys Minet from St. Paul." *Business Insurance* (April 14, 1997).

———. "Willis Move, IPO Spark Speculation." *Business Insurance* (April 23, 2001).

Robinson, Jeffrey. "Goldfinger's Game: How a Maverick Upset Staid Old Lloyd's of London." *Barron's* (August 30, 1982).

———. "Will the Empire Strike Back?" *Barron's* (September 20, 1982).

Schiff, David. "Inside America: The Early Days of Insurance Broking." *Schiff's Insurance Observer* (September 1999).

Schut, Jan H. "Personal Injury: What Do You Call a Disgruntled Employee These Days? A Plaintiff." *Institutional Investor* (May 1993).

———. "Who Pays for Superfund Reform?" *Institutional Investor* (October 1994).

Shapiro, Stacy. "Melding of Aon, A&A Raises Questions." *Business Insurance* (January 27, 1997).

Sheppard, William J. "Reinsurance Recoverable Write-Offs." *ReActions* (February 3, 1988).

Sherer, Robert A. "Frank B. Hall: The Rise and Fall of an 'Alphabet House.'" *Insurance Journal* (March 30, 1992).

Snider, H. Wayne. "Risk Management: A Retrospective View." *Risk Management* (April 1991).

Souter, Gavin. "AIG, Chubb, Goldman Form Bermuda Insurer." *Business Insurance* (December 3, 2001).

———. "New Marsh Enterprise." *Business Insurance* (March 27, 2000).

Souter, Gavin, and Sally Roberts. "Willis Planning $230 Million IPO." *Business Insurance* (May 21, 2001).

Spencer, Leslie. "The Tort Tax." *Forbes* (February 17, 1992).

Spiller, Richard, and Oliver Mellman. "ART Prospers in the Soft Market." *ReActions* (January 7, 1999).

Sturm, Paul W. "The Megabrokers." *Forbes* (April 2, 1979).

Swiss Re. "Alternative Risk Transfer (ART) for Corporations: A Passing Fancy or Risk Management for the 21st Century?" *sigma* no. 2 (1999).

Thomas, John D., comp. "Tales of Marsh & McLennan." *M* 14, no. 2 (1987).

Veysey, Sarah. "Asbestos Hitting Equitas." *Business Insurance* (July 30, 2001).

———. "Equitas Strategizes to Face Asbestos Threat—Again." *Business Insurance* (September 10, 2001).

———. "Jaffray Names Fight Lloyd's Immunity." *Business Insurance* (April 30, 2001).

———. "Judge Denies Request for Jaffray Appeal." *Business Insurance* (January 8, 2001).

———. "Lloyd's Hoping for Turnaround." *Business Insurance* (April 15, 2002).

———. "Lloyd's Market to Face More Losses Ahead." *Business Insurance* (September 3, 2001).

———. "Lloyd's Ups Its Estimates of Sept. 11 Losses." *Business Insurance* (December 3, 2001).

———. "Murray Lawrence Rebuts Jaffray Claims." *Business Insurance* (May 22, 2000).

———. "Names Lose Jaffray Case." *Business Insurance* (November 6, 2000).

———. "Reserves Upped for Asbestos Claims: Equitas." *Business Insurance* (September 18, 2000).

Vinson, Ronald W., and John Cosgrove. "Challenging Risks: Our Story." *Independent Agent* (April 1988).

Webb, Bernard L. "Notes on the Early History of American Insurance." *The Annals of the Society of Chartered Property and Casualty Underwriters* 29 (June 1976).

Wilson, Leonard M. "Reed Stenhouse Acquisition Is a Strategic Move for A&A." *Business Insurance* (January 14, 1985).

Wojcik, Joanne. "Asbestos Funding Uncertain." *Business Insurance* (June 10, 2002).

———. "E-risk Exclusions." *Business Insurance* (December 24, 2001).

———. "Reinsurers Competing for Captive Business." *Business Insurance* (November 1, 1993).

Woolley, Suzanne, with Gail DeGeorge. "Why Insurance Rates Have Lost Their Old Bounce." *Business Week* (May 10, 1993).

Zinkewicz, Phil. "A&A Looks for Expanded Role in International Brokerage." *Journal of Commerce* (October 24, 1980).

Zolkos, Rodd. "Acordia, Heath Form Global Broker Network." *Business Insurance* (April 2, 2001).

———. "Alternative Risk Transfer Tools Growing in Popularity." *Business Insurance* (May 14, 2001).

———. "Risk Financing Alternatives Increasing as Market Grows." *Business Insurance* (March 20, 2000).

Articles in Newspapers

Abelson, Reed. "Surge in Bias Cases Punishes Insurers, and Premiums Rise." *New York Times* (January 9, 2002).

Ascarelli, Silvia. "British Insurers to Merge in $11.72 Billion Stock Swap." *Wall Street Journal* (February 26, 1998).

Ashworth, John. "Merrett Will Not Work in Lloyd's Again after £M Deal." *Times* (London) January 10, 1997.

Atkins, Ralph and John Mason. "Lloyd's Names Win Battle Against Gooda Agency." *Financial Times* (October 5, 1994).

Becket, Michael. "Posgate the Midas-Touch Underwriter Who Was Never Far from Controversy." *Daily Telegraph* (London) August 18, 1989.

Brasier, Mary. "The Ups and Downs of Goldfinger." *The Standard* (London) September 21, 1982.

Bray, Nicholas. "Judge Finds Firm Negligent in Lloyd's Case." *Wall Street Journal* (November 1, 1995).

———. "Lloyd's Compensation Plan Encounters a Hail of Criticism." *Wall Street Journal* (December 16, 1992).

———. "Lloyd's Finds Success Luring Corporate Funds." *Wall Street Journal* (November 16, 1993).

———. "Move Set to Bring Corporate Capital into Lloyd's Market." *Wall Street Journal* (January 13, 1993).

Broad, William J. "Does the Fear of Litigation Dampen the Drive to Innovate?" *New York Times* (May 12, 1987).

Bruce, Robert. "Compelling Case for Legal Liability Reform." *Times* (London) September 10, 1992.

Bunker, Nick. "Fraud Squad Arrests Posgate and Others in Howden Affair." *Financial Times* (July 16, 1987).

———. "Posgate Loses Fight to Rejoin Lloyd's." *Financial Times* (July 11, 1986).

———. "The Sting of Lloyd's Tail." *Financial Times* (June 14, 1989).

Chernow, Ron. "The Birth of a Bureaucratic Mastodon." *Wall Street Journal* (April 9, 1998).

Clark, Chris. "Questions over Liability." *Financial Times* (September 9, 1999).

Coppack, Lee. "Tax Problems Foil Sedgwick/A&A Link." *Lloyd's List* (July 31, 1981).

"Crisis Drags Lloyd's to Brink of Closure." *Independent on Sunday* (London) April 23, 1995.

Danforth, John C. "Revising Product Liability Law: A Need for Uniform Laws." *New York Times* (September 1, 1985).

David, Garth, Anthony Hilton and Lorna Bourke. "Ian Posgate Suspended by Committee of Lloyd's." *Times* (London) September 21, 1982.

Dougherty, Bridget. "Lloyd's and Dixon Settle out of Court." *Lloyd's List* (March 15, 1990).

DuBois, Martin. "ING's Offer May Signal More Mergers." *Wall Street Journal* (November 13, 1997).

Dvorak, Phred. "Big Bank Merger Shows Old Ties Persist in Japan." *Wall Street Journal* (April 20, 2000).

Evans-Pritchard, Ambrose. "Chipping Away the U.S.A." *Sunday Telegraph* (London) June 20, 1993.

Fialka, John J. "Last Hurdle to Lloyd's Reordering Cleared." *Wall Street Journal* (August 28, 1996).

———. "Lloyd's Agrees to Reduce Debts of U.S. Members of Its Syndicates." *Wall Street Journal* (July 11, 1996).

———. "States Take Up Cases of Lloyd's U.S. Names." *Wall Street Journal* (March 28, 1996).

Fields, Randolph. "Meeting Old Public Liability Claims." *Financial Times* (March 26, 1992).

———. "They Figured We're Colonials Says U.S. Name." *Financial Times* (May 24, 1996).

Fox, David R. "70 Execs Leave Willis Corroon." *Nashville Tennessean* (May 9, 1994).

Fuhrmans, Vanessa. "AXA Swells U.K. Presence with a $5.6 Billion Deal." *Wall Street Journal* (February 2, 1999).

Goldsmith, Charles. "British Insurer Willis Corroon Agrees to Takeover." *Wall Street Journal* (July 24, 1998).

Gray, Tony. "Frank B. Hall Accounts for 1986 to Be Qualified." *Lloyd's List* (March 24, 1987).

"Grob's Words Linger On." *Independent* (London) January 4, 1992.

Hertzberg, Daniel, and George Anders. "Alexander & Alexander Negotiations on Acquisition by Sedgwick Are Ended." *Wall Street Journal* (July 15, 1983).

Hilder, David B. and Leonard Zehr. "Insurance Broker Agrees to Buy Reed Stenhouse." *Wall Street Journal* (December 5, 1984).

Ingrassia, Lawrence and Dana Milbank. "Hit by Huge Losses, Lloyd's of London Struggles to Survive." *Wall Street Journal* (May 15, 1995).

Ion, Edward. "Catastrophe Firms to Be Launched." *Lloyd's List* (June 24, 1993).

———. "Merrett Group Quits Underwriting." *Lloyd's List* (November 30, 1993).

———. "New Lloyd's Asbestos Blow." *Lloyd's List* (September 7, 1993).

———. "U.S. Tort Costs Nearly Double Those of Europe." *Lloyd's List* (November 25, 1992).

Jenkins, Patrick. "Alternative Risk Transfer." *Financial Times* (June 25, 1999).

"Kenneth Grob." *Times* (London) January 4, 1992.

Key, Janet. "N.Y. Firm Grabs Saudi Prize." *Chicago Tribune* (May 3, 1979).

Knight, Jerry. "Taking on an Insurance Icon." *Washington Post* (May 1, 1996).

Labaton, Stephen. "Justices Throw Out $1.5. Billion Asbestos Settlement Citing Possible Conflict of Interest." *New York Times* (June 24, 1999).

Lapper, Richard. "The Revolt of the Names." *Financial Times* (May 3, 1991).

Lipin, Steven and Stephen E. Frank. "One-Stop Shopping Is the Reason for Deal." *Wall Street Journal* (April 7, 1998).

Lipin, Steven and Leslie Scism. "Marsh to Buy Rival Johnson & Higgins." *Wall Street Journal* (March 12, 1997).

"Litigation Abuse Ruining U.S. Company." *Daily Telegraph* (London) August 3, 1992.

"Lloyd's Loss Led Name to Kill Himself." *Manchester Guardian* (August 26, 1994).

Lohse, Deborah. "ACE's Purchase of Cigna Unit Moves Firm to Forefront." *Wall Street Journal* (January 13, 1999).

———. "AIG's Deal Signals Faith in Annuities." *Wall Street Journal* (August 21, 1998).

———. "Allstate Plans Direct Insurance Sales by Phone, Internet." *Wall Street Journal* (November 11, 1999).

Mackenzie, Gordon. "Jardine Quits U.S. Property/Casualty." *Lloyd's List* (September 12, 1995).

"M&M Admits Others Were Involved in Bond Deals." *Lloyd's List* (January 17, 1984).

Marckus, Melvyn. "Posgate Tells It His Way." *Observer* (London) (October 17, 1982).

McEwen, Charles. "Automobile: For Better or Worse, the Car Turns 100." *New York Times* (June 9, 1996).

McGeehan, Patrick. "Investment Bankers Are Moving Fast to Offer Securities Backed by Pools of Insurance Policies." *Wall Street Journal* (June 16, 1998).

Milbank, Dana. "Lloyd's of London Is Losing Merrett, Its Deputy Chairman." *Wall Street Journal* (September 9, 1995).

———. "Lloyd's Offer to Investors Is Rejected." *Wall Street Journal* (February 15, 1994).

———. "Recovering Their Losses Is Proving Costly for Lloyd's of London Names." *Wall Street Journal* (April 13, 1995).

Moore, John. "Davison Tries to Clear the Mist." *Financial Times* (August 2, 1984).

———. "Lloyd's Suspends Posgate Over Howden Affair." *Financial Times* (September 21, 1982).

———. "Multi-Million Dollar Deficit in Alexander Howden Assets." *Financial Times* (September 2, 1982).

———. "PCW Victims Hit at Lloyd's Offer." *Independent* (London) October 4, 1987.

———. "Rise and Fall of the Dynamic Ian Posgate." *Independent* (London) July 16, 1987.

———. "Top Insurance Brokers Plan Link-Up." *Financial Times* (November 17, 1978).

Moore, Robert H. "Expanding Risks in a Shrinking World." *Lloyd's List* (May 26, 1994).

———. "Pressure for a Strong Federal Role in Regulation." *Lloyd's List* (October 16, 1991).

Mulrenan, Jim. "Captives Break Down Barriers." *Lloyd's List* (June 17, 1991).

Niedzinski, Joe. "Catastrophe Bond Market Is Poised for Growth in Wake of Significant Storm Damage Last Year." *Wall Street Journal* (June 12, 2000).

Nol, Michael. "Citigroup to Spin Off Travelers Insurance Unit." *Washington Post* (December 20, 2001).

Oster, Christopher. "AIG Raises Loss Estimate to Pretax $800 Million, Plans Charge." *Wall Street Journal* (October 10, 2001).

———. "Risky Games: Companies Scrimp on Insurance Costs." *Wall Street Journal* (August 1, 2002).

———. "Some Insurers Face Shortfall in Reserves for Costly Claims Related to Asbestos." *Wall Street Journal* (May 7, 2001).

Parker-Pope, Tara. "Lloyd's of London Raises Settlement to $4.72 Billion." *Wall Street Journal* (May 13, 1996).

Poole, Anthony. "CNA Set to Buy Out Rival." *Lloyd's List* (December 8, 1994).

"Posgate: Gadfly at Lloyd's." *Manchester Guardian* (June 26, 1982).

Quint, Michael. "A&A Gets Infusion and Hires a New Chief." *New York Times* (June 8, 1994).

Rapoport, Michael. "Marsh & McLennan Unit Agrees to Settle EEOC's Age-Bias Case for $28 Million." *Wall Street Journal* (July 30, 1999).

"R. B. Jones Agrees to Merge." *Kansas City Star* (August 31, 1978).

Rhoads, Christopher and Margaret Studer. "Credit Suisse Plans to Buy Winterthur in Transaction Valued at $9.51 Billion." *Wall Street Journal* (August 12, 1997).

Rocca, Tony and Maurice Chittenden. "Life of Luxury Ends with the Squeal of Police Tyres." *Sunday Times* (London) September 19, 1987.

Scism, Leslie. "Alexander & Alexander to Get Infusion of $220 Million; New Chief Named." *Wall Street Journal* (June 8, 1994).

———. "Johnson and Higgins Considers Going Public or Sale." *Wall Street Journal* (March 11, 1997).

———. "Marsh & McLennan Shares Jump 5.7% on News of Pact for Johnson & Higgins." *Wall Street Journal* (March 13, 1997).

Shirouzu, Norihiko. "Three Insurers to Join Japan's Merger Wave." *Wall Street Journal* (October 18, 1999).

Spinner, Jackie. "Terrorism Insurance Bill Passed by Senate." *Washington Post* (June 19, 2002).

Steinmetz, Greg. "Alluring Island: New Bermuda Insurers Are Draining Business from London Market." *Wall Street Journal* (August 31, 1993).

"Stenhouse Name Lives on after Global Merger." *Business Scotsman* (November 5, 1985).

Stokes, Peter. "Brokers in Shock Plan to Combine." *Lloyd's List* (November 17, 1978).

Studer, Margaret and Leslie Scism. "Zurich Insurance to Acquire About $1 Billion of Premiums from Trygg-Hansa's U.S. Unit." *Wall Street Journal* (December 28, 1994).

Sullivan, Aline. "Why Jilted Johnson & Higgins Decided to Go It Alone in the U.K." *Lloyd's List* (July 2, 1991).

Tanauya, Elyse. "The Vaccine Business Gets a Shot in the Arm."

Wall Street Journal (February 25, 1998).

Tickell, Tom. "Sedgwick's Plan for U.S. Merger Collapses." *Manchester Guardian* (July 31, 1981).

Treaster, Joseph, B. "Allstate Poised to Sell Insurance Over Telephone and Internet." *New York Times* (November 11, 1999).

———. "An Insurer Goes Against the Odds: ACE Bucks the Trend and Expands in Commercial Coverage." *New York Times* (January 26, 1999).

———. "Big Bermuda Insurer Acquiring U.S. Reinsurer." *New York Times* (February 19, 1999).

———. "Marsh & McLennan to Buy Big British Insurance Broker." *New York Times* (August 26, 1998).

———. "So Much for Table Manners: Directors Squabble Over How to Carve up Firm's Spoils." *New York Times* (December 27, 1997).

Truell, Peter. "Mess at Lloyd's May Have a Darker Side." *Wall Street Journal* (March 17, 1994).

Tyerman, Robert. "U.S. Clean-Up Fund Worries Insurers." *Sunday Telegraph* (London) August 21, 1994.

Van Dam, Anthony. Insurance office ad. *New-York Gazette* (August 27, 1759).

Waters, Richard. "AIG Injects $200 M into A&A." *Financial Times* (June 8, 1994).

———. "Broking Tough Man Rejoining the Fray." *Financial Times* (June 9, 1994).

"Well Remembered." *Clarksburg News* (July 28, 1899).

"Willis Corroon." *Sunday Times* (London) March 12, 1995.

"Willis Corroon Still Looks Weak." *Lloyd's List* (March 13, 1995).

Wysocki, Bernard Jr. "Oil Megadeal Signals a World of Low Inflation: The Progeny of Standard Oil." *Wall Street Journal* (December 2, 1998).

Zuckerman, Gregory and Deborah Lohse. "Weather Bonds Hedge Against Mother Nature's Profit Effects." *Wall Street Journal* (October 20, 1999).

Public and Corporate Documents

Alexander & Alexander Services Inc. *Annual Report.* 1969–1995.

Alexander, Charles B. "West Virginiana: Letters from a Father to His Son." State of West Virginia, Department of Archives and History, vol. 30, pp. 607–624, Charleston, West Virginia, July 1969.

American International Group Inc. *Annual Report.* 1999–2001.

Aon Corporation. *Annual Report.* 1995–2001.

Chubb Corp. *Annual Report.* 1998–2001.

Clarksburg City Directory. 1900, 1902, 1905, 1907.

Clarksburg Daily Telegraph. 1900–1909.

Corroon & Black Corporation. *Proxy*. August 27, 1990.

———. *Proxy Supplement*. September 28, 1990.

General Re Corporation. *Annual Report*. 1997.

Frank B. Hall & Co. Inc. *Annual Report*. 1969–1990.

Harrison County Chamber of Commerce. *A Warm Welcome to Harrison County, WV*, n.d.

Johnson & Higgins. *Annual Review*. 1983–1989.

Marsh & McLennan Companies, Inc. *Annual Report*. 1962–2001.

Sedgwick Group plc. *Statement to Shareholders: Proposed Merger with Fred. S. James Group*. June 7, 1985.

United Kingdom. Department of Trade and Industry. "Alexander Howden Holdings plc (formerly Alexander Howden Group plc)." Investigation under Section 165(1)(b) of the Companies Act 1948. Interim and Final Reports by Sir Robert Alexander Gatehouse and Ian Glendinning Watt FCA. London, 1990.

U.S. Congress. Senate. Committee on Commerce, Science, and Transportation. *Availability and Cost of Liability Insurance*. 99th Cong., 2d sess., 1986. Committee Print.

U.S. Congress. *Congressional Record*. 99th Cong. 2d sess., 1986. Vol. 132, pt. 20.

U.S. Geological Survey. *Earthquake History of the United States*. U.S. Department of Commerce and U.S. Department of the Interior. Geological Survey—Publication 41–1. Boulder, Colorado, 1982.

Unpublished Manuscripts

Aetna Life & Casualty Co. "Aetna Timeline." Typescript, March 1993.

Alexander, Herbert Lee. "Alexander Family of Virginia and Jefferson Co., W.Va." Typescript, Martinsburg, W.Va., April 16,1948.

Braidwood, John. "History of Stenhouse & Partners." Typescript, Reed Stenhouse, n.d.

Deloitte, Haskins & Sells. "The Howden Affair." Typescript, December 1985.

Frank B. Hall Co. "Joint Venture. . . . A History of Frank B. Hall." Typescript, February 1979.

Hatcher, Robert V. "Memorandum to Johnson & Higgins directors and branch managers concerning proposed merger between Willis Faber and Corroon & Black, June 4, 1990."

Kilbourn, Joseph A. "The Sinking of R.M.S. Titanic." Typescript, Bigham Englar Jones & Houston. New York, n.d.

Kielholz, Walter B. "Capital and Financial Markets and Reinsurance in the 21st Century." Paper presented to Association of Corporate Treasurers, London, April 21, 1998.

Moore, Robert H. "Critical Issues in the Clinton Era." Paper presented to the National Association of Manufacturers, Captiva Island, Florida, February 1, 1993; excerpt published in *Insurance Advocate*, February 13, 1993.

————"The Implications of Toxic Tort Liability for Industry." Paper presented to Brookings Institution Seminar, "Compensating Toxic Tort Victims," Washington, D.C., September 18, 1985; excerpt published in *Insurance Advocate*, September 28, 1985.

Oil Insurance Association. "The Oil Insurance Association." Typescript, n.d.

Pritchard, Jack. Notes and recollections on Alexander & Alexander history, and interviews with A&A employees. Typescript, n.d.

Reed Shaw Stenhouse. "Spotlight—On Reed Shaw Stenhouse—USA." Manuscript, 1979.

Seabury, C. W. "The President's Letter." Typescript, No. 78, a history of Marsh & McLennan, April 1948.

Souder, William F. Jr. "Marsh & McLennan: A Century of Insurance Services, 1871–1971." Paper presented at the Newcomen Society, Chicago, May 18, 1971.

Travelers. "The Travelers." Typescript, lectures by Hartford, Connecticut home office officials, 1920.

Vinson, Ronald W. and John Cosgrove. "Challenging Risks: The Saga of American Insurance." Typescript, draft manuscript and notes, 1988.

Unpublished Interviews and Letters

I conducted a number of interviews in person, by correspondence, and by telephone from New York City in the late 1980s and early 1990s. The most significant were with George P. Jenkins, Richard A. Alexander, Roswell Dunn, Hugo Standing, Cora Seiler, Kenneth Soubry, and Jack Pritchard. Some of these and other particularly helpful interviews are cited below.

Alexander, Charles B. Letters to National Association of Local Agents, Boston, Massachusetts, 21 and 25 January 1905, 20 February 1905 and 20 March 1905.

Alexander, Richard A. Letters to the author, 22 February 1977, 24 March 1977 and June 1988.

Alexander, W. F. Conversations with his son, Richard, which were taped and provided to author by Hugo Standing, n.d.

Barr, Joseph R. Letter to the author, 28 December 1999.

————. Letter to Richard M. Dugan, 14 August 1990.

Calvert, Geoffrey. Letter to Ruth Rose, 9 January 1979.

Dunn, Roswell C. Letters to the author, 18 December 1988, 31 January 1989, 22 January 1990 and 24 February 1990.

Ness, Philip W. Interview with Robert H. Moore, Osterville, Mass., 20 August 1990.

———. Letter to Robert H. Moore, 19 December 1990.

Parry, Alan. Letter to J. H. Swinglehurst, 10 July 1990.

Swinglehurst, J. H. Letter to the author, 18 July 1990.

Tucker, John W. Letter to author, 26 April 1989.

Vance, Cyrus. Letter to Barbara Rosenbaum, 25 January 1990.

Illustration Credits

Cover and title page: Courtesy Catherine and Shelby Cullom Davis Library, St. John's University; Photo by John Lei

Page 6: Historical Picture Archive/CORBIS

Page 9: Courtesy Lloyd's of London

Page 17: Museum of the City of New York

Page 24: Collection of the New-York Historical Society, 74988

Pages 34-35: Courtesy Bancroft Library, University of California, Berkeley

Page 41: Library of Congress, LC-USZ62-42794

Page 55: Museum of the City of New York

Page 58: Library of Congress, LC-USZ62-69755

Page 69: CORBIS

Page 73: Library of Congress, LC-USZ62-55109

Page 81: Library of Congress, LC-USZ62-5834

Page 85: West Virginia State Archives

Pages 92-93: California Historical Society, FN-04024

Page 96: Collection of the New-York Historical Society, 72723

Page 97: Collection of the New-York Historical Society, 72724

Page 105: Collection of the Author

Page 110: The National Automotive History Collection, Detroit Public Library

Page 117: Library of Congress, LC-USZ62-099987

Page 120: Library of Congress, LC-USZ62-073871

Page 129: American Airlines, C.R. Smith Museum

Page 142: Bettmann/CORBIS

Page 145: The George Meany Memorial Archives

Page 153: Courtesy IBM

Page 157: Collection of the Author

Page 165: Boeing

Page 173: Greenbrier Resort

Page 181: Collection of the Author

Page 187: Academy Foundation, Margaret Herrick Library

Page 199: Collection of the Author

Page 207: Richard Townshend/CORBIS
Page 221: Hulton-Deutsch Collection/CORBIS
Page 233: NOAA, wea00711
Page 237: *Financial Times* of London
Page 251: Natalie Fobes/CORBIS
Page 254: Joseph Sohm; ChromoSohm Inc./CORBIS
Page 263: Collection of the Author
Page 267: Bettmann/CORBIS
Page 281: Bettmann/CORBIS
Page 283: Bettmann/CORBIS
Page 291: Reuters/CORBIS
Page 297: Roger Ressmeyer/CORBIS
Page 303: Patrick Bennett/CORBIS
Page 306: National Gallery of Art
Page 315: Raymond Gehman/CORBIS
Page 327: AFP/CORBIS
Page 337: Vince Streano/CORBIS
Page 341: Courtesy William Bridge

Index

Page numbers in **boldface** indicate illustrations; *italics* refer to captions.

Bailey, Glenn, 282
Bailie, Robert, *120*
Bain Clarkson, 321n
Bain Hogg Group, 318n, 321n, 322
Baker, William, 170n
Baldwin Ehret Hill, 282
Balfour, Guthrie & Co., 116
Balis, Mark, 169
Baloise Holding Company, 23n
Baltimore, Maryland: A&A office Christmas parties, 138; B&O rail line, 36; clipper ships, 39; early insurance companies, 23, 32; first telegraphic message (1844), 40; great fire (1904), 94; opening of A&A office (1914), 98; relocation of A&A office (1921), 115; *see also* Abell Building; Fort McHenry; Johns Hopkins Hospital; Standard Oil Building
Baltimore and Ohio Railroad (B&O), 36, 48, 58, 85; insurance, 97–98, 114
Baltimore Equitable Society for Insuring Houses from Loss by Fire, 23
Baltimore Insurance Fire Company, 20
Banham, Russ, 303
Bank of England, 230, 238, 239, 244, 247
Bank of North America, 19
Bank of Nova Scotia, 292n
Banque du Rhône et de la Tamise S.A., 211, 215–22, 225
Banque Paribas, 220
Barbados: captive insurance companies, 288n
Barber & Baldwin, Inc., 122
Barbon, Nicholas, 5
Barclays de Zoete Wedd Research, 293
Barings plc, 324
Barr, Joseph, 133, 157
Barrett Company, 107n
Barros, Justo, 186
Barros & Carrión, 186
Bartholomay, Henry, 178n
Bartholomay and Clarkson, 157, 158
Batterson, James, 49
Bayly Martin & Faye, 321n
Beddom Brown Insurance Agencies, 272n
Beech Aircraft Corporation, 124n
Bekouw Mendes B.V., 264, 264n
Bell, Alexander Graham, 64
Bellehaven (Alexandria), Virginia, 80
Benedict & Benedict, 190
Benefacts, 158, 188
Benz, Carl, 59
Berardi, Ronald, 226
Berkshire Hathaway, 331, 339
Berlin, Germany: Rembrandt exhibition (1991), 307
Bermuda, 209, 210, 211, 335, 340; captive insurers, 288n, 302; reinsurance companies, 314, 341; as tax haven, 288n
Berry, James D., 262, 318, 318n
Betelgeuse (oil tanker): explosion (1979), *221*, 233
Bicycles: accident insurance, 60, 69; advertisement, **69**; biking craze (1890s), 59–60, *69*; impact of, 69; safety concerns, 59–60
Bissell, Richard M., 32

Cosden Petroleum, 100–101, 101n, 115
Cosgrove, John, 28, 30, 46, 59, 64
Cosgrove & Co., 147–48
Cotton Insurance Association, 118
Council of Insurance Agents and Brokers, 168n, 191n
Council of Lloyd's, 219, 237–38, 241, 250, 257
Covello, Vincent, 60
Crédit Suisse, 324
Critchell, R. S., 68
Cronyn, Pocock and Robinson Ltd., 271, 272, 272n
Crum & Forster Group, 27, 121
Cunard Lines, 47n, 159n

D

D. W. Burrows & Comapny, 70, 70n
Daimler, Gottlieb, 59
D'Alessandro, Angelo, 318n
Davis, John W., 132
Davis, Maynard, 31
Davis & Reid, 29–30
De Gaulle, Charles, 111n
Deere, John, 38
Deloitte Haskins & Sells, 214, 224, 273
Democratic Party, 21–22, 83n, 132, 273
Denver, Colorado: hailstorm (1990), 313
Denver and Rio Grande Western Railway, 65, 114
Department of Trade and Industry (DTI), 209n, 221, 222, *237*, 257
Destein, Joseph, 179
Detroit, Michigan: A&A office, 108, 307
Detroit Insurance Agency, 75n, 124, 170, 170n
Detroit Insurance Ltd., 170
Deutsche Banc, 324
Devine, John, 274n
Dewey, Oklahoma: rain insurance for rodeo (1920), 95n
Dividend Mutual Insurance Company, 44
Dixey, Paul, 217
Dixon, Cromwell, *81*
Dixon, Peter, 224–25
Donnaldson, John, 20
Drake, Edwin L., 47
Drake, Frederick T., 111–12, 130, 141
Drake Insurance Company, 207, 211
Dumas & Wylie Limited, 196
Dunn, Roswell, 109, 109n, 125, 128, 144, 159n
Durante, Jimmy, 244n
Duryea brothers, 61–62

E

E. D. English & Co., 180
E. H. Crump Cos., Inc., 294n
E. L. McLean, Ltd., 148
E. Uzielli & Company, 70, 70n
E. W. Payne & Co., 196–97
Eads, James, 58

Fulton, Robert, 26
Furman Selz, 324

president (1946), 140–41; as first A&A executive vice president, 128; move to Baltimore (1915), 98; retirement (1962), 156–57; role in New York office, 115, 135

Knickerbocker Casualty Company of New York, 64
Knickerbocker Fire Insurance Company, 20n
Knickerbocker Plate Glass and Accident Insurance Company, 64
Kohlberg Kravis Roberts & Co. (KKR), 329, 342

L

Landrum, Baylor, 264
Lane, Julia, 80
Las Vegas, Nevada: hotel fire (1980), 294–95
Lassus, Larry, 139, 139n
Latham, Watkins & Hills, 262
Laughlin, Mary, 308
Law, Arthur, 271–72
Lawrence, Murray, 291
Lee, Hutson, Sr., 99n
Legg, A. D., 99n
Lehman, Robert, 123n
Leslie & Godwin Limited, 200
Lethbridge & Davidge, 72
Lewis, Gwillym, 119
Liechtenstein: *anstalts*, 219–20, 219n, 221; *settlements*, 219, 219n
The Life Insurance Company of Virginia, 322
Lincoln, Abraham, 46
Lincoln, Nebraska, 172, 173, 187, 290
Lincoln National Corporation, 22n
Liverpool & London & Globe, 271
Lloyd, Edward, 7
Lloyd's, 229–42, 243–58
  asbestos claims, 247, 249–50, 254, 258, 283–86
  Central Fund, 226, 252–53, 253n
  changes in eligibility for membership, 230
  clerks (early 20th century), **221**
  computer system, 245
  debt collection unit, 255
  early history, 6–12
  environmental pollution claims, 231, 247, 249–50, 254, 284
  future prospects, 257–58, 342
  headquarters, **207**
  Hurricane Betsy, impact of, 230, *233*
  kidnap and ransom insurance, 263
  loss from September 11 attacks, 258, 339
  Names system, 10–11, 229–30, 229n, 243–44, 253
  restrictions on foreign brokers, 197–200, 202
  scandals: Brooks & Dooley, 239; Howden, 205, 213–27, 237, 238–39, 241–42; PCW, 224–25, 226, 238–39, 241; Sasse, 235–36; *Savonita*, 234–35, 236
  self-regulation, 244, 257
  terrorism insurance, 340
Lloyd's TSB Group, 325
LMX. *see* London Market Excess
Loma Prieta, California: earthquake (1989), 248, 297
London, England: coffeehouses, 6–7; excess-of-loss market, 249–50, 313; fraud trial (1989), *237*, 241–42; Great Fire (1666), 5; jazz orchestra, 139n; World War II, 204, 307; *see also* Globe Theater; Lloyd's; National Gallery;

National Aniline & Chemical Company, 107n
National Association of Insurance Agents, 54, 108
National Association of Insurance Brokers, 191n, 407, 408
National Association of Insurance Buyers, 179n
National Association of Local Fire Agents, 54
National Association of Local Fire Insurance Agents, 90
National Board of Fire Underwriters, 54–55, 57, 68n
National Gallery, London, England: Rembrandt exhibition (1991), 307
National Gallery of Art, Washington, D.C.: "blockbuster" exhibitions, *306*;
    visitors, **306**
National Insurance Company of Great Britain, 268
National-Nederlanden NV, 324
National Reinsurance Corporation, 22n, 331
The Neale-Phypers Company, 75n
Neely, Richard, 279
Neill, Sir Patrick, 240
Ness, Phillip, 130–31, 144, 152, 155, 158–59, 166, 174; retirement, 178, 178n
The Netherlands, 264, 264n, 307, 318, 321n, 322n, 324
New Hampshire: establishment of insurance department (1852), 44
New Haven Fire Insurance Company, 35
New Madrid, Missouri Territory: epicenter of earthquake (1811), 26
New Orleans, Louisiana: flood (1965), *233*
New Southern Reinsurance Company, S.A., 220
New York: early insurance companies, 24, 27; foreign insurers banned (1814),
    32; insurance regulations, 43–44; underwriting (mid-1790s), 24; *see also*
    Albany; East River; New York City
New York Board of Insurance Brokers, 54n
New York Central Railroad, 48
New York City, New York
    A&A office Christmas parties, 138
    coffeehouses, 16
    creation of fire department (1865), 57
    early insurance, 16, 20, 22, 27
    fires, 41–42; early fire engine, 18; fire of 1835, **17**, 37–38; fire safety
        measures, 16, 17
    first midtown plane crash (1929), **120**
    newspapers, 38–39, 45
    opening of A&A office (1919), 100
    railroads, 36, 40n, 45; locomotive construction, 36
    relocation of A&A office, 115, 178, 320
    shipping, *27; see also* Metropolitan Museum of Art; South Bronx; Tontine
        Coffee House; World Trade Center
New York Insurance Exchange, 236
New York Stock & Exchange Board, 28
New York Stock Exchange, 28, 262, **263**, 288n
Newport, Rhode Island: distilleries, 23; West Indies trade, 22–23
Newton, William, 7
Niagara Fire Insurance Company, 44n, 326
Nikkei Stock Exchange, Tokyo, Japan, **327**
Nikols Sedgwick, 329
NL Industries, Inc., 262
Noble Grossart Limited, 274n
Noble Hall & Co., Pty Ltd., 270n
North Carolina: insurance regulations, 180; *see also* Kitty Hawk

233; oil refinery explosion, 248; oil spills, 233, 248, **251**
Pew, J. Howard, 138
Pew, Joseph Newton, Sr., 91
Philadelphia, Pennsylvania
  banks and banking, 19, 25, 28
  brokerage commission rates (nineteenth century), 68
  coffeehouses, 15
  colonial era, 13–16
  early insurance companies and offices, 14, 19–21, 25–28, 40, 44
  fires: 1866 and 1869 fires, 56; creation of fire department (1871), 57; fire
    engines, 18, 25; fire safety measures, 16, 17–18; firefighting brigades, 25,
    27n
  population statistics: 1781, 19; 1808, 25
  port, 15, 20
  underwriting agreement issued (1762), 15–16
Philadelphia Contributionship for the Insurance of Houses from Loss by Fire
  (Hand-in-Hand), 18, 18n, 20, 25n
Philadelphia Gas Company, 97
Phillips Petroleum, 248
Phoenix, Arizona: annual A&A meeting, 160
Phoenix Assurance Company of London (Phoenix Assurance), 19, 30, 31, 35
Phoenix Insurance Company, 26, 45, 51, 56, 64n
The Phoenix Office, 5
Piersol, Rodney, 109, 109n, 124, 159n
Pittsburgh, Pennsylvania: early accident insurance claim, 50; fire (1845), 42;
  railroad, 40; steel-beam production, 59
Platt, Charles, 62, 67–68
"policy," origin of term, 4, 6
Polytechnic Club, 51
Pope, A. A., 59
Portland, Maine: destruction by fire, 55
Posgate, Ian, 207–10, 213, 216–19, 222, 238–39; criminal trial (1989), 241
Posgate & Denby (Agencies) Ltd., 210, 218
Price, Charles, 196
Price, Ezekiel, 16n, 19n
Price, Forbes & Co. Ltd., 196, 200
Prince William Sound, Alaska: oil spill, **251**
"privity," 113
Protection Insurance Company, 23, 37, 37n, 45
Protective National Insurance Co., 295
Providence, Rhode Island: distilleries, 23
Providence Bank, 23
Providence Insurance Company, 23, 23n
Providence Washington Insurance Company, 23n
Prudential Insurance Company, 128, 313
"purchasing groups," 288
"pure risks," 302–3
Putnam Investments, LLC, 159
PW Investors, Inc., 23n

Q

Quadricycle (horseless carriage), 62, 62n
Quebec Fire Assurance Company, 35
Quemahoning Coal Company, 97

R

R. A. Corroon Company, 118
R. A. Waller, 54, 68–69
R. B. Jones Corporation, 75n, 108, 108n, 189–91
R. E. Kelley, 178
R. L. Glover & Co. (Underwriting Agents) Ltd., 219
Railroad insurance, 48, *73*, *81*, 114, 117–18, 144
Railroad Insurance Association, 48n, 98
Railway Underwriters, 48n
Rain policy, first, 95n
Ralston & Lyman, 36
Raphael, Adam, 251, 281–82
Rawle, Francis, 14
Ream Wrightson, 134
Red Cross, 137n
Reed, Joseph, 271
Reed Shaw & McNaught, 271, 272
Reed Shaw Osler Ltd., 198, 271–73
Reed Stenhouse Companies LTD., 198, 200, 265–74; acquisition by A&A, 265–67, 265n, 274, 274n
Regan, Jack, 143n
Reid, Charles, **120**
"reinsurance," principle of, 8, 8n
Reliance Group Holdings, Inc., 292, 294
Reliance Insurance Company, 27n, 295
Republic of Texas Corporation, 262
"respondentia," concept of, 4
Revere, Paul, 22
Rhode Island: early insurance entities, 22; *see also* Newport; Providence
Rice, Fred W., 51
Richmond, Virginia: introduction of electric trolley line (1887), 59
Risk and Insurance Management Society (RIMS), 179n
"risk premium," 3
"risk retention groups," 288
RKO Radio Pictures, 131
Robertson & Barnewell, 36
Robins, Ephraim, 37
Robinson, James, 320
Rock Island Railroad, 40
Rockefeller, John D., *41*, 47, 66
Rogers, G. B., 122
"rollers," use of, 246
Rollins, Charles, 72
Rollins Burdick Hunter, 12, 72, 72n, 292, 321
Roman Empire: early forms of insurance, 4
Romeyn & Company, Ltd., 148
Roosevelt, Franklin D., 123n, 127–28, 132
Roosevelt, James, 127
Roosevelt, Theodore, 74n
Root, Martin, 99, 106, 178n
Ropner, 200
Roseman, Sue, 99n
Rottencutter, Lena ("Miss Lena"), 91–92, 109
Rowland, David, 252, 253

Royal Dutch Petroleum, 119

Royal Exchange Assurance Corporation, 7

Royal Exchange Building, London, England, 5, 7–8, 196

Royal Insurance Company, 134, 172n

Ryan, Patrick G., 321, 322, 328

Ryder System, 294

S

S. G. Warburg, 197n

Saint Paul Fire and Marine Insurance Company, 45, 45n

Salem, Massachusetts: early insurers, 22

Salomon Brothers, 333

San Francisco, California: earthquakes, 11–12, **92–93**, 94, **297**; emergence as insurance center, 51

San Francisco Bay, California: clipper ship and steamer, **34–35**; earthquake damages (1989), 297

Santa Fe Railway, 70

Sasse, F. H. (Tim), 235

"Sasse Affair," 235–36

Satterthwaite, Thomas, 31n

Saudi Arabia, Kingdom of, 192

Saudi Arabian Basic Industries Corporation, 297

Savage, Samuel Phillips, 16n

Savonita (ship), 234, 236

Schiff, David, 67

Schmidt, Fred, 109

Schwindt, Walter, 164

Scotland: Alexander family, 79–80, 79n; golf, 65; insurance brokers, 269n

Scull & Field, 172n

Seabury, Charles W. ("Ward"), 143–44

Securities and Exchange Commission (SEC), 226–27, 290n

Sedgwick, Collins & Co. Ltd., 109n, 119, 134, 143, 200, 265, 265n; acquisition by M&M (1998), 329; acquisition of James Co. (1985), 265, 294, 322; history, 73, 196; PCW reinsurances, 224; ties to F. B. Hall, 73, 200

Sedgwick, Henry B., 73, 196

Sedgwick, Moger & Co., 196

Sedgwick-Alexander Canada, 264

Sedgwick Forbes Bland Payne Ltd., 201

Sedgwick Forbes Holdings LTD, 200–201

Sedgwick Group, 292

Seeley, Donald, 318n

Seiler, Cora, 109, 109n

Selfride, Thomas W., 122

Semet-Solvay Corporation, 107n

Sentry Insurance Company, 210

Sexton, Charles, 169, 169n

Shand, Morahan & Company, Inc., 184, 184n, 321

Shaw, George, 271

Shaw, Samuel, 271

Shaw & McNaught, 271

Shaw & Son, 271

Shell Oil Company, 138, 148

Shell Petroleum Corporation, 119, 123

Shenandoah (warship), 45–46

Steamboats: accidents, 39, 42–43, 48, 93–94, *96*; earliest recorded use, 20; first steam warship, 26; insurance risks, 20, 39, 43; iron steamers, 47, 47n; steel steamer, 203; *see also General Slocum; John L. Stephens*
Steinberg, Saul, 295
Stenhouse, Alexander R., 268–70
Stenhouse, Hugh, 269–71, 269n, 270n
Stenhouse Fincham & Co. Ltd, 270–71
Stenhouse Holdings, 273
Sterling Offices, 210–11
Stevens, John, 36
Stevens, Sinclair, 266–67
Stewart, Cecil P., 54, 73–74, 118, 125
Stewart, Henry, 53, 54, 74, 167
Stewart, James, 167
Stewart, Latimer, 111, 131, 154, 166, 169
Stewart Smith, 197–98
Stewart Wrightson Holdings plc, 198, 322
Stock market crash (1929), *120*, 124–25, *142*
Strategis, 290
Stryker, Manley & Buck, 70
Stuyvesant, Peter, 17
Sultana (steamboat), 48
Sun Life of Canada, 131
Sun Oil Company, 91, 115
Sun Shipbuilding and Dry Dock Company, 138
SunAmerica Inc., 334
Surplus lines broker, 198, 198n
Swann & Everett Holdings, Ltd., 205
Swann & Everett Underwriting Ltd., 205, 206
Swett & Crawford, 200
Swift & Co., 72
Swiss Reinsurance Co., 324, 324n, 341
Synercon, 293

T

T. L. C. J. Davies, 204
Taddington's Insurance Pty Ltd., 270n
Tahmoush, Al, 295
Tasco, Frank, 292–93
Technologies, new, as insurance challenges, 151, 231–32, 301, 304, 337, 343
Tempest Re, 332
Terry, Nathaniel, 32
Texaco, 121n
Texas: insurance laws, 111–12; oil production, 120; *see also* Galveston
Texas and Pacific Railroad, 112, 115
The Texas Company, 74, 121n
The Insurance Finance Company (TIFCO), 183, 289–90
Thomas Willing and Company, 15
Thompson, Helen, 100n
Thorn Agency, 119
Three Mile Island, Pennsylvania: nuclear plant, **267**
TIFCO. *see* The Insurance Finance Company
Tillinghast, Stephen, 33
Tillinghast (actuarial firm), 278

The Authors

John A. Bogardus Jr.

John A. Bogardus Jr. joined Alexander & Alexander as a trainee in 1950 and spent his entire professional career with that premier insurance brokerage. Rising through the ranks, he performed years of distinguished service in the positions of vice president (1962–1973), executive vice president (1973–1977), president and chief operating officer (1977–1978), president and chief executive officer (1978–1982), chairman and chief executive officer (1982–1987), chairman of the board (1987–1988), and director (1963–1995).

Respected as well outside of the insurance industry, he has served as a director of Donaldson, Lufkin & Jenrette, Inc.; Security Capital Corporation; and United States Surgical Corporation. In the nonprofit realm, Jack was a trustee of Pomfret School and he also held leadership positions in organizations in the town of Greenwich, Connecticut.

A featured speaker at insurance industry meetings, Jack is the author of articles in various professional journals. He served as a director of the Insurance Brokers Association of New York and a director and chairman of the governing committee of the National Association of Insurance Brokers. He was also a member of the U.S. Chamber of Commerce Insurance Committee, and a board member of the American Institute for Chartered Property Casualty Underwriters and of the Insurance Institute of America.

Born in New York City, he was graduated from Princeton University in 1950. He served two tours of active duty in the U.S. Navy, the first as an enlisted man, subsequently as an officer.

Robert H. Moore

Robert Moore has been Mr. Bogardus's colleague for a quarter of a century. He earned a bachelor's degree from Davidson College, a master's from the University of North Carolina, and a doctorate from the University of Wisconsin. Commissioned a U.S. Army officer, he taught at the Military Academy at West Point and was an associate professor on the graduate faculty at the University of Maryland.

Robert worked for Alexander & Alexander from 1977 to 1995 and served as a senior vice president of Alexander and Alexander Services Inc., as well as chairman and president of A&A Government and Industry Affairs Inc. In 1985 he was elected president of the National Association of Insurance Brokers, and from 1989 to 1993 he served as chairman of that organization's Past Presidents' Advisory Council.

He has written and spoken extensively on corporate issues. As The Conference Board's emerging issues coordinator, he identified and responded to public policy issues of concern to the business community. He is coauthor of *School for Soldiers: West Point and the Profession of Arms,* which was selected as a *New York Times* "Noteworthy Book."

Spreading the Risks: Insuring the American Experience
was designed by Susan Lehmann of Washington, D.C.

The text type throughout is Minion, a modern face
reminiscent of Renaissance forms which was designed
a decade ago by Robert Slimbach. It is noted for its
versatility and clarity, and for the harmony
of its roman and italic faces.

The chapter titles are set in Clarendon, a slab serif
typeface, designed in 1845 as a heavy face to
accompany lighter serif faces.

The book was printed on 70# Finch Vanilla
Vellum at The Stinehour Press in Lunenburg,
Vermont, and bound by Acme Bookbinding in
Charlestown, Massachusetts.